Prevention, Pre-emption and the Nuclear Option

Despite its portrayal as a bold departure, the Bush Doctrine was not the "new" or "revolutionary" policy instrument that many at the time portended. This work seeks to argue that while it was clear that the Bush Doctrine certainly qualified as a preventive war policy, it is apparent that the adoption of this strategy did not mark a total break with American tradition or earlier Administrations.

Warren seeks to dispel arguments pertaining to the supposed "radical" nature of the Bush Doctrine—based on comparisons with previous National Security Strategies and previous Administrations' penchant for prevention. However, the work also highlights that what *was* new and bold about the Bush Administration's National Security Strategy of 2002 was its willingness to embrace reinvigorating a nuclear option that could ultimately be used in the context of preventive war.

While Obama has struck bold rhetorical notes and promises in relation to limiting the role of nuclear weapons, he has stopped short of changing the status quo on critical issues that have lingered since the Cold War—such as tactical nuclear weapons and keeping missiles on alert. This book's final section examines the extent to which Obama has attempted to "adjust" the nuclear option with the recent release of the congressionally mandated Nuclear Posture Review (NPR).

Offering new insights into the Bush doctrine and providing a comprehensive analysis of the current status of the US nuclear weapons strategy, this volume will be of great interest to scholars and students of American foreign policy, security studies, and international relations.

Aiden Warren is a lecturer in the School of Global Studies, Social Sciences and Planning at RMIT University, Australia.

Routledge Studies in US Foreign Policy

Edited by Inderjeet Parmar
University of Manchester
and
John Dumbrell
University of Durham

This new series sets out to publish high quality works by leading and emerging scholars critically engaging with United States Foreign Policy. The series welcomes a variety of approaches to the subject and draws on scholarship from international relations, security studies, international political economy, foreign policy analysis, and contemporary international history.

Subjects covered include the role of administrations and institutions, the media, think tanks, ideologues and intellectuals, elites, transnational corporations, public opinion, and pressure groups in shaping foreign policy, US relations with individual nations, with global regions and global institutions and America's evolving strategic and military policies.

The series aims to provide a range of books—from individual research monographs and edited collections to textbooks and supplemental reading for scholars, researchers, policy analysts, and students.

1 **United States Foreign Policy and National Identity in the 21st Century**
Edited by Kenneth Christie

2 **New Directions in US Foreign Policy**
Edited by Inderjeet Parmar, Linda B. Miller and Mark Ledwidge

3 **America's 'Special Relationships'**
Foreign and domestic aspects of the politics of alliance
Edited by John Dumbrell and Axel R. Schäfer

4 **US Foreign Policy in Context**
National ideology from the founders to the Bush doctrine
Adam Quinn

5 **The United States and NATO since 9/11**
The transatlantic alliance renewed
Ellen Hallams

6 **Soft Power and US Foreign Policy**
Theoretical, historical and contemporary perspectives
Edited by Inderjeet Parmar and Michael Cox

7 **The US Public and American Foreign Policy**
Edited by Andrew Johnstone and Helen Laville

8 **American Foreign Policy and Postwar Reconstruction**
Comparing Japan and Iraq
Jeff Bridoux

9 **Neoconservatism and American Foreign Policy**
A critical analysis
Danny Cooper

10 **US Policy Towards Cuba**
Since the Cold War
Jessica F. Gibbs

11 **Constructing US Foreign Policy**
The curious case of Cuba
David Bernell

12 **Race and US Foreign Policy**
The African-American foreign affairs network
Mark Ledwidge

13 **Gender Ideologies and Military Labor Markets in the U.S.**
Saskia Stachowitsch

14 **Prevention, Pre-emption and the Nuclear Option**
From Bush to Obama
Aiden Warren

Prevention, Pre-emption and the Nuclear Option

From Bush to Obama

Aiden Warren

Routledge
Taylor & Francis Group
LONDON AND NEW YORK

First published 2012
by Routledge
2 Park Square, Milton Park, Abingdon, Oxon, OX14 4RN

Simultaneously published in the USA and Canada
by Routledge
711 Third Avenue, New York, NY 10017

Routledge is an imprint of the Taylor & Francis Group, an informa business

First issued in paperback 2013

© 2012 Aiden Warren

The right of Aiden Warren to be identified as author of this work has been asserted by him in accordance with the Copyright, Designs and Patent Act 1988.

All rights reserved. No part of this book may be reprinted or reproduced or utilized in any form or by any electronic, mechanical, or other means, now known or hereafter invented, including photocopying and recording, or in any information storage or retrieval system, without permission in writing from the publishers.

Trademark notice: Product or corporate names may be trademarks or registered trademarks, and are used only for identification and explanation without intent to infringe.

British Library Cataloguing in Publication Data
A catalogue record for this book is available from the British Library

Library of Congress Cataloging in Publication Data
Warren, Aiden.
Prevention, pre-emption and the nuclear option : from Bush to Obama / Aiden Warren.
p. cm. – (Routledge studies in US foreign policy)
Includes bibliographical references and index.
1. United States–Foreign relations–2001–2009. 2. United States–Foreign relations–2009– 3. Preemptive attack (Military science)–Government policy–United States. 4. Terrorism–Prevention–Government policy–United States. 5. Nuclear weapons–Government policy–United States. 6. National security–United States. 7. Bush, George W. (George Walker), 1946– Political and social views. 8. United States–Foreign relations–Philosophy. 9. United States–Foreign relations–20th century–Case studies. 10. Preemptive attack (Military science)–Government policy–United States–Case studies. I. Title.
JZ1480.W39 2011
355.02'170973–dc22 2011014681

ISBN13: 978-0-415-66995-5 (hbk)
ISBN13: 978-0-415-70511-0 (pbk)
ISBN13: 978-0-203-80208-3 (ebk)

Typeset in Times
by Wearset Ltd, Boldon, Tyne and Wear

Contents

Abbreviations and acronyms ix

Introduction 1

1 The Bush Doctrine: definitions and interpretations of prevention and pre-emption 6

Pre-emption or preventive war? 8
The decision to undertake preventive war 11
International law 13
Real world preventive considerations 19

2 The Bush Doctrine: preventive war in Iraq 25

The choice of Iraq 26
Early indications of prevention 34
The National Security Strategy of 2002/"Bush Doctrine" 36
Clarifying the preventive strategy 37
Linking the preventive strategy to Iraq 39
Planning for preventive war 42
The lead up 46
Bush announces war with Iraq 47

3 The Bush Doctrine and prevention: evident in twentieth-century US foreign policy–case studies 53

Case study one: preventive war and the USSR, 1945–1954 55
Case study two: preventive war and China, 1960–1963 65
Case study three: preventive war and North Korea, 1993–1994 76
In the context of the Bush Administration 88

4 The Bush Doctrine and the nuclear option: the transition from Clinton to Bush 93

Defense Counter-Proliferation Initiative (CPI) 1993 96
Nuclear Posture Review (NPR) 1994 99
Doctrine for Joint Nuclear Operations (Joint Pub 3-12) 1993 103
Doctrine for Joint Nuclear Operations (Joint Pub 3-12) 1995 104
Doctrine for Joint Theater Nuclear Operations 1996 105
Quadrennial Defense Review 1997 106
Presidential Decision Directive 60 1997 108
National Security Strategy (NSS) 1999 110
From Clinton to Bush 111

5 The nuclear option: Bush and the "real" doctrine 119

Nuclear Posture Review 2002 121
National Security Strategy of 2002 126
National Strategy to Combat Weapons of Mass Destruction 2002 128
CONPLAN (Concept Plan) 8022 (Global Strike) 132
Doctrine for Joint Nuclear Operations (Joint Publication 3-12) 2005 136
Quadrennial Defense Review (QDR) 2006 140
National Security Strategy of 2006 141
Strategic Operations Joint Operating Concept Version 2.0 2006 143
Reliable Replacement Warhead (RRW) 144

6 The nuclear option: from Bush to Obama 156

The Prague speech 156
The National Security Strategy of 2010 158
The Nuclear Posture Review of 2010 159
New START Treaty 164
2010 NPT Review Conference 172
The Nuclear Security Summit 176
The Comprehensive Nuclear-Test-Ban Treaty (CTBT) 179
Closing words on Obama 182

Conclusion 184

Notes 193
Bibliography 227
Index 250

Abbreviations and acronyms

ADW	Agent-Defeat Weapons
ALERTORD	Global Strike Alert Order
BMDR	Ballistic Missile Defense Review
BUR	Bottom-Up Review
BW	Biological Weapon
BWC	Biological Weapons Convention
CBW	Chemical and Biological Weapons
CENTCOM	Central Command
ChiCom	Communist China
CIA	Central Intelligence Agency
CONPLAN	Concept Plan 8022 Global Strike
CORM	Commission on Roles and Missions of the Armed Forces
CPI	Counter-Proliferation Implementation
CTBT	Comprehensive Nuclear-Test-Ban Treaty
CTR	Cooperative Threat Reduction
CW	Chemical Weapon
CWC	Chemical Weapons Convention
DCI	Director of Central Intelligence
DOD	Department of Defense
DOS	Department of State
DOE	Department of Energy
DMZ	Demilitarized Zone
EUCOM	European Command
FAS	Federation of Atomic Scientists
FY	Financial Year
GWAPS	US Gulf War Air Power Survey
HDBTs	Hardened and Deeply-Buried Targets
HEU	Highly Enriched Uranium
IAEA	International Atomic Energy Agency
ICBMs	Intercontinental Ballistic Missiles
INR	Department of State's Bureau of Intelligence and Research
JCS	Joint Chiefs of Staff
Joint Pub 3-12 1993	Doctrine for joint Operations 1993

Joint Pub 3-12 1995	Doctrine for joint Operations 1995
Joint Pub 3-12 2005	Doctrine for Joint Nuclear Operations 2005
Joint Pub 3-12.1 1996	The Doctrine for Joint Theater Nuclear Operations 1996
LEP	Life Extension Program
MIRV	Multiple Independently Targeted Re-entry Vehicles
NATO	North Atlantic Treaty Organization
NBC	Nuclear, Biological, Chemical
NIE	National Intelligence Estimate
NNSA	National Nuclear Security Administration
NNWS	Non-Nuclear Weapons States
NPR	Nuclear Posture Review
NPT	Non-Proliferation Treaty
NSC	National Security Council
NSC-68	National Security Council Paper 68
NSCWMD	National Strategy to Combat Weapons of Mass Destruction
NSG	Nuclear Suppliers Group
NSPD	National Security Presidential Directive
NSS	National Security Strategy
NTM	National Technical Means
NUWEP	Nuclear Weapons Employment Policy
NWC	Nuclear Weapons Convention
OPEC	Organization of Petroleum Exporting Counties
OSD	Office of the Secretary of Defense
PDD	Presidential Decision Directive
PLYWD	Precision Low-Yield Weapons Development
QDR	Quadrennial Defense Review
R&D	Research and Development
ROK	Republic of Korea
RRW	Reliable Replacement Warhead
SLBM	Submarine-launched Ballistic Missile
SSBN	Strategic Submarine Ballistic Nuclear
START I	Strategic Arms Reduction Treaty
START II	Strategic Arms Reduction Treaty
START III	Strategic Arms Reduction Treaty
STRATCOM	US Strategic Command
UCS	Union of Concerned Scientists
UN	United Nations
UNSC	United Nations Security Council
UNSCR	United Nations Security Council Resolution
WMD	Weapons of Mass Destruction

Introduction

To President George W. Bush, September 11, 2001 represented "the Pearl Harbor of the 21st century;"[1] the first salvo in a new era of asymmetrical warfare against an enemy bent on the abolition of Western culture and a willingness to go to extremes as a means to attain that objective. Moreover, it signified an epic struggle between darkness and light. "We are here in the middle hour of our grief," Bush acknowledged at a national prayer service held on September 14. "But our responsibility to history is already clear: to answer these attacks and rid the world of evil."[2] Six days later, speaking to a joint session of Congress, he expanded on this theme, declaring:

> What is at stake is not just America's freedom. This is the world's fight. This is civilization's fight.... Great harm has been done to us. We have suffered great loss. And in our grief and anger we have found our mission and our moment. Freedom and fear are at war. The advance of human freedom—the great achievement of our time, and the great hope of every time—now depends on us. Our nation—this generation—will lift a dark threat of violence from our people and our future. We will rally the world to this cause by our efforts, by our courage. We will not tire, we will not falter, and we will not fail.... The course of this conflict is not known, yet its outcome is certain. Freedom and fear, justice and cruelty, have always been at war, and we know that God is not neutral between them.[3]

The grand work awaiting America in a dawning age of "new and uncertain challenges" demanded bold action[4]—this was to come in the form of the National Security Strategy of 2002.[5]

The release of the National Security Strategy on September 20, 2002, was perceived by many as marking an end of an era in US security strategy and policy. In response to the September 11, 2001 terrorist attacks, the previous structures of US security strategy were replaced with an explicit strike policy that advocated both the identification and destruction of terrorist threats "before" they were able to "reach" the United States' "borders;" even if this entailed acting alone and using what was referred to as "pre-emptive" force.[6] Indeed, the increasing possibility that chemical, nuclear, and biological weapons could fall into the hands of stateless terrorists, coupled with the al Qaeda attack in the United States, signaled the breakdown of the strategy that had served the United States military throughout the Cold War and first phase (1991–2001) of the post-Cold War period. Having witnessed firsthand the terrible destruction wrought by a comparatively small and unsophisticated attack upon New York, Washington, DC and rural Pennsylvania, the Bush Administration unanimously proclaimed that keeping the "world's worst weapons out of the hands of the world's worst people" would henceforth become Washington's highest national security priority for the foreseeable future. True to its word, President George W. Bush and his Administration formalized and put into action a grand strategy designed to compensate for America's new-found perception of vulnerability and more importantly, prevent a "nuclear 9/11."[7]

The National Security Strategy of the United States of America declared that: "WMD—nuclear, biological, and chemical—in the possession of hostile states and terrorists represents one of the greatest security challenges facing the US" and "Our enemies have openly declared that they are seeking WMD … the US will not allow these efforts to succeed … as a matter of common sense and self defense, America will act against such emerging threats before they are fully formed."[8] These two assertions—that the most defining threat to the national security of the US was the synthesis of "radicalism and technology" and that the US would view these developments as unacceptable and act to destroy them "before they are fully formed"[9]—provided the basis for what would become known as the "Bush Doctrine." Not without its critics, the so-called Bush Doctrine came to dominate American political discourse from 2002 to 2004 as political leaders, academic scholars and the general public debated the implications of this broad and contentious initiative. Whereas its proponents contended that an urgent and unprecedented threat revolution was well under way that required new and proactive approaches to using force, critics of the Bush Doctrine viewed its espousal of preventive war to combat the proliferation of WMD as further testimony to American unilateralism, and perhaps most importantly, a fundamentally unnecessary departure from the traditional, time-tested strategies of deterrence and containment that figured so prominently in defeating the Soviet Union during the Cold War.[10] Their political inclinations notwithstanding, both sides agreed that the Bush Doctrine was something entirely "new," "candid," "bold" and "revolutionary," a radical doctrine the likes of which the world had never seen and "perhaps the most sweeping reformulation of US strategic thinking in more than half a century."[11]

However, as this book will argue, despite the frequent portrayal of being radically "new" or "revolutionary," the Bush Doctrine in terms of counter-proliferation and preventive war advocacy was not the era-defining departure that many at the time portended. In fact, it will become evident during the course of the first three chapters that such concepts have been very much implicit in previous US Administrations; in the context of both their National Security Strategy releases and preventive war considerations extending back to the end of World War II. However, if notions of assertive counter-proliferation and preventive war considerations were neither new nor groundbreaking, then what *was* defining about the Bush Doctrine?

In simple terms, and as the second assertion of this book will attest, the "doctrine" attempted to place the nuclear option back to the fore; a defining policy that punctuated, updated, refined and reaffirmed its core nuclear endorsement through the unclassified and classified documents it spawned. These nuclear arteries may be viewed as formal policy that established a willingness to use nuclear weapons on states deemed to be adversarial. Indeed, the 2002 Nuclear Posture Review, the 2002 National Strategy to Combat Weapons of Mass Destruction, the 2005 Doctrine for Joint Nuclear Operations, the 2006 Quadrennial Defense Review, the 2006 Strategic Operations Joint Operating Concept Version 2 and the Reliable Replacement Warhead (RRW) program, clearly illustrate that the Bush Doctrine cannot be defined as a doctrine of preventive intervention alone, but rather as one that advocated nuclear weapons reactivation. It is these documents that signified the Bush Administration's push to modernize US offensive forces, deploy missile defenses, upgrade communication and satellite systems, and overall, reinvigorate the nuclear military complex. Behind the Administration's rhetoric of post-Cold War restraint were expansive plans to revitalize US nuclear forces and all the elements that supported them within a so-called "New Triad" of capabilities, combining nuclear and conventional offensive strikes with missile defenses and nuclear weapons infrastructure.[12] Not since the escalation of the Cold War in Ronald Reagan's first term was there such an emphasis on nuclear weapons in US defense strategy. Indeed, the deeper policy within the Bush Doctrine, carried forward in the above-mentioned policy documents, foreshadowed a new nuclear era in which the once-termed "weapon of last resort" returned as a distinctly usable, and "necessary" tool, or, what Russell and Wirtz described as a "quiet revolution" in which the specter of nuclear reactivation was pursued both arrogantly and assertively.[13]

Chapter 1 will seek to establish, clarify and perhaps even resolve the debates associated with the meanings and definitions pertaining to pre-emption and prevention. The task of confirming the core meanings and disparities between these two "strategic concepts" is an imperative requirement that will allow coherent and greater exposition in evaluating the extent to which preventive war has been an implicit consideration in US security strategy. Additionally, this chapter will convey the degree in which such concepts and accompanying interpretations have challenged and transcended the many facets of international relations and US security policy—within the context of history, doctrine, international law and use within a Presidential rhetorical framework.

Chapter 2 will investigate the question that, if preventive war was considered a viable option by the Bush Administration, then why was Iraq the state of "choice?" It is evident that from 2001 to 2003, Iraq, Iran and North Korea were all considered rogue proliferators and defined by the Administration as "grave and gathering threats." Assuming that the US was determined to act preventively against at least one of them, one would expect to find evidence that the Bush Administration sought and/or planned to attack all three. However, as this chapter will argue, it appears from the outset that the Administration's preferred target was Iraq. The chapter will evaluate the extent to which the cultivation of the preventive war doctrine (rhetorically and formally in the context of the National Security Strategy of

2002) was aligned to the sovereign state of Iraq and will include an analysis into the process involved in the orchestration and lead up to the preventive war action undertaken on March 20, 2003. It will assert that despite its appearance of being a radically new approach, at its core, the Bush Doctrine's push for preventive war (acted on in Iraq) long pervaded the strategic thought of policy-makers, officials and military planners at the highest levels of the US government.

As *Chapter 3* will argue, since the commencement of the nuclear era in 1945, at least three other US Presidents (Dwight D. Eisenhower, Lyndon B. Johnson and William J. Clinton) have faced the potential threat of nuclear technology in the possession of states hostile to their respective Administrations and each wrestled with the same decision faced by President Bush in 2003: whether to use preventive military force as a means to counter the proliferation of such nuclear weapon development. The above Administrations had to evaluate the costs of preventively striking a state perceived to be developing nuclear weapons against the costs of abstaining from employing such preventive actions. Indeed, as this chapter will posit, the historical record of the last half century is replete with examples of high-level US decision-makers who considered the undertaking of major unilateral preventive military actions as a means to impede the proliferation of nuclear weapons by rogue states. Prior to the invasion of Iraq in 2003, the US had considered waging preventive war against no less than three additional rogue proliferators—the Union of Soviet Socialist Republics (Soviet Union) from 1945 to 1954; the People's Republic of China (China) from 1960 to 1964; and the Democratic People's Republic of North Korea (North Korea) from 1993 to 94. This chapter will investigate these case studies as a means to evaluate the extent to which the US seriously considered undertaking preventive war against these states, and in the final analysis, will assess whether Bush's preventive advocacy can be considered a "new," "radical" and "revolutionary" strategy.

Indeed, while the early chapters appraise the extent to which the Bush Doctrine can be perceived as being implicit in US security policy—based on comparisons with previous National Security Strategies and previous Administrations' preventive considerations—the next "section" will evaluate the degree to which the National Security Strategy of 2002 engendered the reinvigorated nuclear option with the potential to be used in a preventive context. *Chapter 4* will argue that while the motivation and consideration of preventive war has been an integral part of US policy-makers strategic thought since 1945, and while it can be argued that the preventive actions of the Bush Doctrine stalled in Iraq, the nuclear dimension encompassed in the Doctrine can be viewed as the aspect that is truly the "bold" and "radical" assertion. As revealed, Bush's policy instruments signified a renewed role for nuclear weapons and the quest of his Administration to upgrade US offensive forces, deploy missile defenses, reconfigure communications and satellite systems, and overall, revitalize the nuclear complex. However, to look at this development as purely a Bush Administration initiative would be historically inaccurate.

Thereby, this chapter will explain how the Clinton Administration retained much of the existing US nuclear weapons policy and force posture in the decade after the demise of the Soviet Union and affirmed the role of nuclear weapons in US security strategy. Furthermore, the Clinton Administration investigated the merit of employing targeting options for the use of nuclear weapons in response to chemical or biological attack from states other than Russia, and, in its own documental instruments, did not put out of consideration the first use of nuclear weapons in extreme circumstances. It was here that military planners and policy-makers—through the Defense Counter-Proliferation Initiative (CPI) 1993, Nuclear Posture Review (NPR) 1994, Doctrine for joint Operations (Joint Pub 3-12) 1993/1995, Doctrine for Joint Theater Nuclear Operations 1996, Quadrennial Defense Review (QDR) 1997 and Presidential Decision Directive (PDD) 60 1997—maintained the significance of nuclear weapons throughout the 1990s.

However, as *Chapter 5* posits, despite the "base" provided and maintained by Clinton, it was the Bush Doctrine and its accompanying guidance documents that expanded the role that nuclear weapons would play in US security strategy. This chapter will evaluate the nuclear arteries that the National Security Strategy engendered, in particular, the 2002 Nuclear Posture Review (NPR), the 2002 National Strategy to Combat Weapons of Mass Destruction (NSCWMD), the 2005 Doctrine for Joint Nuclear Operations, the 2006 Quadrennial Defense Review, the 2006 Strategic Operations Joint Operating Concept Version 2.0, and in recent times, the Reliable Replacement Warhead (RRW) program. Based on this document analysis and policy evaluation it will be argued that the Bush Doctrine should not be simply dismissed or defined as a doctrine of preventive war advocacy alone, but as one that endorsed and invigorated—during the period of 2002–2008—the nuclear option as a necessary war-fighting device. For the Bush Administration, it was a "new" and necessary "approach to warfare … exploiting US intelligence advantages, taking full advantage of science and technology."[14]

With the election of Barack Obama to the White House, *Chapter 6* will focus on the transition between the Bush and Obama Administrations, and more importantly, the extent to which Obama has attempted to "adjust" the nuclear option. Beginning with the vision posited in the 2009 Prague Speech and reaffirmed in the National Security Strategy of 2010, the chapter will outline and evaluate the declaratory policies, initiatives and multilateral efforts that the Obama Administration has pursued since this declaration. While focusing on the congressionally mandated Nuclear Posture Review (NPR) and drive to sign and ratify the New START Treaty, the chapter will also consider the impact made by the Administration at the Nuclear Security Summit and the NPT Review Conference. Additionally, the chapter will also assess the Obama Administration's efforts towards Comprehensive Test Ban Treaty ratification. It will be argued that despite some symbolic inroads, the lofty goals posited in Prague have been difficult to translate into reality in their attempt to deviate away the nuclear path pursued by the Bush Administration. Indeed, cautious rather than bold, Obama's policies and initiatives have ended up being transitional, rather than transformational.

1 The Bush Doctrine

Definitions and interpretations of prevention and pre-emption

Released in 2002, the National Security Strategy of the United States of America defined the Bush Administration's strategic response to the events of September 11, 2001. In essence, the controversial document made two significant declarations: "WMD—nuclear, biological, and chemical—in the possession of hostile states and terrorists represents one of the greatest security challenges facing the US" and "Our enemies have openly declared that they are seeking WMDs ... the US will not allow these efforts to succeed ... as a matter of common sense and self defense, America will act against such emerging threats before they are fully formed."[1] Taken together, these two assertions—that the most vital threat to the national security of the US was the linkage of "radicalism and technology" and that the US would view such developments as intolerable and act to destroy them "before they are fully formed"—created the basis for what became known as the "Bush Doctrine." Not without its critics, the so-called Bush Doctrine came to dominate American political discourse from 2002 to 2004 as political leaders, academic scholars, and the general public debated the ramifications of this broad and contentious initiative.

While its advocates argued that an urgent and unprecedented threat was well under way which required new and proactive approaches in the use of force, critics of the Bush Doctrine viewed its espousal of preventive war to combat the proliferation of WMD as further testimony to American unilateralism and arrogance; "a reckless setting of a dangerous precedent that other states will exploit to mask aggression" and, perhaps most importantly, a fundamentally unnecessary departure from the traditional, time-tested strategies of deterrence and containment that figured so prominently in defeating the Soviet Union during the Cold War.[2] While the Bush Doctrine's assertiveness may have been "candid" and "bold," it was not necessarily the radical departure in US security policy that many portended. As a means to placate some of these debates, this chapter will seek to clarify and establish the meanings and definitions associated with pre-emption and prevention, the legal dimension associated with these meanings and the extent to which preventive war was framed and considered a viable option for the Administration. By establishing the meanings pertaining to these two "strategic concepts," a significant platform will be established and will enable latter analysis; that being, the extent to which preventive war has long been a deep and implicit consideration in US security strategy.

The most controversial assertion of the Bush Doctrine was the official adoption of "anticipatory self-defense," in which the United States was prepared to "act against such emerging threats before they are fully formed." As stated by George W. Bush:

> The grave threat our nation faced lies at the crossroads of radicalism and technology.... We must be prepared to stop rogue states and their terrorist clients before they are able to threaten or use WMD against the US and our allies and friends.... Given the goals of rogue states and terrorists, the US can no longer solely rely on a reactive posture as we have in the past. The US has long maintained the option of pre-emption actions to counter a sufficient threat to our national security.[3]

Through these words of the National Security Strategy of 2002, Bush formally endorsed the use of pre-emptive measures, or, what will be discussed during the course of this chapter, preventive war. He argued that international law recognized that nations "need not suffer" an attack before they could lawfully take action to defend themselves against forces that presented an imminent danger of attack. Bush highlighted how legal scholars and international jurists often conditioned the legitimacy of pre-emption on the existence of an imminent threat—most often a "visible mobilization of armies, navies, and air forces preparing to attack."[4] For the Administration, he continued, the United States must adapt the concept of imminent threat to the capabilities and objectives of today's adversaries. As stated, "rogue states" and terrorists did not seek to attack the United States using conventional means as they "know such attacks would fail." Instead, they "employ acts of terror" and, potentially, the use of weapons of mass destruction; "weapons that can be easily concealed, delivered covertly, and used without warning."[5]

In emotive fashion, Bush's National Security Strategy of 2002 referred to the events of September 11, 2001 as a means to illustrate and punctuate his "pre-emptive" assertions. He pointed to the mass civilian casualties as being the specific objective of the terrorists and that these losses could be exponentially more severe if "terrorists acquired and used weapons of mass destruction."[6] It was this emotional reference that provided Bush with the ultimate platform on which to launch his vision of pre-emption or preventive war. Indeed, as further posited, the United States has "long maintained the option of pre-emptive actions" to impede or "counter a threat to their national security ... the greater the threat, the greater is the risk of inaction" and the more compelling the case for taking "anticipatory action" to defend the United States, even if, he argued, "uncertainty remains as to the time and place of the enemy's attack." The conclusion of this endorsement came with one of the most defining statements of his "doctrine," that being, "to forestall or prevent such hostile acts by our adversaries, the United States will, if necessary, act pre-emptively."[7]

As a means to qualify the above statement, Bush signified that the United States would not use force in all cases to pre-empt emerging threats, nor should nations use pre-emption as a "pretext for aggression." However, as emphasized, "in an age where the enemies of civilization openly and actively seek the world's most destructive technologies," the United States cannot stand still while perils gather momentum.[8] As a means to support a pre-emptive option Bush clearly described what he deemed to be necessary for the future of US national security: that being, the building of better, more integrated intelligence capabilities to provide timely, accurate information on threats, wherever they may emerge; the close coordination with allies to form a common assessment of the most dangerous threats; and "the transformation of our military forces to ensure our ability to conduct rapid and precise operations to achieve decisive results."[9]

Pre-emption or preventive war?

At the time of its release, many scholars and commentators argued that the most defining assertion of the Bush Doctrine was encompassed in the statement that the US would now "act against such emerging threats before they are fully formed,"[10] clearly implying that the US would enact a type of proactive response, or, "anticipatory self-defense." Anticipatory self-defense has often been aligned to notions either of "pre-emption" or "prevention" and while they have been periodically used interchangeably, the terms are actually two distinct strategic concepts. Indeed, the specific dichotomy between the two is based in the relative timing of their application and the immediacy of the perceived threat. Pre-emption, in the most basic sense, is nothing more than a quick draw. Upon detecting evidence that an adversary is about to attack—traditionally a visible mobilization of armies, navies, and air forces preparing to attack—a threatened state beats the opponent to the punch and attacks first as a means to thwart the impending strike.[11] It is employed "downstream," in response to a more specific, direct, and immediate threat where "the necessity of self-defense becomes so instant and overwhelming that it leaves no choice of means and no moment for deliberation."[12] As Jack S. Levy stated, "pre-emption involves the initiation of military action because it is perceived that an adversary's attack is imminent and that there are advantages to striking first or at least in preventing the adversary from doing so." It is a tactical response to a direct threat, "designed to forestall the mobilization and deployment of the adversary's existing military forces."[13] For example, the 1967 Six-Day War in which Israel launched an "unprovoked" attack upon the Egyptian, Syrian, and Jordanian armies massing on its borders was, in the purest sense, a pre-emptive war.

In contrast, prevention pertains to the military strategy undertaken by states as a means to address long-term tensions emanating from hostile and/or powerful rivals. Like preventive medicine, preventive war is employed "upstream" as a means to confront factors that are likely to contribute to the development of a threat before they have a chance to become specific, direct, or immediate. The preventive motivation of conflict or war is structured on the premise that military conflict, while not necessarily imminent, is probably inevitable, and that it is better to undertake the conflict now while the costs and/or risks are low(er) than later when the costs are high(er). In most instances, a preventive war is fought in order to preclude the diminishing level of an individual state's power in relation to an ascending adversary. The dominant state strives to take advantage of a window of opportunity—"a period during which a state possesses a significant military advantage over an adversary"—before a window of vulnerability—"a window of opportunity from the perspective of the disadvantaged side"—appears likely to open.[14] As Levy stipulated, "prevention involves fighting a winnable war now in order to avoid the risk of war later under less favourable circumstances … [it] is a response to a threat that will generally take several years to develop … [and] aims to forestall the creation of new military assets." Additionally, he argues, "the consequence of non-action … is the gradual deterioration of … relative military power and the risk of a more costly war from a position of inferiority."[15]

The classic example of preventive war is the Peloponnesian War, which, according to Thucydides, was made inevitable by the "growth of Athenian power and the fear which this caused in Sparta."[16] More recently, the 1981 Israeli attack against the Iraqi Osirak nuclear reactor was indiscriminately portrayed as a preventive operation which was designed to keep Iraq's nuclear weapons capability from "happening or existing a number of years down the road."[17] Although pre-emption and prevention signify two very different paths to conflict, they both derive from a crucial assessment that inaction is not viable and "that the future will be bleak unless [some anticipatory action] is undertaken or at least a belief that this world will be worse than the likely one produced by the war."[18] As Victor Cha articulated, "in a pre-emptive situation doing nothing means being the victim of imminent aggression. In a preventive situation, doing nothing means growing inferiority."[19] In both instances, the expected costs of peace are higher than the potential costs of conflict, and thereby, necessitate a state to act proactively and assertively. Nonetheless, regardless of their similarities and differences—and the Bush Administration's seeming attempts to confound the two concepts—it is apparent that what was really being pursued in the Bush Doctrine was a strategy of preventive war.

For Colin Gray, preventive war was not a concept akin to deterrence and containment, despite the sentiments to the contrary made by Bush. Preventive action was an option that very occasionally was necessary, however, it did not have the character of a reasonably reliable default strategy, like deterrence and containment.[20] To attain an improved "theoretical understanding of preventive war," Gray posited the following prime observations and suggestions:

1 Preventive war is simply war, distinguished only by its timing.
2 Since preventive war is simply war, it is already explained adequately by Clausewitz.
3 Preventive war, in common with all war, is a gamble.
4 The "preventor" begins with the advantage of the initiative, but if success is

not achieved swiftly and decisively, that advantage will rapidly diminish as the enemy recovers and counterattacks.

5 The assessment of a preventive war option has to be on the basis of cost-benefit analysis (or guesswork).

6 The anticipation of high costs to prevention action need not be a showstopper. It depends upon the value of the stakes.[21]

As Gray further conveyed, the main dichotomy between pre-emption and prevention was that the former option was exercised in or for a war that was certain, the timing of which has not been chosen by the pre-emptor. In every instance, by definition, the option of preventive war, or of a preventive strike, must encompass speculation that war, or at least a major negative power shift, was probable in the future. The preventor had a choice. It could choose to absorb and tolerate the predicted adverse power shift. Alternatively, it could "function grand strategically, and endeavor by, say, diplomatic, economic, subversive, as well as military competitive means, to lessen the growing peril."[22] Obviously, temporally the more distant the danger, the greater has to be the uncertainty. In the early 1990s, Americans were assailed by a fashionable theory that tomorrow's great enemy would be superpower Japan. Less than a decade later, the status of the super threat of the future was shared between Islamic fundamentalism and China.[23]

As will be discussed more extensively in the next chapter, the attack on Iraq was the manifestation of the Bush Doctrine's form of "pre-emption"—or in reality, preventive war—formalized in the National Security Strategy of 2002. The Bush Administration identified rogue states seeking to attain nuclear weapons—in conjunction with "their terrorist clients"—to justify the elevation of preventive military intervention from a last resort option to one that many critics argued was the new centre of US security policy. Indeed, while many admonished that the Bush Doctrine was a defining shift, in reality, the United States has long maintained the option of "pre-emptive" actions to counter adversaries deemed as threats to US national security. The National Security Strategy of 2002 put forth a doctrine of "pre-emptive" military action which it acknowledged was based on "the existence of an imminent threat."[24] However, in its formulation the strategy argued that, "we must adapt the concept of imminent threat to the capabilities and objectives of today's adversaries.… We cannot let our enemies strike first."[25] In essence, this described the notion of prevention—attacking when there was little to no threat of an imminent attack.

The introduction of a policy legitimizing preventive attack on sovereign states for the purposes of self-defense engendered contentious debate, as well as associated political and diplomatic implications. Critics argued that attacking potential enemies before a threat had actually materialized potentially increased the specter and likelihood of unintended consequences, and made it vital that the US national security system act with an extremely high degree of accuracy in any first move. Critics also contended that the US risked establishing a precedent of defensible inter-state preventive attacks in which the actual use of preventive force would motivate other international actors to also incorporate "preventive approaches" into their security planning. Preventive military intervention was aligned to notions of vigilante justice in that the act of a state preventively attacking another violated both the UN Charter and the NATO Charter. Furthermore, an assertive policy raised the capacity to engender nuclear proliferation amongst weaker states instead of deterring them.[26] Finally, critics argued that, in simple terms, the National Security Strategy of 2002 proposed the initiation of violence as a means to prevent it. As John Steinbruner stated, "it appears to neglect and indeed to disdain international legal restraint. In the judgment of much of the world, that formula is more likely to generate violence than to contain it.[27]

Preventive military intervention has always been an option for states but its inclusion in the National Security Strategy of 2002, combined with the US preventive intervention in Iraq, elevated its legitimacy (in the eyes of the Bush Administration) as a viable, defensible tool that states could undertake in the pursuit of their foreign policy goals.[28] This scenario would not necessarily translate to a realm of security and order as expressed by some in the Administration, but an environment in which states themselves could consider prevention a potential option. A policy brief from the Brookings Institution contended, "[that] today's international system is characterized by a relative infrequency of interstate war. Developing doctrines that lower the threshold for pre-emptive action could put that accomplishment at risk, and exacerbate regional crises already on the brink of open conflict."[29]

Conversely, however, Ellis and Kiefer argued that it was unclear as to whether a non-proliferation regime alone "would ultimately be capable of preventing the further proliferation of WMD or weapon-related technologies or expertise, let alone be capable of rolling back existing capabilities in key states of proliferation concern."[30] They challenged the notion that a reactive, diplomatic-oriented, multilateral approach would deter the possibility of a rogue state or non-state actor attacking the United States any more than a proactive, military-operational, unilateral approach would. As stated:

> Rather than a recipe for further proliferation, the Bush National Security Strategy of 2002 is a direct outgrowth of an existing post-proliferated and terror-prone security environment. It is both the logical culmination of more than a decade's worth of experience with recalcitrant proliferants in key regions and a sound premise on which to base US national-security planning in the years ahead.[31]

The decision to undertake preventive war

The use of force is one of the most extraordinary decisions a leader can make. Even more extraordinary is the decision to use force preventively—to attack another state when there is no imminent threat—because international law makes no provision for preventive wars as it does for those of a pre-emptive nature. In a modern context, preventive intervention is often associated with the deployment of military personnel and/or the execution of air strikes against targets across recognized borders for the purpose of precluding the target state from obtaining and utilizing nuclear technology. In simple terms, military intervention is preventive if it is authorized when there is no threat of an imminent attack from the target state. As discussed earlier, the definitions of the concepts of both prevention and pre-emption are based on "better now than later" logic, which explains why they can engender ambiguity in their usage. Referring again to Levy, the term prevention encompasses notions of fighting a winnable battle or simply employing military action now in order to avoid the risk of battle later under less favorable conditions. Conversely, pre-emption involves the initiation of military action because it is perceived that an adversary's attack is imminent.[32] As argued by Levy, "the theoretical significance of preventive war derives from the importance of the phenomenon of changing power differentials between states arising from uneven rates of growth."[33] In essence, preventive military force is the proposition that the dominant power initiates preventive action in order to impede an ascending adversary while the latter is still too weak to pose a serious threat.[34] The preventive motivation for battle arises from the perception that one's military power and potential are declining relative to that of a rising adversary and from the fear of the consequences of that decline. Importantly, apprehension at the decline in power stems from the potential decline; not only of one's military power but also of one's bargaining position in international affairs and the corresponding decline in political, economic, and cultural benefits one receives from the status quo. The power shift may be the result of an advance in military technology or the acquisition of nuclear technology in the weaker state.

As a means to define the preventive motivation, Levy suggested several reasons why a state may prefer to initiate war now rather than war later. First, leaders may be prepared to precipitate a conflict as a means to maintain credibility if they have been challenged.[35] This assumes the preventor is militarily stronger than its adversarial target, which Levy argued is most often the situation. Levy also signified that decision-makers may initiate a preventive attack because they perceive that a victorious war may increase their domestic political support. That is, winning a "conflict" may "satisfy specific interest group pressures, exploit more generalized jingoistic sentiment, or distract the public's attention from internal social or economic problems through the creation of an external scapegoat."[36] Moreover, decision-makers may elect to utilize preventive force if they perceive critical national interests to be directly under threat.

Randall Schweller aligned domestic structure and preventive force, arguing that preventive force was an unrealistic policy for declining democratic leaders, as the strength of public opinion in democratic states often generated a complex set of factors which lessened the motivation to enter into a preventive war.[37] Furthermore, he argued, such declining democratic leaders have attempted to counterbalance rising authoritarian challengers through the formation of defensive alliances rather than through the use of preventive force. Richard Ned Lebow also made the connection between domestic political factors and a leader's decision-making process in relation to the use of force. Like Schweller, he argued that public opinion and other domestic political forces could sway the decision-making of leaders, even if they perceived that the national interest required military action. In referring to World War II he stated, "Pacific or divided public opinion forestalled American intervention in the two world wars until either enough American ships had been sunk or the country itself had been attacked."[38] Moreover, it is clear that the shock of the September 11 events evoked a crisis vortex that may have reduced public skepticism about both "diagnoses of threats and proposed solutions,"[39] and may have invigorated an upsurge in public willingness to embrace an "unusually high cost (economic and human) for international military engagement."[40] Indeed, as Levy noted, regardless of the motivations, variables or stimuli, "a decision to initiate war for preventive purposes involves enormous risks and uncertainties, and the risk propensities of decision makers can have a significant impact."[41]

International law

On September 11, 2001, the United States suddenly found itself in what appeared to be a new and perplexing world in which the old structures no longer seemed adequate. President George W. Bush and his advisors in their new national security policy defined the main lines of that policy which were by no means kept secret.[42] US policy, the Bush Administration declared openly, would no longer be based on the principle of deterrence "while dangers gather." It had to identify the threat and impede such threats before they reached "our borders;" taking "whatever action [was] necessary." It had to be prepared to act "pre-emptively" and, indeed, alone if necessary against "rogue states and their terrorist clients before they are able to threaten or use weapons of mass destruction against the United States and our allies and friends." It had to be proactive and "take the battle to the enemy, disrupt his plans, and confront the worst threats before they emerge." In this "new world," Bush declared that "the only path to peace and security is the path of action."[43]

Reading the Bush Doctrine in the context of international Law, the intention to act "pre-emptively" as a means to stymie the emergence of terrorist networks also became the subject of controversy in international public arenas. Part of the international legitimation controversy the Administration encountered in justifying the change in American foreign policy was its inconsistency with previous instantiations of American military doctrine. Many argued that for decades, the United States' war doctrine was justified based on international law, agreements and norms. Robert Tucker's examination of American doctrine in *The Just War* posed questions concerning the proper limits of defensive war, the grounds in which a pre-emptive war had been condemned, as well as the ramifications incurred in maintaining a Cold War nuclear deterrence strategy. In depicting the "just war" he articulated the overarching legal and moral limitations on military engagement. As stated:

> The American doctrine is distinguished by the assumption that the use of force is clearly governed by universally valid moral and legal standards; it is distinguished further by the insistence with which these standards are interpreted as making the justice or injustice of war primarily dependent upon the circumstances immediately attending the initiation of force. In substance, the just war is the war fought either in self-defense or in collective defense against an armed attack. Conversely, the unjust and, of course, the unlawful-war is the war initiated in circumstances other than those of self or collective defense against armed aggression.[44]

The United States has had a long history of insisting that "whatever its grievances, a state cannot justify initiating war, [and] that whatever its interests, a state should not resort to war to preserve or protect those interests."[45] Its adherence to the Charter of the United Nations, as well as the various security arrangements it entered after World War II, were used by Tucker as confirmatory evidence of the orthogonal nature of the United States' moral standards to those of international law. For decades after World War II, the US military engaged in pre-emptive action to address imminent threats to the nation's interests. With the exception of the Kosovo campaign, the Clinton Administration acted in concert with the United Nations when engaging in military conflict. As stated by Harries:

> There were clear UN resolutions to use force to expel Iraq from Kuwait; to preserve the no-fly zones in Bosnia; for the United States to act under Article 51, the right of self defense, in Afghanistan; to intervene in Sierra Leone and, more ambiguously, in Kosovo.[46]

While the legitimacy of the Kosovo campaign was contested, the US acted with a commitment to internationalist purposes in accord with a "coalition of willing nations" to impede ethnic conflict in the Balkans.

In contrast to these Clinton Administration conflicts, as well as former President George H.W. Bush's campaign against Iraq's incursions into Kuwait, Iraq's military threat presented no immediate danger to another state. Hence, the United States' validation for confronting Iraq's failure to disarm in 2002/2003 was perceived to be steeped with national interest. Furthermore, although the United States vied for an international commitment to justify its intervention efforts, the rationale for military intervention presented a prima facie case contravening international law against pre-emptive war. The Bush Administration justified the Iraq intervention within a security strategy structure that would enable "pre-emptive" action to be undertaken in the absence of an imminent threat. It redefined national security strategy to encompass "pre-emptive" actions taken as a means to prevent rogue states and terrorists from exacting mass civilian casualties upon the United States. In so doing, however, the Administration attempted to create the moral equivalence between historical actions taken by the United States to pre-empt an enemy attack, and the current ambiguous security actions needed to "prevent" terrorist acts. In essence, the Bush Administration argued that the level of proof for executing a "pre-emptive" strike should be lowered as a means to adapt to "non-traditional" objectives of terrorist states and networks. Furthermore, the Administration questioned the legitimacy of international law in the post-September 11 security environment. As already indicated in the above, the new security strategy created an ambiguous new meaning for justified pre-emptive action in the sense that the new meaning would encompass understandings of traditional war fighting conducted as preventive war. As the National Security Strategy of 2002 posited:

> For centuries, international law recognized that nations need not suffer an attack before they can lawfully take action to defend themselves against forces that present an imminent danger of attack. Legal scholars and international jurists often conditioned the legitimacy of pre-emption on existence of an imminent threat—most often a visible mobilization of armies, navies, and air forces preparing to attack. We must adapt the concept of imminent threat to the capabilities and objectives of today's adversaries. Rogue states and terrorists do not seek to attack us using traditional means.... Instead, they rely on acts of terror and, potentially, the use of weapons of mass destruction—weapons that can be easily concealed, delivered covertly, and used without warning.... As was demonstrated by the losses on September 11, 2001, mass civilian casualties is the specific objective of terrorists and these losses would be exponentially more severe if terrorists acquired and used weapons of mass destruction.[47]

The subsequent prevarication between preventive and pre-emptive war was a rhetorical device used with clear intention.

As defined earlier, a legitimate pre-emptive strike under international law required that states demonstrate that aggressive states have both the capacity and intention of executing extreme harm. In contrast, preventive war was without such requirements, but rather engendered mutual fear of a surprise attack. The result may increase global instabilities as motives for arming can be misconstrued. As argued by Crawford:

> Some states may defensively arm because they fear the "pre-emptive/preventive" state; others may arm offensively because they resent the preventive-war aggressor who may have killed many innocents in a quest for total security. A pre-emptive doctrine which has—because of great fear and a desire to control the international environment—become a preventive war doctrine is likely to create more fearful states and more aggressor states.[48]

Furthermore, such an equivocation between preventive and pre-emptive war actions undermined United Nations legal doctrine and diplomatic means of communicating security concerns. While Article 51 of the UN charter defined acts in self-defense as only legitimate in the face of attack, the doctrine of preventive war as posited in the National Security Strategy of 2002 risked making this article irrelevant.

The National Security Strategy of 2002, nonetheless, maintained that the right of pre-emption had been recognized under international law "for centuries," although not in the expanded sense of the concept that the Bush Administration had framed it. Reference to the writings of various classical international jurists lent support to this argument. Gentili, for example, argued in favor of pre-empting impending threats while also preventing the development of potential future threats. He maintained that "[a] defence is just which anticipates dangers that are already meditated and prepared [i.e. pre-emption], and also those which are not meditated, but are probable and possible [i.e. prevention]."[49] He emphasized, however, that there must be a clearly defined basis for apprehending the threat in which "a just cause for fear is demanded; and suspicion is not enough."[50] Nor is hostile intent alone sufficient justification for anticipatory action. As Gentili stated, "one ought not to be punished merely because of his desire to do harm … [but for] an impulse which was accompanied with action, as is made clear elsewhere."[51]

Like Gentili, Grotius acknowledged that pre-emptive action may be taken to forestall or thwart an imminent attack. He also argued that mere suspicion or speculation was not enough to justify such action:

> War in defence of life is permissible only when the danger is immediate and certain, not when it is merely assumed. The danger, again, must be immediate and imminent in point of time. I admit, to be sure, that if the assailant seizes weapons in such a way that his intent to kill is manifest the crime can be forestalled.… But those who accept fear of any sort as justifying anticipatory slaying are themselves greatly deceived, and deceive others.[52]

Pre-emptive action was a measure of last resort, to be taken up only when all other remedies have been exhausted:

> Further, if a man is not planning an immediate attack, but it has been ascertained that he has formed a plot, or is preparing an ambuscade, or that he is putting poison in our way, or that he is making ready a false accusation and false evidence, and is corrupting the judicial procedure, I maintain that he cannot lawfully be killed, either if the danger can in any other way be avoided, or if it is not altogether certain that the danger cannot be otherwise avoided. Generally, in fact, the delay that will intervene affords opportunity to apply many remedies, to take advantage of many accidental occurrences; as the proverb runs, "There's many a slip 'twixt cup and lip."[53]

De Vattel maintained that the greater the likelihood and destructiveness of an impending attack, the greater the justification for taking pre-emptive actions:

> One is justified in forestalling a danger in direct ratio to the degree of prob-

> ability attending it, and to the seriousness of the evil with which one is threatened. If the evil in question be endurable, if the loss be of small account, prompt action need not be taken; there is no great danger in delaying measures of self-protection until we are certain that there is actual danger of the evil. But suppose the safety of the State endangered? ... Are we to delay averting our destruction until it has become inevitable?[54]

In such circumstances, a state need not wait until the danger is apparent, but may act on the basis of a "reasonable presumption" of threat, "but presumption becomes almost equal to certitude if the Prince who is about to acquire enormous power has already given evidence of an unbridled pride and ambition."[55]

The cornerstone of the UN Charter *jus ad bellum* regime is the general prohibition on the use of force found in Article 2(4), coupled with the self-defense exception found in Article 51. Is the preventive or pre-emptive use of military force lawful under the regime anchored on these two provisions? First, it is clear from other provisions of the Charter that the Security Council can resort to the preventive or pre-emptive use of force under its Chapter VII powers.[56] As per Article 39, the Council may pursue forcible measures in response to "any *threat to the peace* [emphasis added], breach of the peace, or act of aggression."[57] The reference to "threat to the peace" suggested that the Security Council may act (or authorize members to act) before a breach of the peace or an act of aggression had actually taken place. This is confirmed in rhetoric used elsewhere in Chapter VII, Article 50, for example, that referred specifically to "preventive or enforcement measures against any state ... taken by the Security Council."[58] The question, however, was as to whether states are permitted to unilaterally (i.e. without prior and explicit Security Council authorization) act in a preventive or pre-emptive military capacity as a measure of self-defense. The answer to this of course depended upon the interpretation of Article 51, and specifically, as to whether the a rticle permitted the anticipatory use of force in self-defense.

The debate over the legitimacy of anticipatory self-defense, that is, unilateral measures of military force taken by a state to prevent an expected armed attack, has been one of the most controversial and extensive disputes connected with the Charter *jus ad bellum* regime. On a general level, there have been two competing interpretations of Article 51. The restrictive or *narrow* interpretation posited that a state may exercise its right of self-defense *only in response to* an actual armed attack. The non-restrictive or *broad* interpretation, conversely, emphasized that a state may also undertake this strategy in *anticipation of* an impending armed attack. Both sides of the equation have articulated and conveyed powerful arguments in support of their respective positions. But while there may be a substantial and admittedly controversial basis for pre-emptive counter-proliferation strategies in international law, there is much less so for preventive strategies. It seems reasonable to recognize the legitimacy of anticipatory self-defense in the face of a clearly defined imminent threat. As has often been said, international law in general—and the UN Charter regime, in particular—is not a suicide pact. No state can be expected to sit passively to absorb an aggressor's impending attack. At the same time, however, active defense does not necessarily imply that pre-emptive action should be taken in all circumstances against all threats.

Nevertheless, there is a place for pre-emption both in a state's national security policy and, more to the point of this section, in international law. This does not extend, however, to the brand of prevention/pre-emption set out in the Bush Doctrine, in so far as it does not meet the conditions of necessity and proportionality that regulate the anticipatory use of defensive force under the current interpretation of the Charter *jus ad bellum* regime. The reason is, quite simply, that the strategic option enshrined in the Doctrine—as argued extensively throughout the above—is not pre-emption but, rather, prevention cloaked in the rhetoric of pre-emption. This is more than just semantics. As also demonstrated in the above, the international community had serious reservations concerning preventive military action. Such action, based often on ambiguous evidence of potential long-term threats has engendered greater scope for abuse, that is, for the pursuit of aggressive ends under the guise of anticipatory self-defense, as well as for major informational mistakes in which thousands die as a result. In order to make its preventive strategy more palatable to the international community—and hence, lessen its instinctive opposition to the strategy—the Bush Administration attempted to convey this strategic option as pre-emption. It drew the conceptual link to pre-emption through its emphasis on an expanded notion of imminence, a key element in the condition of necessity as it related to pre-emption. Here again, the Bush Doctrine embellished the concept of imminence beyond the semantic breaking point. The Doctrine pushed imminence back to the early research and development stage of the nuclear threat cycle, where the time to develop an operational nuclear weapons capability was measured not in days, weeks or even months but, rather, in years. Nuclear activities at this stage of the threat cycle do not pose an imminent threat in the true meaning of the word. This is not to argue for complacency in the face of such a potential long-term threat, and it may call for determined non-military action in order to prevent its realization. But it is not an imminent threat in the sense of a clear and impending attack, the basis for truly pre-emptive action.[59]

This leads to the second component of the necessity condition on which the Bush Doctrine's brand of pre-emption faltered. Traditionally, necessity requires that force be used as a last resort after all reasonable non-military alternatives have been exhausted. It is difficult to credibly make the argument that there is no alternative to the use of force when dealing with a WMD capability whose emergence to the point where it actually poses an existential threat to the target state is measured in years. In such circumstances, the target state certainly has time for "a hundred visions and revisions" of its counter-proliferation efforts. The Bush Doctrine attempted to bypass the issue of time by portraying conflict with the adversary as inevitable. It assumed that the irrational hostility of the leaders of rogue proliferators was such that, once they acquired nuclear weapons, they would—not might—use them against the US and its friends either directly or through their terrorist proxies. That being the case, it was better to "impede now" when there was a better chance of success at relatively low cost, than later when the threat was more fully developed.[60]

The last point where the Bush Doctrine's version of pre-emption faced limitations pertained to the second condition of regulating the defensive use of force on proportionality. The target state should not, for example, incinerate an aggressor's city in response to a rifle shot at a border post. For pre-emption of a perceived nuclear threat, in particular, the severity of the response turns critically on the characterization of that threat. In its public pronouncements, the Bush Administration focused on the worst-case scenario imaginable—a nuclear holocaust unleashed on American cities at the cost of hundreds of thousands, if not millions, of lives—to underpin its preventive/pre-emptive strategy. Can this scenario be completely ruled out? Obviously not. It was not only the consequences of a catastrophic event but the likelihood of that event that must be assessed in order to place a particular threat scenario in its proper perspective among the panoply of other possible threats to the nation's security. This was particularly important when the threat response under consideration was preventive military action, with all the intended—and unintended—consequences that can flow from such action. The target state must have the ability to gather and assess accurate, reliable and timely intelligence on the capabilities and intentions of the adversary.

As several American committees studying the 9/11 and Iraqi WMD intelligence failures have revealed, the US intelligence system did not demonstrate that it had this capacity, certainly to the degree necessary to underpin a strategy of prevention. In the absence of such a capacity, falling back on worst-case scenario planning to "cover the bases" had the associated consequence of rendering the concept of proportionality irrelevant. The hypothesized demise of millions of innocents effectively served to justify any level of preventive military action. It is here that while there may have been grounds, at least in principle, under the UN Charter *jus ad bellum* regime for a counter-proliferation strategy of pre-emption that satisfied the conditions of necessity and proportionality, the Bush Doctrine's brand of pre-emption—prevention by any other name—was extensively limited in this context of international law.[61]

Real world preventive considerations

The National Security Strategy of 2002 deemed the proliferation of nuclear weapons as being unacceptable for a number of compelling reasons. In simple terms, proliferation adds vast complexities to US foreign policy: crisis instabilities are likely to be more extreme; the likelihood of inadvertent or accidental use is likely to be greater; transfers to non-state groups are more likely; and at least some of the future possessor states are likely to be politically volatile, aggressive, and are hard to deter.[62] Important as these were, however, it appears that the real reason the US considered waging preventive war against Iraq, Iran, and North Korea was to ensure the maintenance of its overwhelming superiority in the Persian Gulf, East Asia, and the world.[63] Indeed, it was evident that the Bush Administration was determined to "prevent any hostile power from dominating regions whose resources would allow it to attain great power status (like Iraq or Iran in the oil-rich Middle East); discourage attempts by any other nation to challenge US leadership or upset the established political and economic order and should prevent the emergence of any potential competitors."[64]

Accordingly, the National Security Strategy of 2002 reasserted such sentiments in its depiction of the US—a state that: "enjoyed unparalleled military strength and economic and political influence;" would maintain its effort to "keep military strengths beyond challenge;" sustain forces "strong enough to dissuade potential adversaries from trying to equal or surpass the power of the US;" and "build a balance of power that favors freedom."[65] Therefore, if rogue actors were permitted to attain nuclear weapons, not only would the US become more deterred; rogue proliferators would become less deterred. The emergence of rogue proliferators would threaten the security of the US and its allies, strengthen bargaining positions on both sides in any future political negotiations, increase militancy, entrench hard-liners, destabilize the regional balance, and finally, encourage other states or non-state actors to follow suit. For the Bush Administration this situation was completely unacceptable and had to be avoided. As a result, the National Security Strategy of 2002 emphasized that the US would undertake preventive war against rogue states that were deemed to be close in acquiring nuclear weapons as a means to preserve an imbalance of power favorable to the US and to preclude any potential aggression by emboldened nuclear adversaries. Despite such concerns, many commentators questioned the perceived necessity and efficaciousness of using preventive war to address the issue of rogue proliferation. More specifically, many analysts challenged the notion as to why the US "needed" to wage preventive war against Iraq, Iran, or North Korea in the first place, even if they did pose a threat to US pre-eminence.

Some critics argued that a strategy of preventive war was not necessary because many of the threats to the US were over-exaggerated and could be challenged with assertive, but less militarized policies, such as deterrence and containment.[66] Indeed, there is a substantial body of evidence which suggests that not all rogue proliferators were inherently unhinged and undeterrable. As Record contended, because rogue states, like other states, have "return addresses" in the form of attackable assets such as territory, population, armed forces, governmental and economic infrastructure, and most importantly, leaders who value their lives, they can be held hostage by credible threats of US retaliation.[67] Michael O'Hanlon, Susan E. Rice, and James B. Steinberg similarly posited that deterrence tends to work against even brutal autocrats, "who tend to value highly their hold on power and their lives—as National Security Advisor Condoleezza Rice herself wrote, 'these [rogue] regimes are living on borrowed time, so there need be no sense of panic about them. Rather the first line of defense should be a clear and classical statement of deterrence—if they do acquire WMD, their weapons will be unusable because any attempt to use them will bring national obliteration.' "[68]

Additionally, Lawrence Korb elaborates, "history has demonstrated that even the most ruthless tyrants understand and respect the logic of robust containment and active deterrence." Even if a rogue state ruled by a terrorist and tyrant such as Saddam Hussein attained [nuclear weapons], its weapons "would cause little tangible harm because any attempt to use them would bring national obliteration." When dictators have undertaken acts of aggression, "it has been as a direct result of the United States' failure to communicate credibly its intent to retaliate. On those occasions, deterrence did not fail us; it was just poorly implemented."[69] For example, Saddam Hussein reportedly decided to wage war against Kuwait in July 1990, but before sending in his troops, he approached the US to find out how it would react. In a now infamous interview with the Iraqi leader, US ambassador April Glaspie told Hussein, "we have no opinion on the Arab-Arab conflicts, like your border disagreement with Kuwait." Furthermore, in a previous communication, the US State Department had told Hussein that Washington had "no special defense or security commitments to Kuwait." The US may not have intended to give Iraq a green light, but in essence, that is what it did.[70] This suggests that deterrence worked in 1991, and furthermore, that the despots atop even the most offensive, seemingly reckless rogue regimes were still fundamentally rational calculators that sought some degree of political survival above all else, and understood the logic of deterrence. In other words, "rogue state behaviour so far provides no convincing evidence of immunity to deterrence via the credible threat of unacceptable retaliation."[71] If this is correct, then a strategy of preventive war may not be the most efficacious or cost-effective way to thwart the emergence of rogue proliferators.

Moreover, other scholars and commentators have posited the notion that even if a state was perceived to be both rogue and proliferating, there was still no guarantee that it sought to initiate hostilities, upset the status quo or extend its sphere of influence. After all, "blackmail and aggression are not the only reasons rogue states seek [nuclear weapons]; they may also see in such weapons a means of, deterring or at least raising the price of, US military action against themselves."[72] As posited in the above, the US perception of threat has often derived from the interaction of capabilities with intentions; and while a state's capability to do harm might not be in dispute, there is always the potential for its motives and intentions to be misinterpreted or change, sometimes in unexpected and even positive ways. As Neta Crawford conveyed, the strategy of preventive war assumes sound knowledge of an adversary's ill intentions when such presumptions may be premature or false:[73] "While preventive war doctrines assume that today's potential rival will become tomorrow's adversary, diplomacy or some other factor could work to change the relationship from antagonism to accommodation."[74] Charles W. Kegley and Gregory A. Raymond further explained:

> Preventive war is based on the proposition that it is possible to foretell with certainty what is to come. But predicting another state's future behavior is difficult because leadership intentions are hard to discern. Information on an adversary's long-range goals may be obscured by its attempts to shroud policy planning in secrecy. Evidence on the options being considered for attaining those goals may be misinterpreted due to a carefully crafted deception campaign. Finally, signals of impending moves may be distorted by background noise. Acknowledging these difficulties, [US Administrations]

> often try to predict an adversary's future behavior by evaluating its military capabilities. However, capability estimates can be misleading, especially when being made over a long time horizon without reliable data on possible changes.... Another drawback is divining whether projected capability enhancements are earmarked for offensive or defensive purposes.[75]

Sharing this analysis, numerous statespeople over the years have warned against undertaking wars predicated upon assumptions and speculation about adversaries or the future. As Randall L. Schweller argued:

> Above all, preventive wars are "wars of anticipation," and therefore their justification, if any is given, can rest only upon the inherently unprovable assumptions of human foresight. As Abbe Galiani posited: "the misfortunes of mankind derive from foresight ... the actual cause of wars. Because one foresees the House of Hapsburg will increase, because the French, a hundred years from now, will do such a thing, we begin to cut one another's throats right now."[76]

Even the consummate statesman Otto von Bismarck had difficulty assessing the immediate costs of war against alternative futures, stating that, "the idea of undertaking a war because it might be inevitable later on and might then have to be fought under less favorable conditions has always remained foreign to me, and I have always fought against it." Furthermore, "I would ... never advise Your Majesty to declare war forthwith, simply because it appeared that our opponent would begin hostilities in the near future. One can never anticipate the ways of divine providence securely enough for that."[77] For this reason, promulgating a strategy of preventive war is said to be both imprudent and "defeatist," for "who knows what hopes the passage of time may bring to realization?"[78]

Conversely, proponents of the Bush Doctrine and preventive war have argued that it was imperative for the US to "do something big" after September 11 as a means to restore its damaged deterrent capability. While the Afghanistan campaign was a sufficiently strong response to the September 11 acts themselves, it was not expected to be assertive enough to effectively signify US resolve in preventing the acquisition of nuclear weapons by rogue states. To be an effective treatment for proliferation, preventive war must not only remove the direct threat, it must also dissuade would-be proliferators. For Galia Press-Barnathan, the US has demonstrated its willingness to utilize force since the end of the Cold War, however, most of its activities were limited to the air and to relatively small-scale missions. It was, therefore, not at all clear that a US Administration would be willing and able to engage in a serious ground war that was not preceded by an attack on the US itself.[79] In light of this problem, it was necessary to wage "a preventive war as to serve the goal of re-establishing the credibility of the US deterrent capability, which was undermined after September 11, and, in turn, to give credibility to the new preventive doctrine."[80] Indeed, rogue states such as Iraq, Iran, and North Korea, it was argued, needed to be shown that significant challenges to US supremacy, especially the proliferation of nuclear weapons, would not go unnoticed and would be countered by a prompt and devastating response. As argued by Mead, the enemy had to learn who was the strongest and, if it came to that, the most ruthless. From this standpoint "the invasion of Iraq was in the nature of a warning shot: a warning that future attacks on the pre-eminence of the US will be followed by even more overwhelming responses."[81]

Unfortunately, the main avenue for the US to effectively communicate this new and powerful determination would be to actually engage in a preventive war. As asserted by Robert J. Pauly and Tom Lansford, for any strategy to be deemed credible, decisive action to back rhetorical promises is essential. That is why the Bush Administration's release of "the National Security Strategy coincided with the President's issuance of an ultimatum to Saddam to disarm and desist from sponsoring terrorist organizations … and that is why the Bush Administration ultimately decided to use force to remove Saddam from power."[82] Indeed, even former US Secretary of the Treasury Paul O'Neill, an ardent opponent of undertaking preventive war against Iraq, conceded that taking such action could "act as a 'demonstration model' of what other countries that were considering actions hostile to the US might face … [preventive war] would persuade other countries to change what they've been doing by harboring or supporting terrorists [and developing nuclear weapons]."[83] In essence, after the September 11 attacks, the US needed to make a "big, fast, bold, simple move that would send a signal at home and abroad, a signal that said 'don't mess with Texas or America,'" and according to its proponents, waging preventive war was quite simply the only way in which this could be achieved.[84]

Finally, John Lewis Gaddis and others have posited that the US had to engage in a preventive war relatively soon after its operations in Afghanistan if it was to sustain the already waning momentum of the Bush Doctrine and its expected "domino effect" upon other rogue proliferators. According to Gaddis, the invasions of Afghanistan and Iraq were meant to topple selected dominos with a view of destabilizing and thwarting others. The purpose was as much psychological as military: "to eliminate individuals, gangs, and regimes who commit to support terrorism and acquire nuclear weapons, but also to intimidate so … prevention, by this logic, could produce a deterrent effect … in order for this new domino theory to work, however, the pace had to be kept up; there couldn't be too much time between topplings."[85] Similarly, Vice President Dick Cheney exclaimed: "Afghanistan was only the beginning of a lengthy campaign. Were we to stop now, any sense of security we might have would be false and temporary."[86] Indeed, whereas fighting a preventive war against one rogue proliferator may convince others to relinquish their arrant hostility and nuclear desires, without a "swift, sure, and clear" preliminary action there could be no subsequent reaction. In this view, for the US to attain any long-term deterrent benefits vis-à-vis other existing or potential rogue proliferators, it would be necessary to quickly and successfully set an example by executing a preventive war against at least one rogue proliferator, if not more.

Ultimately defined in this chapter in the context of preventive war, the National Security Strategy of 2002 should be considered an "active" Doctrine. During the 1950s, Paul Nitze argued that the term "doctrine" could be used in two related but different senses, the "action sense" and the "declaratory sense." The action sense referred to the broader guidelines that policy-makers believed should and would in fact govern the movement of the US in various contingencies. The declaratory aspect pertained to policy statements that were gauged principally towards political and/or psychological effects.[87] Although the Bush Doctrine, like most doctrines, may have, at various intervals, served both active and declaratory functions, throughout this volume it will be assumed that its principal aim was to guide and inform the definitive actions of US foreign policy. Regardless of the apparent misuse of the terms pre-emption and prevention, and the interchanging of these terms in Bush's rhetoric via speeches and documental instruments, this chapter in essence has subscribed to the belief that what Bush was advocating all during the period after 9/11 (2001), the release of the National Security Strategy (September 2002), through to the Iraq War (March 2003), was the consideration, endorsement and, ultimately, use of preventive war against those actors deemed as a major threat to the United States' security and well-being. Indeed, the definitions and interpretations of both pre-emption and prevention during this period challenged and transcended every facet of international relations and US security policy in the context of history, doctrine, international law, and their use within a Presidential rhetorical framework. Having defined these concepts (pre-emption and prevention), the next chapter will focus on the perceived threats or "rogue proliferators" that were apparent at the time of the National Security Strategy of 2002, and why the US deemed it both appropriate and necessary that preventive war be both seriously considered (in the context of the "axis of evil") and actually undertaken (in the state of Iraq).

2 The Bush Doctrine

Preventive war in Iraq

Having established the meanings and definitions associated with pre-emption and prevention, and the extent to which preventive war was considered a viable option by his Administration; the next task for Bush was to "choose" a state in which to undertake the preventive war strategy. It was clear that from 2001 to 2003, Iraq, Iran, and North Korea were all perceived to be "grave and gathering threats"—and were all considered rogue proliferators. Assuming that the US was determined to act preventively against at least one of them, one would expect to find evidence that the Bush Administration sought and/or planned to attack all three. From the beginning, however, it appeared that the Administration's preferred target was Iraq. As indicated by Clarke, the US "planned early on to eliminate Saddam Hussein."[1] That is, on November 21, 2001, only two months after the September 11 terrorist attacks, Bush reportedly asked Secretary of Defense Donald Rumsfeld, "what kind of a war plan do you have for Iraq? How do you feel about the war plan for Iraq?"[2] Furthermore, within days of the publication of the National Security Strategy, the Bush Administration announced that a senior State Department official would travel to Pyongyang in October to reengage the North Koreans on security issues, while others were quietly working to secure Iranian neutrality in the case of a war with Iraq.[3] Why was this the case? If the Iranian and North Korean regimes were just as despicable and dangerous as Iraq, why did the Bush Administration seek conciliation with the former and war with the latter? Or, as Senator Richard Durbin inquired in a September 10, 2002 speech to Congress, "If all three are threats and enemies to the US, why is it that the Administration has focused on Iraq."[4] Indeed, if preventive war was to be undertaken, why was Iraq the state of "choice" for the Administration? These questions, together with those pertaining to the events surrounding the justification and lead up to the actual declaration of war, are addressed in this chapter, and thereby, will enable later analysis on the extent to which the National Security Strategy (in its preventive endorsement and aspirations) has been evident and perhaps even implicit in US security strategy since the end of World War II.

The choice of Iraq

From 2001 to 2003, Iraq was widely perceived to be a rogue proliferator, having previously defied no less than 17 different UN Security Council Resolutions. Moreover, it had: allegedly developed an extensive arsenal of WMD; impeded and deceived international weapons inspectors over the span of 12 years; used WMD against its own Kurdish population; invaded two neighboring states (Iran and Kuwait); and supported and harbored well known terrorist organizations. At varying intervals, Iraq had challenged the security of the US and its allies and participated in military confrontation during the first Gulf War. As stated by Gordon, Indyk and O'Hanlon:

> Certainly the US has good reasons to want to get rid of Saddam Hussein. Saddam is a menace who has ordered the invasion of several of his neighbors, killed thousands of Kurds and Iranians with poison gas, turned his own country into a brutal police state and demonstrated an insatiable appetite for WMD. He is currently funding Palestinian terrorists who attack Israeli civilians as well as trying to disrupt world oil supplies. He is also, almost surely, still trying to build nuclear weapons. And he is powerfully motivated to seek revenge against his personal and political nemeses, as demonstrated most vividly in his … attempted assassination of former President George Bush in 1993. That is why there is a general consensus in the US that overthrowing Saddam would be a good thing.[5]

In addition, it appeared that Iraq may have served as a haven, transit point and operational base for groups and actors who directed terrorism and violence against the US, Israel and other Western states. According to the US Department of State, Baghdad overtly assisted two categories of Iraq-based terrorist organizations—Iranian dissidents (Mujahedin-e-Khalq) devoted to toppling the Iranian government and a variety of Palestinian rejectionist groups opposed to peace with Israel. Baghdad provided material assistance to other "Palestinian terrorist groups that were at the forefront of the Intifada. The Popular Front for the liberation of Palestine—General Command Hamas and the Palestine Islamic Jihad were the most important groups to whom Baghdad had extended outreach and support efforts."[6] Several expatriate terrorist groups "continued to maintain offices in Baghdad including the Arab Liberation Front, the inactive 15 May Organization, the Palestinian Liberation Front and the Abu Nidal organization."[7] Moreover, the 9/11 Commission reported that Osama Bin Laden was also willing to explore possibilities for cooperating with Iraq in which Bin Laden himself "met with a senior Iraqi intelligence officer in Khartoum in late 1994 or early 1995. Bin Laden is said to have asked for space to establish training camps, as well as assistance in procuring weapons." In March 1998, after Bin Laden's public fatwa against the US, two al Qaeda members reportedly went to Iraq to meet with Iraqi intelligence, while "in July, an Iraqi delegation travelled to Afghanistan to meet first with the Taliban and then with Bin Laden … Iraqi officials offered Bin Laden a safe haven in Iraq."[8]

Aside from the alleged "connections" to al Qaeda, many in the Bush Administration believed that Iraq had demonstrated an ability to construct a large, clandestine nuclear weapons program.[9] In the decade before the first Gulf War, Iraq had invested more resources into nuclear programs than any other developing state in the world and came very close to becoming the first Arab state to actually produce and deploy such weapons. As stated in the Nuclear Threat Initiative:

> In the early 1970s, Baghdad initiated a bomb program under direct orders from then Vice-President Saddam Hussein. The plan called for developing a civilian fuel cycle and related expertise first; the weapons program was to parallel and build off of these efforts. Accordingly, Baghdad acquired a French nuclear reactor in 1975. After Israel destroyed the [Osiraq nuclear] reactor in June 1981 air strike, Iraq explored a number of clandestine uranium enrichment methods. By the time of Desert Storm in 1991, Iraq had a robust covert nuclear weapons program, with a completed—though untested—nuclear weapon design. Baghdad was perhaps one to three years away from building a nuclear weapon at the onset of the war.[10]

While it was difficult to ascertain the extent to which Saddam Hussein was able to rebuild his nuclear weapons program after the first Gulf War, the view of the CIA and US Department of Defense was that Iraq's nuclear aspirations and accumulated technical expertise had remained intact, and coinciding with this, the capacity to reignite a proliferation program quickly and covertly. As the Rumsfeld Commission reported, "Iraq has maintained the skills and industrial capabilities needed to reconstitute its long range ballistic missile program." Prior to the invasion of Kuwait in 1990, "Iraq could have had nuclear weapons in the 1993–1995 time frame.... Iraq has the capability to reconstitute its nuclear weapon program; the speed at which it can do so depends on the availability of fissile material."[11] Indeed, it was believed that Iraq had a workable design for the weaponization of a nuclear weapon in 2002, to the extent that the only significant impediment to producing such a weapon was its ability to attain fissile material. According to a CIA Unclassified Report to Congress, Iraq engaged in extensive concealment efforts and probably used the period since it refused inspections to attempt to reconstitute prohibited programs. As stated, "a sufficient source of fissile material remains Iraq's most significant obstacle to being able to produce a nuclear weapon. The intelligence community is concerned that Baghdad is attempting to acquire materials that could aid in reconstituting its nuclear weapons program."[12] If Iraq were able to obtain the said material from another state, it was perceived that it could have constructed a nuclear device within months.[13]

Aside from Iraq's potential to develop nuclear weapons, considerations pertaining to varying aspects of international law and precedents dating as far back to the first Gulf War were posited as potential justification for preventive war. According to William Taft and Todd Buchwald, given Iraq's repeated breaches of UN Security Council Resolutions, any military action taken by the US against Iraq would be wholly justifiable:

> [United Nations Security Council Resolution (UNSCR) 678] was the authorization to use force for the Gulf War in 1991. In April of that year, the Council imposed a series of conditions on Iraq, including most importantly extensive disarmament obligations, as a condition of the ceasefire declared under UNSCR 687. Iraq has "materially breached" these disarmament obligations, and force may again be used under UNSCR 678 to compel Iraqi compliance.... Just last November, in resolution 1441, the Council unanimously decided that Iraq has been and remains in material breach of its obligations. 1441 then gave Iraq a "final opportunity" to comply, but stated specifically that violations of the obligations, including the obligation to cooperate fully, under 1441 would constitute a further material breach. Iraq has clearly demonstrated such violations and, accordingly, the authority to use force to address Iraq's material breaches is clear.[14]

According to those in the Administration, as well as proponents of the "Iraq choice," previous UN Security Council resolutions had provided the US with sufficient authority needed to legally justify attacking Iraq. The US would be acting on the basis of implied authority from Resolution 578, which automatically authorized individual member states to use "all necessary means," including force, to enforce Iraqi compliance with any of the conditions stipulated in previous resolutions—especially resolutions 687 and 1441. As stated by Press-Barnathan, "Iraq had a previous 'criminal record' that gave at least some legitimacy to the allegations that it had sinned again and would allow for military action against it."[15] This may have been true, however, it was unlikely that the Bush Administration would have formulated its decision to go to war strictly on legal terms. After all, there was very little historical evidence that US decisions to use force abroad had been cultivated on notions of efficacy and permissiveness of the relevant legal arguments.

On the contrary, the traditional view of international law and the use of force has been that "it is a sham, something that international lawyers talk and write about but to which statesmen pay no attention, except perhaps when they want to justify something that they have made up their minds to do in any case."[16] This may be relatively extreme—the presence of a robust legal argument was certainly important and probably enabled to make the case for war in Iraq—but it was doubtful that any US Administration would focus a decision to wage war strictly on the legality of such actions. Moreover, there was reason to believe that the US would be able to construct equally viable legal arguments based on emerging norms of "conditional" or "contractual" sovereignty and/or existing UN resolutions to facilitate the justification of military action in both Iran and North Korea. As explained by Lawrence Korb:

> This country has long respected the principle of non intervention established by the 1648 Treaty of Westphalia.... Yet, in recent times, international law

> has evolved to recognize a countervailing principle that qualifies the norm of non intervention: regimes may surrender the right to rule over their people if they systematically deviate from established international human rights standards and consistently pose a threat to regional and global peace and stability. A state that condones or practices terrorism, or seeks to use WMD as weapons of choice or retains its hold on power by violating virtually every norm of morality and law known to mankind forfeits its claim to sovereignty.[17]

Indeed, the emerging legal doctrine, also known as the "Responsibility to Protect" required that states had a responsibility to protect the "lives, liberty, and basic human rights of their citizens, and that if they to fail or are unable to carry it out, the international community has a responsibility to step in."[18] This international "duty" also applied to states where the population was experiencing serious harm as a result of internal conflict, insurgency, repression or state failure, as well as those forces that undermined global stability and security via state sponsored terrorism and/or acquisition of WMD.

Furthermore, the US could also plausibly argue that it was within its legal rights to take military action against Iran based on UN Resolution 1373 which, in essence, imposed binding obligations upon states to prevent and suppress the financing of terrorist acts, "to refrain from providing any support to terrorists, to deny safe haven to terrorists, to develop effective border controls, and to bring to justice those who commit terrorist acts, among other requirements."[19] As articulated by Richard N. Gardner:

> [I]n Resolution 1373, the Security Council imposed a legal requirement on all UN members [including Iran] to suppress al Qaeda and other transnational terrorist groups. Read in the context of the long-recognized principle of international law that states must not permit their territory to be used for the purpose of launching attacks on other states, I believe the decisions of NATO and the UN provide a sufficient legal basis for military actions the US needs to take to destroy terrorist groups operating in countries that do not carry out their legal obligations to suppress them.[20]

In relation to the state of North Korea, a solid legal case could be made for military action based on its abrupt withdrawal and dismissal from the legally binding Nuclear Non-Proliferation Treaty (NPT) and/or the regime's egregious human rights abuses. Certainly, Pyongyang's contravention of nuclear safeguards during 1994 could provide a relatively sound legal basis for US military actions. Hence, in the unlikely event that the Bush Administration based its decision exclusively on legal parameters, it would have had no better reason to attack Iraq than either Iran or North Korea

The next point of consideration pertaining to the US's determination in waging war against Iraq was based on Iraq's alleged complicity in the September 11 terrorist attacks and links to the al Qaeda terrorist organization. This viewpoint did not seem plausible, particularly as the Administration struggled to produce any compelling evidence associating Saddam Hussein to al Qaeda; and very few commentators believed that this was the "real" reason as to why the US went to war with Iraq. As Wirtz and Russell reported, many observers found the connection between Saddam Hussein and al Qaeda to be far-fetched and "unlikely that Iraq's secular regime would support religious fundamentalists, or that Saddam, who has plenty of personal and political enemies, would give 'outsiders' control of chemical, biological, or radiological weapons."[21] Indeed, prior to the war most believed that the evidence adduced for the Security Council was, at best, "unconvincing and in part misrepresented and falsified ... very few nations accepted that credible evidence could be shown of an operational link between al Qaeda and the regime in Baghdad."[22] Additionally, as Brent Scowcroft acknowledged, "the only thing that Osama [Bin Laden] and Saddam Hussein have in common is they hate the US. There is scant evidence to tie Saddam to terrorist organizations, and even less to the 11 September attacks."[23] Therefore, it did not appear that the Bush Administration would have chosen to undertake war against Iraq based primarily upon its supposed ties or connection to al Qaeda. In fact, as Chaim Kaufman alerted, "Hussein provided far less practical support to terrorism than did Syria, Iran, Yemen, or sources in some friendly countries such as Saudi Arabia and Pakistan."[24] If any of the three rogue proliferators were to have links to the September 11 attacks or al Qaeda, it would most likely have been the state of Iran. As Clarke exhorted:

> When the Bush Administration talked about Iraq as a nation that supported terrorism, including al Qaeda, and was developing WMD, those comments perfectly suited Iran, not Iraq. It was Tehran that had funded and directed Hezbollah since its inception. It was Hezbollah that had killed hundreds of Americans in Lebanon. Hezbollah, with Iranian support has also killed hundreds of Israelis. While the 'ties' and 'links' between Saddam and al Qaeda were minimal, al Qaeda regularly used Iranian territory for transit and sanctuary prior to September 11. Al Qaeda's Egyptian branch, Egyptian Islamic Jihad operated openly in Tehran. It is no coincidence that many of the al Qaeda management team ... moved across the border into Iran after US forces finally invaded Afghanistan.[25]

Another possible reason as to why the Bush Administration may have "chosen" to wage war against Iraq (rather than Iran and North Korea) was centered upon Baghdad's endemic and deplorable record of human rights abuses. As the US Department of State reported:

> Iraq's human rights record [in 2002] remained extremely poor, and it continued to commit numerous, serious human rights abuses. Citizens did not have the right to change the regime. The regime continued summarily to execute alleged political opponents and leaders of the Shi'a religious community. Reports suggested that persons were executed merely because of

> their association with an opposition group. The regime continued to be responsible for disappearances and to kill and torture persons suspected of or related to persons suspected of oppositionist politics, economic crimes, military desertion, and a variety of other activities.... The UN ... issued a report ... detailing ongoing, grievous violations of human rights by the regime.[26]

There is no doubt that Iraq's human rights record was appalling, however, so too was Iran and North Korea's. According to the same report, Iran's human rights record in 2002 was "poor, and deteriorated substantially during the year, despite continuing efforts within society to make the Government accountable for its human rights policies."[27] Additionally, the State Department highlighted how the Iranian government had "denied citizens the right to change their government" while also undertaking "systematic abuses" including "summary executions; disappearances; widespread use of torture and other degrading treatment, reportedly including rape; severe punishments such as stoning and flogging; harsh prison conditions; arbitrary arrest and detention; and prolonged and incommunicado detention."[28] The situation in North Korea pertaining to humanitarian conditions was reported to be even worse.

The State Department in 2002 also rated North Korea's human rights record as "poor" and indicated that the North Korean government had continued to commit serious human rights abuses. As stated, "Citizens did not have the right to peacefully change their government, and the leadership viewed most international human rights norms, particularly individual rights, as illegitimate, alien, and subversive to the goals of the State and the Party."[29] Moreover, the North Korean situation was complicated by the fact that the government was unable to feed its population; the country relied on international aid and trade to supplement domestic production, which has been hobbled by disastrous agricultural policies. From 1995 to 1997, famine caused internal dislocation, widespread malnutrition, and an estimated one to two million persons—or possibly as much as ten percent of the population—died from starvation and related diseases.[30] In simple terms, all three states had deplorable human rights records and thus could not sufficiently account for the Administration's decision to undertake war against Iraq over the states of Iran and North Korea.

Various commentators and scholars have argued that the reason the Bush Administration may have "chosen" to undertake preventive war with Iraq rather than Iran and North Korea, was because it was "Iraq obsessed" and saw the terrorist attacks as an "opportunity to mobilize support for forcible regime change in Iraq even absent of evidence of Iraqi complicity in 11 September."[31] Indeed, it was apparent that the sensational events of September 11 engendered a "crisis atmosphere that may have reduced public scepticism about both diagnoses of threats and proposed solutions" and may have "spurred an upsurge in public willingness to accept an unusually high cost (economic and human) for international military engagement."[32] Nonetheless, even if the Bush Administration was able to exploit a state of emergency to mobilize public support for a more assertive foreign policy, it did not necessarily lead to a choice of force against Iraq. Indeed, given their respective histories, it would appear that both Iran and North Korea had also been persistent irritants to the US as indicated by the US Department of Defense in December 2001:

> North Korea, Iraq, and Iran ... are among the countries that could be involved in immediate, potential, or unexpected contingencies. All have longstanding hostility toward the United States and its security partners; North Korea and Iraq in particular have been chronic military concerns. All sponsor or harbor terrorists and all have active WMD and missile programs.[33]

Furthermore, the nine independent Commissioners of the Rumsfeld Commission were adamant in their sentiments and concluded that concerted efforts by a number of "overtly or potentially hostile nations" to acquire ballistic missiles with biological or nuclear payloads "pose a growing threat to the US, its deployed forces and its friends and allies." These newer, "developing threats in North Korea, Iran and Iraq are in addition to those still posed by the existing ballistic missile arsenals of Russia and China..." The "extraordinary" level of "resources North Korea and Iran are now devoting to developing their own ballistic missile capabilities poses a substantial and immediate danger to the US, its vital interests and its allies."[34] As Mann articulated, the Rumsfeld Commission report was a "prominent manifestation of the way these three countries were being increasingly bracketed by the Washington's foreign policy and intelligence communities, well before George W. Bush arrived in the White House."[35] Finally, Iran and North Korea were also highlighted by the Bush Administration as being members of the now infamous "axis of evil." Such evidence strongly suggests that the US may have also been "obsessed" with Iran and North Korea.

In the lead up to the 2003 invasion of Iraq, many commentators throughout the US came to believe that the decision to wage preventive war was predicated primarily upon Washington's burgeoning need and desire to gain unimpeded access to Iraq's oil reserves. Given the Bush Administration's links to the oil sector and the rising costs of gasoline, many considered the "oil rationale" to be the most compelling of all. Indeed, it was argued that a combination of US direct influence over Iraq's share of oil reserves—the world's third largest—and a long-term military presence in Iraq, would enable the US to have much greater leverage and control over world oil supplies and policies, and thereby provide American and British companies (ExxonMobil, Chevron-Texaco, Shell, and British Petroleum) a potential windfall of hundreds of billions of dollars. Simultaneously, a successful war could weaken the Organization of Petroleum Exporting Counties (OPEC) oil cartel, limit the influence of other major oil suppliers such as Russia, Mexico, and Venezuela and, finally, reduce the dependency upon oil from Saudi Arabia—the world's single largest supplier of oil.[36] However influential this alleged yearning for oil may have been, it too cannot adequately explain why the US chose to wage preventive war against Iraq; if the US was determined to wage war against a threatening state on account of oil, why did it not attack Iran, the world's second largest holder of proven oil reserves?[37]

In addition to the explanations and variables provided above, the Bush Administration's decision to "choose" Iraq may have been based on other considerations. That is, one of the residual objectives of the Bush Doctrine and the operation in Iraq was to provide the platform for the transformation of the Middle East into a liberal, democratic and economically viable region. In a speech on the future of Iraq, Bush declared that, "a liberated Iraq can show the power of freedom to transform that vital region, by bringing hope and progress into the lives of millions."[38] It was perceived that removing the Iraqi threat and replacing it with a democratic polity could demonstrate the merits of integration and engagement to neighboring Muslim states, and thereby facilitate the desire for democratization and political liberalization in the Persian Gulf. As further articulated by Mann, some of the Bush Administration "hoped that in overthrowing Saddam Hussein, the US could turn Iraq into a model for democracy that would transform Arab political culture and the politics of the entire Middle East."[39] Indeed, "as far as the Bush Administration was concerned, a democratic Iraq at the heart of the Arab world could become a liberal beacon in the region, promoting demands for openness and real reform inside neighboring states."[40]

In contrast to the above explanations, it is plausible that the Bush Administration's decision to undertake preventive war against Iraq rather than Iran and North Korea was viewed as a strategic choice based primarily upon practical considerations. This included notions pertaining to the relative military capacities and capabilities of the targeted states, which represented the most quantifiable measure of a states' ability to defend/retaliate against an armed attack. As explained by Richard Ned Lebow, relative military capability has the further appeal in that it appears "to lend itself to quantification more readily than do other possible measures of deterrence. Relative military strength is frequently described in terms of the respective makeup and size of adversarial forces and the performance characteristics of their most important weapons systems."[41] Certainly no relatively rational US Administration would consider waging war without first taking into account the war-fighting capabilities of the designated state. In assessing the use of force against rogue proliferators, a primary concern must be the capability of the target state to retaliate. Indeed, there are obvious ramifications involved in undertaking a preventive war and these costs vary directly with the military capabilities of the state in question. Holding all aspects to be more or less equal, if we find that Iraq was considerably weaker than both Iran and North Korea from 2001 to 2003 then, presumably, these large asymmetries had a significant impact on the Bush Administration's risk calculus and ultimate decision to attack Iraq first.

In essence, perhaps the real reason the Bush Administration "chose" to undertake preventive war against Iraq, rather than Iran and North Korea, was because it was perceived to be the weakest, least costly of the three threats—and was "the most feasible place where the US could strike the next blow."[42] Although many arguments have been proposed to account for the US decision to attack

Iraq rather than Iran or North Korea—given the varying similarities between them—it appears that one of the major palatable differences between the three threatening states at the time was their relative military strength and relative military capabilities. However, even though Iraq may have been deemed as the weakest of the three states in the eyes of the Bush Administration, it was still perceived as being a dangerous "rogue proliferator." Regardless of some of the varying considerations posited above—it was clear—Bush and his Administration chose Iraq because it argued that it allegedly had WMDs, had supposed links to al Qaeda and posed an extensive threat to the United States' security. While these arguments were highly debatable and contentious, they nonetheless remained the core thrust of the Administration's platform and justification in the lead up to its preventive war with Iraq in March 2003.

Early indications of prevention

Hints that the Bush Administration was considering a counter-proliferation strategy of preventive war were foreshadowed in statements made well before the publication of the National Security Strategy of 2002. Speaking at the Citadel on September 23, 1999, then-Presidential candidate Bush hinted that the US under his presidency would take preventive/"pre-emptive" action to thwart challenges to America's security: "When direct threats to America [emanating from the "troubled frontiers of technology and terror"] are discovered, I know that the best defense can be a strong and swift offense—including the use of Special Operations Forces and long-range strike capabilities."[43] Of course, the 9/11 attacks brought the option of "pre-emption" to the fore. The Administration's first explicit mention of pre-emption came in the statement of the Chairman of the Joint Chiefs of Staff in the Quadrennial Defense Review Report issued 19 days after 9/11.[44] The Report stated that "defense of the US homeland is the highest priority for the US military.... The US must deter, prevent and defend against aggression targeted at US territory sovereignty, domestic population, and critical infrastructure."[45]

Secretary of Defense Donald Rumsfeld followed up on this theme in a speech on the transformation of the US armed forces delivered in January 2002. He noted that the defense of the United States:

> requires prevention, self-defense and sometimes pre-emption. It is not possible to defend against every conceivable kind of attack in every conceivable location at every minute of the day or night. Defending against terrorism and other emerging 21st century threats may well require that we take the war to the enemy. The best, and in some cases, the only defense is a good offense.[46]

President Bush's post-9/11 statements continually moved toward advocating the explicit adoption of prevention as a key weapon in America's global war on terror. In a teleconference broadcast to the Warsaw Conference on Combating Terrorism on November 6, 2001, he indicated that the US would act proactively to prevent terrorist groups from acquiring WMD. He told the assembled audience that "we will not wait for the authors of mass murder to gain the weapons of mass destruction."[47] Bush extended this determination to act proactively to prevent the spread of WMD to include rogue states in his State of the Union address on January 29, 2002. He listed the second objective in the global war on terror as preventing state sponsors of terror—specifically, the "axis of evil" states of North Korea, Iran, and Iraq—from acquiring WMD with which they could threaten the US and its allies.[48] He warned the nation and the world at large that, "by seeking weapons of mass destruction, these regimes pose a grave and growing danger. They could provide these arms to terrorists, giving them the means to match their hatred. They could attack our allies or attempt to blackmail the United States."[49] He vowed that the US would not permit the world's most dangerous regimes to threaten the US with the world's most destructive weapons.[50]

The President explicitly raised the prospect of prevention in the global war on terror in his speech to the West Point graduating class on June 1, 2002. He asserted that the US must "confront the worst threats before they emerge"[51] and warned that "if we wait for threats to fully materialize, we will have waited too long."[52] Further, President Bush again stipulated the need for robust options encompassing those of a military pre-emptive nature as a means to—should it be necessary—prevent attacks from either states or terrorist groups using weapons of mass destruction. Amplifying this theme, Administration officials emphasized that conventional military technologies were being developed as part of a Joint Stealth Task Force that could launch "no warning" pre-emptive raids on suspected nuclear, biological, and chemical weapons facilities. In addition, officials also spoke of using nuclear weapons, especially against biological weapons where the extreme heat of a nuclear blast could vaporize toxic biological agents.[53]

The Administration's interest also extended to the development of a new, low-yield nuclear weapon (including in the sub-kiloton range) that could be used with earth-penetrating missiles to destroy underground command and control bunkers and hidden facilities used for developing or storing weapons of mass destruction. These various strands in elevating pre-emption (or, in reality, preventive war) to a more prominent role in American defense strategy became further crystallized in the President's National Security Strategy report that was made public on September 20, 2002. The relevant section of the report regarding pre-emption was encompassed in Chapter V, entitled "Prevent Our Enemies from Threatening Us, Our Allies, and Our Friends with Weapons of Mass Destruction." The very title of the chapter was clear in its emphasis on preventive war; that the United States would act to prevent potential foes, whether states or terrorist groups, from even threatening to use, much less actually using, weapons of mass destruction. As Chapter V emphasized, the strategy rested on three fundamental components: proactive counter-proliferation efforts (including counterforce capabilities); strengthened non-proliferation efforts; and effective responses to the effects of WMD use.

The National Security Strategy of 2002/"Bush Doctrine"

It was the National Security Strategy of 2002 that provided the official articulation of a strategy of preventive war against hostile states and terrorist groups developing weapons of mass destruction. The document stated that the United States would destroy terrorist organizations and state actors through direct and continuous action using all the "elements of national and international power."[54] Its focus would be those terrorist organizations of global reach and any terrorist or state sponsor of terrorism which attempted to gain or use WMD or their precursors. Bush argued that defending the United States, the American people, and US interests at home and abroad—by identifying and destroying the threat before it reaches its borders—was paramount. In linking the Bush Doctrine to Iraq and the need to impede what has been referred to throughout this book as a "rogue proliferator," Bush emphasized how the US at the time of the Gulf War obtained "irrefutable proof" that Iraq's designs were not limited to the chemical weapons it had used against Iran and its own people, but also extended to the acquisition of nuclear weapons and biological agents.[55] Therefore, he argued, the United States was prepared to thwart such rogue states and their terrorist clients before they were able to threaten or use weapons of mass destruction against the United States and its friends. Alluding to the Administration's willingness to undertake preventive war, Bush pointed to the notion that "minimizing the effects of WMD" use against "our people" would require a need to respond to the effects of WMD use against US forces abroad.[56] That is, given the goals of rogue states and terrorists, the United States could no longer solely rely on a "reactive posture" as it had done in the past. For Bush, the inability to deter a potential attacker, combined with the apparent immediacy of "today's" threats, as well as the magnitude of potential harm that could be executed by adversaries, dispelled future notions of US reaction and pragmatism. As stated, "we cannot let our enemies strike first."[57]

Bush contrasted the Cold War period of deterrence to what he argued was the necessity of today. In the Cold War, especially following the Cuban missile crisis, the United States was generally faced with a "status quo, risk-averse adversary."[58] During this period, deterrence was an effective defense, however, in the post-Cold War era the threat of retaliation was "far less likely to work against leaders of rogue states more willing to take risks, gambling with the lives of their people, and the wealth of their nations."[59] As further explained by Bush, during the Cold War, weapons of mass destruction were considered weapons of last resort whose use risked the destruction of those who used them:

> Today, our enemies see weapons of mass destruction as weapons of choice. For rogue states these weapons are tools of intimidation and military aggression against their neighbors. These weapons may also allow these states to attempt to blackmail the United States and our allies to prevent us from deterring or repelling the aggressive behavior of rogue states. Such states also see these weapons as their best means of overcoming the conventional superiority of the United States.[60]

For Bush, the threat confronting the US in the twenty-first century was based in the nexus of transnational terrorism and WMD proliferation. Again emphasizing the significance of "today's threats," he stated:

> [N]ew deadly challenges have emerged from rogue states and terrorists.... [T]he nature and motivations of these new adversaries, their determination to obtain destructive powers hitherto available only to the world's strongest states, and the greater likelihood that they will use weapons of mass destruction against us, make today's security environment more complex and dangerous.[61]

As a result, the Administration believed that notions of employing traditional concepts of deterrence would not be effective against a terrorist enemy whose avowed tactics were "wanton destruction and the targeting of innocents; whose so-called soldiers seek martyrdom in death and whose most potent protection is statelessness."[62] Again, implying a link with Iraq, the Bush Doctrine argued that states that sponsored terror and those that pursued WMD would compel the United States into preventive action. Interchanging the term preventive with the more "acceptable" term of pre-emption, Bush made it clear that, "the United States has long maintained the option of pre-emptive actions to counter a sufficient threat to our national security."[63] Or in other words, the US has long reserved the right to take pre-emptive action in the face of an imminent security threat. However, it was necessary, the document continued, to adapt the concept of imminent threat to a new era of security circumstances, i.e. to the determination of rogue states and terrorists to use weapons of mass destruction in attacks aimed at US civilian and military targets.

This extended understanding of imminent threat connected logically to a consideration of pre-emption (or preventive war) as a strategic option in confronting that threat. As stated, "the greater the threat, the greater is the risk of inaction—and the more compelling the case for taking anticipatory action to defend ourselves, even if uncertainty remains as to the time and place of the enemy's attack."[64] The Bush Doctrine hastened to add that pre-emption would not necessarily be the first or the only option considered when confronting these threats. Nor, it warned, should other states use this option as a pretext for aggression. But henceforth, it insisted, the US retained the option of acting pre-emptively when the cause was just—in other words, pre-emption if necessary, but not necessarily pre-emption. As articulated, to forestall or impede such hostile acts by our adversaries, the United States would be prepared to "act pre-emptively (preventively).... To support pre-emptive actions (preventive war), it will ... continue to transform its military forces."[65]

Clarifying the preventive strategy

As indicated in the previous chapter, the preventive option set out in the National Security Strategy of 2002 produced extensive controversy within both domestic and international circles. In response, senior Administration officials followed up the release of the document with statements intended to elaborate on, reinforce, and, to some extent, qualify the basic tenets of this option. Administration spokespersons emphasized that the US had not completely forsaken previous strategic doctrines in favor of prevention/"pre-emption," nor had it enshrined this strategy as the cardinal element in its overall national security policy.

In a speech before the Manhattan Institute in New York in October 2002, National Security Adviser Condoleezza Rice maintained that prevention/"pre-emption" was only one of a range of strategic options open to the US in the global war on terror:

> The National Security Strategy does not overturn five decades of doctrine and jettison either containment or deterrence. These strategic concepts can and will continue to be employed where appropriate. But some threats are so potentially catastrophic—and can arrive with so little warning, by means that are untraceable—that they cannot be contained. Extremists who seem to view suicide as a sacrament are unlikely to ever be deterred. And new technology requires new thinking about when a threat actually becomes "imminent." So as a matter of common sense, the United States must be prepared to take action, when necessary, before threats have fully materialized.[66]

Secretary of State Colin Powell echoed Rice's argument in an article written for *Foreign Affairs:*

> As to pre-emption's scope, it applies only to the undeterrable threats that come from non-state actors such as terrorist groups. It was never meant to displace deterrence, only to supplement it. As to its being central, it isn't. The discussion of pre-emption in the NSS takes up just two sentences in one of the document's eight sections.[67]

Rice also emphasized in her October 2002 speech that pre-emption (preventive war) was an option of last resort, to be taken only when the threat is grave and all other means of confronting it have been exhausted:

> [T]his approach must be treated with great caution. The number of cases in which it might be justified will always be small. It does not give a green light—to the United States or any other nation—to act first without exhausting other means, including diplomacy. Pre-emptive action does not come at the beginning of a long chain of effort. The threat must be very grave. And the risks of waiting must far outweigh the risks of action.[68]

State Department Legal Adviser William H. Taft IV stipulated the two-pronged requirement of necessity for preventive/"pre-emptive" action—i.e. a credible imminent threat and the exhaustion of peaceful remedies—implicit in Rice's remarks.

In a memorandum presented to the Council on Foreign Relations, he maintained that, "after the exhaustion of peaceful remedies and a careful, deliberate consideration of the consequences, in the face of overwhelming evidence of an imminent threat [in the Administration's expanded understanding of that term], a nation may take pre-emptive action to defend its nationals from unimaginable harm."[69] These qualifying statements from senior Administration officials sought to dispel what they maintained was the misconception that the Bush Doctrine signaled the adoption of a use-of-force doctrine in which preventive/"pre-emptive" military action was the method-of-choice in the Administration's fight against the twin evils of international terrorism and WMD proliferation.[70]

Linking the preventive strategy to Iraq

The lead up to the National Security Strategy, the formalization and release of the document itself, and the justification and re-emphasis of prevention (conveyed above and referred to as "pre-emption") from Bush Administration officials, were key components of the Administration's post-9/11 security agenda. But also coinciding with such developments was a drive to link such notions of preventive war to the state of Iraq—deemed as the "rogue proliferator" of choice. It was the likes of Vice-President Cheney who stipulated what appeared to be the defining reason as to why the United States should undertake preventive war against Iraq. In late August 2002, in the most aggressive speech given to date by an Administration official on Iraq, Cheney argued that Saddam Hussein's possession of a nuclear arsenal posed a serious threat to the US because Iraq possessed ten percent of the world's oil reserves. According to Cheney, Saddam Hussein could be expected to:

> seek domination of the entire Middle East, take control of a great portion of the world's energy supplies, directly threaten America's friends throughout the region, and subject the United States or any other nation to nuclear blackmail. Simply stated, there is no doubt that Saddam Hussein now has weapons of mass destruction. There is no doubt he is amassing them to use against our friends, against our allies, and against us.[71]

Cheney's assertive tone on Iraq was embraced by many in the Bush Administration—including the President himself.

In his weekly radio address in September 2002, Bush noted that Saddam Hussein "has broken every pledge he made to the United Nations and the world since his invasion of Kuwait was rolled back in 1991," and emphasized how close Iraq was to attaining nuclear weapons. As stated, "should his regime acquire fissile material, it would be able to build a nuclear weapon within a year."[72] In the same address, Bush described Iraq as a gathering danger:

> By supporting terrorist groups, repressing its own people and pursuing weapons of mass destruction in defiance of a decade of UN resolutions, Saddam Hussein's regime has proven itself a grave and gathering danger. To suggest otherwise is to hope against evidence. To assume this regime's good faith is to bet the lives of millions and the peace of the world in a reckless gamble.[73]

Bush also warned that Iraq would use its association with Osama bin Laden to attack the US. As stated to a group of reporters on September 25, 2002:

> [A]l Qaeda hides. Saddam doesn't, but the danger is, is that they work in concert. The danger is, is that al Qaeda becomes an extension of Saddam's madness and his hatred and his capacity to extend weapons of mass destruction around the world.... [Y]ou can't distinguish between al Qaeda and Saddam when you talk about the war on terror.[74]

In the fall of 2002, the Bush Administration's rhetoric on the threat Iraq posed to US security escalated. Public speeches by Bush's foreign policy team became rather shrill, often making the assertion that the only way to disarm Iraq was to oust Saddam Hussein through military intervention. Cheney went on NBC's "Meet the Press" and argued that Iraq was aggressively developing nuclear weapons in which "the United States may well become the target of those activities."[75] Rice told CNN's Wolf Blitzer that "there will always be some uncertainty to obtaining a nuclear weapon," but "we don't want the smoking gun to be a mushroom cloud."[76] On Fox News Sunday, Colin Powell added to these preventive war sentiments, stating that the Bush Administration believed that the best way to disarm Iraq "is with a regime change."[77]

Once the preventive doctrine had been made public in the National Security Strategy of 2002, Bush was both forthright and consistent in his quest to convince the American public of the threat that Saddam Hussein posed and of the possible ramifications should he acquire nuclear weapons—an attack similar to, but potentially more devastating than the events of 9/11. It was apparent that Bush was laying the platform for war and his rhetoric suggested that this was clearly on the Administration's agenda. As stated in a speech in early October 2002 in Cincinnati:

> If the Iraqi regime is able to produce, buy, or steal an amount of highly enriched uranium a little larger than a softball, it could have a nuclear weapon in less than a year.... The Iraqi dictator must not be permitted to threaten America and the world with horrible poisons and diseases and gases and atomic weapons. America must not ignore the threat gathering against us. Facing clear evidence of peril, we cannot wait for the final proof of the smoking gun that could come in the form of a mushroom cloud.

In the same address, the President again linked Saddam Hussein to al Qaeda:

> We know that Iraq and al Qaeda have had high-level contacts that go back a decade. Some al Qaeda leaders who fled Afghanistan went to Iraq.... We've learned that Iraq has trained al Qaeda members in bomb-making and poisons and deadly gases. And we know that after September the 11th, Saddam Hussein's regime gleefully celebrated the terrorist attacks on America.[78]

Aside from the American public, Bush also had to convince Congress that the use of force in disarming Iraq was both necessary and imperative.

Reminding key Senate and House members that they had voted for a policy of regime change in 1998, Bush told the assembled policy-makers that "doing nothing is not an option."[79] Congress responded by requesting more information on Iraq's WMD program from the CIA. The October 2002 National Intelligence Estimate (NIE) concluded in its key judgments that "Iraq has continued its weapons of mass destruction programs in defiance of UN resolutions and restrictions … if left unchecked, it probably will have a nuclear weapon during this decade." Moreover, "since inspections ended in 1998, most analysts assess Iraq as reconstituting its nuclear weapons program." The intelligence community concluded that "if Baghdad acquires sufficient weapons-grade fissile material from abroad, it could make a nuclear weapon within a year.… Without such material from abroad, Iraq probably would not be able to make a weapon until the last half of the decade."[80] Notably, the Department of State's Bureau of Intelligence and Research (INR) held a dissenting opinion on the rest of this assertion, which was clearly referenced in this first key judgment:

> The activities we have detected do not, however, add up to a compelling case that Iraq is currently pursuing what INR would consider to be an integrated and comprehensive approach to acquire nuclear weapons. Iraq may be doing so, but INR considers the available evidence inadequate to support such a judgment.[81]

Three days prior to the Congressional vote (October 7, 2001), DCI George Tenet provided the following information on ties between Iraq and al Qaeda and permitted their use in unclassified discussions. In a letter to the Senate on Baghdad's intentions, it was posited:

- We have solid reporting of senior level contacts between Iraq and al Qaeda going back a decade.
- Credible information indicates that Iraq and al Qaeda have discussed safe haven and reciprocal nonaggression.
- Since Operation Enduring Freedom, we have solid evidence of the presence in Iraq of al Qaeda members, including some that have been in Baghdad.
- We have credible reporting that al Qaeda leaders sought contacts in Iraq who could help them acquire WMD capabilities. The reporting also indicates that Iraq has provided training to al Qaeda members in the areas of poisons and gases and making conventional bombs.[82]

Notably, Tenet did not identify the threat from Iraq as immediate and posited that Saddam Hussein would restrain himself from undertaking terrorist attacks against the US as long as the US did not attack Iraq. As again stated:

> Baghdad for now appears to be drawing a line short of conducting terrorist attacks with conventional or CBW chemical, biological weapons against the United States. Should Saddam conclude that a US-led attack could no longer be deterred, he probably would become much less constrained in adopting terrorist actions.[83]

In other words, if the US didn't attack Saddam, he was unlikely to attack the US, signifying the CIA's view that Saddam Hussein's Iraq was not an immediate or even intermediate threat to the US … *unless it was attacked.* Nevertheless, on October 10 and 11, both houses of Congress authorized President Bush to "use the armed forces of the United States as he determines to be necessary and appropriate … against the continuing threat posed by Iraq."[84]

Planning for preventive war

When Bush asked Rumsfeld to define and construct a war plan for Iraq in November 2001, he had two major options to choose from in deciding how to disarm Iraq. The first pertained to the notion of improving the pre-9/11 policy of containment, including the development of a new sanctions package. The second option was, of course, the disarmament of Iraq through the use of military force and/or covert action as a means to attain regime change. In the late winter and spring of 2002, Bush commenced a review of the options for Iraq involving a review group that comprised of second and third-ranked people from the foreign policy agencies. This included: Deputy Secretary of Defense, Paul Wolfowitz; Undersecretary for Defense Policy, Douglas Feith; Deputy Secretary of State, Richard Armitage; Deputy National Security Adviser, Stephen Hadley; the regional specialist on Iraq from the National Security Council (NSC), Zalmay Khalilzad; Deputy Director of the CIA, John Mclaughlin; and Vice Chairman of the Joint Chiefs of Staff, Peter Pace.[85] This group came to the conclusion that dealing with Iraq using a strategy of containment was no longer viable and that the most appropriate means to impede the threat from Saddam Hussein was to remove him from power—or topple his regime. According to biographer James Mann, Khalilzad said "the belief was that as long as you had Saddam [in power], he could change his mind [about weapons of mass destruction]."[86] The rationale was clear—Iraq could not be disarmed while Saddam Hussein ruled the country and if he was removed, the dissolution of Iraq's WMD program would follow suit. This change in policy objective—in practice and not just theory—significantly altered the nature of the available alternatives to execute it. To achieve disarmament through regime change, Bush's advisers laid out five options from which to choose: tough new UN inspections designed to cause the regime to implode; a coup d'état engineered by the CIA; the Enclave Strategy; Iraqi opposition forces; and, finally, a full-scale, preventive invasion of Iraq.[87]

The eventual and preferred option pertained to a full-scale preventive invasion and occupation of Iraq as a means to remove Saddam Hussein's regime and ultimately destroy his nuclear arsenal. This option comprised of two components:

first, fighting the war to overthrow Saddam Hussein; and second, occupying and rebuilding post-Saddam Iraq. When Rumsfeld began working on a plan for regime change in Iraq, the initial war plan called for a force of 500,000 and envisaged a similar scenario to the Gulf War of 1990/1991—that being, provocative action by Saddam Hussein that would necessitate a large military response, while also allowing ample time (at least seven months) for a force build-up prior to military action.[88] This strategy "draft," however, shifted as Rumsfeld and General Tommy Franks' Central Command (CENTCOM) planning staff vied for a faster and smaller solution. Both men had spent 18 months planning an Iraq invasion, an endeavor which started in earnest in December 2001 two months after the invasion of Afghanistan.[89] The goal of the new war plan was to "conduct military operations to remove Saddam from power, eliminate the threat of any possible weapons of mass destruction, and choke off his suspected support of terrorism."[90]

The first version of the Iraq war plan was the Generated Start or "90–45–90" plan. The first 90 referred to the 90 days it would take to move forces and otherwise prepare for the 45 days of bombing and Special Operations activity. The second 90 days was the period in which ground forces would engage in combat operations to overthrow Saddam Hussein's regime.[91] The Generated Start Plan evoked concern among Bush's foreign policy team, particularly the "Fortress Baghdad" scenario in which Saddam's forces would retreat to the city and force the US to engage in urban warfare—a high-risk endeavor in a foreign state where the enemy had the potential to attain an asymmetrical advantage. According to Franks, there were varying considerations that Bush needed to put into place before undertaking this strategy option. While not an extensive list, they included the attainment of host nation support, the creation of a sustainable supply line, the movement of the alternate air command and control centre into Qatar, and the prepositioning of aircraft around the world in order to transport forces and equipment.[92] In essence, this meant that Bush would need to orchestrate the groundwork for war in advance of a decision to execute it. In the event that the President only gave them short notice (less than the 90 days), a second version of the plan, "Running Start," would go into effect. This scaled-down version would begin with air operations and would escalate over time. Running Start planned for a bare minimum of troops (50,000) to move into Iraq with plans to send two more divisions within the span of three weeks.[93]

The third version of the Iraq war plan—the Hybrid Plan—in simple terms, merged aspects of the Generated Start and the Running Start plans. First and foremost, it vied for a dramatic time frame in which the front end would move forces into place prior to the commencement of offensive military operations. It comprised of four phases—Phase One would take 16 days: five to establish an air bridge and 11 to transport initial forces. Phase Two would entail 16 days of air attacks and Special Force operations. Phase Three consisted of 125 days of combat operations and, finally, Phase Four which comprised of post-war stability operations, but included no time limit as it was not defined at that stage.[94] The idea was to pressure Saddam Hussein's regime to the breaking point, and thereby, avoid a long war. In terms of feasibility, the Bush Administration judged that a full-scale, preventive invasion had a greater chance of achieving the policy goal than the other, more limited options. For example, when asked by the Armed Services Committee why the Iraq proliferation problem could not be solved with air strikes against its nuclear facilities only, Rumsfeld replied:

> The problem with doing it piecemeal is this: First, we do not know where all of Iraq's WMD facilities are. We do know where a fraction of them are. Second, of the facilities we do know about, not all are vulnerable to attack from the air. Some are underground. Some are mobile. Others are purposefully located near population centers—schools, mosques, hospitals, etc.—where an air strike could kill large numbers of innocent people. The Iraq problem cannot be saved with airstrikes alone.[95]

Moreover, the Pentagon assessed that the Iraqi army was even weaker than it had been in the 1991 Gulf War, making the probability of a successful campaign high. This was mainly due to economic sanctions which had prevented Saddam Hussein from modernizing the military and seriously diminished its offensive capability.

The second part of the preventive option focused on rebuilding the Iraqi government without Saddam Hussein. Although a State Department team had been working on a project entitled "The Future of Iraq" for months, the Pentagon's Undersecretary for Policy, Douglas Feith, became responsible for planning a post-Saddam Iraq, while CENTCOM was to orchestrate the invasion and removal of the regime. Feith delegated the actual planning to CENTCOM, however, after several months, the work was largely discarded due to criticisms that it did not reach out "to real-world people and information."[96] On January 20, 2003, the White House issued a National Security Presidential Directive that established the Pentagon post-war planning office—the Office of Reconstruction and Humanitarian Assistance. In essence, post-war planning encountered several false starts and in many instances could be deemed as relatively ad hoc. In fact, the apparent last minute nature of the post-war planning indicated that Bush and his advisers did not take the occupation portion of the preventive option into account when deciding which option to choose.

Although the Bush Administration had assessed the probability of a successful preventive war against Iraq as being fairly high, they also acknowledged the risks associated with such an attack. As a means to ensure that the President understood the types of impediments and problems the US may encounter in the effort to oust Saddam Hussein's regime, Rumsfeld sent a three page memo to Bush on October 15, 2002, detailing the risks of a preventive attack on Iraq. As stated:

> Another state could try to take advantage of the US involvement of preoccupation with Iraq; oil disruption could cause international shock waves; Iraqi intelligence services, who have a global presence including inside the US, could strike the US, our allies or other deployed forces in

> unconventional ways; there could be higher than expected collateral damage; Fortress Baghdad could prove to be long and unpleasant for all; Iraq could experience ethnic strife among the Sunnis, Shiites and Kurds as had happened before; Iraq could use chemical weapons against the Shiites and blame the United States; and Iraq could successfully beat the US in public relations and persuade the world that it was a war against Muslims.[97]

This option was considered the riskiest as it posed the widest variance in outcome. That is, disarming Iraq through regime change and taking the first step in spreading democracy to the Middle East would be considered a success. However, an Iraq response that entailed a WMD counter attack that caused thousands of US casualties, increased the cost and length of war, as well as potentially inciting ethnic strife or increased anti-Americanism, would obviously be deemed the worst case scenario. Nonetheless, the decision was clear. Likening the terrorist attacks in New York, Washington and Pennsylvania to another tragic day in US history, Bush described the events in his diary on the night of September 11, 2001. He stated, "The Pearl Harbor of the 21st century took place today."[98] The preventive war undertaken against Iraq on March 20, 2003 initiated the second "theatre" in the War of Terror and the second major response by the US to the events of 9/11.

Bush later acknowledged that despite George Tenet's warnings about bin Laden, prior to the events of 9/11 he had not "felt that sense of urgency."[99] In simple terms, 9/11 motivated Bush's movement from a cautious policy of containment to a risk-seeking one of prevention. As indicated above, the President's heightened sensitivity to external threats and keen sense of crisis in the aftermath of 9/11 influenced how he began to view Saddam Hussein and the risks he was willing to take as a means to disarm Iraq and topple his government:

> The threat comes from Iraq … and its drive toward an arsenal of terror. It possesses and produces chemical and biological weapons. It is seeking nuclear weapons.… We also must never forget the most vivid events of recent history. On September the 11th, 2001 America felt its vulnerability—even to threats that gather on the other side of the earth. We resolved then, and we are resolved today, to confront every threat, from any source, that could bring sudden terror and suffering to America.… The evidence indicates that Iraq is reconstituting its nuclear weapons program.… Some citizens wonder, after 11 years of living with this problem, why do we need to confront it now? And there's a reason. We've experienced the horror of September the 11th. We have seen that those who hate America are willing to crash airplanes into buildings full of innocent people. Our enemies would be no less willing, in fact, they would be eager, to use biological or chemical, or a nuclear weapon.[100]

Before the attacks, Bush advocated a policy of containment for Iraq, however, after 9/11 he viewed Iraq's threat to the US as more acute and immediate—as the influence of this event became his frame of reference. As stated:

> Before September the 11th, many in the world believed that Saddam Hussein could be contained. But chemical agents, lethal viruses and shadowy terrorist networks are not easily contained. Imagine those 19 hijackers with other weapons and other planes this time armed by Saddam Hussein. It would take one vial, one canister, one crate slipped into this country to bring a day of horror like none we have ever known.[101]

Despite a lack of credible intelligence linking Iraq to either 9/11 or al Qaeda, and the unfounded assumption that Saddam Hussein would give nuclear weapons to terrorists if he had them, Bush's new view of Iraq as an intolerable threat and probable culprit of a horrific future attack on the US suggested that once 9/11 put the President in a domain of loss, his reference point became the pre-9/11 status quo; an America impervious to external, asymmetric attacks, which he felt he could regain only by dismantling the Iraqi regime.

The lead up

At least six weeks before the completion of the UN inspections, Bush made the decision to use preventive force as a means to topple Saddam Hussein's regime. Convinced that the inspections were not going to put enough pressure on Iraq and subsequently force the government to fall, Bush, according to Woodward, informed Rice that "time is not on our side here. Probably going to have to, we're going to have to go to war."[102] Indeed, when Blix's February 14, 2003 announcement to the UN Security Council was made, it only worked to embolden Bush's resolve. Despite "more than 400 inspections covering more than 300 sites" across a wide range of facilities, inspectors had "not found any such [WMD] weapons, only a small number of empty chemical munitions, which should have been declared and destroyed."[103] While this was a key finding which fundamentally undermined the rationale for war—it did nothing to deter Bush from his decision to launch a preventive action against Iraq.[104]

At Tony Blair's request, Bush went back to the UN for two reasons: in hope of garnering a coalition to assist in or at least support an attack against Iraq and to seek a second UN resolution authorizing military force. Despite Powell's efforts to persuade the President to keep war as a last resort and to continue with stern UN inspections, Bush requested that the Secretary of State present the US case for war in Iraq.[105] Powell's February 5, 2003 UN speech illustrated his shift from periodical objector within the Administration to what appeared to be defender of Bush's determination to end the Saddam regime in the pursuit of disarmament, defining the threats from Iraq as "real and present dangers to the region and the world," and the "sinister nexus between Iraq and the al Qai'da terrorist network."[106] Bush and Blair's desire for endorsement from the UN were lost when the leaders of France, Russia, and Germany issued a statement calling for extended weapon inspections, stating that "Nothing today justifies war. Russia, Germany and France are determined to ensure that everything possible is done to disarm Iraq peacefully."[107] With failure imminent, Powell pulled the vote. Undaunted, Bush went to war with a small and unimpressive coalition, at least in comparison to his father's 1991 standards. That Bush proceeded with his plans for regime change in Iraq with substantial and material support from only three countries—Great Britain, Australia, and Spain—made his decision to wage preventive war in Iraq all the more risk-acceptant.

Bush announces war with Iraq

On March 19, just hours after he had ordered the first attacks on Iraq, Bush announced his decision to attack Iraq to the American public and spoke of the Iraqi threat. As stated, "we meet that threat now, with our Army, Air Force, Navy, Coast Guard and Marines, so that we do not have to meet it later with armies of fire fighters and police and doctors on the streets of our cities."[108] Even as he announced the commencement of war with Iraq, Bush reconnected with 9/11—an event wholly unrelated in practical terms to Iraq—to justify the action. Bush chose the preventive option because he believed it could allow him to recoup the pre-9/11 status quo of American invulnerability and this could be attained by ousting Saddam Hussein, disarming Iraq, and therefore averting future attacks similar but more deadly than 9/11. The preventive option had the highest outcome value if it succeeded, but one of the lowest outcome values if it failed. Bush selected the riskiest option in order to take a chance at recouping previous losses, re-establishing the previous status quo, and averting future losses. According to Cheney:

> After we got hit on 9/11 the President said no more and enunciated in the Bush doctrine that we will hold states that sponsor terror, that provide sanctuary for terrorists to account, that they will be treated as guilty as the terrorists themselves of whatever acts are committed from bases on that soil.[109]

From 2001 to 2003, when faced with the prospect of having to wage preventive war against one of three rogue proliferators—Iraq, Iran, and North Korea—the Bush Administration chose to preventively attack Iraq, a decidedly weaker state. This seemed to provide strong evidence to support Richard Ned Lebow's basic claim that:

> a [major] consideration militating against war can be its expected costs. In some circumstances they may be high enough to dissuade policy-makers from using force regardless of the magnitude of the expected gains.... The absolute cost of war ... was probably an important restraining factor for American policy-makers.... This indicates that as the absolute cost of war increases, the importance of relative gains diminishes and may ultimately become irrelevant to the decision for war or peace.[110]

Although many arguments have been proposed to account for the US decision to attack Iraq rather than Iran or North Korea, given the vast similarities between them, it appears that the main palatable difference between the three threatening states at the time was their relative military strength. Nonetheless, it was evident that Bush's regular public refrain about the threat from Iraq centered on the dangers and risks inherent in doing nothing to thwart the suspected Iraqi WMD programs and Saddam Hussein's intent to use them against the US. In simple terms, the President framed the options in public on Iraq as merely twofold: preventive war or "trusting in the sanity and restraint of Saddam Hussein."[111] In seeking to avert future losses similar to those suffered by the US on 9/11, Bush took a worst-case scenario perspective and thus gave little credence to the middle of the road alternatives involving weapons inspections or sanctions that might have worked to disarm Iraq, but not to remove Saddam Hussein from power.

The fact that Bush ordered the invasion before inspections had been completed indicated that when it came to Iraq, preventive military force was not a last resort. A tendency to disregard information both from the intelligence community and from his advisers, specifically Powell, which ran contrary to his goal of regime change, also suggested that Bush sought war with Iraq as a way to re-establish the pre-9/11 status quo and avert a future loss to US national security. A March 2005 White House-commissioned report on NBC intelligence was extremely critical of American intelligence on Iraqi NBC prior to the 2003 Iraq War, "noting the thin body of information."[112] Similarly, Greg Thielmann, former head of the Office of Strategic Proliferation and Military Affairs in the State Department's Office of Intelligence and Research, admonished that "the effectiveness of any first-strike military doctrine depends on reliable intelligence. The US intelligence community's inability to produce accurate information on enemy threats renders such a doctrine feckless and reckless."[113] In essence, Bush and his team disregarded intelligence analysts whose conclusions did not coincide with their own and who, at the same time, challenged intelligence that questioned the existence of Iraqi WMD or Saddam's ties to al Qaeda, or generally, called into question the ultimate goal of regime change in Iraq. Powell, who believed disarmament could be achieved without war, was regularly "outweighted" by Cheney, Rumsfeld, and Wolfowitz, all of whom embraced Bush's view that war was necessary to permanently disarm Iraq. Illustrating how removed Powell was from influencing the "final" decision, Bush chose preventive war and conducted it in a manner that contradicted Powell's doctrine of overwhelming force. Rumsfeld's speed and mobility won out and the post-Saddam occupation occurred without a clear vision for the future or an exit strategy.

In making the decision on how to handle the perceived proliferation of nuclear weapons in Iraq, Bush gave small thrift to options other than preventive war on the grounds that they had been tried to no avail, albeit not during his Administration. The President also chose the preventive option despite the lack of solid evidence indicating Saddam Hussein was complicit in 9/11, that he had ties to al Qaeda or that Iraq's suspected nuclear program was close to producing a nuclear weapon. He made repeated declarations regarding the dire nature and immediacy of threat from Iraq and embedded these declarations with images of a nuclear 9/11 orchestrated by Saddam Hussein—even when there was little evidence to link Saddam to terrorism or to 9/11—and in fact—a statement by the CIA expressing a view that Saddam would not attack the US unless attacked first. That Bush viewed the 9/11 attacks as a type of harbinger of extreme consequences to follow if he did not act to avert it, also likely played a role in his decision to opt for preventive war. As he later stated in the National Security Strategy of 2006:

> For America, the September 11 attacks underscored the danger of allowing threats to linger unresolved. Saddam Hussein's continued defiance of 16 UNSC resolutions over 12 years, combined with his record of invading neighboring countries, supporting terrorists, tyrannizing his own people, and using chemical weapons, presented a threat we could no longer ignore. The UNSC unanimously passed Resolution 1441 on November 8, 2002, calling for full and immediate compliance by the Iraqi regime with its disarmament obligations. Once again, Saddam defied the international community.[114]

Condoleezza Rice's decision-making process was also heavily defined by the events of 9/11.

As late as 2000, Rice felt Iraq could be deterred much as the Soviet Union had been over the last 40 years. Against Iraq and North Korea, she advocated that "the first line of defense should be a clear and classical statement of deterrence—if they do acquire weapons of mass destruction, that weapon will be unusable because any attempt to use them will bring national obliteration."[115] Yet, after 9/11, Rice's views on how to conduct foreign policy underwent a sea change. She saw 9/11 as a sign that it was time to change the direction of American foreign policy. As stated:

> The international system has been in flux since the collapse of Soviet power. Now it is possible—indeed probable—that the transition is coming to an end.... This is, then, a period akin to 1945 to 1947, when American leadership expanded the number of free and democratic states—Japan and Germany among the great powers—to create a new balance of power that favored freedom.[116]

Within this context, Rice stressed the new vulnerability facing the United States in the wake of 9/11:

> It will take years to understand the long-term effects of September 11th. But there are certain verities that the tragedy brought home to us in the most vivid way. Perhaps most fundamentally, 9/11 crystallized our vulnerability.... Today's threats come less from massing armies than from small, shadowy bands of terrorists—less from strong states than from weak or failed states. And after 9/11, there is no longer any doubt that today America faces an existential threat to our security. [117]

Rice clearly discussed both the loss on 9/11 of America's sense of security and the future threats which must be averted.

In the same speech, she also illustrated how the September 11 attacks influenced her thinking on how the US should respond to other actors perceived as threatening in order to avert future losses similar to 9/11: "since 9/11, our nation is properly focused as never before on preventing attacks against us before they happen."[118] A manifestation of Rice's new perspective was the National Security Strategy of 2002, which embodied the Bush Doctrine and created a framework for foreign policy which Rice arguably believed would allow the US to recoup the pre-9/11 status quo of a feeling of security. Using 9/11 as context, Rice asserted that adopting the Bush Doctrine did not constitute throwing out containment or deterrence, but that these traditional concepts were not enough to prevent future losses caused by terrorist attacks. As stated:

> Some threats are so potentially catastrophic—and can arrive with so little warning, by means that are untraceable—that they cannot be contained. Extremists who seem to view suicide as a sacrament are unlikely ever to be deterred. And new technology requires new thinking about when a threat actually becomes "imminent." So as a matter of common sense, the United States must be prepared to take action, when necessary, before threats have fully materialized.[119]

In authoring the National Security Strategy of 2002, Rice married the threat and dangers of terrorism to warnings about Saddam Hussein and his desire to acquire weapons of mass destruction.

In a formula seemingly designed to recoup the pre-9/11 status quo of security and to avert future losses, Rice suggested the threat may come in the form of terrorist attacks similar to, but even deadlier than those perpetrated on 9/11. On this basis, Rice made the case for going after Iraq as part of the war on terrorism.

> Terrorists allied with tyrants can acquire technologies allowing them to murder on an ever more massive scale. Each threat magnifies the danger of the other.... For these reasons, President Bush is committed to confronting the Iraqi regime, which has defied the just demands of the world for over a decade.... The danger of Saddam Hussein's arsenal is far more clear than anything we could have foreseen prior to September 11th. And history will judge harshly any leader or nation that saw this dark cloud and sat by in complacency or indecision.[120]

When it came to choosing between the available options, Rice was not diametrically opposed to seeking a UN resolution on Iraq or renewing inspections, because this method of disarmament had actually worked in South Africa. She initially advocated going to the UN to obtain a new resolution on Iraq and encouraged the President to at least try new weapons inspections, likely because, even if they failed, US efforts at the UN could justify and possibly garner international support for a war in Iraq. However, Rice ultimately believed that the only way to remove the perceived threat of Iraqi WMD was to launch a preventive war. She told House minority leader Nancy Pelosi at a meeting at the White House on February 5, 2003, that "we tried sanctions, we tried limited military options, we tried resolutions. At some point, war is the only option."[121]

Although Rice entered the Bush Administration as a well-known realist who advocated a foreign policy that focused on big, powerful countries in pursuit of the national interest, after the 9/11 terrorist attacks, she began to frame external threats to the US differently. When asked by Bush if he ought to pursue war, Rice answered:

> Yes, because it isn't American credibility on the line, it is the credibility of everybody that this gangster can yet again beat the international system.... To let this threat in this part of the world play volleyball with the international community this way will come back to haunt us someday. That is the reason to do it.[122]

Indeed, the Bush Administration's ideologically driven framing of the Iraq issue, and the mindset that regime change in Iraq was necessary to prevent another 9/11, resulted in a tendency to overlook nuance and to reduce complex issues to simple, Boolean choices which produced an all or nothing perspective on the decision problem regarding Iraq. Even before he went to the UN, Bush publicly cast the decision on how to handle Iraq as a choice between two options—doing nothing or toppling the regime—while ignoring any options in the middle. In a November 2002 speech, he stated that there is a "risk in all action we take. But the risk of inaction is not a choice, as far as I'm concerned. The inaction creates more risk than doing our duty to make the world more peaceful."[123] This characterization of the options did not in fact reflect the way Bush approached his available alternatives, suggesting that his depiction of the options as: a) go to war; b) do nothing and put your fate in the hands of Saddam Hussein, was rhetoric constructed as a means to persuade the American people to back military action.

Bush never considered inaction an option and he appears to have viewed all options other than military action as distinctly limited. His conviction that regime change was a necessary step in preventing another 9/11 manifested itself to the extent that the President believed that options other than military force had already been exhausted. For example, in the weeks before he made the decision on Iraq, Bush dismissed two new options proposed by UN members with the justification that they had been tried in some shape or form and had failed: a German and French proposal for a tougher program of coercive inspections and renewed UN inspections under an explicit threat of force—until it was established with certainty that Saddam Hussein had dismantled his weapons program or inspectors were obstructed from completing their jobs.[124] Bush was convinced regime change was the only viable option for achieving Iraqi disarmament, and thus, making the US more secure, suggesting that the President approached the UN, not to prevent a war with Iraq, but to justify one. Such logic would again be prevalent in the National Security Strategy of 2006. And once again, replacing preventive war with pre-emption, he stated:

> When the consequences of an attack with WMD are potentially so devastating, we cannot afford to stand idly by as grave dangers materialize. This is the principle and logic of pre-emption. The place of pre-emption in our national security strategy remains the same. We will always proceed deliberately, weighing the consequences of our actions. The reasons for our actions will be clear, the force measured, and the cause just.[125]

In terms of the "choice" of Iraq, the cultivation of the preventive war doctrine (rhetorically and formally in the context of the National Security Strategy of 2002), the alignment of the preventive war option to Iraq, as well as the orchestration and lead up to the preventive war itself—it appears that the Bush Doctrine could be deemed as overzealous, extreme, and unprecedented. In fact, when looking at Bush's unbridled determinism to wage war with Iraq, this seemed to be nothing short of the truth. However, despite such appearances of a radically new approach, at its core, the Bush Doctrine's push for preventive war in Iraq in 2003 has long pervaded the strategic thought of policy-makers, officials, and military planners at the highest levels of the US government. As the next chapter will argue, since the end of World II, each time a rogue state has attempted to acquire nuclear weapons, the US has seriously considered taking unilateral preventive action as a means to impede this development—even in the dubious case of Iraq where action was *actually* undertaken. Indeed, the second half of the twentieth century is sated with examples of prominent US decision-makers who have contemplated the undertaking of major unilateral preventive military actions as a means to forestall the proliferation of nuclear weapons by rogue states. Although much attention has been paid to the recent actions in Iraq and the potential for future wars in Iran and North Korea, precious little has been written about the three other earlier preventive war targets. The next chapter will thus seek to investigate and analyze each of those cases in order to assess the extent to which the US considered waging preventive war against them, and to uncover why in the final analysis, US decision-makers in each case decided to refrain from such action. If we find that the US abstained from preventive war against these three states primarily because of practical concerns directly related to military costs (i.e. the size and strength of the enemy and its prospects for retaliation), then perhaps a strong case can be made for the effectiveness of deterrence in mitigating the US drive for preventive war against rogue proliferators in both the past and present.

3 The Bush Doctrine and prevention

Evident in twentieth-century US foreign policy—case studies

The core theoretical thrust underpinning the Bush Doctrine, and specifically, the preventive motivation for war, has long been an intrinsic strategic thought of policy-makers, officials, and military planners at the highest levels of the US government. While it has often been depicted as a distinct and markedly new National Security Strategy, the Bush Doctrine was, in fact, neither new nor era-defining. As Peter Lavoy contended, the Bush Administration's "new" strategy read much like "old wine in a new bottle" and hardly represented the fundamental policy shift that many portend.[1] As this chapter will argue, since the dawning of the nuclear era in 1945, at least three other US Presidents (Dwight D. Eisenhower, Lyndon B. Johnson, and William J. Clinton) have faced the potential threat of nuclear technology in the hands of states hostile to their respective Administrations and each dealt with the same decision faced by President Bush in 2003: whether to use preventive military force as a means to counter the proliferation of such nuclear weapons technology. Each was forced to make their decision regarding the preventive use of force in the face of uncertainty. Each had to weigh the costs—many of them unknown—of preventively striking an adversarial state perceived to be developing nuclear weapons against the costs of refraining from preventive intervention and employing more conservative diplomatic methods, even while the threat of future military conflict hovered.

Indeed, the historical record of the last half century is replete with examples of high-level US decision-makers who seriously considered the undertaking of major unilateral preventive military actions as a means to thwart the proliferation of nuclear weapons by rogue states. As early as January 1946, in a foreboding memorandum on the military implications of the development of nuclear weapons, US General Leslie Groves, then wartime commander of the Manhattan Project, expressed the simple but compelling temptation of preventive war thinking: "If we were ruthlessly realistic, we would not permit any foreign power with which we are not family allied and in which we do not have absolute confidence, to make or possess nuclear weapons. If such a country started to make nuclear weapons we would destroy its capacity to make them before it had progressed far enough to threaten us."[2] Prior to the invasion of Iraq in 2003, the US had considered preventive options against no less than three additional rogue proliferators: the Union of Soviet Socialist Republics (Soviet Union) from 1945 to 1954; the People's Republic of China (China) from 1960 to 1964; and the Democratic People's Republic of North Korea (North Korea) from 1993 to 1994. This chapter will investigate these case studies as a means to appraise the extent to which the US seriously considered executing preventive war against these states, and in the final analysis, will reveal that what Bush advocated in 2002/2003, was not "new," "radical," and certainly not "revolutionary."

According to Schneider, for any leader to order a preventive counter-proliferation strike a "very special set of circumstances" was required. As stated:

> The nuclear aspirant would have to be approaching the nuclear weapons threshold and be led by a hostile government that appears ready to take extreme risks. Such a government is unlikely to be deterred from future warlike actions. Moreover, the developing scenario would have to directly and immediately threaten a vital interest of the country considering the pre-emptive strike. It would require information on important nuclear target locations of the adversary and the ability to achieve tactical surprise. Moreover, the adversary should not be able to threaten the pre-emptor with nuclear arms or other weapons of mass destruction or have a strong ally who is likely to do so on its behalf. All other reasonable options should have been exhausted before such a strike is undertaken. The head of state should have adequate domestic and international political support for the action and for bringing any military campaign to a successful conclusion before choosing this type of non proliferation activity.[3]

That these conditions were not met in the American invasion of Iraq in 2003 is less noteworthy than the fact that the invasion constituted the application of the preventive war doctrine in US national security strategy. The Bush Doctrine, at its core, gave primacy to the use of preventive military intervention both as a central component of US foreign policy and a method of counter proliferation. However, prevention has not only been a common motive for war, it has actually been "quite routine."[4] As argued by Gray, it is difficult to find historical cases of warfare wherein prevention was not a motivator: "Wars typically occur for several, even many, reasons. Prevention is nearly always prominent in the cluster of those reasons. The concept of preventive war has an ominous ring to it that is not entirely deserved. Poor historical understanding is the explanation."[5] What this book suggests is that considerations of prevention typically played a sometimes greater, sometimes lesser, role. As Gray further asserted, it has been rare to find a conflict "wherein there was no spore of a preventive motive to be found."[6] With regard to the Cold War of 1947–1989, it was standard to cite

> the deadly trio of geopolitics, ideology, and personality as combining to produce the fatal brew which resulted in 42 years of nuclear shadowed global menace. But, austerely viewed, in 1946–47 both Washington and Moscow decided to wage preventive non-military conflict.[7]

The United States was determined to prevent the USSR from expanding its sphere of control any further, while "the USSR was no less determined to prevent the United States from rolling back its hard won gains."[8]

In relation to the National Security Strategy of 2002, many of the Administration's critics denounced the policy as new and dangerous, while the Administration itself argued the need to go beyond past practice, warranted by the novel and dangerous threats facing the United States. But as indicated by Steinberg, the use of preventive force—including the debates over its legality and wisdom—predate the Bush Administration's post-9/11 strategy. As stated, a "careful examination of the history, rationale, costs and benefits of using preventive force suggests that while rare, preventive force has had a legitimate role to play in tackling some of the most dangerous security problems facing the United States."[9] For Trachtenberg, the claim that the Bush strategy of dealing with developing threats "preventively" marked a total break with American tradition was an argument that needed to be both examined and challenged:

> It turns out that preventive war thinking played a much greater role in shaping US policy than most people realize. During the early Cold War period, this sort of thinking was by no means limited to the lunatic fringe. Could the United States simply sit back and allow first the Soviets and then the Chinese to develop nuclear capabilities of their own? Many people, both inside and outside the government, were worried about what would happen if America did nothing and thought that the possibility of preventive action had to be taken seriously. In the post-Cold War period, the Clinton Administration seemed ready to do whatever was necessary to prevent North Korea from going nuclear; it seemed prepared, in fact, to go to war over the issue. Even in the pre-nuclear world, preventive war thinking played a major role in shaping policy: American (post-war) policy was strongly influenced by this kind of thinking.[10]

Case study one: preventive war and the USSR, 1945–1954

Preventive considerations

As World War II came to an end, it became increasingly evident that the first unallied foreign power that would attempt to revise the international system by acquiring nuclear weapons would be the second greatest power in the world, that being the USSR. Following the cessation of hostilities, the once expedient wartime alliance between the US and the Soviet Union quickly unraveled into an ideological and strategic chasm. As Russell Buhite and William Hamel argued, in the years immediately following World War II basic conflicts of interest, not to mention mutual suspicion and misperception, tore the Grand Alliance apart and precipitated "a dramatic deterioration of relations between the United States and the Soviet Union. Since their pre-war relationship had provided nothing solid on which to build, it is not surprising that their conflicting world views and objectives in the post-war period" gave way to the rise of the Cold War.[11] With Germany and Japan devastated, Great Britain severely weakened, and the rest of Western Europe on the cusp of political and economic collapse, the US and the Soviet Union after World War II enjoyed a unique period of uninhibited strength and opportunity with which to expand their relative influence throughout the world and especially in Western Europe. Given their vast disparities and mutual interest in this contested region, it was not surprising that by the end of 1945 most US government officials and military planners, to say nothing of the American public, viewed Soviet aggression, expansionism, and intransigence as the most serious threat to the future of US and world security. Indeed, concerns pertaining to the perceived actions, motives, capabilities, and intentions of the Soviet Union informed, and to a certain degree, distorted, American attitudes during this time of great uncertainty.

With a diametrically opposed ideology that espoused sentiments of a worldwide "communist revolution," "capitalist encirclement," and "inevitable conflict;" an estimated four to six million troops already mobilized in Eastern Europe, and an estimated 10.5 million in reserve (more than enough to overturn and occupy all of Western Europe); alleged aggression in Berlin, the Baltic republics, Finland and Hungary; and a perceived desire and ability to develop nuclear weapons, the Soviet Union represented a clear threat to the US and its European allies. As articulated by Michael Nacht, concern over the Soviet Union was predicated on the threatening "character of Soviet communist ideology, consolidation of Soviet political control of Eastern Europe," the potential threat posed by Soviet conventional forces against Western Europe, "the subversive techniques of this international communist movement controlled by Moscow, and the intransigent character of Soviet negotiating behavior on a wide range of post war issues."[12] The supposed Soviet desire to attain nuclear weapons was of specific concern to the US during this volatile period. As conveyed by Trachtenberg, "if the Soviets were allowed to develop nuclear forces of their own there was no telling what might happen." If they were so "hostile and aggressive" in the period of America's nuclear monopoly, "what would they be like once this monopoly had been broken.... wouldn't the Soviets someday try to destroy the one power that prevented them from achieving their goals by launching a nuclear attack on the US?"[13] For many observers during this period the very specter of such an outcome led to a "surprisingly widespread" espousal of Bush Doctrine-like preventive war thinking.

From 1945 to 1949 the US held a clear nuclear monopoly in which no other state in the world had nuclear weapons. From 1949 to 1954, although the Soviet Union had developed a diminutive nuclear capability, the US still enjoyed a vast nuclear superiority and thus, it was argued, still had the capacity to remove the burgeoning Soviet nuclear program. Once this monopoly/superiority was lost, however, most American observers believed that the Soviet Union would likely undertake an even more aggressive, expansionist foreign policy or potentially undertake a quasi-"nuclear Pearl Harbor" against the US mainland. Indeed, shortly after Stalin's emotive ideological address to the Soviet citizenry on

February 6, 1946, William Bullit, the first American ambassador to the Soviet Union warned, “as the conquest of the earth for Communism is the objective of the Soviet government, no nation lies outside the scope of its ambitions.”[14] Furthermore, as Trachtenberg reported, the assumption that the Soviets were intent on world domination and thus on “the destruction of American power, and the belief that they were absolutely ruthless and that their policy was ‘guided only by considerations of expediency,’ implied that they would strike when they had developed [a nuclear] capability.”[15]

In this light, it was viewed by policy-makers in the US and Western Europe that the only reason the Soviet Union had not yet pressed its interests any further west was the fact that the US held a clear nuclear deterrent. Once the Soviet Union was securely in possession of a large nuclear weapons arsenal of its own, however, it was feared that the US line would no longer hold and that the Soviet Union would swiftly move to overthrow or undermine the existing status quo in Western Europe. As Campbell reported: “once Stalin obtained nuclear parity … he would use it to cancel out the American arsenal, move his vast almost omnipotent conventional forces into the ‘Eurasian land mats’ and dare the Americans to risk World War III by stopping him.”[16] As a result, many policy-makers in the US and Western Europe at the time argued that the attainment of nuclear weapons by the Soviet Union would be completely unacceptable and would have to be “rolled back.” It was perceived that the surest way to do so was to “strike first and strike hard,” before it was too late. It was with this in mind that preventive war thinking during this time received an extensive level of support in which, according to Trachtenberg, the “impact on actual policy was both enormous and pervasive.”[17]

The call for preventive war against the USSR came as early as mid 1945, when several high-ranking members of the US government began discussing the need to address the expanding “Soviet problem.” In what is now viewed as an infamous phone conversation with General Joseph T. McNamey, General Dwight D. Eisenhower’s deputy at the time, General George S. Patton—one of the most vocal and anti-Soviet advocates of preventive war—first conveyed the emerging preventive war sentiment:

> Hell, why do you care what the Goddamn Russians think? We are going to have to fight them sooner or later within the next generation. Why not do it now while our army is intact and the damn Russians can have their hind ends kicked back into Russia in three months? We can do it ourselves easily with the help of the German troops we have, if we just arm them and take them with us; they hate the bastards. In ten days I can have enough incidents happen to have us all at war with those sons of bitches and make it look like their fault. So much so that we will be completely justified in attacking them and running them out.[18]

While Patton was one of the first and most overt proponents of preventive war against the Soviet Union, he was certainly neither the last nor the most extreme.

Over the course of the next nine years many others would reiterate his proactive view of assertive counter-proliferation. For instance, later in 1945, the State War Navy Coordinating Committee constructed an official government memorandum which audaciously declared that when it "becomes apparent that forces of aggression are being arrayed against us by a potential enemy, we cannot afford, through any misguided or perilous idea of avoiding an aggressive attitude, to permit the first blow to be struck against us."[19] Furthermore, in September 1946, the Joint Chiefs of Staff recommended in clear fashion that the US needed to "press the issue to a prompt political decision while making preparations to strike the first blow if necessary … the US should demonstrate its readiness … to take prompt and effective military action abroad to anticipate and prevent an attack on the US."[20]

Additionally, in a report to the Secretary of War (now Secretary of Defense), General Henry H. Arnold of the US Air Force staunchly asserted that "the only certain protection against [Soviet] aggression is to meet it and overcome it before it can be launched or take full effect."[21] Furthermore, in August 1950, Secretary of the Navy, Francis Mathews reportedly stated:

> The US should be willing to pay any price to achieve a world at peace even the price of instituting a war to compel cooperation for peace.… [The Communists] would brand our program as imperialist aggression. We could accept that slander with complacency, for in the implementation of a strong affirmative, peace-seeking policy, though it casts us in a character new to a true democracy—an initiator of a war of aggression—it would win for us a proud and popular title—we would become the first aggressors for peace.[22]

Finally, as recounted by Buhite and Hamel:

> Other officers joined the chorus … [they] assumed that in the next war the nation that struck first with nuclear weapons would win; therefore, preventive war seemed like an attractive option. According to General Carl Spaatz, the way to deal with a possible Soviet air attack was "to get them at the place they start before they are launched." And in response to concerns that the Soviet Union might acquire and use the nuclear bomb, General Arnold argued that the "one defense against the nuclear bomb" was to "hit it before it starts." "The first blows" in the next war, wrote Ira Eaker, "would be struck through the air, and to prevent destruction of this country in the event of such an attack, we must strike the enemy first." General Orvil Anderson subsequently spoke out in favour of a surprise attack.[23]

Proponents of preventive war were not limited to the US military. It became clear that notions of preventing the USSR from attaining nuclear weapons by offensive means gained a substantial following among some of the most renowned government officials, journalists, and political scientists in the western world. Of these, many were in favor of a proposal that would take the onus away from the US, placing it firmly upon the Soviet leadership. In this way, the US would present the Soviet Union with an unambiguous nuclear ultimatum: cease research and development efforts on nuclear weapons or face an American preventive war. Indeed, several US government officials and military planners, some of considerable prominence and authority, endorsed this potentially catastrophic assertive proposition. That is, Ambassador Bullit suggested that the US should threaten Moscow with "annihilation" and "if that failed," he wrote, "then the US, should annihilate the Soviet Union."[24] Moreover, according to Trachtenberg, William Laurence, the science correspondent for the *New York Times* and then America's leading writer on nuclear issues, wanted to force the Soviets in 1948 to accept nuclear disarmament through an ultimatum if necessary.[25] If they turned down this American demand, Laurence argued, "their nuclear plants should be destroyed before bombs could be produced." If that meant war, he said, it would be one forced on America by Soviet "insistence on a nuclear armament race which must inevitably lead to war anyway. Under the circumstances, it would be to our advantage to have it while we are still the sole possessor of the nuclear bomb."[26]

Preventive war-thinking garnered even more support following the outbreak of the Korean War. Given the Soviet Union's apparent complicity with the North Korean communists, several officials within and outside of the Truman Administration—and now containing what they deemed to be a "legitimate" pretext for which to justify a war with the Soviet Union—began considering an even more aggressive stance vis-à-vis Moscow. One of these mainstay advocates of preventive war against the Soviet Union included the aforementioned General Anderson, then commandant of the Air University at Montgomery, Alabama, who, on September 1, 1950, stipulated the reasons as to why confrontation was necessary:

> Since we're at war, damn it, I don't advocate preventive war, I advocate the shedding of illusions. I advocate saying to Stalin: "Joe, you're not kidding anybody. You are saying you are going to destroy us." And if he says "yes"—and he has been saying "yes" all the time—we must conclude civilization demands that we act. Give me the order to do it and I can break up Russia's five A-bomb nests in a week! When I went up to Christ I think I could explain to Him that I had saved civilization.[27]

Dwight D. Eisenhower

Under the Eisenhower Administration, it was evident that preventive war options were put on the table on at least two different occasions: first, as an additional option in Project Solarium and, second, after the Soviets tested their first thermonuclear bomb in August 1953. The Project Solarium preventive option was summarily dismissed (and containment favored) as Eisenhower saw prevention as too extreme given the nature of the perceived Soviet threat at the time. However, once the Soviets displayed their formidable and unexpected progress in thermonuclear weapons development one year ahead of US expectations, the President began to view the Soviet nuclear threat as more acute and became willing to at least consider the preventive option in addition to those already posited as part of Project Solarium. Indeed, the status quo after the Soviet thermonuclear test constituted the reference point in which Eisenhower gave serious consideration to launching preventive strikes against the Soviet Union. In a memorandum he sent to Secretary Dulles on September 8, 1953, he stated:

> Among other things, we should describe the capabilities now and in the near future of the H-bomb, supplemented by the A-bomb. We should patiently point out that any group of people, such as the men in the Kremlin, who are aware of the great destructiveness of these weapons—and who still decline to make any honest effort toward international control by collective action—must be fairly assumed to be contemplating their aggressive use. It would follow that our own preparation could no longer be geared to a policy that attempts only to avert disaster during the early "surprise" stages of a war, and so gain time for full mobilization. Rather, we would have to be constantly ready, on an instantaneous basis, to inflict greater loss upon the enemy than he could reasonably hope to inflict upon us.[28]

Additionally, Eisenhower posited further preventive war considerations when he admonished that:

> if the contest to maintain this relative position should have to continue indefinitely, the cost would either drive us to war—or into some form of dictatorial government. In such circumstances, we would be forced to consider whether or not our duty to future generations did not require us to initiate war at the most propitious moment that we could designate.[29]

Ultimately, Eisenhower was unwilling to accept the cost of employing the preventive option against the Soviet Union, as it potentially risked tens of thousands and maybe millions of deaths from a retaliatory strike.

Prevention was also viewed by some decision-makers as morally questionable; a violation of US founding principles and unlikely to produce a successful outcome—that being, the total demolition of the Soviet Union's nuclear capabilities and its ability to threaten the US with complete destruction. From a position of gains in which no lives had yet been lost, Eisenhower judged the options which would prevent a massive loss of life and cautiously chose containment over the preventive option. On January 1955, Eisenhower formally put a halt to the preventive consideration and signed NSC-5501, entitled "Basic National Security Policy." He declared that:

> The United States and its allies must reject the concept of preventive war or acts intended to provoke war. Hence, the United States should attempt to make clear, by word and conduct, that it is not our intention to provoke war. At the same time the United States and its major allies must make clear their

> determination to oppose aggression despite risk of general war, and the United States must make clear its determination to prevail if general war eventuates.[30]

The document argued that the notion of undertaking a preventive war had passed, and hence signified the end of the 1945–1954 "preventive war era." Instead, Eisenhower's national security strategy involved "deterring further Communist aggression and preventing the occurrence of total war" by using a "flexible combination of military, political, economic, propaganda, and covert actions which enables the full exercise of US initiative." Taking the Soviet Union's imminent nuclear parity into account, the national strategy noted that "programs for the general strategy between now and the time when the USSR has greatly increased nuclear power should be developed as a matter of urgency."[31] Containment was thus instituted as a long-term solution to the emerging problem of impending Soviet nuclear parity. Eisenhower showed cautious restraint in dealing with Soviet nuclear proliferation and the threat it posed to the US. Later, in 1956, despite the capability of the US to launch a decisive strike against the Soviet Union, Eisenhower also took the cautious path and rejected the preventive option.

Preventive restrictions

While the record clearly illustrates that the US enjoyed either a clear-cut nuclear monopoly or vast superiority during this time frame, it ultimately chose not to exploit this extraordinary advantage—despite the grave and gathering proliferation threat posed by its main adversary. Why was this the case? Why did neither Truman nor Eisenhower, despite their intense repugnance towards the Soviet Union and the strong pressures upon them to act, ever authorize a preventive war against the rising power of the USSR? Why exactly did the US not then use this monopoly to force some major political concessions on the Soviet Union, perhaps even to force on Moscow what was imposed on Tokyo and Berlin, a surrender and disarmament and democratization?

First, it was apparent that several powerful US government officials and military planners, including some preventive war advocates, believed that the very concept of preventive war was "out of step" with America's political traditions and strategic culture. That is, preventive war was both "aggressive" and "dishonorable," "the kind of thing inflicted on the American people, not initiated by them."[32] As Richard Smoke explained:

> It is worth recalling the option of preventive war, because more recently people have forgotten the moral significance of the fact that the US never considered it. America is the one nation in all of recorded history that for a few years probably had—to put it bluntly—the chance to rule the world. The nuclear monopoly would almost certainly have carried the US to victory in a war against the Soviet Union.... Thereafter the US might have enforced

> pax Americana on the world indefinitely, either directly, or through a UN that America controlled. This possibility was never seriously entertained in Washington, and that fact has a permanent moral meaning. However uncomfortable Americans may have felt, and still feel, about Hiroshima and Nagasaki, and more recently about the war in Vietnam, it will always be to their nation's credit that the US possessed the one opportunity in history to be master of the globe, and was not even seriously tempted.[33]

Indeed, in the history of the US, preventive war had long been equated with aggressive war. As posited by Scott Silverstone, "in normative or moral terms, one problem with preventive war is that throughout history it has been closely tied to the concept of 'wars of aggression.' Witness the cast of characters most frequently cited as engaging in preventive war: Louis XIV, Frederick the Great, Napoleon, Kaiser Wilhelm, Hitler, Imperial Japan."[34] Additionally, as conveyed by Walter Slocombe, "preventive war is not only in violation of international law, but an unbounded invitation to use of force on mere suspicion of the ambitions or intent of another nation; it is indeed a negation of the very concept of international law."[35]

Distinctly conscious of prevention's traditionally negative and unlawful connotation, Army Chief of Staff Matthew Ridgway and several others regularly condemned preventive war as a viable means to impede the Soviet Union from proliferating nuclear weapons—as it was "wholly contrary to every principle upon which our Nation has been founded," and "utterly abhorrent to the great mass of American people."[36] Furthermore, in the now infamous NSC-68, Eisenhower and his advisors maintained:

> It goes without saying that the idea of "preventive" war—in the sense of a military attack not provoked by a military attack upon us or our allies is generally unacceptable to Americans ... [a] surprise attack upon the Soviet Union, despite the provocations of recent Soviet behavior, would be repugnant to many Americans. Although the American people would probably rally in support of the war effort the shock of responsibility for a surprise attack would be morally corrosive. Many would doubt that it was a "just war" and that all reasonable possibilities for a peaceful settlement had been explored in good faith.... The US therefore cannot engage in war except as a reaction to aggression of so clear and compelling a nature as to bring the overwhelming majority of our people to accept the use of military force.[37]

Moreover, many during this period believed that it would be difficult for the US to undertake an aggressive war against the Soviet Union while maintaining its credibility as a benevolent state attempting to engender liberal democracy and notions of world peace. As articulated by Ray Reuther, the United States "rejects the theory of preventive war as the answer to Soviet aggression. We could not live with ourselves nor stand before the world as defenders of human freedom ... if we accepted the 'moral responsibility' for launching a war of aggression."[38]

Finally, and perhaps more significantly, both Truman and Eisenhower were concerned with the contravention of American values and ideals that a preventive war against the Soviet Union would signify. In 1954, for example, James Reston of the *New York Times* asked Eisenhower what he thought of preventive war. Eisenhower replied: “a preventive war, to my mind, is impossibility.... I don’t believe there is such a thing, and frankly I wouldn’t even listen to anyone seriously that came in and talked about such a thing.”[39] Truman was especially clear that preventive war was contrary to American principles and could not be perceived as a policy option in an action sense. On varying occasions, Truman renounced preventive war thinking, having declared: “We do not believe in aggression or preventive war. Such a war is the weapon of dictators, not of free democratic countries like the US,” and “Starting a nuclear war is totally unthinkable for rational men,” and finally “There is nothing more foolish than to think that war can be stopped by war. You don’t ‘prevent’ anything but peace.”[40]

Aside from the moral considerations presented in opposition to preventive war, many US observers at the time were also concerned about the logistic and strategic practicality of such an action. Indeed, there were a plethora of such “practical” variables from 1945 to 1954; three that specifically appeared to be the most defining: a lack of US bombs and bombers; the prospect of Soviet retaliation against Western Europe; and the enormous costs of post-war occupation/reconstruction. In the first instance, the US quite simply did not possess a sufficient amount of nuclear bombs and bombers with which to execute a major preventive campaign against the USSR as envisaged by military war planners. As explained by Quester:

> While the world was led to believe that the US had a sizable stockpile of nuclear weapons ... one of the best kept secrets of the post-war years was that the total of nuclear weapons in the US arsenal was indeed quite small.... By some accounts, moreover, even the few bombs for which components had been assembled ... were no longer functional or usable. The actual totals of nuclear weapons possessed by the US, counting components as if they were assembled into bombs, rather than badly maintained, is something like the following: perhaps three or four at the end of 1945, and nine by the middle of 1946, and perhaps thirteen by the middle of 1947 ... by the middle of 1948 the total had climbed to perhaps fifty.[41]

While an intensive bomb building campaign resulted in a stockpile of approximately 250 nuclear bombs by the end of 1949, the USSR had already developed its own nuclear bomb by that time. Aside from this, the burgeoning US military complex demanded more bombs than those that existed in the US arsenal during the early 1950s. David Allan Rosenberg posited that, during the era of American nuclear monopoly, the nation’s stockpile and delivery capability were extremely limited. There were very “few weapons available and none of these weapons was assembled ... when nuclear war planning began in earnest, this focus was diluted reflecting scarce resources, poor intelligence, and operational difficulties.”[42]

Moreover, even if the US had been in possession of a sufficient amount of nuclear bombs—as a means to meet its preventive war plan objectives—it still would have been palpably limited in executing an attack by virtue of the fact that it lacked a satisfactory delivery capability. In 1946/1947 the US possessed only 27 modified B-29 bombers suitable for delivering the enormous nuclear bombs (each weighed over 10,000 pounds and had to be delivered one at a time); in 1948 it had only 32; and through 1949 that number continued to hover around 30, not nearly enough to ensure a successful delivery capability.[43] Further, compared to modern bombers, the B-29 had a relatively short range of only 1,500 to 1,700 miles depending on the payload. If deployed from the US, American pilots would be forced to undertake costly and inefficient one-way suicide missions. Finally, until the technology and operational capacity improved in 1950, it took approximately 39 men close to a week to assemble the bombs, prepare the modified planes and move them to the appropriate bases for an attack.[44] In short, from 1945 to 1954 the nuclear wherewithal of the US, in terms of having both the quality and quantity of bombs and bombers, was far too inadequate and unreliable to undertake a preventive war on a level necessary to efficiently nullify the Soviet threat.

In addition, while there was no distinct concern in relation to a nuclear retaliation against American cities from 1945 to 1954, there was a legitimate fear of Soviet conventional retaliation against Western Europe. As posited earlier, it was widely perceived that the only reason that the USSR had not yet advanced to occupy and/or devastate all of Western Europe was based on US nuclear deterrence. Indeed, "if we see American nuclear weapons and extended nuclear deterrence as the crucial barrier to Soviet conventional attack one might thus in reverse see the Soviet conventional grip on Western Europe as a necessary and sufficient counter to the American nuclear grip on Soviet cities."[45] Therefore, a defining concern for high-level US government officials and military planners from 1945 to 1954 was the Soviet Union's ability to retaliate against Western Europe. According to Buhite and Hamel, nothing could prevent the Soviet Union, with its overwhelming superiority in conventional forces in place in Eastern Europe, from occupying Western Europe. Short of "using nuclear bombs—an obvious impossibility—nothing the US could do would then dislodge them." Moreover, "any nuclear attack on the Soviet Union would result in a stalemate—the US could devastate a large portion of the Soviet Union, but the Soviets could hold on to the western section of the continent indefinitely."[46] As elaborated by Quester, a more certain explanation of the American failure to initiate a preventive war "must therefore go back to the limitations on the potency of the American nuclear stockpile" as "it was not widely expected that the Russians would surrender even if their cities were regularly being hit by nuclear weapons, as long as they could install themselves in the cities in Western Europe."[47]

Finally, it was evident that the US was "self-deterred" from undertaking a large-scale preventive war against the Soviet Union because of the significant, indeed, unmanageable costs it would incur while attempting to occupy and/or reconstruct the largest state in the world. In November 1947, Air Force General Hoyt Vanderberg admonished, "in a war with the Soviet Union is our purpose to destroy the Russian people, industry, the Communist party, the Communist hierarchy, or a combination of these?… Will there be a requirement to occupy, possibly reconstruct, Russia after victory…?"[48] Years later, Eisenhower exhibited the same concern, stating:

> What do you do with the world after you have won victory in such a catastrophic nuclear war? The colossal job of occupying the territories of the defeated enemy would be far beyond the resources of the US at the end of such a war … the only thing worse than losing a global war was winning one.[49]

In essence, even if a general preventive war could be won in any meaningful sense, the logistical issues that the US would encounter in the post-war period were both overwhelming and, quite obviously, prohibitive.

Case study two: preventive war and China, 1960–1963

Preventive considerations

By the time President John F. Kennedy took office in early 1961, a second major strategic competitor emerged to alter the nuclear balance—China. While having some similarities to the USSR, the case of Chinese proliferation from 1960 to 1963 was extensively distinct from that of the USSR during the period 1945–1954. The USSR epitomized a proliferation threat. It was unequivocally an antagonistic and expansionist state with both the will and the means to challenge the US in strategically significant regions throughout the world. China on the other hand, although clearly hostile towards the US and a formidable regional power, was never considered a threat to the very survival of the US or a legitimate contender for global dominance. As argued by Robert H. Johnson, a high-ranking US State Department Policy Planning Council East Asian specialist in the 1960s:

> We do not believe that the explosion of a first device, or even the acquisition of a limited nuclear weapons capability, would produce major changes in Communist China's foreign policy in the sense that the Chinese would adopt a general policy of open military aggression, or ever become willing to take significantly greater military risks. China's leaders will recognize that their limited capabilities had not altered the real power balance among the major states and could not do so for the foreseeable future. In particular, they would recognize that they remained unable either to remove or neutralize the US presence in Asia … so long as the ChiComs only have soft, vulnerable delivery means, they will have to take account of the danger of a US nuclear or non-nuclear counterforce attack as a possible response to major ChiCom aggression. This could increase ChiCom caution.[50]

Roger Hilsman, director of the State Department's Intelligence Bureau, also subscribed to Johnson's view when commenting in public in 1962 that as "dramatic" as the prospect of China's exploding a nuclear device may have been, "it [would] not change the balance of power in Asia, much less throughout the world."[51] Moreover, in late July 1963, a CIA report on China's anticipated response to the Limited Test Ban Treaty further discounted the possibility of Chinese aggressiveness, stating that the Chinese "over the past few years, in spite of their warlike oratory, have followed a generally cautious policy.... The Chinese have thus far shown marked respect for US power, and we do not expect them to change this basic attitude."[52] In essence it was apparent that several US government officials and military planners from 1960 to 1963 believed that the unique variables surrounding China's nuclear proliferation program—specifically, its historically cautious military policies and weak strategic position vis-à-vis the US—would make its nuclear movements more of a "tolerable inconvenience" than an ominous threat. Many in Washington were therefore unmoved by China's attainment of nuclear weapons and their capacity to effectively challenge the US military.

Of course, not all observers during this period embodied this optimistic assessment. According to Nacht:

> many US policy-makers saw Communist China as, other than the Soviet Union, the most powerful threat to American security interests, especially in Asia but in other regions of the developing world as well. The decade of the 1950s included the Sino-American armed conflict in Korea and several major crises over Taiwan and the neighboring offshore islands.... The Sino-American relationship, prior to Chinese nuclear weapons acquisition, was wholly adversarial, and those Americans who thought it should be otherwise either had no influence or were summarily discredited if they voiced their views too loudly.[53]

Indeed, the acrimony that had characterized the Sino-American relationship during the previous ten years, in which China and the US had recently concluded a bitter war on the Korean Peninsula, almost came close to another conflict over the status of the Taiwanese-held offshore islands of Quemoy and Matsu. This encompassed extensive exchanges of bellicose rhetoric in which many US government officials and military planners, not least of which included President Kennedy, were inclined to view Communist China through a decidedly suspicious and guarded lens. According to William Burr and Jeffrey T. Richelson, "implicit to Kennedy's view, shared by area specialists at the CIA and State Department that the position of the Soviet leadership on peaceful coexistence and the dangers of nuclear escalation was substantially more responsible and less dangerous than Beijing's."[54] For example, in a classified report entitled, "China as a Nuclear Power," a group of high-ranking US State Department policy planners portentously concluded that:

> As China goes down the road of becoming a nuclear power she will do her utmost to exploit her new weapons to achieve her goals. These goals are

> perfectly evident. China is determined to gain status, as a world power, primarily by reducing US power and influences in Asia and the Western Pacific. The Chinese Communists seem determined to eject the US from Asia. We can be sure that they will be seeking ways to exploit their nuclear weapons to this end. China is determined to seize the leadership of the Communist movement. This is to be done by ... proving by example that China is the only militant and reliable source of aid to revolutionaries seeking to overthrow the existing order by force.... Hopes that nuclear weapons will bring greater caution to the Chinese are made to appear rather forlorn by the Chinese criticism of the Soviets for having been too timid in the use of their nuclear deterrent to aid the spread of Communism.[55]

More significantly, it was apparent that Kennedy himself viewed China as an aggressive state with an expansive agenda.

According to Robert Garson, Kennedy at various intervals had described China as being "intrinsically hostile to the US," a "dangerously radical nation that preached and encouraged world revolution that would take any opportunity to eliminate American influence from Asia."[56] Moreover, as reported by Burr and Richelson, "Kennedy was hostile to Mao's regime and found the prospect of a nuclear China disquieting. The President ... saw a Chinese nuclear test as likely to be historically the most significant and worst event of the 1960s."[57] Furthermore, Kennedy's closest advisers regularly overheard him bemoaning China as "the great menace in the future to humanity, the free world, and freedom on earth," who was "prepared to sacrifice hundreds of millions of [Chinese] lives to carry out Mao's aggressive and militant policies."[58] Defining Kennedy's stern position on the Chinese nuclear program was "the perception of Mao's China as fundamentally more dangerous and irresponsible than the Soviet Union (with which the terms of 'peaceful coexistence,' as Khrushchev put it, could be negotiated)."[59] As stated by Alice Langley Hsieh, even the Soviet Union—at this stage China's communist ally and exemplar—had intimated that the real reason the Chinese vied to develop its own nuclear capacity independent of Moscow was to "pursue special aims and interests which could not be supported by the military forces of the socialist camp."[60] The basic foreign policy objectives included the incorporation of Taiwan into Peking's domain, the achievement of hegemony in the Far East, and the removal of US power and influence from the area. Additionally, "the Chinese had little alternative but to seek to rely on their own military potential" and to develop their own nuclear weapons, in order to "make gains where Soviet military support or assistance could not be expected, or where Soviet aid would be subject to conditions and controls imposed by Moscow."[61]

It was of course difficult to fully know the underlying motivations or potential consequences of the Chinese desire for nuclear weapons from 1960 to 1963. Nonetheless, it was quite apparent that any such development, whether intended for "peaceful" or aggressive purposes, was widely perceived in the US to be a potential threat to national and international security. In the first instance, once

China had nuclear weapons there was always the real prospect that it may use them against the US. While China had no intercontinental ballistic missiles at the time, it did have a comparatively sizeable fleet of military aircraft that could reach all parts of Asia, including US military installations and allied structures in Japan, Taiwan, and South Korea. Moreover, as one writer from the *National Review* warned in 1965, "even today a ship can carry a Chinese bomb into the harbors of New Orleans, San Francisco, New York, or London."[62] In fact, the US navy even suggested that "the Chinese might consider initiating a 'catalytic war' ... attacking the US with submarine-launched missiles in such a way as to make the US believe the attacker was the Soviet Union and respond accordingly."[63] This rather extreme scenario in itself may have engendered a sufficiently strong justification for acting against China's nuclear weapons program. However, based on the empirical record, it is evident that it was not, as a matter of policy, Washington's primary concern. For the US, the potential for continuous negative political-psychological effects (particularly in the context of the Cold War), together with an increase in China's involvement in low-level border wars, as well as an expected "chain reaction" of nuclear proliferation in Asia, proved even more distressing (and realistic) than the prospect of an overt Chinese nuclear attack.

According to some US officials, Chinese nuclear proliferation had the potential to engender politically significant "psychological effects" on both allies and enemies throughout the region and around the world. As Johnson observed in early 1964, "the ChiComs will value their nuclear capability for ... its psychological effects in weakening the will of countries resisting insurgency, inhibiting their requests for US assistance, and in stimulating and exploiting divisions within Asia and between Asian countries and the West."[64] It will be used to put political pressure on the US military presence and "to obtain support for Chinese acknowledgement of claims to pre-eminence in Asia and status as a world power."[65] Hence, if the Chinese were allowed to attain nuclear weapons, a heightened sense of China's power could create a "bandwagon effect with greater political pressures on states in the region to accommodate Beijing and loosen its ties with Washington ... [this] could only weaken Washington's influence in the region and its capabilities to intervene on behalf of its allies there."[66] In short, the political and psychological effects following the detonation of a Chinese nuclear weapons was expected to raise China's "stock" or prestige while at the same time undermining the US presence in Asia.

A second and related concern pertained to the possibility of how a dramatic increase in international power and prestige may encourage China to use its new capability as a type of "political weapon ... to earn respect, to promote [and] encourage revolutionaries."[67] Given its storied history of actively supporting communist Marxist and Maoist revolutionary movements along its borders, the US certainly had legitimate reason to believe that an emboldened nuclear China would "feel very much stronger and this mood would doubtless be reflected in their approach to conflicts on their periphery."[68] While Johnson and other policy-makers believed it to be unlikely that China would risk a general war on the continent for such revolutions, they did believe that Beijing would come to doubt America's willingness to intervene on the Asian mainland. As a result, China's policies were expected to grow more assertive. This could very easily translate into increased Chinese "political pressures and the indirect support of local 'wars of liberation,'" as well as a more direct play towards hegemony on the Asian continent.[69]

Third, and finally, many US government officials and military planners at the time were concerned that the acquisition of nuclear weapons by China would foster an unwelcome "chain reaction" of nuclear proliferation in the greater Asia region and beyond. As posited by Johnson, the possibility of "development of additional national nuclear capabilities has been one of the central concerns of our interdepartmental Chinese nuclear exercise because of the general possibility that Asian nations might be tempted in this direction."[70] Similarly, as indicated by Burr and Richelson, in early 1961, CIA analysts "mused" that if China or Israel were to go nuclear, other states might enter the field if only to counter the power and "prestige which their rivals or their enemies might gain.… Intelligence reports from the capitals of two key countries, Japan and India, suggested that heads of state there were considering the possibility of developing national nuclear weapons programs."[71] It was envisaged that if this scenario was to take place, a major level of "global instability would result," in which even a minor increase in the number of states "possessing nuclear weapons will add to the dangers inherent to critical situations when they arise … an increase in the number of states with nuclear-threat capabilities would increase the chances for irrational and desperate action."[72]

Although there is substantially less corporeal information pertaining to the prevalence of preventive war thinking in the US from 1960 to 1963 than from 1945 to 1954, a number of recently declassified government documents signify that the logic of preventive war had in fact infiltrated some of the most influential offices of the US government—including that of the President. In February 1963, the Secretary of Defense Robert McNamara drafted a secret memorandum for Kennedy on the prospects and implications of the "diffusion of nuclear weapons," concluding that their spread was "clearly not in the interest of the US" and "in some cases … would probably have to [be met] with stronger incentives and sanctions than has seriously been considered so far," encompassing both economic and military "penalties."[73] Furthermore, in July 1963, Secretary of State Dean Rusk reportedly informed the US ambassador to West Germany that robust coercion would be undertaken against Beijing "not to go down the nuclear path," and if China persisted, "other action might have to be taken to prevent this."[74] In a meeting with Taiwan's powerful "security czar" in October 1963, National Security Assistant McGeorge Bundy made clear that the US was "very interested in whether something could be planned … that could have a delaying and preventive effect on the nuclear growth of China."[75]

McGeorge Bundy, National Security Adviser

When Gordon Chang revealed in 1988 that President Kennedy had seriously considered using preventive military force to destroy China's nuclear installations, McGeorge Bundy denied that such action had ever been considered. He wrote, "there had been talk in Washington about the possibility of pre-emptive action against the Chinese bomb—talk, not serious planning or real intent."[76] However, Bundy's denial directly contradicts the paper trail of documents declassified in 1997 which portray him as "the point man in countering the Chinese nuclear effort, passing Kennedy's instructions to the CIA, holding secret discussions with Nationalist Chinese officials and seeking to enlist Soviet diplomats in joint efforts against China's nuclear program."[77] Indeed, it appears that Bundy was more in favor of preventive attacks on Chinese nuclear sites than Johnson's other senior advisors. His willingness to seriously consider preventive force began during the Kennedy Administration from the period when China's nuclear program was discovered. Bundy continued to hold this position despite the opposing views of colleagues and key subordinates in the subsequent Johnson Administration. Motivating his proclivity for preventive military action was his belief that a nuclear China presented a grave threat to United States national security. Bundy believed that while the Soviet Union under Khrushchev was a cautious nuclear power, China under Mao was volatile. As stated, "Mao regularly insisted that nuclear war would bring the end of imperialism and the final victory of socialism, while Khrushchev argued that the right way to victory was by the peaceful proof that socialism was better."[78]

Throughout 1963 and the beginning of 1964, Bundy continued to favor some type of preventive military action despite contrary opinions from his colleagues. Following an informal Planning Group lunch on November 5, 1963 at which Communist China's nuclear developments and US possible responses were posited, NSC staffer Robert Komer reported to Bundy that "[while] there was much discussion on how to 'strangle the baby in the cradle' before the Chinese developed a capability,"[79] the essential conclusion was that the "ChiCom acquisition of a semi-nuclear capability will not have much more than a marginally significant impact and can probably be coped with by some marginal stepping up of existing programs."[80] However, in spite of Komer's virtual dismissal of preventive action, Bundy wanted to see more work and planning done in the "preventive action field." In response to another memo from Komer on February 26, 1964, in which he wrote, "WWR [Walt Rostow] is also poking around in the preventive action field. Do we want this?" Bundy wrote in the margin, "I'm for it."[81] In short, Bundy appeared to be willing to take on the "option."

John F. Kennedy

As indicated in the above, it was evident that Kennedy himself had taken a considerable interest in the notion of using preventive military action as a means to "strangle the baby in the cradle" and impede China's expanding nuclear weapon program. Indeed, since his untimely assassination on November 22, 1963, a wide range of previously classified and significant information regarding Kennedy's thinking on China and preventive war has been released. As Burr and Richelson stated:

> Less than a year after President John F. Kennedy's assassination, Arms Control and Disarmament Agency Director William Foster told a historian that Kennedy had been rivalling to 'consider politically dangerous moves ... to coerce the People's Republic of China into complying with the 1963 Limited Test Ban Treaty.' Foster, whose comments remained classified until 1994, asserted that Kennedy was willing to ... secure Soviet cooperation 'in taking action, if necessary physically, against China.' Moreover, Foster told his interviewer that the President would 'think out loud' saying 'You know, it wouldn't be too hard if we could somehow get kind of an anonymous airplane to go over there, take out the Chinese facilities ... they've only got a couple ... and maybe we could do it, or maybe the Soviet Union could do it, rather than face the threat of a China with nuclear weapons.'[82]

Kennedy also articulated his concerns in a conversation with Director of Central Intelligence, John McCone, in which he stated that "[a nuclear China] would so upset the world political scene [that] it would be intolerable."[83] According to Bundy, Kennedy felt that "we should be prepared to take some form of action unless they [China] agreed to desist from further efforts in this field."[84] Specifically, at the January 22, 1963 National Security Meeting, Kennedy said that the Chinese would be "our major antagonists of the late 1960s and beyond," such that the US' main purpose in treaty negotiations with the Soviet Union should be to "halt or delay the development of an atomic capability by the Chinese Communists."[85] China's nuclear efforts had so concerned Kennedy that since June 1961 he had been considering approaching the USSR in hopes of exploiting the widening Sino-Soviet split and persuading Khrushchev to work with the US in countering or delaying China's nuclear program.[86]

It was the possibility of joint action by the US and the Soviet Union, combined with his concerns about the political implications and consequences of a nuclear China, that spurred Kennedy to seriously consider the use of preventive military force to stop China from obtaining nuclear weapons. In February 1963, Paul Nitze, Assistant Secretary of Defense for International Security Affairs, asked the Joint Chiefs of Staff (JCS) to conduct a study on using "persuasion, pressure, or coercion" to persuade China to sign a test ban treaty. Influenced by the thinking of Ambassador-at-Large Averell Harriman, Kennedy felt a US and Soviet Union agreement to stop nuclear development in China would create enormous pressure on China to give up their nuclear program or at least provide justification for a military strike by the US—but blessed by the Soviet Union.[87] However, while the report submitted to Nitze by the JCS in April 1963 included a myriad of indirect measures involving propaganda campaigns and diplomatic schemes, as well as direct coercive measures including both multilateral and unilateral military options, the Acting Chairman General Curtis LeMay ultimately concluded that because there was no guarantee that China would actually adhere to a nuclear test ban treaty, it was "unrealistic to use military force" to try to achieve that goal. However, the report also stated that Soviet cooperation, in the event the US decided to conduct air strikes against Chinese nuclear facilities, could "well be the difference between escalation and quick acquiescence by the ChiComs."[88]

In July 1963, Kennedy sent a secret cable to Assistant Secretary of State, Benjamin H. Read, the US official responsible for communications with the Soviet Union. It related to what he referred to as the largest Chinese nuclear development and clearly affirmed his preventive war inclinations vis-à-vis the Chinese. As articulated by Kennedy:

> I remain convinced that the Chinese problem is more serious than Khrushchev's comments in the first meeting suggest, and believe you should press question in private meeting with him. I agree that large stockpiles are characteristics of US and USSR only, but consider that relatively small forces in hands of people like ChiComs could be very dangerous to us all.... You should try to elicit Khrushchev's view of means of limiting and preventing Chinese nuclear development and his willingness either to take Soviet action or to accept US action armed in this direction.[89]

While Kennedy did not clearly specify the type of "action" he had in mind, it was apparent that he was advocating something more than mere diplomatic or political strategies. Moreover, at a meeting of the National Security Council on January 22, 1963, Kennedy explained that "our primary purpose in the ongoing Nuclear Test Ban Treaty negotiations with the Soviet Union is to halt or delay the development of an atomic capability by the Chinese Communists."[90] Finally, in response to a question on how a nuclear test ban treaty would thwart China and other states from acquiring nuclear weapons, Kennedy argued that "the ban" should stipulate that signatories would "use all the influence that they had in their possession to persuade others not to grasp the nuclear nettle." Further, Kennedy added, "quite obviously," countries pursuing nuclear weapons "may not accept this persuasion and the, as I say, they will get the *false* security which goes with nuclear diffusion."[91] While such words are hardly conclusive, they do signify that Kennedy was at least attuned to the consideration of waging preventive war against China.

Despite the general advantages in taking such an approach—the elimination of the Chinese nuclear capability would eliminate the need for US consideration and action in responding to Communist aggression or ChiCom use of nuclear weapons; deprive the ChiComs of the political psychological and military-defense advantages of a nuclear capability; and greatly reduce the incentive and justification for Indian development of nuclear weapons and the possible subsequent movement of Japan [and Taiwan] in the same direction—"the preventive war option was, quite obviously, never made a reality."[92] Shortly after Kennedy's assassination, newly appointed President Lyndon B. Johnson, who was said to be "rhetorically more cautious about China" and "wholly averse to confrontation with China," quickly and quietly decided to put aside the preventive war option, and instead, put in place a more cautious, less intrusive means of counter-proliferation, including trade and export controls, assertive military containment and continued intelligence monitoring.[93] These efforts came to no avail. On October 16, 1964, China detonated its first nuclear weapon and thus ended the 1960–1963 preventive war era. Johnson described his perspective on the Chinese nuclear test in his memoir, seven years after his cautious decision to try again with the Soviets:

> Peking's accomplishment came as no great surprise because we had been expecting it for some time. Nonetheless, the fact that a large country with a hostile government had mastered the technology of nuclear explosives was necessarily a source of worry. I was not concerned for the immediate future. A long and expensive road separated setting off a nuclear blast and developing the powerful and accurate missiles to carry nuclear weapons across seas and continents. But what of my successor? Or his successor? Some future President would have to face the question of how to deal with this situation. The problem was not just a matter of China. It was a question of how to deal with a great many nations, of all sizes and levels of political stability, equipped with nuclear weapons. All I could do was to move as fast and as far as possible during my Presidency to slow the arms race, to achieve international agreements on their control, and to prevent the continuing proliferation of weapons that could mean an end to civilization as we knew it.[94]

In the months that followed, Johnson Administration officials continued to evaluate the use of force, however, officials at the top no longer viewed such a strategy as being viable unless Beijing first launched a major aggressive act against its neighbors. Johnson and his advisers "would monitor China's nuclear progress closely and search for ways to delay it through trade controls, but it was clear that the President had tacitly decided to live with the Chinese bomb."[95]

Preventive restrictions

The 1960–1963 period was the second time in ten years that the US had an extraordinary opportunity to preclude a major strategic competitor from acquiring nuclear weapons via preventive action—but refrained from doing so. As indicated in the case of the Soviet Union, when faced with a similar situation, both Truman and Eisenhower were apt to forgo a preventive course of action on the basis of both moral and practical considerations. In the case of China, however, it appears that only latter restraint proved politically influential. Indeed, very little evidence exists to support an argument that the Kennedy Administration was dissuaded from taking preventive action against China on account of morality. This is not to say that the Kennedy Administration completely eschewed international norms or American traditions regarding the use of force—after all, during the Cuban missile crisis President Kennedy and his brother, US Attorney General Robert Kennedy, ultimately condemned a surprise US air strike against Soviet missile sites under construction in Cuba because they believed it was morally repugnant.

At one point in the famous "Excom" debates, Robert Kennedy passed a note to President Kennedy which read, "I know now how Tojo felt when he was planning Pearl Harbor" and "[attacking Cuba] would be a Pearl Harbor in reverse, and it would blacken the name of the US in the pages of history" as a great power who attacked a small neighbor. However, regardless of this, the fact remains that neither legal nor moral questions were explicitly addressed in any of the available government documents concerning preventive action in China.[96]

Nevertheless, Kennedy's political advisers did frequently express concerns pertaining to the potential for "heavy foreign policy costs," "adverse international political reactions," and "difficult international opinion" that were expected to accompany an unprovoked US preventive attack on China. As Burr and Richelson indicated, the Kennedy Administration well understood that "an unprovoked US attack could entail heavy foreign policy costs," "was dangerous and likely to fail and ... could hurt the US image and weaken its prestige."[97] Moreover, Johnson concluded that any US action "with no justification than a general argument that the US was seeking to preserve the peace of the world through depriving a potential aggressor of nuclear weapons would be subject to [adverse international political reactions]."[98] Finally, acting Chairman of the Joint Chiefs of Staff, Curtis LeMay, concluded that it was unrealistic to "use overt military force" against China because if "the US took unilateral action, whether initiating a blockade or military action, policy-makers had to consider the strong prospects for retaliation and escalation, not to mention the difficulty of justifying such an action to international opinion."[99] While such statements hardly prove that the Kennedy Administration had a strong moral aversion to preventive war, they may imply that there was, at least on some level, a general concern for the "rightness" or "wrongness" of such action.

Whereas morality seemed to play a very small role in restraining the Kennedy Administration from taking preventive action against the Chinese nuclear program, the practicality (or impracticality) involved in such an attack was ever present. Indeed, as posited by Robert H. Johnson in one of his many studies on the Chinese Communist nuclear capability and some "unorthodox" approaches to the issues of nuclear proliferation: "It is evident ... that the significance of a ChiCom nuclear capability is not such as to justify the undertaking of actions which would involve great political costs or high military risks."[100] In particular, many observers believed that the chances of operational failure (à la "Bay of Pigs" fiasco) and Chinese retaliation were far too great. First, it was evident that the intelligence "portfolio" on China from 1960 to 1963 was inadequate. According to Burr and Richelson:

> the US intelligence collection capabilities, particularly with respect to China were limited. Satellite imagery of China became available only in August 1960, and at first on an intermittent basis. Meanwhile, the location deep in China's interior of critical nuclear facilities ... made it difficult to cover such targets with U-2 spy planes ... with all the gaps in intelligence about the PRC's nuclear program, Washington may not have identified all relevant targets.[101]

Moreover, Johnson concluded, "there is considerable uncertainty regarding the location of critical facilities … we have no certainty, even now, that we have identified all nuclear production facilities."[102] Clearly, this was a major impediment for the Kennedy Administration and the preventive war option, for without accurate intelligence, it would have been near impossible for the US to "have full assurance that its action [would] eliminate the ChiCom capability."[103] Not eliminating the Chinese nuclear program would, of course, have undermined the very purpose of launching a preventive attack in the first place.

The second and perhaps more important restraint upon the US was the strong possibility of Chinese retaliation against Taiwan or US bases in East Asia. Indeed, there was a clear apprehension among US leaders at the time that Beijing or Moscow would misconstrue a "limited war action" on select Chinese nuclear installations as the beginning of a major attack on the Chinese mainland, and such developments could engender a massive communist retaliation against allied positions by China, the Soviet Union, or both. The possibility of military retaliation by Communist China or the USSR was difficult to estimate because it would depend in "some significant measure upon the particular circumstances in which the US action was taken." However, "some kind of ChiCom retaliation cannot be ruled out.… In general, action against Communist Chinese facilities … is highly dangerous, involving grave risk of precipitating war in Asia and even bringing the Soviets to the support of the Chinese."[104] In essence, it appears that the Kennedy Administration—like the Truman and Eisenhower Administrations before it—was deterred from waging a preventive war against China based on perceived practical concerns pertaining to the uncertainty of targets, as well as the potential physical costs and/or risks of retaliation. Shortly after the Chinese Communists detonated their first nuclear device, Kennedy's successor, President Lyndon Johnson, directly addressed this development in a speech to the American people.

The President made a point of assuring US allies that Washington was carefully monitoring the nuclear situation in China, that it had expected the nuclear test, could specify where and when it had occurred, and emphasized that it would not lead to immediate dangers of war:

> As Secretary Rusk noted on 29 September, we have known for some time that the Chinese Communists had a nuclear development program which was approaching the point of a first detonation of a test device.… The explosion came as no surprise to the US Government. It has been fully taken into account in planning our own defense program and nuclear capability. Its military significance should not be overestimated. Many years and great efforts separate testing of a first nuclear device from having a stockpile of reliable weapons with effective delivery systems. Still more basic is the fact that if and when the Chinese Communists develop nuclear weapons systems, free world nuclear strength will continue to be enormously greater.[105]

Three days later, the Chinese Government issued a statement, setting forth in detail China's position on the question of nuclear weapons: "China's mastering of nuclear weapons is entirely for defense and for protecting the Chinese people from the US nuclear threat."[106] The Chinese government also announced it would never be the first to use nuclear weapons and stated their position against all nuclear weapons. The Chinese immediately began acting like a cautious nuclear power, validating CIA and State Department political analysis. However, examination of debris picked up by US Air Weather Service aircraft revealed that the bomb exploded by the Chinese had in fact contained U-235, proving wrong the CIA's conclusion that the first Chinese bomb would be fuelled by plutonium. It was evident to US officials that China was likely to become a full nuclear power sooner than originally had been expected.[107]

Case study three: preventive war and North Korea, 1993–1994

Preventive considerations

The third and final case in which preventive options were extensively considered pertains to the state of North Korea in 1993–1994. Once again, the US was confronted with a "strange, secretive, dangerous, and deeply troubled small country" actively working to acquire a nuclear capability.[108] Often known as the "hermit kingdom," North Korea was, in short, viewed by many US policy-makers as an extremely volatile and highly militarized old-fashioned communist state dominated by a ruthless dictator committed to reunification of the Korean peninsula. As contended by Michael O'Hanlon and Mike Mochizuki, North Korea was a "major military threat to South Korea ... as well as American forces in the ROK, Japan's nearby population centers, and the region as a whole with the possibility of a second unprovoked war, including massive artillery and missile attacks."[109] Indeed, North Korea at the time had the second largest military in Asia (behind China), including one million troops out of a population of only 22 million. In per capita terms, this represented the highest percentage in the world and ten times the global average. Moreover, North Korea also devoted a far greater share of its gross domestic product to its armed forces than any other state in the world, thus contributing to the characterization of the DMZ as the "densest concentration of firepower in the world."[110]

Aside from creation of a nuclear weapon for its own individual use, the specter of newly developed and inadequately safeguarded North Korean nuclear materials becoming "lost" was a further concern. As Carter and Perry reported, if nuclear weapons are controlled by a state "enmeshed in social and political turmoil," they might end up "commandeered, bought or stolen by terrorists. Who knows what might happen to North Korea's nuclear weapons as that state struggles to achieve a transformation, possibly violent, to a more normal and prosperous nation."[111] Such potentiality garnered sentiments of striking first, because once North Korea had produced nuclear materials—given the small size of a critical mass of plutonium and the porous nature of international borders—thwarting their transfer would be virtually impossible. As confirmed by Wit *et al.*, "this scenario is as stealthy as it is worrisome.... A detonation somewhere might well be the first evidence of such a transfer.... The US could not expect to prevent, deter, or defend against such an act."[112] Additionally, the US was once again concerned that North Korea's acquisition of nuclear weapons could engender a "chain reaction." As explained by Carter and Perry, the US had successfully persuaded South Korea to forgo nuclear weapons "on the grounds that North Korea had none and with the US as an ally the South did not need nukes for its defense." That argument could be undermined if North Korea attained a nuclear weapon—"the next dominoes to fall might be Japan and Taiwan."[113] Indeed, it was viewed that if North Korea was able to develop nuclear weapons, a regional arms race could result, producing significant and destabilizing tensions within Japan, South Korea, and Taiwan, as well other states within the region. If such an arms race began, it was hard to predict where it might lead and how it might end. As Secretary of State Dean Rusk argued in 1961, "[if the US abetted nuclear proliferation], it would start us down a jungle path from which I see no exit."[114] It is with this in mind that when confronted with the 1994 North Korean nuclear crisis—in which a rogue state was actively engaging in the proliferation of nuclear weapons—the Clinton Administration, like its predecessors, seriously "contemplated its own act of pre[vention] against the strange, isolated regime then considered the greatest threat to US national security."[115]

Unlike the cases of the Soviet Union and China, however, preventive war thinking towards North Korea developed in response to a single, very specific, and highly publicized nuclear crisis. Beginning in March 1993 with North Korea's rejection of the International Atomic Energy Agency's (IAEA) request for a "special inspection" of two suspected nuclear waste sites at the Yongbyon nuclear complex—of which the North Koreans were required to permit as a signatory to the NPT—and the controversial announcement that it would soon secede completely from the NPT, the 1994 nuclear crisis lasted approximately 15 months and almost ended in outright conflict. At its peak, the US and North Korea came very close to the brink of conflict, particularly when the latter indicated that it had already started removing spent nuclear fuel rods from the Yongbyon reactor—containing enough plutonium to produce up to five nuclear bombs. When the US threatened to impose economic sanctions on the embattled regime, Pyongyang responded by stating that "sanctions mean war and there is no mercy in war."[116] Clinton's advisers viewed this declaration with varying degrees of alarm, but agreed that it would have been irresponsible for the US to ignore the warning. As Daniel Poneman explained:

> The North Koreans had said that they would view the imposition of UN Security Council sanctions an act of war. Now we were not shaking in our boots when they said this but, you know, if you're Bill Perry, Secretary of Defense, you cannot ignore that. Therefore, what we were doing quietly and pretty much continuously, with the exception of the Patriots which got hung up politically, was we were enhancing our force presence and our posture in the Korean peninsula and in that theater. The view of the Principals was that

> at such time as the UN Security Council sanctions would actually kick into force, that we should have a sufficiently robust presence in theatre to deter the North Koreans from any foolish military action and response to sanctions, so effectively, to call their bluff and say "You're going to call that an act of war … well let me put enough forces in here that you don't treat it as such.' And so the trick is to put enough force in to deter but not so much in that you provoke the attack you're trying to deter.[117]

Aside from the outcomes or provocative nature of sanctions, the actual notion of using preventive military force to preclude North Korea from obtaining a nuclear arsenal became a distinct possibility based on the issue of defueling.

Reprocessing was a further possible trigger: if the US learned that the North Koreans had begun reprocessing—the step after defueling in which the plutonium would be easier to transport and hide—the preventive option certainly would have moved to the forefront of deliberation. This is not to say that such sentiments were not already on the agenda; the DOD had been studying the requirements for attacking Yongbyon since the discovery of the existence of the nuclear facility in 1989. The methods of preventive strikes considered by the Pentagon ranged from targeting single buildings to the entire installation, employing everything from cruise missiles to raids carried out by commandos.[118] Assistant Secretary of Defense Ashton Carter and Secretary of Defense William Perry have at varying intervals admitted that a preventive military option was on the table during 1994. As stated, "The two of us, then at the Pentagon readied plans for striking at North Korea's nuclear facilities and for mobilising hundreds of thousands of American troops for the war that probably would have followed."[119] Indeed, a successful attack required "timely intelligence, accurate targeting, tight command and control, and pinpoint timing" as the "option" needed to take place just as the North Koreans were moving the spent fuel to the reprocessing plant, but before the separated plutonium was moved to a different location to manufacture nuclear weapons.[120] Tactically complicating the execution of this attack was the nearby placement of more than 300 anti-aircraft guns and the construction of a half-dozen new surface-to-air missile bases.[121] Despite the complexity of this option, Defense Secretary William Perry declared to Congress in 1995, "I can tell you flatly that we know how to do that."[122]

Not wanting to take any chances with what was perceived as a hostile regime, many in the US advocated "seizing the initiative" and striking first via preventive war. Indeed, due to its unprecedented media coverage, preventive war thinking during the 1994 North Korean nuclear crisis commanded a wide range of support throughout the US government as well as the general population. So popular was the notion that the US should eliminate North Korea's nuclear capability that one high-ranking South Korean diplomat on his first trip to Washington was reportedly "struck by the willingness of the American witnesses—think-tank experts and former US officials—to advocate a preventive strike against North Korea."[123] In June 1994, six out of every ten Americans surveyed thought that US "vital" interests were at stake in North Korea—a far higher figure than for any other international situation at the time (generally speaking, a vital interest is one for which the US would be willing to wage war). While this does not provide a conclusive assessment into those Americans who supported the taking of preventive military action against North Korea in 1994, it does illustrate that "the stakes were both high and well understood; the American people viewed the threat of nuclear proliferation in North Korea as the top foreign policy risk facing the nation."[124]

In addition, various media commentators and think-tank observers throughout the US openly endorsed preventive action against North Korea before it was able to produce a nuclear weapon. As argued by Larry DiRita of the Heritage Foundation, rather than "trying to appease one of the last remaining Stalinist dictatorships in the world," the Clinton Administration "should set a deadline for North Korea to allow international inspectors, or else impose sanctions and consider destroying military headquarters, ballistic missile launch sites, or command and control facilities."[125] Moreover, as exhorted by *Washington Post* columnist Charles Krauthammer, the Administration's response to North Korea's nuclear drive has been "all carrots and no stick." As an inducement to be nice, "we have already given the North Koreans their first direct high-level talks with the US. We have dangled diplomatic recognition. We are now dangling an offer to cancel joint US military exercises with South Korea. These are gestures of weakness.... The time has come for action."[126]

As the crisis deepened, former National Security Council staff member Richard Haas insisted that the Clinton Administration should "launch a preventive military attack against North Korea's nuclear facilities at Yongbyon that is comparable to Israel's attack that destroyed Iraq's reactor in 1981."[127] Meanwhile, within the pages of the *Economist* periodical, various "hawks" and "hardliners" expressed their opinions in which one commentator stated that "at some point the talking has got to stop.... Faced with a chilling choice of risk—between a pre[ventive] strike to cripple North Korea's nuclear program and waiting until its tough talk is backed up by nuclear threats—America would in the end be right to strike first."[128] In a more direct endorsement of preventive action, former Pentagon official Frank Gaffney, Jr. stated that "[the US] should take military steps to neutralize those facilities we know about.... It is a question of risking going to war now, when US military capabilities are still relatively strong and North Korean forces are minimal, if extant, rather than later when such advantageous conditions will almost surely not exist."[129]

Finally, throughout the 1994 North Korean nuclear crisis, preventive war thinking also received a great deal of attention from many high-level US government officials and military planners. On ABC's "Nightline," for example, US Senators John McCain and Bob Kerrey exhibited rare bipartisan agreement when they together argued that resolving the North Korean nuclear crisis warranted running the risk of war. In articulating his case, McCain incorporated preventive logic, querying whether "is it better to act now, while the nuclear weapons program is still in an embryonic state, or is it better to wait two or three or four years when you are facing an enemy with nuclear weapons and the means to deliver them as far away as Japan? I think the answer is we have to act now."[130] Moreover, in the *Wall Street Journal*, US Congresswoman Karen Elliot House observed that "negotiations, pleas and promises of cooperation for good behaviour haven't had the slightest effect [on the North Koreans] ... [instead of sending former President Jimmy Carter to negotiate] President [William J.] Clinton ought to be sending [General] Norman Schwarzkopf—perhaps with a few sample photos of high-tech warfare in the Gulf.... The Administration has to be willing not only to go to war on the Korean peninsula but also to put the US–China relationship on the line."[131] Furthermore, according to Wit *et al.*, "former [George H.W.] Bush Administration officials Brent Scowcroft and Arnold Kanter advocated such a strike unless the North allowed the IAEA continuous, unfettered monitoring to ensure that no further reprocessing took place."[132] Aside from the above, specific policy-makers within the Clinton Administration also considered and weighed up the notion of using the preventive option.

Anthony Lake, National Security Adviser

From the beginning of the crisis, National Security Adviser, Anthony Lake, was prepared to run the risk of a violent North Korean reaction to sanctions and undertake preventive air strikes if it meant stopping Pyongyang from obtaining a nuclear arsenal. For Lake, North Korea's effort to develop a nuclear capability was especially dangerous because of their ballistic missile program and the likelihood that Pyongyang would export both technologies to other rogue states.[133] As stated:

> North Korea has become one of the foremost merchants of such [ballistic missiles] weapons. It has sold Scud missiles to Syria and Iran, and it is actively marketing its next generation of ballistic missiles. In short, if North Korea develops nuclear weapons, we face a greatly increased danger that other hostile, rogue states around the world will soon have them also.[134]

However, despite Lake's thinking on the preventive option, he was convinced that it "almost certainly would have provoked a North Korean attack."[135] Lake characterized preventive air strikes as riskier than sanctions, noting there was a general belief among Clinton Administration officials that a second Korean war would be won by the US but at a considerable cost. "We ... went through intensive planning on what a Korean conflict would entail—concluding that it would be very bloody, with heavy civilian as well as military casualties, but we would win."[136] According to Lake, there were three issues that could hinder the preventive air strikes option:

> One is would they work? Would you get it all? The second is what sort of plume would you create? And the third was what were the chances of the North Koreans then responding with a conventional attack across the parallel? And what would be the consequences of that and how well would we be prepared for it?[137]

William Perry, Secretary of Defense

Secretary of Defense, William Perry, thought this was one of "the most serious crises that we faced during his tenure ... the most serious and [he] did not believe that we could permit the North Koreans to go forward with their nuclear program and was preparing unilateral military options."[138] Underscoring the risk of escalation, however, Perry ruled out the use of force up front, but made it clear that preventive military force would not be taken off the table. At the other end of the spectrum would be the application of military pressure, "but even limited application of military pressure entails the risk of a large-scale war. Although we will not rule out any option for all time, this course should only be considered when all other possibilities have been exhausted."[139] In a June 10 memo to Clinton, Perry cautioned the President against limiting US options, "either in terms of military preparations or preemption."[140] However, Perry stressed that military action was considered a last resort:

> It was serious enough that we had put together a detailed plan to do it but I want to emphasize, it was never something we considered doing without having first exhausted many other alternatives. So, it was something that was on the table but at the end of the table not at the beginning of the table. We would not consider doing it until we had first positively exhausted our diplomatic alternatives and then exhausted all of the non-military coercive diplomatic alternatives. So, it was in the sequence but it was at the end of the sequence.[141]

Perry's aversion to the preventive air strikes option was related to its astronomical consequences.

While he felt confident that the US would win a second Korean war, he judged that the cost would be disastrously high:

> We understood that it would be very costly—very costly to the Koreans and to the American forces as well. So, we considered that we wanted to take every step we could possibly take to avoid that alternative short of allowing North Korea to precede with a full blown nuclear arsenal. The way I presented it to the President was that we had—that if we got to that military option, we would have to consider the choice between two terrible alternatives: one of them was taking action which might precipitate a war and a war which would be very—would have disastrous consequences for everybody or allowing North Korea to precede with a nuclear arsenal which we also believed could have disastrous consequences. Had we gotten to that point, we would have had to choose between two very bad alternatives therefore our whole strategy was to try to figure out—to try to take a course of action which would keep us from having to make that choice.[142]

James Woolsey, Director of Central Intelligence (DCI)

Of the senior-level officials in the Clinton Administration, DCI James Woolsey was the strongest proponent of using preventive war to destroy North Korea's nuclear program, particularly upon their announcement that defueling was imminent. Throughout the crisis, Woolsey had viewed the possibility of a negotiated solution with skepticism, predicting that North Korea would negotiate only as a means to buy time in which they could continue building nuclear weapons. From his viewpoint, Kim Il Sung was "a dictator and a liar and a cheat" and "I didn't think we could trust him as far as we could throw him."[143] This lack of trust for the regime and the knowledge that North Korea could soon process plutonium for more nuclear weapons motivated Woolsey's hawkish stance on the nuclear crisis. According to Gallucci, "In terms of what the [North Korean nuclear] program was all about and therefore, [were] negotiation[s] a reasonable thing to be engaged in—the Director of the CIA at the time, thought we were nuts, absolutely nuts."[144]

While Woolsey did endorse the preventive war option, he also held some misgivings about the long-term effectiveness of launching preventive, surgical air strikes against Yongbyon. That is, Woolsey agreed with Clinton's senior advisers that a surgical strike against the North would not be guaranteed to get all of the nuclear material, as the location of the plutonium was unknown and would likely motivate some response from the North Korean military.[145] As he explained:

> It seems to me you always want to know what the practicality is of the use of force. And, whereas most thinking centers on a surgical strike against Yongbyon, I don't think that would have been very reasonable because of the North Koreans would have attacked the South. I think you had to answer the question, "What would it take to pull their teeth and their capacity—this was now eleven years ago—and their capacity to move effectively against the South?" I don't think it matters that they have a huge army. A huge army is a sitting duck for smart weapons as we've showed time and time again. It's those artillery sites and possibly missile launching sites that could hit South Korea that we would have had to have been able to take out virtually all of them.[146]

In essence, Woolsey rationalized that if surgical strikes were going to lead to armed conflict between the US and North Korea, then it made more sense to launch the initial strike against their artillery sites as well as the nuclear facilities; in effect, to launch a preventive war.

The DCI believed preventive surgical strikes were only a short-term solution, unlikely to permanently halt the North Korean nuclear program, and instead, urged officials to at least consider all variables pertaining to the execution of a preventive attack against North Korea. Woolsey believed such an attack would be less risky than just striking Yongbyon because he judged that a first strike with overwhelming force would give the offensive advantage to the US, whereas preventive surgical strikes could incite a full-scale response in which case the US would be on the defensive. Although Woolsey was the highest-level official opposed to negotiating a solution to the nuclear crisis with North Korea, his role as DCI precluded him from participating in the policy process in the same way other high-level Administration officials did. As stated:

> My opinion wasn't solicited on policy matters at all.... One of the only things that we did talk about was that the DCI really shouldn't be a policy adviser. He asked me what I thought. I said that I did not think he should, that I thought he ought to call it the way he saw it—if the DCI was a policy adviser, people were going to get the idea that intelligence was getting skewed to support the policy beliefs of the DCI.... The President didn't want me to be so I was there to present the intelligence, period.[147]

As a result, Woolsey's assertive position on North Korea played little to no role in the President's ultimate decision on how to deal with Pyongyang's nuclear program.

Clinton: returning to negotiations

Clinton described the North Korean nuclear crisis as "by far the biggest foreign policy issue."[148] The showdown over defueling presented the President with a problem to which every solution involved risks: How to preserve the security of the US by preventing the North Koreans from becoming a nuclear power without provoking a second Korean War. On the one hand, choosing a non-military option diminished the prospect of expeditiously ending North Korea's nuclear program and still stood a chance of provoking a major war if Pyongyang was serious that sanctions equaled war. If he chose not to launch preventive strikes against Yongbyon, and Pyongyang began not only defueling the reactor but also reprocessing the spent fuel, Clinton risked missing the opportunity to destroy the fissile material before it was hidden away. Refraining from preventive strikes also risked allowing the North Koreans to level the playing field for a future war by providing them with the time to develop a nuclear arsenal. On the other hand, launching preventive strikes at Yongbyon would possibly achieve the policy goal of preventing North Korea from building a nuclear arsenal in the short term, but there was no guarantee it would destroy all of the fissile material possessed by Pyongyang. There was also a very good chance striking Yongbyon would provoke a retaliation that could escalate into a costly second Korean War.[149]

The turning point

The commencement of defueling also marked the point when Clinton moved closer to considering preventive strikes against Yongbyon, although this alternative was always an option of last resort. On May 18, as a sanctions package was being pulled together and military preparations continued, Perry and Shalikashvili called in every active four-star general and admiral in the US military to discuss support for Commander, US Forces and Korea and General Luck's war plan for Korea. The ensuing meeting discussed troops, materiel, logistics, and in particular, details of preparatory deployments of troops and transport from other commands, "the shifting of US aircraft carriers and land-based warplanes closer to the Korean coast and plans for massive reinforcements—deployment of roughly half of all US major combat forces—if hostilities actually got under way."[150] According to Don Oberdorfer's account, on May 19, Perry, Shalikashvili and Luck informed the President of the costs and consequences should the nuclear crisis escalate to military conflict and then potentially to general war with North Korea.[151] Luck told Clinton that the US-ROK chances against North Korea in a conventional war were good but success would be costly. In the first 90 days, the generals estimated "52,000 US military casualties, killed or wounded, and 490,000 South Korean military casualties … at a financial outlay exceeding $61 billion, very little of which could be recouped from US allies."[152] Overall, US officials estimated that the damage caused by a second Korean war would be in the range of a million lives and a trillion dollars.[153]

Clinton changes approach

The following day (May 20), now armed with information regarding the human and economic costs likely to result from a war with North Korea, Clinton held a meeting with his senior advisers to discuss the crisis.[154] Here, despite North Korea's defiant defueling of the reactor at Yongbyon, the President changed tactics, moving back to pursuing a diplomatic solution: a far less risky endeavor than sanctions or prevention. Clinton offered to join Pyongyang in a third round of high-level negotiations and attempted to set up a direct meeting between Kim Il Sung and Senators Sam Nunn and Richard Lugar in hopes of communicating directly with North Korean leadership to ease the rising tension. In simple terms, Clinton altered his direction because he hoped to avoid the risks associated with an option that could escalate to war. However, based on the IAEA's June 3 declaration that North Korea had deliberately destroyed information that would reveal the operating history of the reactor, the Nunn and Lugar meeting did not take place.[155] According to Clinton, "they have triggered this, not the United States or anyone else. I just don't think we can walk away from this."[156]

Just as the Clinton Administration began to again consider more assertive options, former President Jimmy Carter intervened, offering to meet with Kim Il Sung. Carter's unofficial "eleventh hour" mission to North Korea was successful and averted what was likely to be a very costly war on both sides. As recalled by Clinton:

> President Carter called me on June 1 and said he would like to go to North Korea to try to resolve the problem. I sent Ambassador Bob Gallucci, who was handling the matter for us, down to Plains, Georgia, to brief Carter on

> the seriousness of the North Korean violations. He still wanted to go, and after consulting with Al Gore and my national security team, I decided it was worth trying. About three weeks earlier, I had received a sobering estimate of the staggering losses both sides would suffer if war broke out.... Al Gore called Carter and told him that I had no objection to his going to North Korea as long as President Kim Il Sung understood that I would not agree to a suspension of sanctions unless North Korea let the inspectors do their jobs, agreed to freeze its nuclear program and committed to a new round of talks with the United States on building a non-nuclear future.[157]

It was here that Carter's diplomatic effort not only helped averting a major crisis, but also served to mark the end of the third era of the preventive war option.

Preventive restrictions

Implementing the preventive war option against North Korea carried significant risks. The augmentation of US force posture in South Korea was meant to pressure North Korea into staying at the negotiating table to avoid sanctions, deter a North Korean attack, and better prepare US-ROK forces in the event that negotiations faltered, deterrence failed, or the US opted to launch air strikes against Yongbyon. But the military build-up necessary to accomplish this could actually provoke the North Koreans to launch an assault below the 38th parallel. Pyongyang had made a study of US actions preceding the 1991 Gulf War, particularly the build-up of US troops in the Gulf prior to the fighting. Kim Il Sung was likely to view any build-up in American forces as a prelude to war with his country. Launching preventive strikes against North Korea's nuclear facilities also risked putting off much needed allies like Japan—who did not want to get involved in a major war but whose involvement was critical to US success—and China—who would not take kindly to US aggression on the Korean peninsula. Launching preventive strikes against North Korea ran the very real risk of potentially provoking a form of Chinese intervention, just as it had done in June 1950. Foremost in terms of risks was the very high probability that North Korea would retaliate against a US military strike and that any retaliatory strike could escalate quickly to a second Korean war. US intelligence and several Clinton Administration officials estimated that the US could not launch preventive surgical strikes against Yongbyon and destroy North Korea's nuclear facilities without facing retaliation, although there was uncertainty about what form this retaliation would take.[158]

Part of the ambiguity relating to this option was the lack of US intelligence on how North Korean leadership thought and how they might react to a US limited strike on Yongbyon. While US knowledge on North Korea's nuclear program was considered to be relatively sound by most high-level Administration officials, intelligence on the intricacies of the leadership and how the regime functioned was limited. Pyongyang's response could range from a contained artillery barrage to a full-scale attack in which the North Korean army moved south over the 38th parallel. Specifically, military planners were concerned about a possible attack on South

Korean nuclear power plants which were vulnerable to sea attack and which, if hit, could shower parts of South Korea with significant radioactive fallout and damage the economy by knocking out much of its power.[159] Additionally, the vast majority of North Korea's troops were gathered just north of the 38th parallel, only 30 miles north of Seoul—the population of which accounted for one fourth of the people in South Korea and close to one half of the country's economic output—increasing the risks associated with any military option.[160]

General Gary Luck, Commander, US Forces Korea at the time of the crisis, thought North Korea would respond to any US strike with an all-out counterattack: "If we pull an Osirak, they will be coming south."[161] In this event, according to Daniel Poneman, "A variety of target sets were looked at including target sets that would interfere with their ability to move south."[162] A former senior US military official assessed the situation, asserting that from a military perspective, preventive surgical strikes were not truly an option if President Clinton wanted to avoid a second Korean war.

> A surgical strike was not really an option because what you did with a surgical strike is you gave them the reason to attack you, which then put the odds in their favor for the first phase of the campaign. If you attack Yongbyon, then you've got to put down the probabilities that go with that; the probability that they'll accept that without retaliating. That's a real small probability. And then you keep doing your math-calculus—if they surprise attacked us while we're in the defensive crouch, what are the losses? If we take the aggressive approach, and attack them, which we would have to do anyway after they attacked us, what are the odds? It made sense that if we felt strongly enough about punishing North Korea for continuing with their nuclear program, the best option would have been for us to launch a full-scale attack as opposed to a few preventive strikes. The third option—you boil all the smoke out of it and that's what you've got.... Preventively attacking Yongbyon would have just been an invitation to the fight. There was nothing clean about this. It was either you're going to fight or you're going to negotiate.[163]

The option was also constrained because of the significant risk that a preventive attack would not necessarily destroy all North Korean plutonium or important bomb-making equipment.

Military planners were concerned that North Korea would unload the fuel rods and move them to the reprocessing facility and separate the plutonium, which could then be transported to a secret location and made into nuclear weapons. According to a former senior US military official:

> We didn't know where they had the stuff. They [the North Koreans] don't have anything else to do up there except dig tunnels. Who knew where they had stored the material? How much credence do you put in an intelligence report from a closed society? We had nothing other than overhead pictures to tell us anything.[164]

In essence, a US preventive strike risked releasing a significant amount of radiation or, if the radioactive material was moved, the attack would fail to destroy it, thus giving the North Koreans a chance to rebuild the foundation of their nuclear program. Moreover, the option was the riskiest of those examined because it offered the largest variance in outcome—the destruction of the North Korean nuclear program—if successful, but also the worst outcome if North Korea responded with an all-out attack on the South, which the Clinton Administration judged it was likely to do.[165]

Litwak further conveyed the potential risk of a preventive war, arguing that the North Koreans "did not distinguish between a narrow US counter-proliferation option on the North's nuclear facilities and general war." From an American viewpoint, "the fear of inadvertent escalation and catalytic war—the possibility that a counter-proliferation strike on the North's nuclear infrastructure would provoke an all-out war on the Korean Peninsula—was a key policy determinant" and prompted the Clinton Administration to pursue "alternative non-military approaches."[166] Indeed, although no one was certain about the extent to which North Korea may respond, most observers agreed that that if attacked, North Korea would undertake some form of massive counterattack against allied positions. According to Philip Saunders, Pyongyang had various options at its disposal:

> North Korean long-range artillery could hit Seoul with artillery shells and chemical weapons, causing panic and massive civilian casualties … it could hit Japan with its … missiles. Seventy percent of North Korean army ground units are located within 100 miles of the demilitarized zone … positioned to undertake offensive ground operations. These units could fire up to 500,000 artillery rounds per hour against South Korean defenses for several hours. Finally, if North Korea does have one or two deliverable nuclear weapons, nuclear retaliation (or nuclear threats) would also be available.[167]

In any event, the results were expected to be disastrous. According to Wit *et al.*:

> If war were to occur, the US and South Korea would win, but it would be costly. Computer projections showed 30,000 American casualties and 450,000 South Korean casualties, but these numbers might be too low; the killed-in-action numbers would likely be higher since the battlefield was far more lethal than during the Korean War in the 1950s … another Korean war would kill or wound 1 million civilians, cost more than $60 billion, devastate the South Korean economy to the tune of at least $1 trillion, cause an Asian recession, and adversely affect the rest of the global economy. When asked by the President … whether the US would win the war, General [Gary] Luck [commander of the US forces in South Korea] replied, "Yes, but at the cost of a million [casualties] and a trillion [dollars]."[168]

In simple terms, the costs in executing the preventive option on the Korean peninsula were so high as to be prohibitive. The significant possibility that a preventive attack on North Korea's nuclear facilities would engender a general war on the Korean peninsula, in essence, effectively removed the US military option from consideration.

In the context of the Bush Administration

Despite claims to the contrary, it appears that the efforts by the Bush Administration to prevent rogue states from acquiring nuclear weapons were not altogether new or groundbreaking. In fact, as evident in the preceding discussion, every single time a state hostile to the US has sought to acquire nuclear weapons, the incumbent Administration—whether composed of Republicans or Democrats—has considered utilizing force as a means to hinder this development. Indeed, not including Iraq, Iran, and North Korea from 2001 to 2003, over the last 50 years, the US has assessed the viability of waging large-scale unilateral preventive wars against three additional rogue proliferators: the Soviet Union from 1945 to 1954; China from 1960 to 1963; and North Korea from 1993 to 1994. Significantly, in all three cases, it is apparent that the US opted not to take preventive action due to a number of overriding moral and practical inhibitions. What can we infer from this record of inaction and how does this evidence help to explain the 2003 War in Iraq?

In the first instance, while it is impossible to fully comprehend the specific reason as to why each respective Administration chose not to employ the preventive war option—analytically it is difficult if not unworkable to separate normative concerns from strategic calculations. As stated by Lebow, the former are "intangible considerations that do not lend themselves to ready assessment let alone to quasi-quantification," and based on the available information, it is fair to assume that the key US decision-makers in all of the cases reviewed in the above were more heavily influenced by the practical costs of said action.[169] To be sure, none of these Administrations were completely unaware or unmoved by the immorality and illegality associated with preventive war, however, it was clear that each one—from Truman and Eisenhower to Kennedy and Clinton—was ultimately willing (if not always able) under the "right" conditions, to embark upon a preventive path of action irrespective of the moral costs. If any of these Administrations were truly concerned with or repulsed by the "moral depravity" of preventive war, we would expect to find an immediate and wholesale dismissal of such thinking. The sheer fact that not a single one was willing to dismiss preventive war in an absolute fashion signifies that morality was not the most significant restraint. As confirmed by Trachtenberg, the reason that a preventive war strategy was never adopted as policy "was not that Eisenhower was shocked or appalled by this … the real problem was that it did not make any strategic sense."[170] While Trachtenberg was referring specifically to the case of the Soviet Union, it would be accurate to attribute such a conclusion to the cases of China 1960–1963, Iraq 2001–2003, and North Korea both 1993–1994 and 2001–2003 as well.

Indeed, one cannot resolutely pronounce that normative objections by themselves restricted American action against any of the aforementioned states. In only one of the three cases reviewed—the Soviet Union 1945–1954—was morality explicitly mentioned and considered; in the other two cases it is evident that very little, if any, discussion was prevalent in the context of morals, arms, or legality. Furthermore, it was apparent that in some cases morality was actually used to endorse and promote preventive war. For example, in the early 1950s James Burnham, a political scientist at Harvard University argued that

> if there is good reason to believe that a sudden and massive blow [to the Soviet Union] would save many lives and goods [in the US], result in less destruction and social disintegration [than if the US waited for the Soviet Union to acquire nuclear weapons and attack first], give a better chance for building a workable world polity, then to strike such a blow, far from being morally wrong, is morally obligatory. If there is to be war in any case, it is hard to comprehend why a war is morally better because it is more difficult, longer, more cruel and costly and bloody."[171]

Four phenomena may assist in articulating this apparent disregard for traditional morality.

First, there exists substantial empirical evidence to support the claim that largely dynamic moral constructs such as the characterization of preventive war as "aggressive" or "dishonorable" may be either refined or deferred in times of supreme national crisis. Many historians and political scientists have explained Japan's 1941 attack on Pearl Harbor in these terms. Second, it was not uncommon for conventional morality to be temporarily suspended whenever the results were expected to produce a more favorable long-term outcome. For example, torturing an individual to gain valuable information which will save a number of lives was widely viewed to be an occasion in which the postponement of morality was acceptable. Similarly, the preventive motivation was based on the belief that war was probably inevitable and that it is better to fight now while the costs and/or risks are low(er), than later when they are expected to be high(er). In both cases, the "ends" were said to "justify the means." Third, it is significant to note a critical difference between the case of the Soviet Union—the only case in which the moral implications of undertaking a preventive war were seriously debated—and the remaining cases.

In the former, a successful preventive strike would have required the US to use nuclear weapons as a means to annihilate both counter-force and counter-value targets, including major Soviet cities; in the latter, it would have been possible for the US to employ superior military technology to eliminate the requisite nuclear programs without causing an overzealous level of collateral damage. In this light, the preventive option in the more recent examples would have required far less violence, and thereby, meant that debates pertaining to notions of morality were far less pressing. Finally, in respect to non-proliferation, it has been apparent in the last 20 years that a strong international norm has developed against the horizontal proliferation of nuclear weapons, to the extent that such proliferation is widely considered to be an unlawful act. In this view, any state actively working to attain weapons is deemed a "criminal" and thus subject to appropriate sanctions and diplomatic condemnation. Moreover, because a nuclear proliferator has already broken the "law," any military action taken against it would be considered reactive, not preventive. Maintaining this position thus removes the moral approbations surrounding the "unprovoked" use of force.

Nonetheless, the fact that none of the aforementioned Administrations were compelled to reject or even thoroughly discuss the moral consequences of preventive war strongly supports the argument that practicality, especially concerns pertaining to enemy retaliation and general war, and not morality, did more to coerce US decision-makers away from waging preventive war against the Soviet Union from 1945 to 1954, China from 1960 to 1963 and North Korea from 1993 to 1994. Indeed, it was apparent that political leaders and military planners during each of the periods in question were not guided primarily by legal or moral reasoning. In any of the cases reviewed, if the extremely prohibitive practical situations had not existed, would the Truman, Eisenhower, Kennedy, Johnson and Clinton Administrations have measured morality in the same way? More importantly, would they have been deterred by morality alone? For instance, if the US had been in possession of a more substantial amount of nuclear bombs and bombers between 1945 and 1954, and the Soviet Union was not able to effectively retaliate against Western Europe or so big as to prohibit a post-war occupation/reconstruction, would things have turned out differently? Would the US have attacked the Soviet Union? We will of course never know for sure; however, if viewed in the context of Iraq from 2001 to 2003, it is evident that morality alone did not impede the US from undertaking a preventive war against a comparatively small and weak rogue proliferator, with no real prospects for retaliation. The circumstances surrounding the Soviet Union, 1945–1954, China, 1960–1963, and North Korea, 1993–1994, and Iraq, 2001–2003 differ in some very distinct and important ways (i.e. the September 11 terrorist attacks and the newly perceived threat of nuclear terrorism may have allayed some of the opposition to preventive war). The application of preventive war in the latter suggests that the historically pervasive anti-preventive war moral sentiment in the US has neither changed dramatically, nor has it been the most significant deterrent when it comes to waging preventive war.

Assuming that the moral purview of preventive war thinking in the US has not changed significantly over the last half century—and recent polls and studies, to say nothing of the academic and political rhetoric, have shown that it has not—and furthermore, that the Bush Administration subscribed to the same morality as its predecessors, it stands to reason that the practical costs of waging preventive war was—and still is—the more critical of the two deterrent variables. In essence, while morality may be a necessary constraining factor of preventive war, alone it is not sufficient. If this is true and if states are more likely to wage preventive attacks when the practical costs and/or risks of retaliation are low, then it lends robust support to the claim that the Bush Administration's decision to pursue the preventive option against Iraq is best seen as a strategic choice primarily based upon practical considerations, especially the relative military capabilities of the targeted states. It also underscores the powerful logic of deterrence and yields some important conclusions.

First, it was evident that from 2001 to 2003, the Bush Administration likely preferred to wage preventive war against Iraq first because it was the weakest of the three perceived threats (Iran being second and North Korea a distant third). If the US continued to believe that the cost of inaction was higher than the cost of action (which, as we have seen may be significant), we can expect that the Bush Administration—if given the chance—would have sought to attack the outstanding threats in that order. Second, if a rogue proliferator emerges in the future, the US will again strongly consider waging preventive war against it. For example, if Syria were to make a serious drive to acquire nuclear weapons, we can expect that the US would seriously consider taking preventive measures to stop it from doing so. Even so, it is highly unlikely that a strategy of preventive war will ever replace or supplant the reality of deterrence or be implemented uniformly against all nuclear proliferators.

Indeed, the fact that the US has historically been extremely reluctant to attack militarily strong rogue proliferators suggests that the US will continue to differentiate between big and small, weak and strong states and also continue to weigh the military costs involved in waging war against them. A commensurate statement was articulated by Feaver and Niou:

> A military strike is simply not a credible option against many countries that might develop nuclear weapons, regardless of the strength of US resolve.... There are obvious costs involved in executing a military strike against proliferators, and these costs vary directly with the military capabilities of the [rogue] proliferators. The costs of a decapitating strike against a Great Power like the Soviet Union would be prohibitive, making the force option not viable ... [strong] enemies are simply too large for such an option to be workable. Indeed, the military option is only credible against small enemies. But even here, the military option is not credible once the country has, in fact, deployed nuclear weapons because of the risk that the proliferator would be able to fire off one of the weapons before the US could destroy the arsenal.... Weighing these factors, our argument draws the following conclusions. The US will never ... attack a large enemy ... [and] the final deployment of nuclear weapons could be thought of as rendering a 'small' country into a 'big' one ... making the costs of a military strike prohibitive.[172]

Similarly, Drell and Goodby have observed that the relevant lessons to be learned from America's experience with preventive war and rogue proliferators was that "military force, or the threat of it," was only usable "when the likelihood of successful retaliation against the homelands of the attacking power by the potential proliferant was low."[173] Military force was not likely to be employed when the costs of doing so were perceived to be higher than allowing proliferation to occur. The conclusion from this analysis, they argued, was "that military force or the threat of using such force is quite circumscribed in its application to the problem of nuclear proliferation."[174]

Indeed, based upon the historical record, we may anticipate that in the future the US will "think twice" before waging war against three kinds of strong rogue proliferators: those that have strong conventional forces capable of defending against a US invasion (i.e. a large, populous Iran); those that have strong conventional forces capable of deterring a US invasion (i.e. North Korea's artillery over Seoul); and those that have nuclear weapons, which can, by themselves, raise the costs/risks of preventive war to an unacceptable level by defending against a US invasion, deterring it, or both (i.e. North Korea with proven nuclear capability). Simply put, in the future it is reasonable to say that the US will continue to "aim at what is feasible, holding in view the real sentiments … that right as the world goes, is only in question between equals in power, while the strong do what they can and the weak suffer what they must."[175] For Trachtenberg, the preventive war term is one that endorses the notion of force being used even if a country has not been attacked, "but we also mean a policy rooted in concerns about the future, about what might happen tomorrow if nothing is done today."[176] By this definition it was evident that the Bush policy certainly qualified as a preventive war policy, however, did the "adoption of that strategy of 'prevention' mark a total break with American tradition, or did earlier Administrations, to one extent or another, also think in 'preventive' terms?" As affirmed by Trachtenberg, "it turns out that the sort of thinking one finds in the Bush policy documents is not to be viewed as anomalous. Under Roosevelt and Truman, under Eisenhower and Kennedy, and even under Clinton in the 1990s, this kind of thinking came into play in a major way. Concerns about the future—about what might happen if nothing were done—weighed heavily on American policy during the period from 1941 through 1963." This continued through to end of the Cold War and the 1990s, and will no doubt continue on in the 2000's and "beyond."[177]

4 The Bush Doctrine and the nuclear option

The transition from Clinton to Bush

As has been established, the motivation and consideration of preventive war has been an implicit part of US policy-makers' strategic thinking since 1945. While it can be argued that the preventive tenets of the Bush Doctrine stalled in Iraq after the quick and easy defeat of Saddam Hussein in 2003, the nuclear dimension encompassed in the Doctrine, and the reassertion of this option, became the legacy of the Bush Administration when he departed in January 2009. As the focus of Chapter 5, Bush asserted nuclear weapons as a distinct pillar within US security strategy, articulating and refining such sentiments through the 2002 Nuclear Posture Review (NPR), the 2002 National Strategy to Combat Weapons of Mass Destruction (NSCWMD), CONPLAN (Concept Plan) 8022 (Global Strike), the 2005 Doctrine for Joint Nuclear Operations, the 2006 Quadrennial Defense Review, the 2006 Strategic Operations Joint Operating Concept Version 2.0, and in recent times, the Reliable Replacement Warhead (RRW) program. While it is clear that Bush attempted to place the nuclear option to the fore in an assertive fashion, acknowledgment of the transition between the Clinton and Bush Administrations is imperative when analyzing and evaluating the extent of the shift that the Bush Doctrine engendered, and will therefore be the focus of this chapter. In many instances, it can be argued that the Clinton Administration ignored its historic opportunity to reverse decades of dangerous and provocative nuclear weapons planning, while the Bush Administration—in its punctuating and reaffirming policy instruments (as posited above)—furthered the process towards increasing the role of nuclear weapons in US policy and security strategy. Indeed, the Bush documents and policy instruments signified a renewed role for nuclear weapons and the quest of his Administration to upgrade US offensive forces, deploy missile defenses, reconfigure communications and satellite systems, and overall, revitalize the nuclear complex.

Nonetheless, it would be both remiss and incorrect to see this as merely the result of the Bush Administration's policies. It was evident that the Clinton Administration retained much of the existing US nuclear weapons policy and force posture in the decade after the demise of the Soviet Union and affirmed the role of nuclear weapons in US security strategy. Furthermore, the Clinton Administration began to develop targeting options for the use of nuclear weapons in response to chemical or biological attacks from states other than

Russia, and, in its declaratory policy, the Administration did not rule out the possible first use of nuclear weapons in these circumstances. It was here that military planners and policy-makers—through the Defense Counter-Proliferation Initiative (CPI) 1993, Nuclear Posture Review (NPR) 1994, Doctrine for joint Operations (Joint Pub 3-12) 1993/1995, Doctrine for Joint Theater Nuclear Operations 1996, Quadrennial Defense Review (QDR) 1997 and Presidential Decision Directive (PDD) 60 1997—maintained the significance of nuclear weapons despite the Cold War's conclusion. Ultimately, it was the Bush Doctrine and its accompanying guidance documents that expanded on this Clinton "base" in a much more defined and assertive posture, foreshadowing a new nuclear era in which the once-termed "weapon of last resort" became a usable and necessary preventive war-fighting option.

During the Cold War, the United States maintained nuclear forces that were sized and structured as a means to deter any attack by the Soviet Union and its Warsaw Pact allies, and if deterrence failed, to defeat the Soviet Union.[1] In the period after the 1989 collapse of the Berlin wall and 1991 demise of the Soviet Union, officials in the US government and analysts outside government pursued numerous reviews and studies of US nuclear weapons policy and force structure. While these studies varied in scope, intent and outcome, most attempted to define a new role for US nuclear weapons, including the appropriate size and structure of the US nuclear arsenal in the post-Cold War era. In positing their recommendations, these analyses addressed not only the end of the hostile US-Soviet global rivalry, but also the emergence of new threats and regional challenges to US security. As stated by Siracusa and Coleman:

> As the defence forces began to look beyond containment, it became readily apparent that the threats to US security had not faded away—they had changed. Rather than giving way to a time of peace and stability as many had hoped, the end of the Cold War paved the way for instability and the surfacing of regional issues that had long been suppressed during the Cold War and introduced other, non traditional threats.[2]

In response, the US Department of Defense conducted several far-reaching reviews—including the 1993 Bottom-up Review, the 1994 Nuclear Posture Review and the 1997 Quadrennial Defense Review—that contributed to the Clinton Administration's response to changes in the international security environment.[3] These formal reviews, when combined with less prominent internal studies, resulted in numerous changes to the structure of US nuclear forces and policy guiding their potential use. It was with this in mind that by the end of the 1990s many critics of the Clinton Administration argued that the US nuclear posture looked very much as it had at the beginning of the decade.

While the number of deployed nuclear weapons had declined—reflected in its implementation of the first Strategic Arms Reduction Treaty (START I) as well as the completed withdrawal of most of its non-strategic nuclear weapons—the

Clinton Administration and others argued that nuclear weapons remained important as a means to deter the range of threats faced by the United States. Indicative of such thinking was expressed by Secretary of Defense Perry in his Annual Report for 1995, noting that "recent international upheavals have not changed the calculation that nuclear weapons remain an essential part of American military power. Concepts of deterrence … continue to be central to the US nuclear posture." Thus, the United States will continue to "threaten retaliation, including nuclear retaliation, to deter aggression against the United States, US forces, and allies."[4] In theory, this deterrent strategy extended beyond Russia in which "the United States must continue to maintain a robust triad of strategic forces sufficient to deter any hostile foreign leadership with access to nuclear forces and to convince it that seeking a nuclear advantage would be futile." Furthermore, according to the Clinton Administration, "nuclear weapons serve as a hedge against an uncertain future, a guarantee of our security commitments to allies and a disincentive to those who would contemplate developing or otherwise acquiring their own nuclear weapons."[5]

Clinton retained the existing US policy on "first use" and, specifically, did not forswear the actual first use of nuclear weapons. His Administration signified that states other than Russia might encounter nuclear retaliation if they attacked the United States with nuclear, chemical, or biological weapons. Indeed, while it reaffirmed the US negative security assurance in 1995, Administration officials indicated that the United States would reserve the right to use nuclear weapons first "if a state is not a state in good standing under the Nuclear Non-proliferation Treaty (NPT) or an equivalent international convention."[6] Furthermore, a state might relinquish its protections under the negative security assurance if it attacked the United States or US forces with weapons of mass destruction (WMD).[7] Hence, regardless of the Cold War's demise, it was apparent that Clinton both maintained and even asserted nuclear weapons as a mainstay of US security strategy and counter proliferation.

For the United States government, the 1991 Gulf War highlighted the significance of being prepared to fight WMD-armed adversaries. While Iraq did not ultimately use chemical or biological weapons in the conflict, post-war intelligence into the nature of Iraqi WMD developments shocked those within the national security community; startling even well informed observers and highlighting the potential susceptibility of US regional security strategies.[8] According to the US Gulf War Air Power Survey (GWAPS):

> The Iraqi nuclear program was massive, for most practical purposes fiscally unconstrained, closer to fielding a weapon, and less vulnerable to destruction by precision bombing than Coalition air commanders and planners or US intelligence specialists realized before Desert Storm. The target list on 16 January 1991 contained two nuclear targets, but after the war, inspectors operating under the United Nations Special Commission eventually uncovered more than twenty sites involved in the Iraqi nuclear weapons program; sixteen of the sites were described as "main facilities."[9]

As Keaney and Cohen further articulated, after the war it was concluded that "the air campaign no more than inconvenienced Iraqi plans to field atomic weapons."[10] The GWAPS study stated that "that the Iraqis' program to amass enough enriched uranium to begin producing atomic bombs was more extensive … further along, and considerably less vulnerable to air attack than was realized at the outset of Desert Storm."[11]

It was in response to such findings that at the Gulf War's conclusion, Defense Secretary Cheney orchestrated the classified Nuclear Weapons Employment Policy (NUWEP), formally advising the military to plan for nuclear operations against nations it deemed to be capable of developing weapons of mass destruction.[12] It was evident that had Iraq used chemical and biological weapons (CBW), the US and allied forces may not have been sufficiently equipped to counter them. This Iraqi "capacity"—albeit somewhat exaggerated by the more conservative sector of the national security community—together with its supposed (and largely undetected) technical progress, defined the emergence of a major post-Cold War defense planning challenge. As the (post-Cheney) Secretary of Defense Les Aspin declared, "we are making the essential change demanded by this increased threat … adding the task of protection to the task of prevention."[13] In his view, while containment remained the United States' main focus, the Defense Department had undertaken a new strategy: developing military capabilities as a means to cope with WMD-armed regional adversaries.[14] As Aspin further articulated, "the American experience in the Gulf War made manifest the implications of NBC proliferation for defense planning. For DOD to do its job in the post-Cold War era, it must take seriously the potential NBC dimension of future conflicts." In this light, he added, "US forces must be properly trained and equipped for all potential missions, including those in which opponents might threaten or use NBC weapons. The Defense Counter-proliferation Initiative is designed to meet these challenges."[15]

Defense Counter-Proliferation Initiative (CPI) 1993

From the outset, there has been much conjecture pertaining to counter-proliferation as a policy based on its inclusion of nuclear weapons in the resources available to US commanders for use against enemy NBC weapon targets. The inclusion of nuclear use doctrines during the 1990s for this purpose, and the potential use of nuclear weapons in regional wars, evoked a dichotomy in viewpoints and opinions. While there is some merit to the notion that Bush merely continued the policies implemented by the Clinton Administration, in reality, it was Bush who took Clinton's "base" and asserted the emphasis of nuclear weapons to one of centrality within US security strategy. Nonetheless, to define the Clinton era as one of unbridled internationalism devoid of any degree of nuclear weapon assertions would be both careless and historically selective. Indeed, while the Bush Administration certainly placed the nuclear option back to the fore, the nuclear dimension of US security during the Clinton era was more than evident—as these following initiatives, documents, and policy instruments will clearly highlight.

Beginning in 1993, it was evident that nuclear considerations would definitely play a role in Clinton's Counter-Proliferation Initiative. That is, pursuant to a Presidential Directive, Secretary of Defense Les Aspin announced on December 7, 1993, that the United States would add a military dimension to its fight against the spread of weapons of mass destruction (WMD). In a speech before members of the National Academy of Science in Washington, DC, Aspin explained the rationale and initial program of what he termed a US "Defense Counter-Proliferation Initiative (CPI)." Aspin signified that the post-Cold War threat of nuclear, chemical, biological, and ballistic missile systems posed by unstable states or terrorist groups required a five-point counter-proliferation drive. He informed the audience that the five points would encompass: an understanding that this was a new mission, not the old Cold War mission; the development of new US weapons to destroy weapons of mass destruction; a reassessment of the strategies used against the new kind of threat; a concentration of intelligence efforts on detecting weapons of mass destruction; and, the facilitation of international cooperation in curtailing the threat of such weapons.[16] As described by Schneider:

> The new program, called the Counter-Proliferation Initiative (CPI), provides funding to prepare for combating foes with nuclear, biological, and chemical (NBC) and missile weapons on future battlefields, improves monitoring for locating rival NBC/missile programs, improves theater defenses, and develops weapons capable of penetrating and destroying underground facilities. US efforts will include a diplomatic offensive to persuade US allies to take similar counter-proliferation steps.... The central thrust of the CPI is to prepare US and allied forces for dealing with future enemies on the battlefield who are armed with weapons of mass destruction.... An important secondary thrust of the CPI is to provide the Commander-in-Chief with the tools to disarm an adversary unilaterally if necessary, before the adversary can initiate the use of WMD in situations where we are on a collision course with such an enemy and no alternative course seems feasible.[17]

Aspin stated that the United States was now undertaking a campaign to improve and specialize military capabilities, doctrine, training, and contingency plans to pursue such counter-proliferation policies, while the Department of Defense was tripling the number of people assigned to gathering counter-proliferation intelligence.

The DOD Counter-Proliferation Initiative would encompass: extra preparations for countering nuclear, biological, chemical (NBC), and missile weapons on future battle zones through changes in contingency planning, doctrine, equipment, and training;[18] increased monitoring of specific NBC/missile programs on a global level, including a sounder coordination of US defense and intelligence operations directed against emerging programs and arsenals; improved non-nuclear weapons capable of penetrating and destroying underground facilities; a US diplomatic offensive aimed at NATO, Japan, and other allies as a means of persuading them to take on similar initiatives—thereby strengthening their own counter-proliferation efforts; and accelerated funding for high-technology defense programs as a means to detect and locate mobile missile systems.[19] Additionally, it would: enlist Japan in a cooperative effort to develop a regional ballistic missile defense program against a potential North Korean nuclear missile threat; renew the focus on creating effective theater missile defenses capable of intercepting missiles with NBC warheads;[20] alter the 1972 ABM Treaty to permit the development, testing, and deployment of an effective US theater defense system and create an interservice body as a means of dealing with defenses against biological weapons.[21]

Aside from such military and intelligence initiatives, Aspin indicated that diplomacy, export controls, treaty restrictions, security assurances, non-military sanctions and economic cooperation would still remain an important component with the US security framework of preventing, and coping with, the proliferation of WMD.[22] Nonetheless, the role of nuclear weapons would remain an integral part of the CPI as it would provide improved US capability to deal with, in Aspin's words, a "Saddam Hussein with nukes," either in a reactive or a pre-emptive mode, primarily the former, but also the latter when no other option provided a better means of defense.[23] As further articulated by Schneider:

> This new US policy anticipates a troubled world in which more states acquire WMD—with some of those states governed by dangerous and hostile radical regimes. Hopefully, leaders of such states can be deterred from WMD use. However, it is for those states who are willing to accept risks, are very dissatisfied with the status quo, and may not be deterred by threats to their people or their nation's economy that the DOD Counter-Proliferation Initiative was designed.[24]

The arms control community regarded Aspin's strategy as a declaration of war on traditional non-proliferation tools such as diplomacy and arms control. For them, Aspin appeared to be suggesting that failure in US and international non-proliferation efforts was preordained, even though he did try to qualify his "declaration" by stating that "prevention remains our preeminent goal.... The CPI in no way means we will lessen our non-proliferation efforts."[25] The dichotomy of opinion at the time was expressed by Angus McColl:

> To some analysts, pursuit of both paths appears to pose a conflict of interest. Many proponents of traditional diplomatic non-proliferation efforts fear that the coercive element of counter-proliferation, especially the threat to use military force, will undermine the international cooperation and consensus upon which non-proliferation depends for its success. They also criticize counter-proliferation as a short-term solution to the WMD proliferation problem because it does not directly confront the long-term security concerns that motivate regional adversaries to acquire WMD in the first place. Others point out that some people view counter-proliferation as a panacea, whereas, at best, it is probably only a stopgap measure that could be stillborn if required tech-

> nologies cannot be developed. They know that military operations are not without risk, pointing to past intelligence and operational failures. Finally, some people fear that counter-proliferation will undermine the traditional US leadership that has been so vital to negotiating, implementing, and improving various non-proliferation treaties and agreements.[26]

Aspin's announcement also engendered reactions from various executive departments and agencies.

The State Department viewed it as a challenge to its preeminent role in dealing with all things related to proliferation. Officials there moved right away to limit the scope of the CPI to protect their role as vicars of non-proliferation policy.[27] The Department of Energy (DOE)—particularly its Defense Programs element—saw the CPI as a means of reversing the downward spiral of its budget. The national laboratories, in particular, saw it as a potential godsend; after all, their primary mission—the development and testing of nuclear weapons—clearly did not have the support of the Clinton Administration. Thus, DOE scientists sought to sustain certain critical skills through challenging projects other than nuclear testing—and the CPI held great promise in that regard. The military services reacted skeptically, seeing the CPI as: (1) a potential drain on service budgets already strained; and (2) as another "initiative" driven by the Office of the Secretary of Defense (OSD), such as the Strategic Defense Initiative, imposed from above without a great deal of forethought and with little or no involvement of the military. Their concern was heightened when Dr Harold Smith, assistant to the Secretary of Defense for atomic energy, speaking at a conference in New Mexico, suggested that the DOD would budget $300–400 million per year on the CPI (Defense Counterproliferation Initiative), mostly for new hardware programs.[28] How would OSD seek to pay for this new, unfunded mandate? Each of the services fully expected to be hit with a "tax" that would further undermine readiness and slow the few remaining modernization projects. The services also reacted negatively to the blunt challenge issued by OSD's Dr Carter. In a July 1994 interview with *Jane's Defence Weekly*, Carter warned that DOD civilians would dictate to the services how much would be spent on the CPI. As stated, if the services "do not hear the music, then we will have to do it ourselves."[29] Such words clearly did not convey a strong willingness on the part of senior OSD officials involved in the CPI to take into account service concerns. Indeed, as observed by analyst Joseph Pilat, the counter-proliferation debate became unnecessarily "complicated by divergent bureaucratic interests and the absence of a widely accepted definition of the term."[30]

Nuclear Posture Review (NPR) 1994

Despite these debates, it was clear that the usage of counter-proliferation and the role that US nuclear weapons would play was given greater weight and clarified within a formal review of nuclear policy and force structure. Initiated in October 1993, the Nuclear Posture Review (NPR) was described as the most ambitious review of US nuclear weapons and nuclear planning in decades. The six working groups were to investigate:[31] the role of nuclear weapons in US security strategy; nuclear force structure and infrastructure; nuclear force operations and Command and Control; nuclear safety, security, and use control; the relationship between alternative US nuclear postures and counter-proliferation policy; the relationship between alternative US nuclear postures and the threat reduction policy with the former Soviet Union.[32] Of the six working groups that were created to review US nuclear policy and force structure, one was specifically given the role of investigating the link between alternative US nuclear postures and counter-proliferation policy.

The group approved incorporation by US Strategic Command (STRATCOM)[33] of regional WMD contingencies into nuclear war planning. During the meeting process, Ashton Carter's special assistant and former professor at the University of Maryland, Dr Steven Fetter, stated vehemently that nuclear weapons could only deter nuclear use or acquisition, although the effect on acquisition was intensely debated. For Fetter, no reasonable contribution was likely to come from nuclear weapons in deterring chemical and biological weapons of mass destruction.[34] For the military leaders of STRATCOM, it was all or nothing if deterrence was to be seen as credible. The documents from the group's meetings provide a sound insight into the inner "ideology" of STRATCOM and its perception of the role of nuclear weapons against proliferating states. For STRATCOM, while nuclear weapons may not have directly impacted Third World countries' acquisition of WMD, maintaining nuclear weapons could support US political aims. This would be accomplished, it was argued, "through demonstrating intent by maintaining an arsenal and continuously providing war plans to support regional CINCs [Commanders-in-Chief]."[35] As stated:

> the US should preserve its options for responding to the situation by maintaining its current policy in which the DOE does not preclude first use of nuclear weapons. While it would not be in our interest to unleash the destructive power of a nuclear weapon, the loss of even one American city, or the endangerment of vital American interests overseas is unacceptable. To counter this threat, the US should not rule out the pre-emptive first use of nuclear weapons. In addition, following the use of WMD, the US should again seek to preserve its options. The US policy should not require retaliation with nuclear weapons, but it should leave that option open as one of a complete spectrum of possible options.[36]

The Nuclear Posture Review of 1994 affirmed the role of nuclear weapons and endorsed STRATCOM's force structure as posited above. Not only did it accept STRATCOM's broad nuclear deterrence vision, it also subscribed to the philosophy that deep and extensive reductions in US nuclear weapons may influence proliferators negatively as they attempt to match US numbers or allies under US protection—such as Japan and Germany—and go nuclear.[37] Within the counter-proliferation group there was a "consensus that [the] full range of nuclear options was desirable to deter proliferant nations," and the majority wanted the "unique contribution of nuclear deterrence to counter-proliferation" to be "stated more forcefully."[38] Additionally, the group also argued that nuclear weapons should remain as the core method of destroying specific types of targets including deeply buried structures and facilities.[39]

It was in relation to the scenario of deterring terrorist use of WMD that the group envisaged limitations to the role of nuclear weapons and stipulated that nuclear deterrence should only be applicable to state sponsored terrorism as non-state actors would not be deterred by the US nuclear posture.[40] However, this inclusion was only temporary as the Joint Chiefs of Staff would later include non-state actors as potential targets for US nuclear weapons in their Joint Theater Nuclear Doctrine publication from early 1996 (discussed later in this chapter).[41] In essence, STRATCOM was pleased with the outcome and impact it had on the NPR, for when the findings were conveyed to Congress in September 1994, nuclear weapons featured extensively in counter-proliferation roles. Interestingly, such findings were largely absent from the "spin the Clinton Administration gave on the NPR in public, which instead portrayed the NPR as a continuation of the disarmament process and a further reduction of the role of nuclear weapons in US national security policy."[42]

In September 1994, the Clinton Administration approved the recommendations of the Pentagon's Nuclear Posture Review (NPR). A significant conclusion of this review was that the United States would retain a triad of strategic nuclear forces with the capacity to deter any potential hostile state or group—who had access to strategic nuclear forces—from acting against US interests and would be able to convince the state or group that seeking "a nuclear advantage would be futile."[43] As a result, the 1994 National Security Strategy of Engagement and Enlargement paper argued that the United States would continue to maintain nuclear forces of sufficient size and capability as a means "to hold at risk a broad range of assets valued by such political and military leaders."[44] Indeed, encompassed in the NPR's "broad range of assets" and strategic nuclear force posture were: 14 Trident submarines, each carrying 24 Trident II submarine-launched ballistic missiles (SLBMs); three wings of Minuteman III intercontinental range ballistic missiles (ICBMs), each equipped with a single warhead; 66 B-52 bombers capable of carrying air-launched cruise missiles; and 20 B-2 bombers capable of carrying gravity bombs.[45]

The Nuclear Posture Review reaffirmed the need for ICBMs and SLBMs and signified that it would undertake "extensive studies to identify how to keep ICBMs and SLBMs on alert for decades to come."[46] Additionally, it highlighted that the DOD would develop an investment plan for ICBM service life extension which would encompass new technologies in the "propulsion systems, guidance systems and re-entry vehicles."[47] Such programs, it was stated, would extend the service life of this system through to 2020. Other programs and initiatives included: the Minuteman III propulsion replacement program—a $2.9 billion effort that included repouring rocket motors; the $1.6 billion

Guidance Replacement Program to provide a full upgrade for aging Minuteman III electronics; modification of the B-1 and B-2 fleet for conventional missions to help keep these strategic-alternative systems ready; investment in a $4.5 billion D-5 backfit program to replace C-4 missiles aboard Trident submarines; and a $250 million Trident Navigation Commonality Program to provide an updated, D-5 compatible navigation suite.[48] The NPR also contained nuclear infrastructure requirements for the DOE as a means to maintain the enduring stockpile, namely to: preserve nuclear weapons capability without underground testing or the production of fissile material; develop a stockpile surveillance engineering base; provide the capability to refabricate and certify weapon types in the enduring stockpile; maintain the capability to design, fabricate, and certify new warheads; maintain a science and technology base; ensure tritium availability; and accomplish these tasks with no new-design nuclear warhead production.[49]

It was evident that the 1994 Nuclear Posture Review reaffirmed the role of nuclear weapons in US security and that such weapons would be retained as a means of deterring "any future hostile foreign leadership with access to strategic nuclear forces from acting against our vital interests and to convince it that seeking a nuclear advantage" would be fruitless. "Therefore we will continue to maintain nuclear forces of sufficient size and capability to hold at risk a broad range of assets valued by such political and military leaders."[50] The Nuclear Posture Review assessed the size and role of US nuclear forces in the global arena and the extent to which the proliferation of nuclear weapons and other weapons of mass destruction, rather than the nuclear arsenal of a hostile superpower, posed a security risk to the United States. However, while it reiterated the significance of the CPI and in the instance of a potential WMD threat or use, senior political and military leaders also required a wide array of options, particularly those of a non-nuclear nature.[51] According to some observers, it was here that in NPR, the Department of Defense attempted to strike a balance between what it deemed to be "leading the way to a safer world" and hedging against the unexpected. As stated by William Perry:

> in the post-Cold War environment the United States continues to require a nuclear deterrent. The strategic triad has been streamlined and adjusted, as have non-strategic nuclear forces, to account for the new role nuclear weapons play in US national security. Major force reductions and cost savings are already underway, leading to a smaller, safer, and more secure US nuclear force.[52]

In one sense, while the Pentagon indicated that the NPR had changed the way it thought about nuclear weapons and the changing nature of their role, it still quietly endorsed the importance of nuclear weapons as a means to counter the proliferation of weapons of mass destruction.[53] As Deputy Secretary of Defense John Deutch explained to the Senate, an examination of the remaining nuclear threat from Russia and the non-Russia republics "that possess nuclear weapons as well as the emerging threat from other countries around the world indicate that the United States will continue to need nuclear weapons for deterrence for the foreseeable future."[54] The NPR was widely reported at the time to provide only non-nuclear responses to hostile use of WMD in regional conflicts. However, nuclear weapons were clearly advocated in counter-proliferation roles pertaining to deterring both acquisition and use. Moreover, several non-strategic nuclear weapon missions in support of the non-proliferation scenarios were, according to Kristensen and Handler, "deleted from public record."[55]

Doctrine for Joint Nuclear Operations (Joint Pub 3-12) 1993

The impact of STRATCOM was also apparent in instruments outside of the NPR domain and needs to be acknowledged in both emphasizing and complementing the role of nuclear weapons within the Clinton security framework. This was evident when on April 29, 1993, the first Doctrine for Joint Nuclear Operations (Joint Pub 3-12) was published, stating that with the conclusion of the Cold War, the reorganization of US military planning for joint operations was needed. The doctrine utilized Weapons of Mass Destruction (WMD) as the key term in defining the role of nuclear deterrence in US security strategy. As stated, "the fundamental purpose of nuclear forces is to deter the use of weapons of mass destruction (WMDs), and to serve as a hedge against the emergence of an overwhelming threat … credible and capable nuclear weapons are essential for national security."[56]

For the main extent, the Joint Pub 3-12 transferred notions and strategies of Cold War deterrence against the Soviet Union over to the new security arena that encompassed a more regional context. STRATCOM's efforts to formulate a regional nuclear deterrence against "rogue" states armed with WMD, engendered notions of nuclear strike options and requirements for new capabilities, including those of a low low-yield nature. As stated:

> WMD used on US forces would cause a significant tactical or operational loss; greatly change the character of the war, putting the outcome in doubt and threatening escalation; leave the United States with a difficult choice: to retaliate or not to retaliate. A selective capability of being able to use lower-yield nuclear weapons in retaliation, without destabilizing the conflict, is a useful alternative for the US National Command Authorities (NCA).[57]

The proponents of Joint Pub 3-12 argued that it caught up with the realities of nuclear planning that was well underway at the time.[58] Even before Joint Pub 3-12 was approved, STRATCOM planners had been undertaking an extensive modernization process of weapon systems and nuclear planning capabilities as a means to target specific states on a global scale. As a result, the "new" doctrine Joint Pub 3-12 was based on existing key nuclear planning documents that directed detailed nuclear planning against rogue states: NUWEP (Guidance for the Employment of Nuclear weapons) issued by Defense Secretary Dick Cheney in November 1992, the Joint Strategic Capabilities Plan—Annex C (Nuclear) FY 1993–1995 from 1992, the National Military Strategy Document—Annex B (Nuclear), and SIOP-93 from April 1993.[59]

Doctrine for Joint Nuclear Operations (Joint Pub 3-12) 1995

During December 1995, the JCS released a newer version of Doctrine for Joint Nuclear Operations (Joint Pub 3-12 1995). As in the case of its predecessor, STRATCOM played a leading role. The 1995 Joint Pub 3-12 was a more thorough document than the 1993 version, expanding on the role of nuclear deterrence, and force posture and deployment considerations in much greater detail. As indicated in the above, the Clinton Administration's NPR affirmed the importance of nuclear weapons and maintained a Cold War-type triad of nuclear warheads on submarines, land-based missiles, and bombers. Joint Pub 3-12 reiterated this expansive role of nuclear deterrence outside of Russia and China to those deemed "rogue" states. While the 1995 Joint Pub 3-12 doctrine was published after the 1995 Congressional ban on precision low-yield nuclear weapons development (the so-called PLYWD legislation), it nonetheless repeated the need for such weapons, particularly in relation to regional conflicts.[60]

The expanded role of nuclear deterrence beyond nuclear to also cover non-nuclear opponents armed with chemical or biological (or just ballistic) missiles had real implications for the NPT. The indefinite extension of the treaty was secured partially because the US (together with the other five original nuclear powers) pledged not to use nuclear weapons to threaten or attack non-nuclear states party to (and in compliance with) the NPT. However, since the NPT only regulates nuclear but not other forms of WMD, the expanded US nuclear deterrence meant that a non-nuclear NPT country could potentially find itself a target for US nuclear weapons threat or use if it possessed chemical or biological weapons. Proponents argued that, as with its predecessor, the 1995 Joint Pub 3-12 brought official nuclear doctrine "up to the realities of nuclear planning as it occurred at the time"[61] and reaffirmed that as per the NPR of 1994, nuclear weapons would remain fundamental to the US security strategy in the post-Cold War era:

> US nuclear forces serve to deter the use of WMD across the range of military operations. From a massive exchange of nuclear weapons to limited use within a theater, US nuclear capabilities must confront an enemy with risks of unacceptable damage and disproportionate loss should the enemy choose to introduce WMD in a conflict.[62]

As a result of the increased focus on regional military operations and nuclear deterrence of "rogue" states armed with WMD, the 1995 Joint Pub 3-12 addressed mainly strategic nuclear operations. Although it did include descriptions of theater nuclear operations, this was from a strategic context and threats from terrorists were only looked at in the context of securing nuclear weapons against theft. Such issues, as well the targeting of "rogue" states and terrorists, were addressed at a more in-depth level in the Doctrine for Joint Theater Nuclear Operations 1996.[63]

Doctrine for Joint Theater Nuclear Operations 1996

Efforts to further align nuclear deterrence with the requirements for regional conflicts resulted in the publication in February 1996 of a doctrine document specifically focused on theater nuclear operations. The Doctrine for Joint Theater Nuclear Operations (Joint Pub 3-12.1) outlined a regional security situation where the risk of use of nuclear and other forms of WMD was said to have increased after the Cold War:

> The dissolution of the Soviet Union has greatly reduced the possibility of a large scale nuclear exchange. However, the loss of the stability inherent in a clearly bipolar world has increased the likelihood of a nuclear exchange by regional powers. In addition, the threat to the United States, its allies, and its deployed forces due to the proliferation of WMD has grown following the end of the Cold War. The flow of advanced technology to potential or actual hostile nations has led to a proliferation of systems (missiles and aircraft) capable of delivering WMD. The possibility of a WMD exchange in a regional conflict has risen dramatically, threatening our forward-deployed forces and challenging our long-range power projection capabilities.[64]

The emergence of a specific doctrine for theater nuclear operations followed on the heels of efforts in 1993–1995 within STRATCOM to more clearly define how nuclear deterrence would work against regional aggressors armed with WMD. With its focus on regional nuclear deterrence, Joint Pub 3-12.1 included important details that were not described in Joint Pub 3-12.

Foremost among these were the kind of targets that might be subject to nuclear strikes in a regional conflict. Enemy combat forces and facilities that may be likely targets for nuclear strikes, included: WMD and their delivery systems, as well as associated command and control, production, and logistical support units; ground combat units and their associated command and control and support units; air defense facilities and support installations; naval installations, combat vessels, and associated support facilities and command and control capabilities; non-state actors (facilities and operation centers) that possess WMD; and underground facilities.[65] As explained by Kristensen:

> The focus was on the regions, and in February 1996 regional nuclear counter-proliferation was formally enshrined into nuclear doctrine when the JCS published its Doctrine for Joint Theater Nuclear Operations (Joint Pub 3-12.1). This document "translates" the overall joint nuclear doctrine from 1995 for use in regional scenarios such as in Europe, the Middle East, and the Korean Peninsula. The emphasis on WMD is striking. Joint Pub 3-12.1

> defines that the threat of nuclear exchange by regional powers and the proliferation of WMD have grown following the end of the Cold War.... Short, medium, and intermediate-range missiles capable of carrying nuclear, biological, or chemical warheads, the doctrine concludes, are "the primary threat" in theaters.[66]

Most of these target categories were "mirrored" from Cold War nuclear targeting onto regional scenarios, but there was one big surprise: "non-state actors."

The 1994 Nuclear Posture Review spent considerable time analyzing the effect of nuclear deterrence against regional opponents, and while the review concluded that nuclear weapons should have a prominent role against "rogue" states armed with WMD, it also concluded that nuclear weapons were unlikely to have any deterrence effect on non-state actors.[67] STRATCOM was a participant in that analysis but apparently did not let the findings affect the language of Joint Pub 3-12.1 which fully endorsed non-state actors as a target. Indeed, it was apparent that while the Clinton Administration retained much of the existing US nuclear weapons policy and force posture and affirmed the role of nuclear weapons in US security strategy, it also began to develop targeting options for the use of nuclear weapons in response to chemical or biological attack from states and regions other than Russia, and as conveyed in its declaratory policy, the Administration did not rule out the possible first use of nuclear weapons in these circumstances. The Doctrine for Joint Theater Nuclear Operations (Joint Pub 3-12.1) was testament to this mode of thinking.

Quadrennial Defense Review 1997

Undertaken in 1997, the Quadrennial Defense Review (QDR)[68] examined US nuclear strategy and force posture and once again reaffirmed the continuing need for "a robust and flexible nuclear deterrent."[69] In simple terms, nuclear forces were assessed and deemed to be an integral part of United States' security strategy. The review of defense "issues" encompassed those pertaining to threat, strategy, force structure considerations, and, finally, resource issues.[70] As the fourth comprehensive review of the US military since the end of the Cold War, the Quadrennial Defense Review (QDR) was an attempt to extend the United States' experience with the policy and forces of the 1991 Base Force Review, the 1993 Bottom-Up Review (BUR) and the 1995 Commission on Roles and Missions of the Armed Forces (CORM). It was argued that as a result of such reviews, the US had made extensive adjustments in its forces, procedures, and organizations. While it had "accumulated a wealth of experience" in a new and constantly changing security environment, it recognized that this was a propitious time to re-examine its assumptions, programs, and operations. Indeed, "the rapid rate of change in the world since the end of the Cold War underscores the importance of undertaking such a re-examination on a regular basis."[71]

The QDR was a collaborative effort between the Office of the Secretary of Defense (OSD) and the Joint Staff, with extensive participation from the Military

Services and the Commanders-in-Chief of the Combatant Commands. The Review was designed to be both bottom-up and top-down: It was bottom-up in the sense that the QDR sought expertise and ideas from the Department and solicited additional ideas and support from beyond DOD. The effort was top-down in the sense that the Secretary of Defense and Chairman of the Joint Chiefs of Staff guided the process to ensure that all choices and alternatives provided the capabilities necessary to execute the strategy.[72] The QDR was structured into three organizational tiers or levels. At the first level, seven panels conducted reviews of strategy, force structure, readiness, modernization, infrastructure, human resources, and information operations and intelligence. At the second level, an "Integration Group" collated the panel results into a streamlined set of "integrated options" designed to be consistent with the defense strategy. At the third level, a Senior Steering Group, co-chaired by the Deputy Secretary of Defense and the Vice Chairman of the Joint Chiefs of Staff, oversaw the entire process and made recommendations to the Secretary of Defense, who, in turn, reviewed the recommendations in consultation with the Chairman and other members of the Joint Chiefs of Staff.[73] It was here that a road map was established, requiring close adherence to the following milestones:

- Start-up and guidance phase (December 1996): Identify issues, provide guidance and direction to panels, and begin evaluation of the threat assessment.
- Strategy and fiscal context phase (January 1997): Present defense strategy and projection of fiscal environment and program risks.
- Analysis phase (February 1997): Report initial results of panel reviews.
- Integration phase (March 1997): Evaluate and refine integrated options within the defense strategy framework.
- Decision phase (April 1997): Present refined alternatives to Secretary of Defense for decision and identify issues for further evaluation.[74]

Drawing on the basic principles of the Review, work in each phase built directly upon the work of the preceding phase, leading ultimately to the decisions that are conveyed below. Work in the second and third phases began simultaneously and was initially conducted largely in parallel because of the enormity of the task and the tight schedule. The second and third phases were then reconciled in the last two phases in order to produce an integrated result. The National Defense Panel received regular briefings on the work of the panels as well as on the integration options and decisions. The National Security Council staff and other Administration agencies also participated at various points in the Review. As the decision options began to take shape, the Department began consultation with Congress. The President reviewed and then approved the defense strategy and the final decisions regarding program directions.[75] For Thomason *et al.*, the QDR process fostered a range of structured comparisons of alternative ways to implement the newly articulated defense strategy—"Shape, Respond, and Prepare."

Through this process the Secretary of Defense made a series of choices among options, or "paths," and selected a path to "balance available resources across the major requirements of the strategy, both for the near and the longer term."[76] Three paths were explicitly described in the QDR report. Each was said to be an equal cost option and the three were compared for their relative prospects of achieving the capabilities to carry out each dimension of the "Shape, Respond, and Prepare" strategic construct at acceptable levels of risk. At the Secretary's direction, each path was examined to ensure that it was fiscally executable.[77] Overall, and most importantly, the QDR review concluded that the policy and strategy to maintain US nuclear forces was "still correct."[78] Indeed, as stated by the Secretary of Defense at the time, William Cohen, it was imperative that the United States "maintain its military superiority" in the face of evolving, as well as discontinuous, threats, and challenges. Without such "superiority, our ability to exert global leadership and to create international conditions conducive to the achievement of our national goals would be in doubt."[79] Moreover, according to Conetta:

> The priority that the QDR places on maintaining military superiority and the role it accords military power as a means of influence constitute a wager about the future character of international competition. A contending view holds that military contests among the great and emerging powers will be less important in the new era than in the old, while economic and other forms of international competition will be more critical. The BUR partially reflected this view in recognizing the primacy of economic and social renewal as a national goal. Against this perspective, the QDR implies that military power is now and will continue to be as relevant as ever to the attainment of national goals.[80]

Presidential Decision Directive 60 1997

During November 1997, and in response to the QDR, President Clinton signed and approved a new Decision Directive (known as Presidential Decision Directive (PDD) 60) on nuclear weapons employment policy guidance. While US nuclear plans had been updated regularly and refined through Presidential Decisions such as the Presidential Nuclear Initiatives and the Nuclear Posture Review, this was the first revision of such guidance in over 15 years.[81] The directive considered the changes in policy and force posture brought on by the end of the Cold War and expanded on the findings of previous policy reviews, such as the NPR and QDR. According to *The Washington Post*, the highly classified Presidential Decision Directive (PDD) 60 contained language that "would permit" US nuclear strikes after enemy attacks using chemical or biological weapons. As stated, "rogue states, a terminology commonly used by the Pentagon for countries such as Iran, Iraq, Libya, North Korea, and Syria, are specifically listed as possible targets in the event of regional conflicts or crises."[82] Aside from positing the broad Presidential guidance for developing operational plans, the directive articulated guidelines for maintaining nuclear deterrence and US nuclear forces.[83] As stated:

> The United States must maintain the assured response capability to inflict "unacceptable damage" against those assets a potential enemy values most. It also posits that the US must continue to plan a range of options to insure that the US can respond to aggression in a manner appropriate to the provocation, rather than being left with an "all or nothing" response. The new guidance also continues the policy that the US will not rely on "launch on warning," but will maintain the capability to respond promptly to any attack, thus complicating an adversary's calculations. However, the new guidance eliminates previous Cold War rhetoric including references to "winning a protracted nuclear war."[84]

Moreover, PDD 60 reaffirmed that the United States should have a triad of strategic deterrent forces as a means to complicate an adversary's attack and defense planning. It also argued that deterrent forces and their associated command and control should be "flexible and survivable, to ensure that the US would be able to make an adequate and appropriate response."[85] In essence, the PDD 60 ordered the military to no longer target Russian conventional forces and industry, but focus on destroying nuclear forces, as well as the military and civilian leadership. In simple terms, it replaced a nearly 17-year old directive signed by President Reagan in 1981 at the height of the Cold War in which "fighting and winning a protracted nuclear war against Russia would no longer be an objective."[86] PDD 60 was drafted by an extremely small and specialized group, led by Special Assistant Robert Bell of the National Security Council and the Assistant Secretary of Defense for International Affairs, Franklin Miller.[87]

There was no review or panel, and while the State Department was supposedly involved, the US Arms Control and Disarmament Agency were not consulted, signifying an inability to consider the impact on non-proliferation efforts.[88] According to Bell, the three basic situations in which the United States might use nuclear weapons were not changed by the new PDD 60.[89] The criteria were as follows: if the attacking country has nuclear weapons; if the aggressor is not in compliance with the international treaty to curb the spread of nuclear weapons; or if it is allied to a nuclear power in its attack on the United States. While Bell emphasized that PDD 60 reflected the reality of the time in which an attacker using weapons of mass destruction could face nuclear reprisal,[90] Kristensen argued that "a reaffirmation of the commitments to non-proliferation and nuclear disarmament by removing chemical, biological, and radiological weapons and facilities from US war planning would be a more fitting post-Cold War measure."[91] As the above Clinton initiatives and documents suggest, planning for nuclear war in "the Third World" against states and non-state actors evolved significantly after the Gulf War of 1991. For nuclear planners, the logical conclusion of proliferation, and the US renunciation of chemical and biological weapons, was that nuclear weapons would now remain prominent in deterring the acquisition and use of WMD.[92] Behind a mask of military secrecy, planning in the form of guidance documents and initiatives progressed virtually unopposed. As Kristensen further lamented, "with little informed opposition and public debate, the result was a nuclear doctrine that borrowed heavily from Cold War nuclear thinking. President Clinton's Decision Directive of November 1997 merely permitted this planning to continue."[93]

National Security Strategy (NSS) 1999

Interestingly, such planning was not mentioned nor addressed in President Clinton's 1999 National Security Strategy (NSS). The report, entitled "A National Security Strategy for a New Century," outlined the President's vision for America's role in the world and discussed the Administration's international priorities. The three core objectives of NSS1999 were: to enhance America's security; to bolster America's economic prosperity; and to promote democracy and human rights abroad. All of these themes were present in NSS1998 and were expanded upon in this document. Central to the President's strategy for achieving these aims was US engagement and leadership in world affairs.[94] The NSS1999 placed less of an emphasis on the role of military power in promoting American interests as it was not considered "a substitute for other forms of engagement, such as diplomatic, economic, scientific, technological, cultural, and educational activities."[95]

While Clinton's NSS placed more of an emphasis on "soft power" and the ability to influence foreign powers through cultural or ideological means,[96] the role of nuclear weapons in US security strategy was conspicuously presented in a non-proliferation "only" fashion. As stated:

> We have a fundamental responsibility to limit the spread of nuclear weapons and reduce the danger of nuclear war. To this end, the United States remains committed to bringing the Comprehensive Nuclear Test Ban Treaty (CTBT) into force … and is encouraging all other states to do the same. We are encouraging all states that have not done so to sign and ratify the CTBT. We remain committed to obtaining Senate advice and consent toward ratification of the CTBT.… The Nuclear Non-Proliferation Treaty (NPT) is the cornerstone of international nuclear non-proliferation efforts and reinforces regional and global security by creating confidence in the non-nuclear commitments of its parties.[97]
>
> To reinforce the international nuclear non-proliferation regime, we seek to strengthen the International Atomic Energy Agency (IAEA) safeguards system and achieve a Fissile Material Cut-off Treaty in the Geneva Conference on Disarmament.… Through the Nunn-Lugar Cooperative Threat Reduction (CTR) Program and other initiatives, we aim to strengthen controls over weapons, usable fissile material and prevent the theft or diversion of WMD and related material and technology from the former Soviet Union.… At the Cologne summit in June 1999, the leaders of the G-8

nations affirmed their intention to establish arrangements to protect and safely manage weapons-grade fissile material no longer required for defense purposes, especially plutonium.[98]

We seek to strengthen the Biological Weapons Convention (BWC) with a new international regime to ensure compliance.[99]

Despite Clinton's willingness to embrace internationalist approaches to nuclear weapons proliferation, his tenure in office saw the continued (and potentially offensive) role that nuclear weapons would play in his security strategy. As evident in the above excerpt from NSS1999, when it came to the public domain, the Clinton Administration emphasized its multilateral nuclear drives and initiatives, but in reality, hedged its approach and kept the nuclear platform intact.

From Clinton to Bush

When looking at the nuclear weapons policy initiatives, policies, documents, and instruments of the Clinton Administration, it would be easy to assume that George W. Bush merely continued the trend. However, if we are to compare both the "Clinton Doctrine" and the "Bush Doctrine" it is apparent that Bush clearly downplayed traditional non-proliferation measures in favor of an assertive counter-proliferation stance; one that encompassed a driving assertion of the nuclear option. Whereas the National Security Strategy of 1999 issued by Clinton detailed action on initiatives such as the Biological Weapons Convention, the Comprehensive Test Ban Treaty, the Nuclear Non-proliferation Treaty and the START agreements, the National Security Strategy of 2002 outlined its non-proliferation activities in one paragraph, mentioning a recent Group of Eight agreement gauged towards the disposal of weapons in Russia. There is no doubt that the Clinton Administration was a key factor in formally defining and maintaining the role of nuclear weapons in US security strategy. However, while the concept of prevention as a means to counter the perceived threat of an adversarial use of WMD was explicit in the Bush Administration's National Security Strategy of 2002, and evident in several of the requirements of the 1993 Defense Counter-proliferation Initiative that called for an "improved counterforce capabilities to destroy adversary WMD,"[100] they cannot be viewed in the same degree.

That is, the National Security Strategy of September 2002, as well as the Nuclear Posture Review (NPR) of 2002, expanded on the Clinton platform in a more vigorous fashion, calling for contingency plans to be made for nuclear attacks on seven nations, in both "pre-emptive" and wartime counter-proliferation operations. While it is apparent that Clinton's guidance documents and instruments (discussed throughout this chapter) emphasized that the significance of nuclear weapons remained a central pillar in US security strategy, they appeared to be at least somewhat balanced with a national strategy predicated on traditional and more non-proliferation measures—albeit at times rhetorically.

Although there were occasions where pre-emptive or preventive measures were actively contemplated by the Clinton Administration against proliferant states, such as North Korea in 1993–1994, the Administration's general approach revolved more around diplomatic dissuasion than military operations.

Perhaps the greatest dichotomy between the two strategies, and certainly the most contentious, was the Bush Administration's unbridled determination in not allowing enemies of the United States to strike first, emphasizing that the risks of inaction or containment in specific cases may outweigh the risks of action. The National Security Strategy of 2002 stated that in the face of a looming threat, the United States "will, if necessary, act pre-emptively" to "forestall or prevent hostile acts by our adversaries."[101] Even though discussion pertaining to "pre-emption" was certainly evident during the Clinton Administration, the sentiments were articulated through terms such as "potential future requirements," "prospective utility," and "potential liabilities"—with the required strategic and operational framework and military capacity to enact such an approach perceived as an impossibility that could derail the Defense Counter-proliferation Initiative (CPI). However, under the Bush Administration, such "issue" considerations were lowered as the nuclear option came to the forefront of national strategy.[102]

The urgency that motivated Bush in 2002 and subsequent years derived from two underlying arguments: that WMD and missile capabilities would continue to proliferate; and that the use of such weapons against US forward-deployed forces, US friends and allies, or even US or allied homelands was increasingly likely. In response, the United States sought to advance its security along two parallel and mutually reinforcing lines: an assertive and proactive drive against security challenges emerging from the proliferation–terrorism nexus, while bolstering homeland and transforming military capabilities as a means to deter, protect against, and nullify the effects of an attack. It is with this in mind that Bush actively sought to devalue the appeal of WMD and missiles and to impede the dire consequences to US interests should adversaries successfully execute such attacks.[103] Therefore, while it has been argued by some commentators that Bush continued a policy that was initiated by the Clinton Administration, his National Security Strategy of 2002, or "doctrine," and subsequent nuclear weapons guidance documents, focused on a more assertive counter-proliferation route as a means to impede or remove existing adversarial holdings of WMD before they could be used.

In the adjoining National Strategy to Combat Weapons of Mass Destruction (NSCWMD), Bush began with an excerpt from his National Security Strategy of 2002, re-emphasizing the path that his Administration would take:

> Our enemies have openly declared that they are seeking weapons of mass destruction, and evidence indicates that they are doing so with determination. The United States will not allow these efforts to succeed … as a matter of common sense and self-defense, America will act against such emerging threats before they are fully formed. We cannot defend America and our friends by hoping for the best. So we must be prepared to defeat our enemies' plans, using the best intelligence and proceeding with deliberation.

> History will judge harshly those who saw this coming danger but failed to act. In the new world we have entered, the only path to peace and security is the path of action.[104]

Furthermore, in the 2002 Nuclear Posture Review, the Pentagon outlined a list of contingencies and targets where nuclear weapons might be used. As stated:

> In setting requirements for nuclear strike capabilities, distinctions can be made among the contingencies for which the United States must be prepared. Contingencies can be categorized as immediate, potential or unexpected ... North Korea, Iraq, Iran, Syria, and Libya are among the countries that could be involved in immediate, potential, or unexpected contingencies. All have long-standing hostility toward the United States and its security partners; North Korea and Iraq in particular have been chronic military concerns. All sponsor or harbor terrorists, and all have active WMD and missile programs.[105]

While it is evident that Bush continued the policy first instituted by Clinton, the above words signified a defining assertion in terms of his counter-proliferation policy. Indeed, the adaptive planning described in the 2002 NPR expanded the role of nuclear weapons beyond the primary role of deterring a nuclear attack, and suggested that nuclear weapons could be employed against targets able to withstand non-nuclear attack or in retaliation for use of biological or chemical weapons.[106]

The 2002 NPR also suggested that the US must develop new nuclear weapon capabilities as a means to defeat "hardened and deeply buried targets" in states that are party to the Non-Proliferation Treaty (including Iran, Iraq, Libya, and Syria). Parts of the 2002 NPR that were leaked to the media illustrated Bush's view on how nuclear weapons could be used in three different scenarios: against targets able to withstand non-nuclear attack; in retaliation for attack with nuclear, biological, or chemical weapons; or "in the event of surprising military developments."[107] The document proposed that the US be prepared to launch a nuclear strike to destroy stocks of chemical and biological weapons as well as to break regional conflicts like an Arab-Israeli conflict, a North Korean attack on South Korea, or a military confrontation between China and Taiwan.[108] The Bush Administration further articulated the notion of threatening the use of US nuclear weapons to prevent the proliferation of NBC weapons to other states or non-state groups in the September 2002 National Security Strategy and December 2002 National Strategy to Combat WMD respectively:

> We know from experience that we cannot always be successful in preventing and containing the proliferation of WMD to hostile states and terrorists. Therefore, US military and appropriate civilian agencies must possess the full range of operational capabilities to counter the threat and use of WMD by states and terrorists against the United States, our military forces, and friends and allies.[109]

In contrast to Bush's nuclear amplification (and as indicated in the above), the Clinton Administration retained much of the existing US nuclear weapons policy and force posture in the decade after the demise of the Soviet Union.

While the Clinton Administration, and the Bush Snr Administration before it, eliminated many specific targets from the US war plan and reduced the size of the US nuclear arsenal, the central tenets of the US deterrence strategy and nuclear employment plans remained relatively unchanged.[110] Furthermore, during the 1990s, the Clinton Administration began to develop targeting options for the use of nuclear weapons in response to chemical or biological attack from states other than Russia, and, in its declaratory policy, the Administration did not rule out the possible first use of nuclear weapons in these circumstances.[111] At the same time, many participants in the public debate over nuclear weapons policy argued that the United States should distinctly redefine its nuclear weapons strategy and force posture. They argued that in the absence of the global threat from the Soviet Union, the United States could maintain its deterrent posture with a far smaller number of nuclear weapons; many proposed reductions to levels of around 1,000 warheads. Some even argued that due to its overwhelming superiority in conventional weapons, the United States could defeat almost any potential adversary without threatening to resort to nuclear weapons.[112] Indeed, several studies came to the conclusion that a policy of "nuclear abolition" could be a practical, albeit long-term, goal for the United States and other nations with nuclear weapons. In the meantime, it was posited that the United States should use its nuclear weapons only to deter the potential use of nuclear weapons by other states. As stated by Michael Gordon:

> As the Cold War waned, so did the notion that nuclear weapons could be used to fight a war. While Washington did not give up its option to make the first use of nuclear weapons against a Warsaw Pact attack, it cast the use of such weapons as a last resort. With the end of the Cold War, the need for nuclear weapons seemed to fade further.[113]

While maintaining the nuclear role as affirmed under Clinton, the Bush Administration also provided a different description of what this role would entail.

Indeed, Bush assumed that nuclear weapons would be a part of US security strategy for at least the next 50 years. Given this time frame, the Nuclear Posture Review (NPR) of 2002 recommended that the United States should undertake a development process of its weapons systems that would enter force in the years between 2020 and 2040. It was clear that the Bush Administration did not assume that the "current systems" in the US nuclear arsenal would be the last, and that to have an efficient nuclear option would involve redevelopment of such systems—even with the potential of creating a new nuclear weapon. It was evident that the Bush Administration amplified the role of nuclear weapons beyond the "weapon of last resort" designed to deter only nuclear attack. The Administration not only argued that nuclear weapons could deter chemical, biological, and conventional attack, it believed that they could also be used to assure allies of US commitments, dissuade adversaries from acquiring weapons of mass destruction or threatening the United States, and defeat adversaries by destroying critical targets if deterrence failed.

The Bush Administration outlined plans to develop a more focused nuclear war-fighting capability for the United States, and emphasized the development of such penetrating nuclear weapons as a means to destroy hardened and deeply buried targets, together with the "capabilities" based approach in which it would seek the ability to destroy threatening capabilities possessed by any potential adversary. Critics argued that these changes in the US nuclear posture made it more likely that the United States would use nuclear weapons in a future crisis. However, according to Doyle McManus, the Bush Administration argued that US plans and capabilities to use nuclear weapons against smaller countries would make nuclear use less likely because it would make the US deterrent more credible and robust.[114] For Sokolsky and Rumer, the Bush Administration's approach had distinct limitations as "leaders of rogue states may not take seriously a US threat to launch massive nuclear strikes on leadership and weapons sites.… Thus, having the capability to destroy such targets with smaller and less destructive weapons would strengthen, rather than erode deterrence."[115] The Bush Administration, however, argued that this expanded role for nuclear weapons did not mean that the United States was increasing its reliance on nuclear weapons. It noted that the addition of missile defenses and precision-guided conventional weapons to US deterrent forces would give the President a greater number of options in a crisis and actually reduce the likelihood of nuclear use.[116]

Critics questioned this mode of thinking, arguing that the Bush Administration's approach would blur the distinction between nuclear and conventional weapons and increase the likelihood of nuclear use. According to Brookings Institute analyst, Ivo Daalder, the Administration outlined a role for nuclear weapons that emphasized war-fighting over deterrence. As stated, "if military planners are now to consider the nuclear option any time they confront a surprising military development, the distinction between nuclear and non-nuclear options fades away."[117] Others also concluded that the Bush Administration's plan did increase US reliance on nuclear weapons. Former Senator Sam Nunn, former Secretary of Defense William Perry and retired General Eugene Habiger argued that the Administration's policy was "expanding options for nuclear attacks, widening the number of targeted nations and developing new nuclear weapons variants." They noted that "each of these ideas may have a plausible military rationale," but "their collective effect is to suggest that the nation with the world's most powerful conventional forces is actually increasing its reliance on nuclear forces."[118] Additionally, other critics of the Bush Administration queried as to whether threats to use nuclear weapons in response to anything other than a nuclear attack would be either necessary or credible. In this regard, according to Peter Scoblic, "the US would be far better served by adopting a genuinely new nuclear posture, one that maintains nuclear weapons only to deter nuclear attack. Given the awesome power of US conventional forces, we do not need nuclear weapons for any other purpose, even to deter a chemical or biological attack."[119] Furthermore, given the long-standing "taboo" against the use of nuclear weapons, some argued that the United States would enhance its standing in the international community if it sought to reduce, rather than expand, the role of nuclear weapons in international affairs.[120]

Regardless of such critical sentiments, the Bush Administration emphasized that nuclear weapons would "continue to be essential to our security, and that of our friends and allies."[121] In simple terms, nuclear weapons would remain the only weapons in the US arsenal that could hold at risk the full range of targets valued by an adversary, and as a result, would continue to play a key role in US deterrent strategy. In contrast to Clinton, the Bush Administration described a more comprehensive and integrated role for nuclear weapons. In outlining the results of the 2002 Nuclear Posture Review, the Administration stated that nuclear weapons, along with missile defenses and other elements of the US military establishment, would not only deter adversaries by promising an unacceptable amount of damage in response to an adversary's attack, they also assured allies of the US commitment to their security by providing an extended deterrent, dissuading potential adversaries from challenging the United States with nuclear weapons or other "asymmetrical threats" by convincing them that they can never negate the US nuclear deterrent; and defeat enemies by holding at risk those targets that could not be destroyed with other types of weapons.[122] According to former Undersecretary of Defense Douglas Feith, "linking nuclear forces to multiple defense policy goals, and not simply to deterrence, recognizes that these forces ... perform key missions in peacetime as well as in crisis or conflict."[123] In addition to expanding the role of nuclear weapons beyond deterrence, Bush altered the role of deterrence in US national security strategy. As will be expanded upon in the next chapter, the Bush Administration through varying guidance documents, instruments, and speeches argued that the United States would not necessarily be able to contain or deter the types of threats "emerging today," and therefore, must be prepared to "pre-empt" these threats by launching strikes against adversaries before the adversary attacks the United States, its allies, or its interests. Some analysts concluded that, with this change in perspective, the Bush Administration foresaw the possible preventive/"pre-emptive" use of nuclear weapons against states or groups that were not necessarily armed with their own nuclear weapons.[124]

In its National Security Strategy of 2002, the Bush Administration stated that the United States would "deter and defend against the threat [of nuclear, biological, and chemical weapons] before it is unleashed." However, the document also stated that the United States would seek to "strengthen non-proliferation efforts to prevent rogue states and terrorists from acquiring the materials, technologies, and expertise necessary for weapons of mass destruction." The report said that the United States would "enhance diplomacy, arms control, multilateral export controls, and threat reduction assistance that impede states and terrorists seeking WMD."[125] According to the Administration, the development of new types of nuclear weapons that could defeat hardened and deeply buried targets, along with the potential use of nuclear weapons in retaliation for non-nuclear attacks, were a part of the US effort to deter and dissuade state and non-state actors from acquiring and threatening to use chemical, biological, or nuclear weapons. Many critics at the time argued that the Administration' approach was likely to undermine US diplomatic efforts to discourage nuclear proliferation and in most instances they have been proven correct. According to one analyst, "by emphasizing the important role of nuclear weapons, the Pentagon is encouraging other nations to think it is important to have them as well."[126] Senator John Kerry conveyed a similar viewpoint when he stated that the 2002 National Security Strategy and the 2002 NPR would undermine US credibility as they sought to convince other states to forego nuclear weapons, noting that "it reduces all our bona fides on the proliferation issue."[127]

Critics of the Bush Administration's policy pointed specifically to the implications its views on the US negative security assurance might have for US non-proliferation efforts. Many at the time noted that, through the negative security assurance, the United States sought to convince other states that they would not need their own nuclear weapons to deter a nuclear threat from the United States. However, there would be "no reason for other countries to refrain from acquiring nuclear weapons" if the United States abandoned that policy.[128] Not only would these states receive no security benefit from the absence of nuclear weapons in their arsenals, they might also conclude that they could only deter a US attack if they were to acquire their own nuclear weapons. Others, however, argued that the negative security assurance has done little to stem proliferation or enhance US security because other states do not consider the US nuclear posture or declaratory policy when making their decisions about the acquisition of nuclear weapons. Even if the United States did not have any nuclear weapons, some states would seek them for themselves to counter their neighbors or offset the US advantage in conventional weapons. Furthermore, some analysts consider the negative security assurance, and its specific focus on nuclear weapons, as an "outdated policy that effectively gives non-nuclear countries a safe haven for developing chemical and biological weapons."[129]

Nevertheless, many critics of the Bush Administration's policy questioned the wisdom of an approach that may have undermined US nuclear non-proliferation objectives, even in the interest of providing new tools to address chemical and biological weapons. They noted that the United States possessed conventional forces that were far superior to those of any other country. If, however, potential adversaries were to acquire nuclear weapons, they may present the United States with an "asymmetrical threat" that could offset US conventional superiority. Therefore, according to Daalder and Lindsay, the United States should have sought to "marginalize as much as possible the role that nuclear weapons play in US defense and foreign policy." States can only negate the overwhelming US conventional superiority with nuclear weapons, so "it is in US interest to keep the firewall between nuclear and conventional high and strong."[130] Despite such sentiments, the Bush Administration vigorously pursued and outlined a posture that reflected the view that nuclear weapons should play a broader role in US national security strategy than just the deterrence of nuclear attack, that a credible deterrent required the capability to effectively threaten and destroy a range of critical targets, and that the United States may need different numbers of nuclear weapons and different types of nuclear weapons to address threats that emerge in the future. Under this formula, the flexibility to restore nuclear warheads quickly, expand the number of deployed warheads over time, and develop new weapons with new capabilities—the doctrine argued—would make it possible for the United States to reduce its deployed weapons in the near term without creating potential risks to its security in the future.[131]

As an extension of the broader National Security Strategy posited two months earlier in September 2002, the National Strategy to Combat Weapons of Mass Destruction (NSCWMD) illustrated that Bush's policy was indeed a deviation in direction that endorsed and advocated an assertive nuclear weapons policy. While the Clinton Administration reaffirmed earlier US pledges not to use nuclear weapons to attack non-nuclear-weapon states-parties to the nuclear Non-proliferation Treaty (NPT), at the same time, it kept open the option to use nuclear weapons, even in nuclear-weapon-free zones. Indeed, as stated by Siracusa and Coleman, for the Clinton Administration "nuclear weapons ... were still a vital part of US efforts to hedge against an uncertain future."[132] In essence, both Administrations found new reasons as to why nuclear weapons would remain vital to US security while they sought to keep the rest of the world denuclearized.[133] Clinton retained much of the existing US nuclear weapons policy and force posture in the decade after the demise of the Soviet Union and affirmed the role of nuclear weapons in US security strategy through the Defense Counter-Proliferation Initiative (CPI) 1993, Nuclear Posture Review (NPR) 1994, Doctrine for joint Nuclear Operations (Joint Pub 3-12) 1993/1995, Doctrine for Joint Theater Nuclear Operations 1996, Quadrennial Defense Review (QDR) 1997 and Presidential Decision Directive (PDD) 60 1997.

However, it was the Bush Administration that expanded on the Clinton "platform" by amplifying the role of nuclear weapons, to the extent that they could be considered and used as a distinct option against potential nuclear, biological, and chemical threats from other states and non-state actors—even preventively. As the next chapter will illustrate, the Bush Administration, through the National Security Strategy of 2002 and the classified and unclassified guidance documents and instruments it implemented—notably the Nuclear Posture Review, the 2002 National Strategy to Combat Weapons of Mass Destruction, the 2005 Doctrine for Joint Nuclear Operations, the 2006 Quadrennial Defense Review, the 2006 Strategic Operations Joint Operating Concept Version 2.0, and in recent times, the Reliable Replacement Warhead program—engendered a new era in which nuclear weapons were not just a mere feature of the United State's security strategy, but were reinvigorated as both an assertive and driving force behind the Bush Administration's view of the world—and can be viewed as one of his legacies when he himself departed office in 2009.

5 The nuclear option

Bush and the "real" doctrine

The Bush Doctrine can be defined as the set of policies that President George W. Bush implemented in response to the September 11, 2001 terrorist attacks and formalized on the September 20, 2002 in his National Security Strategy. Bush declared that the United States would make "no distinction between terrorists who committed these acts and those who harbor them,"[1] a statement that defined "the doctrine" and launched the policy of "pre-emptive" war against potential aggressors before they were capable of launching an attack against the United States. As the core rationale and justification for the 2003 Iraq invasion and subsequent conflict, the National Security Strategy of 2002 has been often depicted as a marked departure from the policies of deterrence that characterized US foreign policy during the Cold War and "Phase 1" of the post-Cold War period (1991–2001). But if one is to thoroughly examine this subject, it is evident that elements of the Bush Doctrine pertaining to pre-emption, preventive considerations and regime change have been implicit in US foreign policy over the course of the last 65 years. Critics and commentators have often viewed the doctrine as a "hawkish" moment in time, the quest of a belligerent warmonger, the beginning of "Phase 2" of the post-Cold War era, and in doing so, define it in isolation. While there may be some merit to these views, they fail to comprehend the broader critical dimension of the doctrine—that being, the nuclear policy instruments and documents that it indirectly and directly sponsored throughout the entirety of Bush's two terms in office. It is with this in mind that the National Security Strategy cannot be moribund to 2002 perceptions, but a document that must be viewed as a dangerous and living catalyst; a document that punctuated, updated, refined, and reaffirmed its core sentiments through the unclassified and classified documents it spawned over the period of 2002–2008.

In simple terms, these nuclear arteries of the Bush Doctrine can be viewed as formal policy instruments that advocated the United States' willingness to use nuclear weapons on states that it deemed to be adversarial. The 2002 Nuclear Posture Review (NPR), the 2002 National Strategy to Combat Weapons of Mass Destruction (NSCWMD), the 2003/04 CONPLAN (Concept Plan) 8022 (Global Strike), the 2005 Doctrine for Joint Nuclear Operations, the 2006 Quadrennial Defense Review, the 2006 Strategic Operations Joint Operating Concept Version 2.0, and in recent times, the Reliable Replacement Warhead (RRW) program, clearly illustrate that the Bush Doctrine should not be simply dismissed or defined as a doctrine of preventive intervention alone, but as one that advocated nuclear weapon reactivation. Specifically, it was these documents that signified the resurgent role of nuclear weapons and the Bush Administration's push to modernize US offensive forces, deploy missile defenses, upgrade communication and satellite systems, and overall, revitalize the nuclear military complex.

Behind the Administration's rhetoric of post-Cold War restraint were expansive plans to revitalize US nuclear forces and all the elements that would support them within a so-called "New Triad" of capabilities that combined nuclear and conventional offensive strikes with missile defenses and nuclear weapons infrastructure.[2] Not since the escalation of the Cold War in Ronald Reagan's first term had there been such an emphasis on nuclear weapons in US defense strategy. The deeper policy within the Bush Doctrine and its accompanying documents foreshadowed a new nuclear era in which the once-termed "weapon of last resort" evolved into a usable and "necessary" device. Russell and Wirtz described this as a "quiet revolution" in which the specter of nuclear reactivation would become the Bush Doctrine's main legacy.[3] As Defense Secretary Robert Gates stated in May 2007, the assertion of nuclear weapons will "play a critical role in the defense of the United States … their unique capabilities contribute in vital and irreplaceable ways to the ability to deter adversaries and dissuade others from pursuing nuclear capabilities on their own."[4] These words coincided with the release of the Reliable Replacement Weapon program,[5] clearly signifying both the culmination and continuum of a nuclear reactivation process that began with the National Security Strategy of 2002.

When the Iraq conflict began on March 20, 2003, the United States' intervention strategy rested on four core principles found in the Bush Doctrine: first, that the United States should act preventively to thwart strikes on US targets; second, that Washington should be willing to act unilaterally, alone or with a select coalition when the United Nations or allies balk; third, that Iraq was the next cornerstone in the global war on terrorism; and, finally, that Baghdad's transformation into a new "democracy" would foster region-wide change. Of course, the Bush Doctrine's quest to legitimize a state intervention based on such pillars was undermined by the initial failure to find WMD, the inability to prove Iraq's ties to al Qaeda, the ongoing specter of violence, limited reconstruction, the US's apparent inability to cope with an asymmetrical threat and mounting Arab disillusionment with the US leadership and occupation.[6] When critics point to the Iraq war as a clear repudiation of the Bush Doctrine, perhaps they are not considering all of the applications of the doctrine in a broader context. True, Iraq was where the Bush Doctrine was most visible and most noticeably put to the test. It was equally true that it failed this test—regardless of the 2007 surge and claims of success made by General Petraeus at the time. But while it is crucial to highlight the doctrine's key tenet failures, it is also imperative to acknowledge that it remained "alive" in the nuclear classified and unclassified instruments it engendered over the course of the Bush Administration's tenure.

Nuclear Posture Review 2002

Of course, the ominous nuclear seeds of the Bush Doctrine were evident when the Bush Administration announced in January 2002 that a congressionally mandated review of US nuclear capabilities had been conducted. Defined as the Nuclear Posture Review (NPR), the examination argued that a "new strategic triad, encompassing nuclear and precision non-nuclear strike forces, inert and active defenses and a revitalized defense infrastructure would be emphasized and implemented."[7] The architects of the review considered nuclear weapons as one option in an array of capabilities designed to adapt to the perceived threats posed by the proliferation of chemical, biological, and nuclear weapons, and long-range ballistic missiles. On a more specific level, the main focus of the Bush Administration's "new strategic triad" was to integrate defenses (i.e. missile defense), nuclear weapons, and "non-nuclear strike forces"[8] into a streamlined capability as a means to dissuade and deter adversaries, while maintaining the ability to undertake conflict should deterrence fail. The NPR stated that the strike elements "could provide greater flexibility in the design and conduct of military campaigns to defeat opponents decisively. Non-nuclear strike capabilities may be particularly useful to limit collateral damage and conflict escalation. Nuclear weapons could be employed against targets able to withstand non-nuclear attack."[9]

While the Nuclear Posture Review advocated the reduction of operationally deployed nuclear forces to 1,700–2,200 warheads by 2012, it ambiguously vied for a "flexible" and "responsive nuclear force" that could be "uploaded within days" and guard against "potential contingencies."[10] This was evident in the NPR's quest to develop hardened and deeply buried targets (HDBTs), considered a key "unmet" capability in US defense. For the Bush Administration, the new triad encompassed a wider range of options available in which the United States would have what it deemed to be "an appropriate way to respond to aggression, thereby bolstering deterrence."[11] The most concerning aspect of the new triad was the greater latitude it gave to the Administration. As Russell and Wirtz posited, it enabled a way to "sidestep bureaucratic resistance to changing what constitutes one of the most respected elements of the nuclear creed that shaped US nuclear doctrine, the sanctity of the old (Cold War) triad of forces and the focus on guaranteeing a massive nuclear response under any circumstances."[12] On a surface level, the Bush Administration argued that the new strategic triad allowed for further reductions in US strategic nuclear forces because it cleared a path for the possible elimination of one of the arms of the old nuclear triad. However, its quest for flexibility and "boutique" nuclear applications only highlighted a willingness to utilize the nuclear option.[13]

The Bush Administration released its classified Nuclear Posture Review to Congress on December 31, 2001, and followed up in September 2002 with the broader and well known National Security Strategy. While the focus of this book has been focused primarily on the Bush Doctrine, the NPR can essentially be defined as an integrated release that provided a more detailed insight into a key artery of the "doctrine" itself, namely, the concept of assertive counter-proliferation.

While both documents called explicitly for pre-emptive (or preventive strikes), taken together they represented an alteration in US "declaratory policy regarding nuclear weapons use."[14] If one is to closely assess the NPR as an implementation strategy for the goals encompassed in the National Security Strategy of 2002, it is evident that the United States was placing itself in a position in which it was more likely to use nuclear weapons first against a perceived threat, or even a potential attacker—whether a state or non-state actor, whether armed with nuclear weapons or not.[15] As the National Security Strategy of 2002 stated, "our enemies … are seeking weapons of mass destruction.… America will act against such emerging threats before they are fully formed."[16] It further argued that deterrence, or at least deterrence defined in its traditional sense, was unlikely to work against terrorists or "rogue" states, warning that the United States "cannot not let our enemies strike first."[17]

The Bush Administration worked to support the "pre-emption" strategy by arguing that the United States was permitted under international law's recognized right of self defense to undertake pre-emptive action against an "imminent attack." However, it is clear that the Administration's approach pushed the boundaries of the traditional definition of "imminent" to include preventing a state or non-state body from obtaining even the capacity to attack the United States or US interests, especially if the state or non-state actor was pursuing WMD as a means of attack.[18] While the NPR did not specifically identify the issue of preventive or pre-emptive nuclear war, the document did endorse at an in-depth level the need for a "flexible" arsenal with weapons that "vary in scale, scope and purpose" to address expanding threats. Specifically, the document emphasized the potential to use nuclear weapons as a means to penetrate secluded targets such as chemical or biological weapons storehouses or factories, or underground command centers. It further advocated new nuclear weapons "options," including "possible modifications to existing weapons to provide additional yield flexibility in the stockpile; improved earth-penetrating weapons (EPWs) to counter the increased use by potential adversaries of hard and deeply buried facilities; and warheads that reduce collateral damage."[19]

In essence, the NPR examined the changes in the post-Cold War security environment and identified contingencies in which nuclear forces could be utilized.[20] The effort defined the relationships among nuclear forces and other military capabilities, set objectives for nuclear and related capabilities, and outlined programs to further these ends. As indicated in the above, the NPR called for the exploration of new nuclear weapons concepts to defeat hard, deeply-buried targets such as underground WMD bunkers, as well as Agent-Defeat Weapons (ADW) to nullify biological and chemical weapons agents and, thereby, required the development of several new nuclear warheads.[21] As the report articulated:

> Greater flexibility is needed with respect to nuclear forces and planning than was the case during the Cold War. The assets most valued by the spectrum of potential adversaries in the new security environment may be diverse and, in some cases, US understanding of what an adversary values may

> evolve. Consequently, although the number of weapons needed to hold those assets at risk has declined, US nuclear forces still require the capability to hold at risk a wide range of target types. This capability is key to the role of nuclear forces in supporting an effective deterrence strategy relative to a broad spectrum of potential opponents under a variety of contingencies. Nuclear attack options that vary in scale, scope, and purpose will complement other military capabilities. The combination can provide the range of options needed to pose a credible deterrent to adversaries whose values and calculations of risk and of gain and loss may be very different from and more difficult to discern than those of past adversaries.[22]

Advocates of the NPR asserted that the new posture was imperative as a means to change the US deterrence stance from a "one-size-fits-all" structure gauged towards the Cold War global posture to one that could defeat all sizes and types of adversaries. Indeed, both the NPR and the National Security Strategy engendered the continuum of policy guidance and reshaped US strategic planning by advocating the transferral of the top-heavy Cold War Single Integrated Operational Plan into a suite of boutique, flexible plans designed to thwart adversaries and those who might seriously undermine the security of the United States.

In conjunction with the National Security Strategy of 2002, the Bush Administration's NPR can be perceived as a significant document that posited long-range nuclear weapons policy, plans, and aspirations. A year in the making, the expansive classified report was presented to Congress at the end of 2001, and was very quickly leaked to the media.[23] Not since the reassertion of the Cold War during the Reagan era had there been such a focus on nuclear weapons in US defense strategy. In many respects, the NPR reversed notions of post-Cold War progress by expanding the range of potential conflicts in which nuclear weapons could be employed; advocating the design and building of a new generation of warheads to meet these perceived needs; and putting in place a planning and command structure that would make it easier to plan and launch nuclear attacks.[24] The Administration believed that its reinvigorated nuclear posture via the NPR and National Security Strategy of 2002 would restrengthen national security by deterring adversaries from using or even acquiring nuclear and other weapons of mass destruction. Yet the evidence from the Russian and Chinese responses to this assertive nuclear posture was not encouraging. It was clear that the United States' intention to retain stockpiles of nuclear weapons and its motives for potentially creating new and more usable weapons have caused competitors to act with varying degrees of countermeasures since the NPR's inception. Russia adjusted its nuclear forces in response to the NSS, NPR and subsequent US nuclear instruments, retaining warhead missiles that have the capability to penetrate the prospective US missile defense system. China also created more missiles and warheads than it originally had envisaged and has possibly deployed MIRVed (multiple independently targeted re-entry vehicles) missiles in response to a US ballistic missile defense system. Similarly, the assertive US stance since the NPR and NSS and its pursuit of reduced-yield weapons—or what has been at times referred to as "boutique" nuclear weapons—have no doubt engendered certain state and non-state actors to seek weapons of mass destruction as leverage against the US.[25]

Nonetheless, the NPR argued that an assertive nuclear policy made the United States more secure, and as such, to articulate the expanded role that nuclear weapons would play in defending US security, it adopted the terminology used in the Quadrennial Defense Review issued in 2001.[26] As stated in the review, the Department of Defense was vying for the expansion of its nuclear framework around four core pillars: to instill confidence in its allies; to deter military competition; to impede threats and coercion against US interests; and to defeat any adversary if deterrence failed. The NPR used similar rhetoric to support the United States' ongoing usage of nuclear weapons when it stated that "US nuclear forces [would] continue to provide assurance to security partners" and would "serve to reduce the incentives for friendly countries to acquire nuclear weapons of their own.... Systems capable of striking a wide range of targets throughout an adversary's territory may dissuade a potential adversary from pursuing threatening capabilities."[27]

Indeed, both the NPR and the NSS can be deemed the cornerstone of the Bush Administration's quest in placing the nuclear option back to the fore. The NPR was clear in urging the United States to retain existing nuclear weapons, while also positing the notion of developing new ones. While the Bush Administration publicly pledged to reduce the nuclear stockpile in the vicinity of 1,700 to 2,200 "operationally deployed strategic warheads" by 2012, the Administration continued to impose unwarranted Cold War levels of secrecy on the changes it was making in the size of the active and reserve nuclear stockpile.[28] It was evident through the NPR and subsequent guidance documents that followed that the Administration pursued a new mix of weapons in a future arsenal. Since 2001, both the Pentagon and the Department of Energy played an assertive role in paving the way for a new generation of nuclear weapons. Through a wide array of programs, they began soliciting a new intercontinental ballistic missile that was to be operational in 2018, a new submarine-launched ballistic missile and a nuclear-powered ballistic missile submarine for 2030, and a new heavy bomber ready in 2020, all presumably needing new or modified warheads.[29]

A central pillar of the NPR was to make nuclear war planning speedier and flexible. The virtue of flexibility in nuclear war conflict is that it enables agility and quick adjustments in "campaigns," even after a mission has begun. It can potentially provide a greater number of nuclear attack options available to the President, while enabling the ability to shift seamlessly from the identification of a target to one of destruction. The NPR's quest was not just limited to notions of "flexibility" and making the nuclear arsenal easier to use, it also advocated the merging of forces as a means to carry out nuclear and conventional "global strikes." That is, an intercontinental ballistic missile could carry either a nuclear warhead or a conventional warhead. It was this that further accentuated Bush's nuclear option quest in that the "assimilation" dispelled the boundaries that had traditionally placed nuclear weapons with an extreme classification. Incorporating the use of nuclear weapons as another step in the defense "suite" only increased the likelihood of usage. Indeed, the NPR's pursuit in combining nuclear and conventional weapons posed a very specific danger in which nuclear warheads could be utilized in regional conflicts as a means to destroy structures or facilities that conventional weapons could not. For instance, the NPR called for the development of nuclear earth-penetrating and low-yield weapons to enhance the capability—meaning utility—of the strike force.[30] The rhetoric that surrounded such weapons—"bunker busters," "mininukes," "micronukes," "collateral-damage limiting nukes"—illustrated a shift that potentially lowered the threshold of utilizing them.[31]

As was clearly outlined in the National Security Strategy of 2002, the Bush Administration expanded the set of adversaries, and coinciding with this, war plans that demanded that the US have a more specialized set of weapons to destroy them. The NPR articulated these sentiments and contributed to the wide array of guidance documents that altered previous large-scale permanent nuclear strike plans, and instead, assembled attack plans in the event of hostilities with another nuclear state. Given the destructive power of nuclear weapons, having fewer warheads in place at all times would not diminish their perceived power to deter enemies. As the NPR emphasized, the Bush Administration had no intention of quashing the planning infrastructure left over from the Cold War. Instead, it reasserted the nuclear option with the notion of creating new and specific types of weapons. Indeed, the NPR's suggested force structure and number of deployed nuclear warheads was intended to support not only the pressing requirements for deterrence, but also to contribute to the further goals of assuring "allies and friends," dissuading potential opponents from taking the path of arms competition or military challenge, and providing a barrier against the possible emergence of more extreme military threats or severe technical issues in the arsenal.[32] As stated in the foreword to the NPR report by Secretary of Defense Donald Rumsfeld, the review "put in motion a major change in our approach to the role of nuclear offensive forces in our deterrent strategy."[33] In Rumsfeld's testimony to Congress and several statements made by other officials, the Bush Administration portrayed the NPR as reducing the role of nuclear weapons, lowering the readiness requirement for nuclear forces and increasing the role of non-nuclear and missile defense capabilities.[34] However, as the rest of this chapter will highlight, both the NPR and NSS only worked to reinvigorate the nuclear option—evident in the subsequent guidance documents that they have spawned.

Indeed, the National Security Strategy of 2002 and "editing" documents (particularly the NPR "foundation document") illustrated the significant contradiction between the Bush Administration's public rhetoric about reducing the role of nuclear weapons and the guidance issued to nuclear planners. That is, while the overall number of warheads was being reduced, the National Security Strategy of 2002, NPR and subsequent guiding planning for the remaining arsenal, reaffirmed the assertive position in relation to having nuclear forces on high alert; ready to be used in an increasing number of limited-strike scenarios against adversaries anywhere, and even preventively. In many ways, the National Security Strategy appeared to be precipitated by anticipation among military planners that deterrence would fail and US nuclear weapons would be used in a conflict sooner or later.[35] While the NPR laid the foundation in articulating requirements for forces and planning tools that re-emphasized operations against regional adversaries armed with WMD—and called for a "New Triad" that intertwined nuclear and conventional weapons in offensive operations,[36] the National Security Strategy of 2002 publicly articulated a preventive doctrine against WMD that required the transformation of military forces to rapidly and precisely impede rogue states before they were able to threaten or use weapons of mass destruction against the United States.

National Security Strategy of 2002

In other words, if the Nuclear Posture Review of 2002 established the nuclear framework and the supposed necessity of "flexible" requirements for forces and planning tools by the US military, it was the National Security Strategy of 2002 (the "Bush Doctrine") that placed the nuclear option back to the fore.[37] As stated by Woolf:

> The Bush Administration's Nuclear Posture Review (NPR), completed at the end of 2001, sought to adjust the US nuclear posture to reflect, on the one hand, the emergence of a more cooperative relationship between the United States and Russia, and, on the other hand, increasing threats from other states and non-state actors, particularly those armed with nuclear, chemical and biological weapons (weapons of mass destruction or WMD). The Administration has highlighted these changes in the international security environment in several documents, including the US National Security Strategy.... The Administration has also emphasized that the United States will use any means necessary to deter or defeat the use of WMD by rogue nations or terrorist groups. One of the issues highlighted in the Nuclear Posture Review is the role that nuclear weapons might play in addressing these emerging threats.[38]

Indeed, the National Security Strategy of 2002 document provided the first official public articulation of a strategy of "pre-emptive" action against hostile states and terrorist groups developing WMD. As the document stated:

> We must be prepared to stop rogue states and their terrorist clients before they are able to threaten or use weapons of mass destruction against the United States and our allies and friends.... The greater the threat, the greater the risk of inaction—and the more compelling the case for taking anticipatory action to defend ourselves, even if uncertainty remains as to the time and place of our enemy's attack. To forestall or prevent such hostile acts by our adversaries, the United States will, if necessary, act pre-emptively.... To support pre-emptive actions, we will ... continue to transform out military forces to ensure our ability to conduct rapid and precise operations to achieve decisive results.[39]

While many commentators have focused on the Administration's endorsement of pre-emptive intervention, it was the latter stages of Chapter Five, and more significantly, the concluding Chapter [Nine] that revealed the "real" doctrine and its reference to nuclear applications. As Chapter Five admonished:

> Proactive counter-proliferation efforts [will continued to be pursued]. We must deter and defend against the threat before it is unleashed. We must ensure that key capabilities—detection, active and passive defenses, and counterforce capabilities—are integrated into our defense transformation and our homeland security systems. Counter-proliferation must also be integrated into the doctrine, training, and equipping of our forces and those of our allies to ensure that we can prevail in any conflict with WMD-armed adversaries.[40]

Through the course of the National Security Strategy of 2002, Bush provided veiled nuclear option references via a broad range of symbols and often undefined rhetoric.

References pertaining to "proactive" forms of counter-proliferation were used at varying levels and no doubt provided an insight into what he would deliver on the nuclear front. As Chapter Five further argued:

> In the Cold War, weapons of mass destruction were considered weapons of last resort whose use risked the destruction of those who used them. Today, our enemies see weapons of mass destruction as weapons of choice. For rogue states these weapons are tools of intimidation and military aggression against their neighbors. These weapons may also allow these states to attempt to blackmail the United States and our allies to prevent us from deterring or repelling the aggressive behavior of rogue states. Such states also see these weapons as their best means of overcoming the conventional superiority of the United States.
>
> Traditional concepts of deterrence will not work against a terrorist enemy whose avowed tactics are wanton destruction and the targeting of innocents; whose so-called soldiers seek martyrdom in death and whose most potent protection is statelessness. The overlap between states that sponsor terror and those that pursue WMD compels us to action. For centuries, international law recognized that nations need not suffer an attack before they can lawfully take action to defend themselves against forces that present an imminent danger of attack. Legal scholars and international jurists often conditioned the legitimacy of pre-emption on the existence of an imminent threat—most often a visible mobilization of armies, navies, and air forces preparing to attack. We must adapt the concept of imminent threat to the capabilities and objectives of today's adversaries. Rogue states and terrorists do not seek to attack us using conventional means. They know such attacks would fail. Instead, they rely on acts of terror and, potentially, the use of weapons of mass destruction—weapons that can be easily concealed, delivered covertly, and used without warning. The targets of these attacks are our

> military forces and our civilian population, in direct violation of one of the principal norms of the law of warfare. As was demonstrated by the losses on September 11, 2001, mass civilian casualties is the specific objective of terrorists and these losses would be exponentially more severe if terrorists acquired and used weapons of mass destruction.[41]

By stating that "we must adapt the concept of imminent threat to the capabilities and objectives of today's adversaries" and "traditional concepts of deterrence will not work," it was apparent that Bush was alluding to the ominous shift in the US military complex as a means to counter such proliferators.

In fact, while the National Security Strategy of 2002 was rife with rhetorical ambiguity, it was clear that "proactive counter-proliferation" was to be the new course, and that such counter-proliferation would entail a reinvigorated nuclear option. Chapter Nine further illustrated this direction:

> Our military's highest priority is to defend the United States. To do so effectively, our military must: assure our allies and friends; dissuade future military competition; deter threats against US interests, allies, and friends; and decisively defeat any adversary if deterrence fails.... A military structured to deter massive Cold War-era armies must be transformed to focus more on how an adversary might fight rather than where and when a war might occur.... Innovation within the armed forces will rest on experimentation with new approaches to warfare, strengthening joint operations, exploiting US intelligence advantages, and taking full advantage of science and technology.[42]

While the above two passages broadly conveyed Bush's nuclear weapon intentions, it was the NPR and the subsequent National Strategy to Combat Weapons of Mass Destruction (NSCWMD) that, in essence, provided the NSS's detailed nuclear expository. Indeed, as indicated above and through the course of this chapter, the Bush Administration consistently released updates of this nuclear strategy, suggesting that while the National Security Strategy of 2002 may appear to lack specific nuclear "detail," it can be perceived as the guiding force that must be viewed as a dangerous and living catalyst—a document that punctuated, updated, refined and reaffirmed its core sentiments through the unclassified and classified documents it sponsored.

National Strategy to Combat Weapons of Mass Destruction 2002

It was only six weeks later on 10 December 2002 that the Bush Administration released the emphatically titled "National Strategy to Combat Weapons of Mass Destruction," which specifically advocated the use of nuclear weapons on states it deemed to be developing WMD. However, what made this expansion of the Bush Doctrine controversial was the classified version of the "National Strategy to Combat Weapons of Mass Destruction"—National Security Presidential Directive (NSPD) 17—which stated that "the United States will make clear that it reserves the right to respond with overwhelming force—including potentially nuclear weapons—to the use of [weapons of mass destruction] against the United States, our forces abroad, and friends and allies." The wording in NSPD 17 used the rhetoric of "potentially nuclear weapons," whereas the declassified version replaced this with the very ambiguous "all of our options;"[43] no doubt an attempt by the Administration to soften and dilute potential international criticism.

The specific detail pertaining to nuclear weapons reassertion that the NSS perhaps lacked was clearly supplemented in the concise NSCWMD, and in particular, the classified NSPD 17. The fact that the NSCWMD was introduced with a direct quote from the NSS illustrated the linkage, continuum and more importantly, guiding pillar that the NSS provided from here on in nuclear instrument formation. As the NSCWMD quoted from the NSS:

> The gravest danger our Nation faces lies at the crossroads of radicalism and technology. Our enemies have openly declared that they are seeking weapons of mass destruction, and evidence indicates that they are doing so with determination. The United States will not allow these efforts to succeed.... History will judge harshly those who saw this coming danger but failed to act. In the new world we have entered, the only path to peace and security is the path of action.[44]

The NSCWMD even specified this link further in its earlier stages by emphasizing how the countering of WMD, including the use and further proliferation, was "an integral component of the National Security Strategy of the United States of America."[45] It then argued that the United States' strategy for homeland security, and its new concept of deterrence, including the ability to combat WMD, represented a fundamental change from the past and that the United States must take advantage of "today's opportunities"—including the utilization and application of new technologies, the increased focus on intelligence collection and analysis, the strengthening of alliance relationships, and the establishment of "new partnerships with former adversaries."[46]

The focus on Weapons of Mass Destruction was further expanded on in the NSCWMD by highlighting how such weapons could enable adversaries to inflict massive harm on the United States, its military forces at home and abroad, and "our friends and allies." That is, some states, including several that have supported and have continued to endorse terrorism, already possessed WMD and were pursuing even greater capabilities, as vehicles of coercion and intimidation. For "them," the NSCWMD emphasized, such weapons were not of the last resort but a militarily useful weapon of choice with the intention of undermining the United States' "advantages in conventional forces," and impeded it from "responding to aggression against our friends and allies in regions of vital interest." In addition, it argued, terrorist groups have sought and are seeking to attain WMDs with the stated goal of killing large numbers of US people and those of friends and allies—"without compunction and without warning."[47]

Notions of counter-proliferation, including the capability and willingness to utilize nuclear weapons, began to emerge as the NSCWMD shifted into its second stage. It was here that the possession and increased likelihood of WMDs being used by hostile states and terrorists was presented as stark "realities of the contemporary security environment."[48] In response to this, the document argued that it was imperative that the US military and applicable civilian agencies be prepared to deter and defend against the full range of possible WMD employment situations. As a result, all capabilities to combat WMD needed to be fully assimilated into the emerging defense transitional plan and into the homeland security structure.[49] Counter-proliferation, it continued, would also be fully integrated into the "basic doctrine, training, and equipping of all forces" as a means to "sustain operations to decisively defeat WMD-armed adversaries."[50] While the NSCWMD advocated a "Strengthened Non-proliferation [effort] to Combat WMD Proliferation," as well as "Consequence Management to Respond to WMD Use," its main focus and further articulation of the National Security Strategy was evident in its rhetoric pertaining to an assertive counter-proliferation with a nuclear dimension. That is, in the section entitled "Interdiction," the NSCWMD argued that the US must enhance the capabilities of the military, intelligence, technical, and law enforcement communities as a means to prevent the movement of WMD materials, technology, and expertise to hostile states and terrorist organizations.

Endorsement of nuclear considerations was made clear in the "Deterrence" section. It stipulated that as a consequence of state and non-state actors' willingness to take high risks to achieve their goals—including the aggressive pursuit of WMD and their means of delivery as critical tools in this effort—new methods of deterrence were imperative. This would entail, it argued, a strong declaratory policy and effective military force as core elements for the United States' contemporary deterrent posture from here on in. While the US would utilize a wide range of political tools to deter potential adversaries from seeking WMDs and the use of WMDs, it unequivocally reserved the "right to respond with overwhelming force—including all of our options [including potentially nuclear weapons][51]—to the use of WMDs against the United States, its forces abroad, and friends and allies."[52] It was here that the willingness to consider or utilize the nuclear option was emphasized in a clear and concise fashion—albeit interchanged in the classified and declassified versions—and can be deemed as a critical juncture in the guidance process that began with the NPR and National Security Strategy.

In addition to the specter of nuclear response and defense capabilities, the NSCWMD signified that the US deterrent platform against WMD threats would be reaffirmed by effective intelligence, surveillance, interdiction, and domestic law enforcement capabilities. Such assimilation in combined capabilities, it emphasized, would improve deterrence by "devaluing an adversary's WMD and missiles," and by positing the notion of an extreme response to any use of such weapons.[53] In the case that deterrence was not successful, the NSCWMD argued, US military forces and applicable civilian agencies must have the capacity to defend against WMD-armed adversaries, including in some instances, the capability to undertake "pre-emptive measures."[54] This would require capabilities as a means to detect and destroy an adversary's WMD structures before such weapons were used.

Furthermore, active defenses that impeded, undermined, or destroyed WMD en route to their targets as well as vigorous air defense and effective missile defenses against threats were required. Conversely, passive defenses needed be shaped to the individual and varying forms of WMD, as well as the means to enable the mitigation of the effects of a WMD attack against deployed forces. The NSCWMD again alluded to the potential development of nuclear weapons or strike force without being overly specific. As with deterrence and prevention, it argued, an effective response needed rapid attribution and a robust strike capability—and thereby, required the acceleration of efforts to create and field new capabilities as a means to defeat WMD-related assets.[55] Further nuclear and preventive emphasis was made when the document stipulated the United States' need to undertake post-conflict operations as a means to destroy or dismantle any residual WMD capabilities of the rogue state or terrorist network. Such a response would not only eliminate the source of a WMD attack but could potentially work as a deterrent to other adversaries that possess or seek WMD or missiles.[56]

While the National Security Strategy of 2002 provided the platform for nuclear option aspirations, the NSCWMD—as an artery of the NSS—began the refining process. This was evident when it was revealed in a top secret appendix to NSPD 17, that Iran, Syria, North Korea, and Libya were specifically named among the states that were deemed to be the central focus of the new US strategy. A senior Administration official briefing reporters on the new strategy stated at the time that the options included nuclear weapons. The motivation, according to one participant in the interagency process that drafted the new strategy, was the conclusion that "traditional non-proliferation has failed, and now we're going into active interdiction."[57] The Joint Chiefs of Staff further explained that the NSPD 17:

> outlines a comprehensive approach to counter nuclear and other WMD. The strategy has three principal pillars: Counter-proliferation to Combat WMD Use—recognising that the possession and increased likelihood of WMD use by hostile states and terrorists are realities of the contemporary security environment; strengthened Non-proliferation to Combat WMD Proliferation—determined to undertake every effort to prevent states and terrorists from acquiring WMD and missiles; and Consequence Management to Respond to WMD Use—to reduce to the extent possible the potentially horrific consequences of WMD use at home and abroad.[58]

It was clear that the National Security Strategy of 2002 was not limited to notions of prevention alone, but would be further articulated and kept "alive" via the nuclear classified and unclassified documents it would engender—the core catalyst in advocating the United States' willingness to use nuclear weapons on states or non-state actors that it deemed to be adversarial.

This is no clearer than the US nuclear war plan that entered into effect in March 2003—including new executable nuclear strike options against regional states seeking or holding weapons of mass destruction. Indeed, the declassified US Strategic Command (STRATCOM) document was a further crystallization of the nuclear option initiated in the NSS and NPR guidance platforms. When sections of the Nuclear Posture Review were leaked in the *Los Angeles Times* in March 2002, Bush Administration officials responded by attempting to devalue the significance of the document and its impact on nuclear option planning. The Chairman of the Joint Chiefs of Staff, General Richard B. Myers, stated that [the NPR]:

> is not a plan, it's not an operational plan.... It's a policy document. And it simply states our deterrence posture, of which nuclear weapons are a part.... And it's been the policy of this country for a long time, as long as I've been a senior officer, that the President would always reserve the right up to and including the use of nuclear weapons if that was appropriate. So that continues to be the policy.[59]

A formal comment articulated by the Department of Defense further highlighted that the NPR "does not provide operational guidance on nuclear targeting or planning," but that the military merely "continues to plan for a broad range of contingencies and unforeseen threats to the United States and its allies."[60] However, such rhetoric was proven folly with the release of the US Strategic Command's (STRATCOM) plan to expand and transform the NSS, NPR and NSCWMD into reality in which a series of new nuclear strikes against regional states would become a physical and viable option.

CONPLAN (Concept Plan) 8022 (Global Strike)

In November 2003, the first CONPLAN (Concept Plan) 8022 (Global Strike) was completed by STRATCOM. When Bush signed the National Security Presidential Directive (NSPD) 17 he enacted the National Strategy to Combat Weapons of Mass Destruction (NSCWMD) as an approach to thwart not just nuclear but also other weapons of mass destruction, including the willingness to use nuclear weapons—even preventively—against any state or non-state actor using weapons of mass destruction against the United States, its forces abroad, and friends and allies. The initial STRATCOM CONPLAN 8022, entitled "Global Strike" was further articulation of this putting in place for the first time a pre-emptive and offensive strike capability. The Concept Plan included processes for designing courses of action and decision-making, target selection, and the forces available.[61] The origins of the STRATCOM CONPLAN 8022–02 were evident when President Bush approved Change 2 to the Unified Command Plan in January 2003, stipulating four missions: Global Strike; missile defense; information operations; and global C4ISR (Command, Control, Communications, Computers, Intelligence, Surveillance, and Reconnaissance).

This was followed in March 2003 by the Nuclear Posture Review Implementation Plan, a 26-page list of specific items from the 2002 Nuclear Posture Review that the armed forces were ordered to implement in creating the force structure that would make up the New Triad.[62] To orchestrate the new guidance, STRATCOM devised a major reconstruction of the strategic war plan, previously known as the SIOP.[63] The new plan, entitled OPLAN 8044 Revision 05, became effective on October 1, 2004, providing "more flexible options to assure allies, and dissuade, deter, and if necessary, defeat adversaries in a wider range of contingencies."[64] As a means to create the New Triad, the new plan encompassed the "integration of conventional strike options" for the first time. As an artery of the New Triad, Global Strike was added to STRATCOM's portfolio by the Unified Command Plan in January 2003, and was deemed to be one of the most significant components of the implementation of the "pre-emption" doctrine.[65] The Unified Command Plan defined Global Strike as "a capability to deliver rapid, extended range, precision kinetic (nuclear and conventional) and non-kinetic (elements of space and information operations) effects in support of theatre and national objectives."[66]

CONPLAN 8022 was not operational at the time in November 2003, but was nonetheless available for activation if instructed by the Secretary of Defense. This occurred in June 2004, when shortly after the NUWEP was issued, Defense Secretary Donald Rumsfeld ordered the military to implement CONPLAN 8022 as a means to provide the President with a prompt, global strike capability. As he stated in the document:

> US nuclear forces must be capable of, and be seen to be capable of, destroying those critical war-making and war-supporting assets and capabilities that a potential enemy leadership values most and that it would rely on to achieve its own objectives in a post-war world.[67]

In response to this, Joint Chiefs of Staff Chairman General Richard Myers signed the Global Strike Alert Order (ALERTORD) on June 30, 2004 which ordered STRATCOM to set CONPLAN 8022 into action in conjunction with the Air Force and Navy. The nuclear option specter came closer to being a reality when on August 17, STRATCOM published Global Strike Interim Capability Operations Order (OPORD) which changed CONPLAN 8022 from a concept plan to an operational contingency plan. This development was further expanded on when on November 18, 2005, the Joint Functional Component Command Space and Global Strike achieved Initial Operational capability after "being thoroughly tested in the nuclear strike exercise Global Lightning 06."[68]

The National Security Strategy of 2002 and subsequent documents and policy instruments pertaining to the reinvigorated nuclear option it engendered (including the Global Strike mission) signified much more than a hypothetical "what if." They illustrated real change in US planning and assumptions about the use of nuclear weapons. CONPLAN 8022 was a new offensive war plan created specifically to support and substantiate the Administration's willingness to strike first.[69] Indeed, it is evident that the nuclear option in CONPLAN 8022 was not about influencing adversaries but about destroying targets that, according to the Administration, could not be destroyed by other means. The underlying premise was that deterrence was ultimately flawed and limited, and as such, when it did fail, nuclear weapons would be available and used accordingly. As again stated by Chairman General Richard Myers at the July 2004 retirement ceremony of Admiral James Ellis as STRATCOM commander in Omaha:

> [You reshaped] the roles and missions of that old command to better posture our military forces to defeat existing and future threats against our nation [after 9/11] .... You did this by expanding the options available to the President, both from a strong nuclear deterrence standpoint and conventional and non-kinetic response options.[70]

The following year, General Myers repeated his description of the expansion of the nuclear option in a statement before Congress:

> Within DOD, the Secretary of Defense has tasked the US Strategic Command to synchronize our efforts to counter WMD and ensure the force structure and the resources are in place to help all combatant commands defeat WMD. STRATCOM has revised our strategic deterrence and response plan that became effective in the fall of 2004. This revised, detailed plan provides more flexible options to assure allies, and dissuade, deter, and if necessary, defeat adversaries in a wider range of contingencies.[71]

A year after the attacks on the World Trade Center and the Pentagon on September 11, 2001, the Bush Administration released the National Security Strategy of the United States of America.

Expanding on the events of 9/11—and a decade or so of gradual development of nuclear doctrine gauged towards Russia and China to one focused increasingly on regional actors armed with weapons of mass destruction—the new strategy defined the combination of terrorism and WMD proliferation as requiring a more assertive US military and nuclear posture. The Administration argued that they must be prepared to stop rogue actors and their terrorist clients before they were able to threaten or use weapons of mass destruction against the United States. As means to impede or "forestall" such hostile acts the United States would need to "transform" its "military forces" as a means to ensure its "ability to conduct rapid and precise operations to achieve decisive results."[72] In 2005, the military and nuclear product of this strategy became operational under the banner of Global Strike; a strike plan created by STRATCOM in conjunction with the Air Force and Navy that would provide global strike options to the President with nuclear, conventional, space, and information warfare capabilities.[73] It is important to understand that the Global Strike mission and CONPLAN 8022 were different from previous missions and plans both in their aims and capabilities. While often defined and portrayed by its advocates at the time as a way of increasing the President's options for deterring adversaries, in reality Global Strike was an offensive and pre-emptive instrument firmly based on the notion that deterrence would fail sooner or later.[74] "Rather than waiting for the mushroom cloud to appear,"[75] a phrase used at various intervals by the Bush Administration, the Global Strike mission was gauged towards defeating a threat before it came to the fore.

At the most extreme end of the spectrum, Global Strike's main premise was to attain "near-invulnerability" for the United States by forcing "vulnerability upon any potential adversary."[76] It is with this in mind that CONPLAN (Concept Plan) 8022 (Global Strike), as a continuum of the National Security Strategy's endorsement of the nuclear option, can be deemed as an instrument focused principally on war fighting rather than deterrence. As stated by William M. Arkin:

> CONPLAN 8022 anticipates two different scenarios. The first is a response to a specific and imminent nuclear threat, say in North Korea. A quick-reaction, highly choreographed strike would combine pinpoint bombing with electronic warfare and cyber-attacks to disable a North Korean response, with commandos operating deep in enemy territory, perhaps even to take possession of the nuclear device. The second scenario involves a more generic attack on an adversary's WMD infrastructure. Assume, for argument's sake, that Iran announces it is mounting a crash program to build a nuclear weapon. A multidimensional bombing (kinetic) and cyber-warfare (non-kinetic) attack might seek to destroy Iran's program, and special forces would be deployed to disable or isolate underground facilities. By employing all of the tricks in the US arsenal to immobilize an enemy country—turning off the electricity, jamming and spoofing radars and communications, penetrating computer networks and garbling electronic commands—global strike magnifies the impact of bombing by eliminating the need to physically destroy targets that have been disabled by other means.[77]

The inclusion, therefore, of a nuclear weapons option in CONPLAN 8022—a specially configured earth-penetrating bomb to destroy deeply buried facilities, if any exist—was particularly disconcerting. The global strike plan held the nuclear option in reserve if intelligence suggested an "imminent" launch of an enemy nuclear strike on the United States or if there was a need to destroy hard-to-reach targets.[78]

Doctrine for Joint Nuclear Operations (Joint Publication 3-12) 2005

The regional strike plans posited and envisaged in STRATCOM's CONPLAN (Concept Plan) 8022 (Global Strike) also found their way into the draft Doctrine for Joint Nuclear Operations (Joint Publication 3-12); further illustrating that the Bush Administration's nuclear option extended outside notions of retaliation, including "pre-emptive" strikes. The second draft from March 2005 listed five scenarios where the use of nuclear weapons might be requested. First, to counter an adversary *intending to use* weapons of mass destruction against US, multinational, allied forces, or civilian populations; second, to counter *an imminent attack* from an adversary's biological weapons that only effects from nuclear weapons can safely destroy; third, to attack adversary installations including weapons of mass destruction, deep, hardened bunkers containing chemical or biological weapons, or the command and control infrastructure required for the adversary to execute a WMD attack against the United States or its friends and allies [this was probably the "target base" in OPLAN 8044 Revision 03]; fourth, to counter potentially overwhelming adversary conventional forces; finally, to demonstrate US intent and capability to use nuclear weapons to deter adversary WMD use.[79]

It is evident with the 2005 Doctrine for Joint Nuclear Operations that the continuum of the Bush Doctrine's nuclear aspirations were further accentuated, reaffirming the strategic planning concept of assimilating "pre-emption" into a US nuclear doctrine with conventional weapons and missile defenses. The document signified how combatant commanders attempted to articulate the Administration's quest to redefine US nuclear policy into operational guidance for military forces. It came nearly five years after the completion of the Bush Administration's Nuclear Posture Review (NPR) in December 2001 and National Security Strategy of 2002, and represented the first revision of basic nuclear doctrine in a decade. In simple terms, the Doctrine for Joint Nuclear Operations formally reaffirmed pre-emption into a joint nuclear doctrine in which the threshold for nuclear use was lowered, endorsed a role for nuclear weapons against all forms of weapons of mass destruction, a role for nuclear weapons against terrorists, and described missile defenses as a means of defending nuclear forces rather than people against attack. Encompassing the findings of the 2001 Nuclear Posture Review, the core sentiments of the National Security Strategy of 2002, and the National Strategy to Combat Weapons of Mass Destruction, it reflected the impact of 9/11 on US strategic thinking in which a focus on all WMD threats—whether from state or non-state actors—would be pursued. As a result of these developments, the updated Joint Pub 3-12 changed significantly in comparison to the previous versions of the document (as discussed in the previous chapter).

Indeed, the decision to update the doctrine dated back to March 2001, when the Joint Chiefs of Staff issued a program directive in which the consolidation of Joint Pub 3-12 and Joint Pub 3-12.1 (theater) was to be undertaken in which a single Doctrine for Joint Nuclear Operations would be established as a means to guide the employment of both strategic and non-strategic (theater) nuclear forces. The format of the new nuclear doctrine changed considerably from the 1995 version. It was 22 pages longer because of a new chapter on theater nuclear operations, a discussion of the role of conventional and defensive forces, and an expanded discussion on nuclear operations. The insertion of a chapter on theater nuclear operations illustrated the post-Cold War focus of US nuclear planners in their quest to dissuade and deter regional aggressors (i.e. rogue states) holding nuclear, chemical, and biological weapons.[80] Importantly, the document also reflected a decade-old rivalry between the regional combatant commanders and US Strategic Command (STRATCOM) over who "owned" regional nuclear strike planning. The document showed that STRATCOM "today" has responsibility for more than "half of the phases in the theater planning support process."[81]

The Doctrine for Joint Nuclear Operations further illustrated the Bush Administration's willingness to utilize the nuclear option, as it gave pre-emption an increasingly flexible component that made nuclear weapons an easy to draw on device. The revised doctrine enshrined notions of nuclear pre-emption into official US joint nuclear doctrine for the first time, defining four key goals that would guide the development of US force capabilities, their development and use:

> assuring allies and friends of the US steadfastness of purpose and its capability to fulfil its security commitment; dissuading adversaries from undertaking programs or operations that could threaten US interests or those of our allies and friends; deterring aggression and coercion by deploying forward the capacity to swiftly defeat attacks and imposing severe penalties for aggression on an adversary's military capability and supporting infrastructure; and, decisively defeating an adversary if deterrence fails.[82]
>
> Developing and sustaining a modern and diverse portfolio of military capabilities serves the four key defense policy goals, identified earlier, that guide the development, deployment, and use of military forces and capabilities, including nuclear forces.[83]

The second final coordination draft of the Doctrine for Joint Nuclear Operations (Joint Pub 3-12) was published by the Joint Chiefs of Staff and reaffirmed a prominent role for nuclear weapons against regional adversaries armed with weapons of mass destruction. As articulated by Kristensen:

> For the first time, JP 3-12 includes descriptions of pre-emptive use of nuclear weapons: an adversary intending to use WMD against US, multinational, or allies forces or civilian populations; imminent attack from adversary biological weapons that only effects from nuclear weapons can safely destroy; attacks on adversary installations including WMD, deep, hardened bunkers containing chemical or biological weapons or the command and control infrastructure required for the adversary to execute a

> WMD attack against United States or its friends and allies; to demonstrate US intent and capability to use nuclear weapons to deter adversary use of WMD.[84]

In nuclear "pre-emption," the goal would no longer be deterrence through threatened retaliation, but the destruction of targets with nuclear weapons in anticipation that deterrence would fail.

As the Doctrine for Joint Nuclear Operations argued, to deter a potential adversary from utilizing WMDs, that adversary's leadership must "believe the United States has both the ability and will to pre-empt or retaliate promptly with responses that are credible and effective."[85] The document also noted that US policy in the past had "repeatedly rejected calls for the adoption of a 'no first use' policy of nuclear weapons since this policy could undermine deterrence."[86] In other words, to deter the use of WMD against the United States, the Pentagon paper endorsed preparations in which the use of nuclear weapons and determination to use them was "necessary to prevent or retaliate against WMD use."[87] Indeed, the use of the nuclear option espoused in the Doctrine for Joint Nuclear Operations depicted a post-Cold War scenario in which the use of nuclear weapons may take place at a much lower intensity level than envisioned during the Cold War. This was evident as the document regularly replaced "war" with "conflict" as a means to convey the lower intensity of hostilities that could involve the use of US nuclear weapons in post-Cold War nuclear battle zones. As further explained by Kristensen:

> the pre-emption language in the draft is accompanied by replacing the word "war" with "conflict" in the war determination section. In proposing this change, STRATCOM argues that it better "emphasizes the nature of most conflicts resulting in use of a nuclear weapon. Nuclear war implies the mutual exchange of nuclear weapons between warring parties—not fully representative of the facts." Echoing STRATCOM's assessment, European Command (EUCOM) further explains that "the use of a bunker-buster 'mini-nuke' might not, in fact, be 'provoked by some action, event, or perceived threat' per se; rather, it may be used simply because it is the only weapon that will destroy the target!"[88]

Unlike the two previous versions of the Doctrine for Joint Nuclear Operations from 1993 and 1995,[89] however, the new doctrine did not mention a need for weapons with lower yields. The paragraph included in the previous version was deleted. Instead, lower yields were mentioned in the section that discussed reducing nuclear collateral damage as a matter-of-fact potential capability. As stated, "specific techniques for reducing nuclear collateral damage may include lower yield weapons, improving accuracy, employing multiple smaller weapons, adjusting the height of burst, and offsetting the desired ground zero."[90]

Another distinct change was the insertion of discussion pertaining to the use of conventional weapons and defensive forces into the sections describing the purpose, planning, and employment of nuclear forces. As the document states, "as non-nuclear strike capabilities and nuclear strike are integrated, targets that may have required a nuclear weapon to achieve the needed effects in previous planning may be targeted with conventional weapons, provided the required effects can be achieved."[91] This no doubt echoed the 2002 Nuclear Posture Review in which the creation of a "new triad" with nuclear weapons was depicted as constituting only part (together with advanced conventional weapons) of one of the pillars in the triad. A second pillar, the NPR stated, would be missile defense, and together the two (conventional weapons and missile defenses) would reduce the role of nuclear weapons by providing the President with other response options than nuclear retaliation.[92] Regardless of this, however, the Doctrine for Joint Nuclear Operations admonished that while "some contingencies will remain, the most appropriate response may include the use of US nuclear weapons."[93] Further, the document appeared to posit another objective, that being, how advanced conventional weapons and missile defenses could be used to increase the survivability and effectiveness of US offensive nuclear forces.

Aside from the specific new components inserted into the Doctrine for Joint Nuclear Operations, the core nuclear mission remained surprisingly similar to that described in previous versions of the document. As such, the major reduction in the role of nuclear weapons promised by the Bush Administration in 2001–2002 was not evident. Instead, the "new" Doctrine for Joint Nuclear Operations can be viewed as opportunistic in both deepening existing missions and defining new roles for nuclear weapons. Despite the continued White House rhetoric about reducing the role of nuclear weapons, the document reaffirmed the significance of maintaining an aggressive nuclear option in which "modernized forces would be on a high readiness level, capable of destroying—even pre-emptively—targets anywhere on the globe."[94] As argued in the above, aside from immersing pre-emption into a nuclear doctrine, the Joint Nuclear Operations doctrine of 2005 lowered the threshold for nuclear use by further reducing the level of hostilities where US nuclear weapons might be used; endorsed a role of nuclear weapons against all forms of weapons of mass destruction; advocated a role of nuclear weapons against terrorists, and described missile defenses as a means of defending nuclear forces rather than people against attack.[95] The doctrine expanded on the arguments and "findings" of the 2002 Nuclear Posture Review, the 2002 National Security Strategy and the 2002 National Strategy to Combat Weapons of Mass Destruction in which a flexible and nuclear option was no longer a last resort, but a defining and strategic device.

As a marked expansion on the Bush Doctrine, the 2005 Doctrine for Joint Nuclear Operations and its intricate definitions of the "pre-emptive" use of US nuclear weapons was so controversial, it provoked the Senate Armed Services Committee to ask for a briefing and 16 lawmakers to protest in writing to President Bush about what they considered to be a "drastic shift in US nuclear policy." The detail of the controversial doctrine was leaked to *Arms Control Today* and in September 2005, the *Washington Post* followed up with a front-page story. Embarrassed by the exposure, the Pentagon cancelled not only the draft doctrine (and four other related doctrine documents) but also the existing Doctrine for Joint Nuclear Operations document that had been publicly available on the Joint Chiefs of Staff website for a decade. A Joint Staff official explained that the documents would not be published, revised, or classified, explaining that they had been found not to be real doctrine documents but "pseudo doctrine" documents discussing nuclear policy issues. The public "visibility led a lot of people to question why we have them," he said.[96]

Quadrennial Defense Review (QDR) 2006

Nonetheless, this was only a minor derailment to the Bush Doctrine's nuclear reactivation process. The apparent relentlessness of the Administration was again evident with the February 6, 2006 release of the Quadrennial Defense Review (QDR). Formally created by the Department of Defense and Donald Rumsfeld, the review articulated the need for "prompt global strike capabilities (that) would be available to attack fixed, hard and deeply buried, mobile and relocatable targets with improved accuracy anywhere in the world promptly upon the President's order. Nuclear weapons will be accurate, safe and reliable, and tailored to meet modern deterrence requirements."[97] The QDR also gave the People's Republic of China more emphasis and reaffirmed its standing as an ongoing strategic competitor. As the review stated, "of the major and emerging powers, China has the greatest potential to compete militarily with the United States and field disruptive military technologies that could over time offset traditional US military advantages absent in US counter strategies."[98] Aside from the China connection, the 2006 QDR furthered continued the refinement of the nuclear option—in which a shift from a "one size fits all" approach to deterrence would be tailored towards an approach it deemed appropriate for advanced military competitors, regional WMD states, as well as non-state terrorist networks.[99]

Indeed, the QDR clearly advocated "full balanced, tailored capability" as means to deter both state and non-state threats—including the utilization of WMD, terrorist attacks in the tangible and information categories, and opportunistic aggression—while at the same time, assuring allies and "dissuading potential competitors."[100] The QDR remained very consistent with the New Triad priorities developed during the 2002 Nuclear Posture Review and consolidated with the National Security Strategy of 2002. That being, the assertion of force and how it would now encompass a wider range of non-kinetic and conventional strike capabilities, while also maintaining a stern and bold nuclear deterrent—the cornerstone of US national power.[101] This included integrated ballistic and cruise missile defenses and a responsive infrastructure that would be supported by an agile and diligent National Command and Control System, superior intelligence, flexible planning systems, and the capacity to maintain access to legitimate, high-quality information for "timely situational awareness."[102]

Of course, the most startling aspect of the document pertained to the notion that the Bush Administration was considering the development of a new nuclear weapon. The document articulated how the Department of Defense was working with the Department of Energy as a means to assess the viability and cost of a Reliable Replacement Warhead and, if required, would begin the development of that system. This "system," it argued, would enable reductions in the number of older, non-deployed warheads maintained as "a hedge against reliability problems in deployed systems," while assisting in the evolution and creation of a smaller, boutique and more responsive nuclear weapon infrastructure. Overall, it was evident that the Quadrennial Defense Review of March 2006 revalidated the 2002 NPR planning assumptions that required defined yet flexible deterrence for rogue powers, terrorist networks, and near-peer competitors. It restated that international conditions "are trending toward—if anything—a more stressing strategic landscape, for example, with respect to North Korea, Iran, and nuclear proliferation."[103] But even more than this, the QDR again reinforced the Bush Doctrine's planning assumptions and the "continuum of transformation in the Department … with strong, sound and effective war fighting capabilities in the decades ahead."[104] Indeed, as stated by Josh White and Ann Scott Tyson in *The Washington Post*:

> The United States is engaged in what could be a generational conflict akin to the Cold War, the kind of struggle that might last decades as allies work to root out terrorists across the globe and battle extremists who want to rule the world, Defense Secretary Donald H. Rumsfeld said yesterday. Rumsfeld, who laid out broad strategies for what the military and the Bush Administration are now calling the "long war," likened al Qaeda leader Osama bin Laden to Adolf Hitler and Vladimir Lenin while urging Americans not to give in on the battle of wills that could stretch for years. He said there is a tendency to underestimate the threats that terrorists pose to global security, and said liberty is at stake. The speech, which aides said was titled "The Long War," came on the eve of the Pentagon's release of its Quadrennial Defense Review (QDR), which sets out plans for how the US military will address major security challenges 20 years into the future. The plans to be released today include shifts to make the military more agile and capable of dealing with unconventional threats, something Rumsfeld has said is necessary to move from a military designed for the Cold War into one that is more flexible.[105]

While the "long war" was an ambiguous title it did nonetheless reflect the Bush Administration's transformative quest and desire for an "agile" nuclear option—a process that began in 2002.

National Security Strategy of 2006

Of course, such nuclear aspirations and force agility was to be further articulated in the National Security Strategy of 2006. Published by the White House in March 2006 as a means to guide military and other areas of strategic planning in the future, the National Security Strategy of 2006 began with four words:

"America is at war." The morbid but perhaps realistic first sentence was distinct to the introductory words stated in the previous National Security Strategy from 2002, in which the "war on terror" focus remained (perhaps strategically) in the background to notions of social struggle between democratic and oppressive societies. Nonetheless, both documents were creations of the post-9/11 attacks which engendered the so-called "pre-emption" doctrine in which the United States would "no longer solely rely on a reactive posture as we have in the past"[106] but strike first if necessary. The NSS2006 document reiterated this bold proclamation when it stated that the United States would "act pre-emptively in exercising our inherent right of self-defence."[107] Since it was first published in September 2002, the Bush Administration's "pre-emption" doctrine has been widely lambasted for conveying an overly aggressive security strategy. While the NSS of 2006 did acknowledge this ("The United States will not resort to force in all cases to pre-empt emerging threats. Our preference is that non-military actions succeed. And no country should ever use pre-emption as pretext for aggression"[108]), it signified that regardless of the fact that US military forces were tied down in Iraq following the preventive invasion in 2003, very little had changed in terms of US security strategy. As the document stated:

> If necessary, however, under long-standing principles of self defense, we do not rule out the use of force before attacks occur, even if uncertainty remains as to the time and place of the enemy's attack. When the consequences of an attack with WMD are potentially so devastating, we cannot afford to stand idly by as grave dangers materialize. This is the principle and logic of pre-emption. The place of pre-emption in our national security strategy remains the same. We will always proceed deliberately, weighing the consequences of our actions. The reasons for our actions will be clear, the force measured, and the cause just.[109]

The 2002 and 2006 National Security Strategy documents, as well as the guidance instruments that have punctuated them since, clearly shifted the emphasis more decisively toward prevention with nuclear aspirations.

Of course, what did change was the geographic positioning and depth of the preventive scenarios, the methods to execute them, and the type of conflict that could necessitate them. While preventive strike options were no doubt still being refined against Russian and Chinese nuclear forces, the NSS2006 pre-emptive planning was focused on developing strike options against regional proliferators armed with weapons of mass destruction, in low-intensity conflicts, even before armed hostilities had broken out—and in doing so, echoed the sentiments expressed in the defunct Doctrine for Joint Nuclear Operations of 2005. As has been emphasized above, the 2002 and 2006 National Security Strategy documents were only a small public insight into the evolution of the Bush Administration's reassertion of the nuclear option. While significant, they form part of a consortium of documents (most of which remain classified) that have been issued since 2001 as a means to guide, refine, and direct the military on how to implement the preventive doctrine. This included over a dozen major new guidance documents issued by the White House and the Office of Secretary of Defense, as well as an entirely new strike plan designed by US Strategic Command (STRATCOM) to provide the President with new nuclear and conventional strike options against regional states and non-state actors. The NSS of 2006 merely reaffirmed this shift and how the nuclear option would continue to play "a critical role" in US national security strategy:

> safe, credible, reliable [nuclear weapons] … will continue to play a critical role. We are strengthening deterrence by developing a New Triad composed of offensive strike systems (both nuclear and improved conventional capabilities) …. These capabilities will better deter some of the new threats we face, while also bolstering our security commitments to allies.… If necessary, however, under long-standing principles of self-defense, we do not rule out the use of force before attacks occur, even if uncertainty remains as to the time and place of the enemy's attack. When the consequences of an attack with WMD are potentially so devastating, we cannot afford to stand idle while grave dangers materialize. This is the principle and logic of pre-emption.[110]

In essence, the National Security Strategy of 2006 further re-emphasized the function of nuclear weapons in pre-emptive military strikes against terrorists and "aggressive" states armed with chemical, biological, or nuclear weapons. As Hans Kristensen stated, the document "was the Bush Administration's last opportunity to demonstrate that it has reduced the role of nuclear weapons after the Cold War.… Instead it has chosen to reaffirm their importance and in the most troubling way possible: prevention and the nuclear option."[111]

Strategic Operations Joint Operating Concept Version 2.0 2006

The extent to which the Bush Doctrine's nuclear option becomes a "Bush only" legacy remains to be seen. But as the 2006 Strategic Operations Joint Operating Concept Version 2.0 indicates, long-term plans were clearly on the Department of Defense's agenda. As stated:

> The challenges identified in the National Security Strategy require a new concept for 'waging' deterrence paired with revised joint force capabilities that provide a wider range of military deterrent options. Deterrence requires a national strategy that integrates diplomatic, informational, military, and economic powers.[112]

The core platform of the document was to stipulate ways to coerce decisively an adversary's decision-making process, and thereby, thwart hostile actions against US key interests. The document's timeframe extended to 2025 and provided what it deemed to be:

> a set of steps necessary to operationalize deterrence planning that supports the National Military Strategy (NMS) objective of 'Prevent Conflict and Surprise Attacks' and the NMS requirement to develop a wider range of options that discourage aggression and coercion. It provided the operational context and conceptual basis for further concept development, capability based assessments (CBA), integrated architectures and experimentation.[113]

The document did not distinguish between nuclear and non-nuclear missions, but combined nuclear, conventional, and non-kinetic capabilities under "Global Strike" means as a way of directly influencing an adversary's decision process by creating deterrence operations to specific adversaries and contexts. As such, the document focused more than its predecessor on how to influence different kinds of adversaries. In simple terms, it provided the "conceptual framework needed to meet the 2006 Quadrennial Defense Review requirements for deterrence activities tailored for rogue powers, terrorist networks and near-peer competitors."[114] While it is often believed to be static and slow to change, US nuclear weapons policy since 2002 was continually punctuated with the above reaffirmative documents as a means to steer and refine the broader nuclear sentiments and ideology posited in the Bush Doctrine. Indeed, the Strategic Operations Joint Operating Concept Version 2.0 merely continued this process.

Reliable Replacement Warhead (RRW)

The deeper policy within the Bush Doctrine and its accompanying documents foreshadowed a new nuclear era in which the once-termed "weapon of last resort" became a usable and "necessary" option. The "quiet revolution" was further accentuated with "Complex 2030" and the encompassing Reliable Replacement Warhead (RRW) program, perceived by many as potentially being the United States' first development of a new nuclear weapon since 1992. Under the US Department of Energy's Complex 2030, it was envisaged that the entire US nuclear weapons complex would be upgraded whilst also designing and producing a series of new nuclear warheads.[115] Such new weapons produced via the Reliable Replacement Warhead program would ultimately replace the entire US nuclear arsenal.[116] The main argument of Complex 2030 was that for the US to maintain warheads that were reliable and safe in the future, it was necessary to develop a responsive weapons complex that could rapidly produce additional warheads, remain cost efficient, and allow the United States to reduce the size of its nuclear arsenal.[117] The Department of Energy (DOE)—through the National Nuclear Security Administration (NNSA) and in partnership with Department of Defense (DOD)—believed that the RRW would enable the United States to have "a safe, secure, and reliable nuclear deterrent."[118] The Complex 2030 document acknowledged the changes implemented 2001 in which strategic deterrence was based on the "premise … of deterring a peer adversary to one of responding to emerging threats."[119]

Indeed, as has been emphasized throughout the course of this book, the National Security Strategy of 2002 directed a change in the platform of the deterrent as a means to adapt to the perceived changing nature of the threat. The NSS and NPR called for the following:

- Changing the size, composition, and character of our nuclear stockpile in a way that reflects the reality that the Cold War is over;
- Achieving a credible deterrent with the lowest possible number of nuclear warheads consistent with our national security needs, including our obligations to our allies;
- Transforming the NNSA nuclear weapons complex (also referred to as the "Complex") into a responsive infrastructure that supports the specific stockpile requirements and maintains the essential US nuclear capabilities needed for an uncertain global future.[120]

As part of the ongoing continuum of nuclear option considerations, Complex 2030 and its accompanying documental instruments illustrated the desire to cultivate a future nuclear weapons enterprise, in which the deployed stockpile would be transformed into one smaller than today.

It is here that the document posited the concept of the Reliable Replacement Warhead in which the "warhead design limitations" imposed on Cold War systems would be more easily and efficiently "manufactured at fewer, modernized facilities with safer and more environmentally benign materials."[121] In an assertive fashion, Jacqueline Cabasso, described "Complex 2030" as the:

> publicly announced United States plan to modernize its nuclear weapons complex and replace its entire nuclear arsenal with new 'Reliable Replacement Warheads' by the year 2030 . . . the proposed project, which could cost more than $150 billion over 25 years, is tantamount to a US declaration of 'nukes forever,' and a repudiation of its obligation under Article VI of the Nuclear Non-Proliferation Treaty (NPT) to end the arms race 'at an early date' and to negotiate 'in good faith' the elimination of its nuclear arsenal.[122]

Proponents of Complex 2030, however, argued that such replacement warheads would have the same military characteristics, could be transferred on the same kinds of delivery systems, and hold at risk the same targets as the warheads they replaced. They would be redesigned to foster a greater sense of safety and security, while enabling an easier production process and maintenance.[123] Moreover, the document contended, confidence in the stockpile would remain high, minus the resurrection of nuclear testing, as the RRW enabled the increase in performance margins based on a sounder understanding of nuclear weapons attained from the Stockpile Stewardship Program (SSP) as well as the accompanying research and development (R&D).[124] The structures that supported this smaller stockpile would be robust and able to efficiently address any technical problems in the stockpile, while simultaneously being able to respond to adverse geopolitical change.[125]

Supporting the NNSA's argument and concern, Congress provided capital for the RRW program in the FY2005 Consolidated Appropriations Act, P.L. 108–447.

The RRW was conveyed in the conference report as a "program to improve the reliability, longevity, and certifiability of existing weapons and their components."[126] Congress provided further authorization in the FY2006 National Defense Authorization Act, P.L. 109–163, Section 3111. As indicated in the above, Congress stipulated several goals for the RRW program, in particular, an increase in confidence that warheads would perform as intended over the long-term without nuclear testing. Other goals pertained to increasing the ease of manufacturing and certification, the reduction in life cycle cost, the increase in weapon safety and use control, and reduction in potential damage to the environment.[127] As expected, the RRW program engendered varying levels of debate. One commentator argued that "the plutonium research results obliterate the chief rationale for NNSA's emerging strategy" of RRW,[128] while the *New York Times* opined that RRW "is a public-relations disaster in the making overseas" and "a make-work program championed by the weapons laboratories and belatedly by the Pentagon."[129]

Indeed, while Complex 2030 and the RRW it encompassed were depicted by the NNSA as developing a smaller and efficient nuclear weapons complex designed for the twenty-first century with safety and security in mind, others were more wary of such developments. As Jacqueline Cabasso testified, while the NNSA claimed that "RRW is not a new weapon providing new or different military capabilities and/or missions,"[130] NNSA chief Linton Brooks was clear that the nuclear option and potential to develop a new nuclear weapon was not a farfetched proposition:

> In 2030, our Responsive Infrastructure can also produce weapons with different or modified military requirements as required. The weapons design community that was revitalized by the RRW program can adapt an existing weapon within 18 months and design, develop and begin production of the new design within 3–4 years of a decision to enter engineering development … goals that were established in 2004. Thus, if Congress and the President direct, we can respond quickly to changing military requirements.[131]

As stern advocates of the RRW and its quest to redesign the physical aspects of the nuclear option, the Bush Administration argued that the current stockpile—most units of which were manufactured between 1979 and 1989—were designed to deter and, if necessary, defeat the Soviet Union. In today's international climate, the threat, strategy, and missions have changed, leaving the United States with an "out of date stockpile."[132] As Brooks further stated, current warheads are wrong technically because "we would [now] manage technical risk differently, for example, by 'trading' [warhead] size and weight for increased performance margins, system longevity, and ease of manufacture." These warheads were not "designed for longevity" or to minimize cost, and may be wrong militarily because yields are too high and "do not lend themselves to reduced collateral damage." They also lack capabilities against buried targets or biological and chemical munitions, and they do not take full advantage of precision guidance.[133] As O'Brien articulated in *Sustaining the Nuclear Enterprise: A New Approach*, the stockpile was wrong because it was too large:

> We retain "hedge" warheads in large part due to the inability of either today's nuclear infrastructure, or the infrastructure we expect to have when the stockpile reductions are fully implemented in 2012, to manufacture, in a timely way, warheads for replacement or for force augmentation, or to act to correct unexpected technical problems.[134]

Moreover, it was argued by RRW advocates that the stockpile was not appropriate in terms of physical security, as it was not designed for a situation in which terrorists may attain control or detonate a nuclear weapon. As further articulated by Brooks, "if we were designing the stockpile today, we would apply new technologies and approaches to warhead-level use control as a means to reduce physical security costs."[135]

Of course, there were those who questioned the notion that the RRW would improve the current stockpile. For the likes of Speed and May, new weapons may not offer much new capability: that is, earth penetrators may not necessarily destroy hardened facilities buried very deeply or at imprecisely known locations, and nuclear weapons are of questionable effectiveness against chemical and biological agents.[136] Medalia expanded on such doubts in his Congress Research Service, 2008 Reliable Replacement Warhead program report:

> They (opponents of the RRW) anticipate that RRWs, like any other product, would have "birth defects," whereas such defects have been wrung out of existing warheads, and believe that such defects could require a larger stockpile. They state that performance margins of current warheads are adequate and can be improved somewhat if needed, such as by new systems to deliver boost gas. They question the argument that RRW would reduce physical security costs on grounds that a terrorist attempt to seize and detonate a nuclear warhead in place is most unlikely given the high level of security currently in place, and doubt that Congress or NNSA would reduce the guard force because of RRW.[137]

During the course of the twentieth century, the nuclear weapons complex has expanded and contracted in response to what the Administration of the day perceived to be the national interest security imperative. Whether it was the rush to produce the first bomb in World War II, the quest to produce many thousands of warheads of many different types during the Cold War, the desire for dismantlement and less production with the conclusion of the Cold War or the current era in which state and non-state actors are both nuclear players, "the US Complex" has attempted to shift and adjust but with varying degrees of success.[138] Indeed, the nuclear stockpile was constructed as a means to address Cold War demands in which, for example, high explosive yield per unit of warhead weight (the "yield-to-weight ratio") was "critically important while cost, ease of manufacture, and reduction of hazardous material were less so."[139] In today's climate, Medalia argued, "yield-to-weight has become less important, the others just mentioned have become more important, new constraints have appeared in the wake of 9/11, and warheads must continue to be safe and reliable."[140] As a result, the Bush Administration asserted, the RRW made it possible to adapt the stockpile to reflect such changes.

The quest to update and reassert the nuclear option to the fore was reflected in the Bush Administration's support of the RRW from the outset. The Administration saw the RRW program as the basis for addressing and complementing the nuclear aspirations stipulated in the National Security Strategy of 2002 and NPR and the subsequent documents, instrument, and plans. This transformation was evident when Representative David Hobson, Chairman of the House Energy and Water Development Appropriations Subcommittee in the 108th and 109th Congresses, presented himself as a major advocate of the RRW. In introducing the FY2005 energy and water bill (H.R. 4614) to the House, he highlighted the need to reconfigure the Complex as a means to adhere to the NPR, but also realign the nuclear option to what he perceived were "today's" requirements. As stated:

> much of the DOE weapons complex is still sized to support a Cold War stockpile. The NNSA needs to take a 'time-out' on new initiatives until it completes a review of its weapons complex in relation to security needs, budget constraints, and [a] new stockpile plan.[141]

For Hobson, the RRW would be an integral part of the Administration's effort to readjust US nuclear strategy, reshape the nuclear weapons stockpile and Complex to hold up that key strategy, pursue weapons programs aligned with that strategy, and reject those that were inconsistent.[142]

Indeed, the RRW further illustrated that notions of transforming the Complex into the responsive infrastructure articulated in the 2002 Nuclear Posture Review and National Security Strategy were becoming a reality. As Thomas D'Agostino, then NNSA Deputy Administrator for Defense Programs, articulated in 2006:

> By "responsive" we refer to the resilience of the nuclear enterprise to unanticipated events or emerging threats, and the ability to anticipate innovations by an adversary and to counter them before our deterrent is degraded ... much remains to be done to achieve stockpile and infrastructure transformation.... The "enabler" for transformation is our concept for the RRW. The RRW will benefit from relaxed Cold War design constraints that maximized yield to weight ratios. This will allow us to design replacement components that are easier to manufacture; are safer and more secure; eliminate environmentally dangerous, reactive, and unstable materials ... RRW, we believe, will provide enormous leverage for a more efficient and responsive infrastructure and opportunities for a smaller stockpile.[143]

It was evident that those who endorsed the nuclear option continuum encompassed in the RRW focused extensively on safety and cost efficiency, rather than the fact that the RRW program also contained the capability to enable the development of a new nuclear weapon. As the Committee stated:

> The RRW weapon will be designed for ease of manufacturing, maintenance, dismantlement, and certification without nuclear testing, allowing the NNSA to transition the weapons complex away from a large, expensive Cold War relic into a smaller, more efficient modern complex. A more reliable replacement warhead will allow long-term savings by phasing out the multiple redundant Cold War warhead designs that require maintaining multiple obsolete production technologies to maintain the older warheads.[144]

Those who were wary of the real potential of new nuclear weapons development expressed concerns about the link between RRW and the nuclear weapon Complex transformation. As Representative Peter Visclosky, Chairman of the Energy and Water Development Appropriations Subcommittee indicated:

> I am also troubled by the apparent unbridled enthusiasm of the nuclear weapons complex over the Reliable Replacement Warhead and wish I saw that same enthusiasm replicated, as far as their dedication to downsizing the complex.... The department [DOE] will have to develop a modernization plan that is near term and demonstrates a recognition that the long-term requirements of the nuclear weapons complex are tied to a much smaller nuclear stockpile.[145]

Of course, proponents for a reinvigorated nuclear option lamented that if nothing was done, confidence in the stockpile would decline, and with it, the ability of the US to assure allies that its deterrent capacity was sound and able "to dissuade competitors from beginning nuclear programs, to deter adversaries, and if necessary to defeat enemies, as called for in the 2001 Nuclear Posture Review and National Security Strategy of 2002."[146]

The Bush Administration attempted to soften the RRW by portraying it as a pathway to attain a replacement weapon option, rather than a new weapon with new military capabilities. It would be one that would be easier to manufacture, maintain, and certify than current warheads; with broader performance margins as a means to instill the confidence as intended.[147] Critics of the Bush nuclear option argued that the RRW would make it more challenging for the United States to negotiate with Iranian and North Korean nuclear programs, and those programs in turn could lead to a follow-on wave of possible proliferators. By conveying to the world that they were willing to emphasize the nuclear option through the RRW program instead of seeking to quell and devalue such weapons, the United States ultimately could undermine its capacity to lead global nuclear non-proliferation efforts.[148] As former Senator Sam Nunn stated:

> On the RRW itself, if Congress gives a green light to this program in our current world environment—and I stress in our current world environment—I believe that this will be misunderstood by our allies, exploited by our adversaries, complicate our work to prevent the spread and use of nuclear weapons ... and make resolution of the Iran and North Korea

> challenges all the more difficult. Also, I think it will make it more difficult to discourage the many new countries that are right on the tipping point of beginning their enrichment process ... we will pay a very high price in terms of our overall national security if Congress goes forward with this program.... So I would not fund additional work on the RRW at this time, certainly not development and going forward with deployment.[149]

Former Secretary of Defense William Perry reiterated the above sentiments when he argued that the development of a new nuclear weapon could be deferred, as this "would put us in a stronger position to lead the international community in the continuing battle against nuclear proliferation, which threatens us all."[150]

Aside from external considerations, the Bush Administration repeatedly downplayed the possibility of a new nuclear weapon. In the medium term, the plan conveyed involved the mixing of existing and RRW warheads in the stockpile as a means to increase the diversity of warheads pertaining to each of the nuclear triad.[151] As highlighted above, the new warheads, the Administration claimed, would have more "flexible design parameters and be simpler and cheaper to maintain without nuclear testing."[152] In the long term, however, all warhead types in the "enduring" stockpile could be replaced. In its justification for the RRW nuclear option, the Administration undermined the original objective of a ban on nuclear testing—that being, the prevention of new nuclear weapons development and production. Now, production was said to be necessary to avoid nuclear testing.

In the latter stages of his Administration, it was apparent that Bush's quest for a new nuclear option was facing extensive opposition from a Congress that was (post-2006 mid-term elections) quite hostile to such aspirations. Throughout the fiscal 2008 budget process, Congress was sceptical of the RRW Program, which the Bush Administration had promoted as a more reliable, proliferation-proof option, and some committees cut funding for RRW dramatically.[153] They felt that it was premature to rush forward with a new warhead design and a production complex before basic questions were answered. Such questions related to the amount of bombs that would be built, and more fundamentally, the role of nuclear weapons in US security policy. In part to address these issues, the Senate Armed Services Committee directed Defense and Energy to submit a new Nuclear Posture Review to Congress in December 2009. The committee advised: "The new NPR would include a review of policy objectives with respect to nuclear forces and weapons and include the relationship among United States nuclear deterrence policy, targeting strategy, and arms control objectives."[154]

Nonetheless, the Bush Administration remained determined in its nuclear option quest. For FY2009, DOE requested ten million dollars and projected a similar amount for each year in the FY2010–FY2013 period.[155] It justified the request as follows:

> $10 million is requested to enable maturation of the RRW design to address questions raised by the JASON review of RRW feasibility study activities.

> Design refinement is necessary to establish parameters for potential impact on certification. Without further design work, there is insufficient detail available to use this design to resolve certification questions raised by the JASON review. This funding will also facilitate documenting the Phase 2A RRW work that has been completed through 2007 (prior to the FY 2008 Consolidated Appropriations Act (P.L. 110–161)) to support future Administration decisions on options for our nuclear weapons stockpile. The Department of Defense and the Joint DOD-DOE Nuclear Weapons Council fully support continuing efforts to examine how the RRW concept can address issues of safety, security and long-term reliability of the nation's nuclear deterrent.[156]

In February 2008, NNSA Administrator Thomas D'Agostino testified that proceeding with the RRW study would provide information crucial to completing the review of the nuclear posture in a "timely manner." Moreover, it would address concerns about the US capacity in maintaining the stockpile for the long-term with LEP, offer the prospect of improving warhead surety and address the maintenance of nuclear skills.[157] At the same hearing, General Kevin Chilton, USAF Commander, US Strategic Command, argued for the necessity in attaining "a warhead that is designed for the 21st century," with greater emphasis on reliability, safety, security, and maintainability, rather than on maximizing yield to weight.[158] According to one report, he also stated that without completing the RRW study "he would be ill-prepared to advise the incoming president next year on how best to modernize the atomic arsenal."[159] Conversely, others maintained their opposition to the RRW and expressed their sentiments accordingly. In relation to the need to improve surety, Daryl Kimball, Executive Director of the Arms Control Association, argued, "should we spend billions of dollars to replace existing warhead types in our arsenal to reduce by an infinitesimal amount [the possibility] that al Qaeda could detonate it?"[160] Similarly, former Senator Sam Nunn said, "in this world atmosphere, in this climate, for us to build a new warhead now would be a real setback to all of our non-proliferation efforts, so I am opposed to it.... At this moment I think it would be a mistake for America to go forward with that program."[161]

Of course, it was apparent that the views of Kimball and Nunn were to prevail as Bush's RRW nuclear option faced an impasse after both the House and Senate had an informal conference on the defense authorization bill. According to the Joint Explanatory Statement, "the result of these negotiations comprised the House amendment to S.3001, which was considered and passed under suspension of the Rules of the House of Representatives on 24 September 2008, by a vote of 392 to 39. By unanimous consent, the Senate agreed with the House amendment to S.3001 on 27 September 2008."[162] The resulting bill had no RRW funds for the Navy or NNSA.[163] It was signed into law, P.L. 110–417, on October 14, 2008. The House Appropriations Committee marked up the FY2009 energy-water appropriations bill on June 25 and released a committee print version of its report in June.[164] The committee eliminated the ten million dollar NNSA request for RRW and based its reasoning in the following:

> The Committee is aware of the advantages of a modern warhead design and strongly supports improved surety. The Committee also understands that high margin provides protection against failure due to compound unknowns. The Committee supports trading off Cold War high yield for improved reliability, in order to move to a smaller stockpile requiring a smaller and cheaper weapons complex with no need for nuclear testing.
>
> That said, the Committee remains to be convinced that a new warhead design will lead to these benefits. The Committee will not spend the taxpayers' money for a new generation of warheads promoted as leading to nuclear reductions absent a specific glide path to a specified, much smaller force of nuclear weapons. Similarly, the Committee finds no logic in spending the taxpayers' money on a new generation of warheads promoted as avoiding the need for nuclear testing, while the Secretary of State insists that "the Administration does not support the Comprehensive Test Ban Treaty."
>
> Before the Committee will consider funding for most new programs, substantial changes to the existing nuclear weapons complex, or funding for the RRW, the Committee insists that the following sequence be completed:
>
> (1) replacement of Cold War strategies with a 21st Century nuclear deterrent strategy sharply focused on today's and tomorrow's threats, and capable of serving the national security needs of future Administrations and future Congresses without need for nuclear testing; (2) determination of the size and nature of the nuclear stockpile sufficient to serve that strategy; (3) determination of the size and nature of the nuclear weapons complex needed to support that future stockpile.[165]

The committee argued that while plans to execute these steps were stipulated in the FY2008 Omnibus Appropriations Act, "none of the required plans have been submitted."[166] The committee approved the bill by voice vote on June 25 and the report (H.Rept. 110–921) was released December 10, 2008. The Senate Appropriations Committee reported S.3258, the FY2009 energy water appropriation bill, on July 14. It recommended no NNSA funds for RRW.[167]

The House and Senate versions of this bill were not brought to the floor. Instead, funding for NNSA[168] and many other agencies was made available through the continuing resolution component of H.R. 2638, Consolidated Security, Disaster Assistance, and Continuing Appropriations Act, 2009, for the period October 1, 2008—March 6, 2009 or until enactment of the applicable regular appropriations bill. Section 104 provided that "No appropriation or funds made available or authority granted pursuant to section 101 shall be used to initiate or resume any project or activity for which appropriations, funds, or other authority were not available during fiscal year 2008."[169] RRW was one such activity; accordingly, the bill provided no NNSA funds for RRW. H.R. 2638 was signed into law, P.L. 110–329, on September 30, 2008. P.L. 111–6, a one-sentence continuing resolution, extended the expiration of P.L. 110–329 through March 11, 2009. P.L. 111–8, Omnibus Appropriations Act, 2009, provided funds for the balance of FY2009. It, also, provided no NNSA funds for RRW.[170] The Bush Administration also requested $23.3 million in RRW funds for the Navy in the Department of Defense appropriations bill. These funds were part of an $80.1 million request for Program Element 11221N, strategic submarine and weapons system support. While the Defense Appropriations Subcommittees marked up the bill, the full committees did not report their respective bills. Instead, the Department of Defense appropriations bill was contained in H.R. 2638, Division C, as a regular appropriations bill. That bill eliminated Navy RRW funds.[171]

With Bush's departure in January 2009, it was not surprising that for FY2010, the Obama Administration requested no funds for RRW and included the program in a list of programs to be terminated. Indeed, an Office of Management and Budget report defined the RRW as "not consistent with Presidential commitments to move towards a nuclear-free world."[172] The House Armed Services Committee reported H.R. 2647, the FY2010 defense authorization bill, on June 18, 2009. Section 3112 of the bill would strike Section 4204a of the Atomic Energy Act directing DOE to establish the RRW program.[173] The bill passed the House, 389–22, with 1 present, on June 25. The Senate Armed Services Committee reported S. 1390, FY2010 defense authorization bill, on July 2. Section 3113 would strike Section 4204a of the Atomic Energy Act.[174] The bill passed the Senate, 87–7, on July 23. No amendments on RRW were offered to either bill. The House Appropriations Committee reported H.R. 3183, FY2010 energy and water development appropriations bill, on July 13. It contained no funds for RRW. The House passed the bill, 320–97, on July 17, with no amendments on RRW. The Senate Appropriations Committee reported its energy-water bill on July 9. It also contained no funds for RRW, and most importantly, appeared to be the final conclusion to the Bush Administration's nuclear drive.

During its two-term tenure, statements and promises posited by the Bush Administration in regard to reducing the dependency on nuclear weapons in US national security through the creation of a "New Triad" were relatively limited. Rather than replacing nuclear weapons, conventional weapons and missile defense systems have been utilized as a means to complement the nuclear posture. Although there has been a stern push in the US Congress to re-examine nuclear policy, there will also be significant resistance as "cutting too deep and changing too much (will be challenged) amid the political development in Russia, the rise of China, and the (continued) fear of proliferation of weapons of mass destruction" by non-state actors.[175] The nuclear doctrine encompassed in the National Security Strategy of 2002 and the subsequent "editing" documents illustrated the stark contradiction between the Bush Administration's public rhetoric about reducing nuclear weapons and the guidance issued to the nuclear planners in the role they will really continue to play.

While the overall number of warheads was reduced, the new doctrine guiding planning for the remaining arsenal reaffirmed an aggressive posture with nuclear forces on high alert, ready to be used in an increasing number of limited-strike scenarios against adversaries anywhere, even preventively. As signified above, the Bush Doctrine and revitalization of the nuclear option has obviously been precipitated by the anticipation among military planners "that deterrence would fail and US nuclear weapons would be used in a conflict sooner or later." Perhaps the best example of how excessive and resilient the US nuclear posture has been since 2001 is that when all the planned reductions have been implemented by 2012, "the US nuclear weapons stockpile will still—nearly a quarter of a century after the Cold War ended—be 15 times greater than when the National Security Council Paper 68 (NSC-68) in 1950 outlined the US justifications for a rapid and massive military build-up to contain the Soviet Union."[176]

It took the Clinton Administration ten years to dismantle more than 11,000 warheads in the 1990s, but it would take more than 15 years to dismantle less than half that number under the Bush Administration's plan. In fact, the Bush Administration dismantled the smallest number of nuclear weapons of any US Administration since 1957.[177] Its rationale was straightforward: the focus was never on disarmament but rather on extending the life of the remaining stock of nuclear weaponry. The Reliable Replacement Warhead program was testament to this in which the US Department of Energy proposed the development of a new generation of nuclear warheads, an attempt to redesign and replace the entire US nuclear arsenal with new warheads. Despite the apparent defeat of the RRW program and election of Barack Obama, there will be immense difficulties in reversing the course on nuclear weapon development. As stated by Michael O'Hanlon, a military expert at the Brookings Institution who has specialized in nuclear issues, Obama and Gates are 'at loggerheads on' the issue of nuclear weapons.[178] While serving under former President Bush, Gates had repeatedly called for the Reliable Replacement Warhead program to be put into operation as the current US nuclear arsenal—mostly produced in the 1970s and 1980s—was ageing and thereby had the potential to undermine both the arsenal's safety and its destructive capacity. As Gates stated in early 2009, "the Reliable Replacement Warhead is necessary ... even though the days of hair-trigger superpower confrontation are over, as long as other nations possess the bomb and the means to deliver it, the United States must maintain a credible strategic deterrent."[179]

For all of Obama's internationalist rhetoric, the sheer fact that he reappointed Gates as Defense Secretary in an unusual step of continuity between Republican and Democratic Administrations, suggests that the nuclear option asserted by Bush may be diluted, but not necessarily removed. As further articulated by Gates, "Congress needs to do its part by funding the Reliable Replacement Warhead Program—for safety, for security, and for a more reliable deterrent"[180] and would give the US the confidence to shrink its overall nuclear arsenal. For the likes of Gates, the RRW in essence trades away explosive force for greater assurance that the new warheads would work predictably in the absence of tests—which the US has refrained from conducting for nearly two decades to help advance non-proliferation goals. Under a self-imposed moratorium, the US has not conducted nuclear tests to assure the reliability and potency of its weapons since 1992. But it does spend more than $5 billion a year conducting analyses and computerized tests to monitor the health of the weapons.[181]

Despite the withdrawal of RRW funding, it is apparent that there is a struggle within the new Administration between the "transformationalists" who seek a new vision to transform US nuclear policy and the "incrementalists" who focus on gradual steps using the techniques of previous years. While Obama has indicated that he does not want to produce "new" nuclear weapons, he has not removed the significance of nuclear weapons in US security policy thus far. Rather than a fully-fledged RRW program, future production of replacement or significantly modified warheads may instead be carried out by expanding the scope of Life Extension Program work to add new features to existing warhead designs. A recently obtained National Nuclear Security Administration document has spoken of "evolving and sustaining the nuclear deterrent"[182] and that the Obama Administration is planning on maintaining and modernizing nuclear weapons and facilities over the next 15–20 years (discussed in the next chapter). Indeed, whether or not a form of the RRW continues is a moot point as "other replacement warheads are likely to emerge in the future under other names."[183] It is this nuclear reality that confirms the notion that while key elements of the Bush Doctrine stalled in the context of the Iraq conflict, the deeper nuclear dimension of the doctrine—reiterated, refined, accentuated, and guided through the 2002 National Strategy to Combat Weapons of Mass Destruction, the 2002 Nuclear Posture Review, CONPLAN (Concept Plan) 8022 (Global Strike), the abandoned 2005 Doctrine for Joint Nuclear Operations, the 2006 Quadrennial Defense Review, the 2006 Strategic Operations Joint Operating Concept Version 2.0 and the recent Reliable Replacement Warhead program—foreshadowed a new nuclear era in which the once termed "weapon of last resort" became a usable and, according to the Bush Administration, necessary war-fighting device.

6 The nuclear option

From Bush to Obama

As the previous chapters illustrate, the Bush Administration viewed arms control treaties and multilateral non-proliferation agreements as inherently unverifiable and overly constraining to their notions of US security strategy. During his tenure in office, Bush ignored the Comprehensive Nuclear Test Ban Treaty (CTBT), withdrew from the Anti-Ballistic Missile Treaty (ABMT) to pursue a national missile defense system, and signed a cursory arms reduction treaty with Russia that didn't even include counting measures, let alone verification. The Administration proposed developing a nuclear bunker-buster weapon, explored the option of putting anti-missile weapons in space and reached a nuclear cooperation deal with India—which is not a party to the non-proliferation treaty. Additionally, Bush attempted to coerce nuclear rogues through threats of "pre-emption"/prevention, while arguing that new nuclear weapons and missile defense systems were needed[1]—or as defined in the previous chapters, a reinvigorated nuclear option. This chapter will focus on the transition between the Bush and Obama Administrations, and more importantly, the extent to which Obama has attempted to "adjust" the nuclear option. Starting with the vision and goals posited in the 2009 Prague Speech and reaffirmed in the National Security Strategy of 2010, the chapter will outline and evaluate various Obama declaratory policies, initiatives, and multilateral efforts—namely, the Congressionally mandated Nuclear Posture Review, the New START Treaty, the Nuclear Security Summit, the Nuclear Non-Proliferation Treaty Review Conference, the Comprehensive Test Ban Treaty—and the extent to which such initiatives have upheld the lofty goals posited in Prague and/or deviated from the nuclear path pursued by the Bush Administration.

The Prague speech

The election of Barack Obama as the 44th President of the United States promised significant changes in US nuclear policy and priorities compared with those of the Bush Administration. During the 2008 Presidential campaign, Obama pledged to "set a new direction in US nuclear weapons policy and show the world that America believes in its existing commitment under the Nuclear Non-Proliferation Treaty (NPT) to work to ultimately eliminate all nuclear weapons."[2]

In his April 2009 speech in Prague, Obama posited a vision of a transformed international security context and the goal of total nuclear disarmament: "So today, I state clearly and with conviction America's commitment to seek the peace and security of a world without nuclear weapons."[3] The positive impression he left on his Prague audience was viewed by many in the international community as a sharp break from policies of the previous Administration, which had banished the term "disarmament" from its official vocabulary and, according to Paul Meyer, "broke with past nuclear policy pronouncements that suggested an expanded role for nuclear weapons in the nation's defenses."[4]

In its opening sections, the Prague address paid its respects to the 1989 Velvet Revolution, subtly linking Obama's apparent nuclear weapons drive with those actions of the Czech revolutionaries of the Cold War:[5] The [Velvet Revolution] "proved that moral leadership is more powerful than any weapon" and such moral leadership now needs to be directed at eliminating the nuclear weapons that represent "the most dangerous legacy of the Cold War."[6] In this push for nuclear disarmament, Obama argued that a leadership role for the United States was needed as not only a function of power or the size of the US nuclear arsenal, but as a matter of "moral responsibility." Having set up the moral imperative for action, which itself is a remarkable change in the Presidential "lexicon for international security policy," Obama enumerated a series of steps his administration would implement to put the vision into practice.[7]

Broadly speaking, the President made a dual pledge: on the one hand, to "take concrete steps towards a world without nuclear weapons," and to "put an end to Cold War thinking" by reducing "the role of nuclear weapons in our national security strategy, and urge others to do the same." On the other, he pledged to "maintain a safe, secure and effective arsenal to deter any adversary, and guarantee that defense to our allies." As a means to reduce US warheads and stockpiles, his Administration would negotiate a new Strategic Arms Reduction Treaty with the Russians in 2010; to achieve a global ban on nuclear testing, the Administration would immediately and "aggressively" pursue US ratification of the Comprehensive Test Ban Treaty; and, finally, Obama would attempt to strengthen the Nuclear Non-Proliferation Treaty as a basis for cooperation.[8] As stated:

> The basic bargain is sound: Countries with nuclear weapons will move towards disarmament, countries without nuclear weapons will not acquire them, and all countries can access peaceful nuclear energy. To strengthen the treaty, we should embrace several principles. We need more resources and authority to strengthen international inspections. We need real and immediate consequences for countries caught breaking the rules or trying to leave the treaty without cause.[9]

For some analysts, the "section" pertaining to the NPT was the weakest component of the otherwise impressive rhetoric of the Prague speech. Aside from reaffirming that "[t]he basic bargain is sound," there was minimal clarity and coherence in Obama's remarks as to what the chief challenges to the NPT were and what remedial action would be necessary.[10] While there was an emphasis on monitoring ("more resources and authority to strengthen international inspections")[11] and enforcement ("we need real and immediate consequences for countries caught breaking the rules"),[12] there appeared to be no overriding commitment to balanced compliance with all three pillars of the treaty—non-proliferation, disarmament, and peaceful uses of nuclear energy. As stated by Meyer, "the problems besetting the NPT go well beyond the defiance of North Korea or the machinations of Iran. To limit the prescription to finding better ways to hold these two states accountable is to overlook the deeper sources of malaise within the NPT."[13] The commitments enumerated in Prague represented the practical content of a speech that radiated idealism and appealed to people around the world to seek security through cooperation rather than confrontation. This vision was a distinct shift to that of the Bush Administration and was further accentuated in the National Security Strategy of 2010.

The National Security Strategy of 2010

Again, the "goal of a world without nuclear weapons" was emphasized. While Obama stated that this goal would not be attained during his Administration, he argued that the active pursuit and eventual achievement would increase global security, maintain the United States' commitment under the NPT, build its cooperation with Russia and other states, and increase its credibility to hold others accountable for their obligations.[14] However, echoing the modest nature of his nuclear policy in real terms—as opposed to the declaratory symbolism espoused at Prague—Obama also cautioned that "as long as any nuclear weapons exist, the United States" would "sustain a safe, secure, and effective nuclear arsenal, both to deter potential adversaries and to assure US allies and other security partners that they can count on America's security commitments."[15]

Despite this qualifying point, Obama highlighted that the US had signed a New START Treaty with Russia which—if ratified—would "substantially limit our deployed nuclear warheads and strategic delivery vehicles, while assuring a comprehensive monitoring regime." Additionally, the Administration sought to reduce the role of nuclear weapons in the US national security approach, "extending a negative security assurance not to use or threaten to use nuclear weapons against those non-nuclear states that are in compliance with the NPT and their nuclear non-proliferation obligations."[16] Emphasizing the sentiments of the Prague Speech, Obama highlighted his Administration's goal of emboldening the NPT through: seeking more resources and authority for international inspections; developing a new framework for civil nuclear cooperation; and implementing an international consensus to insist that all nations meet their obligations. The National Security Strategy would seek ratification of the Comprehensive Test Ban Treaty, while vying for "a new treaty that verifiably ends the production of fissile materials intended for use in nuclear weapons."[17] Finally, Obama's NSS would also pursue a focused international effort to secure all vulnerable nuclear material around the world through enhanced protection and accounting practices, expanded cooperation with and through international institutions, and new partnerships to lock down these sensitive materials.[18] As stated:

> To detect and intercept nuclear materials in transit, and to stop the illicit trade in these technologies, we will work to turn programs such as the Proliferation Security Initiative and the Global Initiative to Combat Nuclear Terrorism into durable international efforts.[19]

For many analysts, the President's address in Prague, together with the National Security Strategy of 2010, were a reassuring assertion of United States' commitment and leadership in the effort to rid the world of its most devastating weapons. In part of the Prague speech, however, Obama affirmed that "[w]ords must mean something." That is, the positive glow of Obama's oratorical and declaratory success would soon fade if his Administration did not follow up with demonstrable action and achievement. It is this point that leads us to the first real test—the release of the Nuclear Posture Review of 2010.

The Nuclear Posture Review of 2010

The Obama Administration's Nuclear Posture Review (NPR) contained assertive language that committed the United States to work for non-proliferation and—for the first time—the goal of elimination of nuclear weapons was enshrined into the NPR. In what appeared to be a broader range of policy issues in defining the nuclear posture, the review represented a shift from the Bush Administration's NPR, which was more focused on military capabilities. At the same time, however, the new NPR can be viewed as a cautious document that recommended curtailing the US nuclear posture further in the future but maintained many of the key nuclear weapons force structure and policy elements of the previous Administration. As stated by David Hoffman, "the document is filled with laudable goals that mark a change from the past and may help advance his dream of a world without nukes. But flying at high altitude also has certain advantages; you can avoid the rough terrain below." At the "ground level," he added, "the President stopped short of changing the status quo on critical issues that have lingered since the Cold War, such as tactical nuclear weapons and keeping missiles on alert."[20]

Despite these sentiments, there were many proponents who argued that the NPR provided a much needed clarification of the US negative security assurance, an important "enticement" intended to help persuade states not to acquire nuclear weapons. While not a new policy by any means, the NPR streamlined the "nuclear enticement" in which the "United States would not use or threaten to use nuclear weapons against non-nuclear weapons states that are party to the Nuclear Non-Proliferation Treaty and in compliance with their nuclear non-proliferation obligations."[21] This was a distinct contrast to the version posited by the Bush Administration in 2002 where the US would not use nuclear weapons against non-nuclear weapon states who were parties to the Treaty on the

Non-proliferation of Nuclear Weapons. The exception would be in the case of an "invasion or any other attack on the United States, its territories, its armed forces or other troops," its "allies" or on a "state toward which it has a security commitment, carried out or sustained by such a non-nuclear weapon state in association or alliance with a nuclear weapon state."[22] There were many exemptions buried in the old version, to the extent that it was at times difficult to comprehend. In contrast, the Obama version addressed this in more simple terms.

In his 2009 Prague speech, Obama pledged that he would "reduce the role of nuclear weapons" to "put an end to Cold War thinking," and reaffirmed in February 2010 that the "Nuclear Posture Review will reduce [the] role…"[23] The document stated in the executive summary that the "fundamental role of US nuclear weapons is to deter nuclear attack on the United States, our allies, and partners."[24] Under the section "Reducing the Role of US Nuclear Weapons" the NPR listed three overall conclusions. First, the United States would continue to strengthen conventional capabilities and reduce the role of nuclear weapons in deterring non-nuclear attack, with the objective of making deterrence of nuclear attack on the United States or its allies and partners the sole purpose of US nuclear weapons. Second, the United States would only contemplate the use of nuclear weapons in extreme circumstances to defend the critical interests of the United States or its allies and partners. Third, the United States would not use or threaten to use nuclear weapons against non-nuclear weapons states that are party to the NPT and in compliance with their nuclear proliferation obligations.[25] The language—"deter nuclear attack" and pursuit of "sole purpose"—was clearly new, and if implemented, would signify a roll-back of the Clinton and Bush Administrations' policy of using nuclear weapons to deter all forms of WMD.

As the document progressed, however, it was apparent that the actual reduction in the nuclear mission was rather moderate. In fact, it was difficult to see the extent to which it truly was a shift in US nuclear planning. That is, the Obama NPR appeared to continue nuclear planning against regional adversaries with weapons of mass destruction and explicitly rejected the adoption of a "sole purpose" policy—in which "sole purpose" was conveyed as a goal "rather than a reality of current US nuclear force posture"[26]—leaving it up to future Presidents to possibly change the policy in that direction. Indeed, the NPR put off to the indefinite future the acceptance of a policy that would "unequivocally limit the role of US nuclear weapons to deterring the use of such weapons by others." For now, this remains the "fundamental" rather than the "sole" role for US nuclear forces.[27] A residual deterrent role was still claimed for potential future biological weapons threats and against nuclear-weapon states and non-compliant states to deal with an unspecified "narrow range of contingencies"[28] in which US nuclear weapons could deter attack by conventional, chemical, or biological weapons. Many analysts were also hoping for a "no first use" declaration—a clear statement that nuclear weapons would only be used in response to a nuclear attack by others. Instead, the NPR promised to "reduce the role of nuclear weapons in deterring non-nuclear attacks, with the objective of making deterrence of nuclear attack on the United States or our allies and partners the sole purpose of US nuclear weapons." While the Obama Administration was not prepared to rule out first use against other nuclear weapons states, it did, however, state that the US "would only consider the use of nuclear weapons in extreme circumstances to defend the vital interests of the United States or its allies and partners," while also promising to "work to establish conditions under which [a sole purpose] policy could be safely adapted."[29] In essence, it appeared that US declaratory policy still wanted to cover "all the bases with its nuclear forces."[30]

Changes in the role of nuclear weapons were also much more difficult to ascertain in the context of Russia and China, to which the NPR merely appeared to continue the Bush Administration's Triad and an upload capability tied to such scenarios. As the document stated, "Russia's nuclear force will remain a significant factor in determining how much and how fast we are prepared to reduce US forces."[31] Moreover, as David Tratchenberg emphasized:

> In some ways, the Obama Administration's NPR looks suspiciously like an endorsement of the Bush Administration's New Triad, without using the term. For example, the new NPR calls for "placing increased reliance on non-nuclear deterrence capabilities (e.g., missile defenses and conventional long-range missiles)." It states that the United States will "develop non-nuclear prompt global strike capabilities ... [that] may be particularly valuable for the defeat of time-urgent regional threats." It declares that "effective missile defenses are an essential element of the US commitment to strengthen regional deterrence against states of concern." And it argues for "a modern physical infrastructure—comprised of the national security laboratories and a complex of supporting facilities—and a highly capable workforce with the specialized skills needed to sustain the nuclear deterrent."[32]

President Obama also pledged in the Prague speech that he would "reduce the number of nuclear weapons."[33] The NPR force structure analysis became the basis for New START limits of 1,550 deployed strategic warheads and 700 deployed strategic delivery vehicles. Those limits represented a reduction compared with previous limits set by the 1991 START and 2002 Moscow Treaty. However, as acknowledged by Obama, while New START reduces the limit for how many warheads can be deployed, it did not limit the actual number of warheads in the arsenal. Additionally, the NPR did not identify how the New START limits would be achieved. Potential areas for the reductions pertained to: a retirement of two SSBNs from the nuclear mission; a cut of about 50–100 additional Minuteman III ICBMs; and conversion of some of the B-52s to conventional-only aircraft. The NPR will continue the conversion of the ICBM force to single-warhead configuration, implementing a decision made in the 1994 NPR, that the Bush Administration modified as a means to allow ICBMs to continue on carrying multiple warheads.[34] As stated by Kristensen, "there were not many, though, so the reduction in warheads from finishing the conversion will be modest, although a decision to reduce the number of ICBMs further would increase the reduction."[35]

The NPR's moderate stance was also evident in the fact that it did not clearly direct a reduction in the size of the total nuclear weapons stockpile—which currently contains approximately 5,000 warheads. The Bush Administration reduced the stockpile by nearly 50 percent between 2004 and 2007 and announced an additional 12 percent reduction by 2012, leaving about 4,600 warheads. However, the Bush Administration's decision in 2001 to retain a Responsive Force of reserve warheads that could be loaded back onto missiles and bombers if necessary received extensive criticism. There are currently an estimated 2,500 active warheads in that hedge. The new NPR was adamant that the US would "significantly reduce the size of the hedge, but that the United States will retain the ability to 'upload' some nuclear warheads as a technical hedge against any future problems with US delivery systems or warheads, or as a result of a fundamental deterioration of the security environment."[36] Overall, it can be argued that the NPR retained the Cold War force structure of nuclear weapons deployed on a Triad of delivery vehicles and concluded that, "the current alert posture of US strategic forces—with heavy bombers off full-time alert, nearly all ICBMs on alert, and a significant number of SSBNs at sea at any given time—should be retained for the present."[37] Obama's campaign assurance to "work with Russia to take US and Russian ballistic missiles off hair trigger alert" appears to have been put on hold. No doubt, retaining a Cold War posture with only modest reductions and delaying decisions about where the cuts would take place, helped his Administration attain crucial votes in the Senate for ratification of the New START treaty. With the modest reductions posited in the text of the new NPR, the report stated that President Obama had already directed a review of future reductions of nuclear weapons. However, such reductions are conditioned on further strengthening regional deterrence, maintaining strategic stability with Russia and China, providing nuclear umbrellas over allies, and building new bomb making factories.[38]

The significance of nuclear weapons in US security strategy was also evident in the NPR's text as it did not recommend reducing or withdrawing the (approximately) 200 nuclear bombs currently deployed at six bases in five European countries. Instead, it stated that the US would "consult with our allies regarding the future basing of nuclear weapons in Europe, and is committed to making consensus decisions through NATO processes."[39] This was probably intended to formally leave the decision to NATO's Strategic Review process scheduled for completion in November 2010. Nonetheless, for a document that emphasized non-proliferation and adherence to NPT obligations, the description of "NATO's unique nuclear sharing arrangements under which non-nuclear members participate in nuclear planning and possess specially configured aircraft capable of delivering nuclear weapons" appears to be inconsistent.[40] Similarly, in terms of the future role of nuclear weapons in regional scenarios, the NPR stated that "US nuclear weapons will play a role in the deterrence of regional states so long as those states have nuclear weapons," but the decisions taken in "the NPR, BMDR [Ballistic Missile Defense Review], and QDR [Quadrennial Defense Review] reflect the US desire to increase reliance on non-nuclear means to accomplish our objectives of deterring such states and reassuring our allies and partners."[41]

There are currently about 4,500 retired nuclear warheads ready to be dismantled. At the low dismantlement rate currently used (200–400 warheads per year) it will take more than a decade to dismantle the build up. More retired warheads will come from the decision to "significantly reduce" the hedge, further extending the timeline. Dismantlements compete with warhead maintenance and production for limited capacity at the Pantex Plant in Texas. The NPR recommended full-rate production of the W76–1 warhead, followed by the B61–12, and possibly the W78. These programs were described as extending the lives of existing warhead designs, although modifications can be significant. The NPR argued that "the United States will not develop new nuclear warheads. Life Extension Programs will use only nuclear components based on previously tested designs, and will not support new military missions or provide for new military capabilities."[42] However, this policy leaves the opportunity for extensive modifications of nuclear warheads—and could potentially enable production of the Reliable Replacement Warhead (RRW)—although officials insist that program is "dead." Indeed, the NPR stated that the full range of warhead work will be considered: refurbishment of existing warheads, reuse of nuclear components from different warheads, and replacement of nuclear components. Mindful of how controversial a decision to build replacement warheads is, the NPR has assured that decisions to modify warheads "will give strong preference to options for refurbishment or reuse" rather than replacement.[43]

However, whereas the President spoke of maintaining a nuclear deterrent in his April 2009 speech, a recently obtained National Nuclear Security Administration (NNSA) document has spoken of "*evolving* and *sustaining* the nuclear deterrent."[44] That is, it was reported that the NNSA had sent Congress the FY 2011 Stockpile Stewardship and Management Plan (SSMP) with new information about what the Obama Administration planned to spend on maintaining and modernizing nuclear weapons and facilities over the next 15–20 years. The Federation of Atomic Scientists (FAS) and Union of Concerned Scientists (UCS) obtained unclassified sections of the document and analyzed the Obama Administration's first nuclear weapons management plan and the extent to which the Prague speech vision will be translated into national nuclear weapons policy. To support the stockpile, the NNSA intended to spend more than $175 billion (in then-year dollars) over the next two decades on building new nuclear weapons factories, testing and simulation facilities, and modernizing and extending the life of the nuclear weapons in the stockpile. The plan has shown for the first time how much will be spent on modernizing and extending the life of three nuclear weapons: the B61 gravity bomb, the W76 sea-based strategic warhead, and the W78 land-based strategic warhead. The cost is approximately $10 billion (in then-year dollars) between 2010 and 2025, peaking at about $1.05 billion in 2017 (at about the same time the New START strategic arms reduction treaty enters into force).[45]

As the previous chapter discussed, over the course of the past decade Congress cancelled or delayed, as NNSA described them, "opportunities to exercise the full suite of design competencies through life extensions and modernizations" of nuclear weapons (presumably the Nuclear Robust Earth Penetrator and the Reliable Replacement Warhead). The new plan is designed for "providing the opportunity to fully exercise design and production skills" and "vastly improved capabilities" of modified warhead components. While this appears to affirm the pledge of reducing the nuclear weapons stockpile, the goal is conditioned on constructing new nuclear weapons production factories and creating a "more agile deterrent."[46] As the plan firmly stated, a "multi-year and steady investment in the modernization of the complex is an essential element of the NPR, allowing the United States to safely reduce the role of nuclear weapons."[47] Attaining a balance between disarmament and deterrence—a balance that conveys a clear transition towards disarmament—will be delicate and the Obama Administration must work to ensure that the goodwill of Prague is not undercut by nuclear modernizations.[48]

New START Treaty

The quest to sign and ratify the New START Treaty can be deemed as the second important pillar to which one can assess the extent to Obama has sought to "adjust" the nuclear option—amplified by the Bush Administration. It was in early April 2009 that "the leadership by the two major nuclear powers, possessing between them over 95 per cent of the world's nuclear warheads" defined their goals for the negotiations on a new START Treaty. Obama and Medvedev issued a joint statement signifying that the basis of the new agreement would "be the reduction and limitation of strategic offensive arms,"[49] however, the new treaty would not address missile defenses, non-strategic nuclear weapons, or non-deployed stockpiles of nuclear weapons.[50] The Presidents also concluded that they would pursue reductions to their respective forces to levels below those in the 2002 Moscow Treaty and that the new agreement would "mutually enhance the security of the Parties and predictability and stability in strategic offensive forces, and will include effective verification measures drawn from the experience of the Parties in implementing the START Treaty."[51] Further refinement of their goals for New START was evident in a Joint Understanding signed at their summit meeting in Moscow in July 2009—indicating the range they were considering for the limits in the treaty. They agreed that the new treaty would restrict each party to between 500 and 1,100 strategic delivery vehicles and between 1,500 and 1,675 associated warheads.[52]

On April 8, 2010, the United States and Russia signed the new strategic arms reduction treaty—known as New START, but officially titled the *Treaty between the United States of America and the Russian Federation on Measures for the Further Reduction and Limitation of Strategic Offensive Arms*.[53] The treaty was designed to replace the 1991 Strategic Arms Reductions Treaty (START), which expired after 15 years of implementation, on December 5, 2009.[54] With the ratification process completed in December 2010, New START has overridden the 2002 Strategic Offensive Reductions Treaty (known as the Moscow Treaty) which was to remain in force until the end of 2012.[55] The Treaty's duration will be ten years—and unless superseded by a subsequent agreement—parties are permitted to extend the Treaty for a period of no more than five years. Additionally, the Treaty has included a withdrawal clause that is standard in arms control agreements.[56]

The New START Treaty follows many of the same conventions as the 1991 START Treaty, encompassing detailed definitions and counting rules that both states will utilize as a means to identify the forces limited by the treaty. It also requires that the parties maintain a comprehensive database, indicating the locations, numbers, and technical characteristics of weapons limited by the treaty.[57] Additionally, the treaty enables the parties to use varying types of displays and on-site inspections to confirm information in the database and to monitor forces and activities limited by the treaty. It contains a verification regime that combines the components of the 1991 START Treaty with new elements adapted to the limitations of the Treaty. Measures under the Treaty include on-site inspections and exhibitions, data exchanges and notifications related to strategic offensive arms and facilities covered by the Treaty, as well as provisions to facilitating the use of national technical means for treaty monitoring. To increase confidence and transparency, the Treaty also provided for the exchange of telemetry.[58]

The new Treaty, however, is by no means an extension of START. Many of the provisions in the original treaty reflected the uncertainty and suspicions that were evident at that time when the two states were still Cold War adversaries and each was still wary of the capabilities and intentions of the other. The New START Treaty is a product of a different era and a different relationship between the United States and Russia.[59] While some of the goals remain intact—the parties have sought provisions that would allow for predictability and transparency in their current forces and future intentions—the United States and Russia have streamlined and simplified the central limits and the monitoring and verification provisions.[60] The new Treaty does not encompass specific levels of limits and sublimits as each side can determine its own mix of land-based ICBMs, SLBMs and heavy bombers. Moreover, in the current international environment, both states appear more focused on facilitating continued co-operation and openness, than "choking off avenues for potential evasion schemes."[61]

Core limits of the New Start Treaty

The New START Treaty specifies three central limits on US and Russian strategic offensive nuclear forces. First, it limits each side to no more than 800 deployed and non-deployed ICBM and SLBM launchers and deployed and non-deployed heavy bombers equipped with the capacity to hold nuclear armaments. Second, within that total, it limits each state to no more than 700 deployed ICBMs, deployed SLBMs, and deployed heavy bombers equipped to carry nuclear armaments. This limit is less than half the corresponding strategic nuclear delivery vehicle limit of the START Treaty.[62] Third, the treaty limits each side to no more than 1,550 deployed warheads, including the actual number of warheads carried by deployed ICBMs and SLBMs, and one warhead for each deployed heavy bomber equipped for nuclear armaments.[63] According to the

Office of the Press Secretary, this limit is 74 percent lower than the limit of the 1991 START Treaty and 30 percent lower than the deployed strategic warhead limit of the 2002 Moscow Treaty.[64] The parties will share information on the locations of these missiles[65] in the database they maintain under the treaty and contact each other when they move these systems. These provisions should provide the means in which both states can monitor the numbers and locations of non-deployed missiles, while deterring efforts to stockpile hidden, uncounted missiles. A party would be in breach of the treaty if one of its non-deployed missiles was identified to be at a facility not included on the list or if one were found at a location different from the one listed for that missile in the database.[66]

Conversion and elimination

In terms of conversion and elimination, New START has stipulated that ICBM launchers, SLBM launchers and heavy bombers equipped to carry nuclear armaments will continue to count under the treaty limits until they are converted or eliminated according to the provisions described in the treaty's Protocol. As the Treaty states:

> ICBMs, SLBMs, ICBM launchers, SLBM launchers, and heavy bombers shall cease to be subject to this Treaty in accordance with Parts Three and Four of the Protocol to this Treaty. ICBMs or SLBMs of an existing type shall cease to be subject to this Treaty if all ICBM or SLBM launchers of a type intended for such ICBMs or SLBMs have been eliminated or converted in accordance with Part Three of the Protocol to this Treaty.[67]

These provisions are substantially less demanding than those posited in the original START Treaty, however, proponents have argued that this "will provide the United States and Russia with more flexibility in determining how to reduce their forces to meet the treaty limits."[68]

New START affirms that *ICBM Launchers* "shall be destroyed by excavating them to a depth of no less than eight meters or by explosion to a depth of no less than six meters,"[69] while silos can be "completely filled with debris resulting from demolition of infrastructure, and with earth or gravel."[70] Additionally, the party undertaking the elimination is permitted to develop other processes to eliminate its silos. Under New START, the elimination process pertaining to *Mobile ICBM launchers* is extensively simpler and far less dangerous. While the elimination process "shall be carried out by cutting the erector-launcher mechanism, levelling supports, and mountings of the erector launcher mechanism from the launcher chassis and by removing the missile launch support equipment … from the launcher chassis," neither the framework nor the chassis itself have to be cut into pieces. If the chassis is going to be used "at a declared facility for purposes not inconsistent with the Treaty"[71] the surfaces of the vehicle that will be visible to national technical means of verification must be painted a different color or pattern than those surfaces on a deployed mobile ICBM launcher.

Under New START, *SLBM launchers* (launch tubes) may be eliminated "by removing all missile launch tube hatches, their associated superstructure fairings, and, if applicable, gas generators."[72] That is, the missile section of the submarine and specific launch tubes can remain intact in the submarine and cease to count under the treaty limits if they are altered so that they can no longer launch ballistic missiles. Additionally, the elimination procedure for *Heavy Bombers* has also been simplified under New START.[73] To eliminate bombers, both states have agreed to cut "a wing or tail section from the fuselage at locations obviously not assembly joints," or, cut "the fuselage into two parts at a location obviously not an assembly joint."[74] Furthermore, to convert a bomber defined under the treaty as a heavy bomber no longer equipped to carry nuclear weaponry, parties can either: adapt the weapons bays and exterior attachments for pylons so that they cannot carry nuclear armaments; or modify all internal and external launcher assemblies so that they cannot carry nuclear armaments; or develop any other procedure to carry out the conversion. As was the case with the conversion and elimination of missile launchers, the party may have to reveal its conversion procedure, but the other party does not have the right to object or reject the method.[75]

New START has also limited the locations of *Mobile ICBMs* and their launchers, enabling the United States to monitor missiles covered by the treaty, while deterring Russian efforts to hide extra missiles away from the deployed force. In simple terms, deployed mobile ICBMs and their launchers must be located only at ICBM bases, while all non-deployed launchers for mobile ICBMs must be located at "production facilities, ICBM loading facilities, repair facilities, storage facilities, conversion or elimination facilities, training facilities, test ranges, and space launch facilities."[76] The locations of non-deployed mobile ICBMs are also restricted to loading facilities, maintenance facilities, repairs, storage facilities, conversion or elimination facilities test ranges, space launch facilities, and production facilities.[77] While some of these facilities may be at bases for operational mobile ICBMs, the non-deployed missiles must remain in the chosen facility and cannot be located in deployment areas. Additionally, when deployed or non-deployed missiles or launchers are shifted from one facility to another, both states will need to update the database so each facility has an updated, comprehensive list of each item contained at that facility, as well as a distinctive identifier associated with each item. It is here, according to the Protocol to the Treaty, that "inspectors shall have the right to read the unique identifiers on all designated deployed ICBMs or designated deployed SLBMs, non-deployed ICBMs, non-deployed SLBMs, and designated heavy bombers that are located at the inspection site."[78] Thereby, both parties will have the opportunity to ascertain that items posited at the facilities are supposed to be there.[79]

Monitoring and Verification

The New START Treaty has also provided a *Monitoring and Verification* structure that parallels the regime in START—particularly as it contains: specific definitions of items limited by the treaty; provisions that define the use of national technical means (NTM) to attain data on each side's forces and activities; a wide database that identifies the numbers, types, and locations of items limited by the treaty; provisions requiring notifications about items limited by the treaty; and inspections allowing the parties to confirm information shared during data exchanges. At the same time, however, the verification regime has become more coherent in an effort to make it less costly and complex than the regime in START.[80] It also has been altered to reflect the limits in New START and the current position in the relationship between the United States and Russia. Specifically, it is gauged on a sustainable transparency to which cooperation and openness—as well as on deterring and detecting potential violations—are the new pathway.

Furthermore, New START will also allow the parties to undertake up to 18 short-notice on-site inspections each year that can take place at both deployed and non-deployed launchers and missiles facilities. The treaty divides these into Type One inspections and Type Two inspections in which both states can conduct up to ten Type One inspections and up to eight Type Two inspections. Moreover, during each Type One inspection, the parties will be able to execute two different types of inspection activities—which are in essence on par with the data update inspections and re-entry vehicle inspections in the original START Treaty. Thereby, the 18 short-notice inspections permitted under New START are essentially equivalent to the 28 short notice inspections permitted under START.[81] According to Oelrich and Kristensen:

> The most important part of the new treaty is that it extends a verification regime at least a decade into the future. According to the White House, the inspections and other verification procedures in this Treaty will be simpler and less costly to implement than the old START treaty. This includes on-site inspections. Each side gets a total of 18 per year, ten of which are actual warhead counts of deployed missiles and the remaining eight being "Type 2" inspections of storage and dismantlement facilities. Exchange of missile test telemetry data has been limited partly because it is not as necessary for verification as previously; there are other means for collecting this information. Even so, the treaty includes exchange of telemetry data for five test flights each year.[82]

Ballistic missile defense

When Presidents Obama and Medvedev met in April 2009, the two states also agreed to address Russia's concerns with US missile defense programs in a discussion separate from the negotiations on a New START Treaty.[83] However, during their meeting in Moscow in July 2010, both agreed that the treaty would include a "provision on the interrelationship of strategic offensive arms and strategic defensive arms."[84] Appearing in the preamble of New START, this statement acknowledged the connection between strategic offensive arms and strategic defensive arms, in which the "interrelationship will become more important as strategic nuclear arms are reduced, and that current strategic defensive arms do not undermine the viability and effectiveness of the strategic offensive arms of the parties."[85] Upon signing New START, Russia and the United States each posited statements affirming their positions on the relationship between New START and missile defenses. As Russia stated:

> The Treaty can operate and be viable only if the United States of America refrains from developing its missile defense capabilities quantitatively or qualitatively. Consequently, the exceptional circumstances referred to in Article 14 of the Treaty include increasing the capabilities of the United States of America's missile defense system in such a way that threatens the potential of the strategic nuclear forces of the Russian Federation.[86]

In its statement, the United States conveyed the following:

> Missile defense systems are not intended to affect the strategic balance with Russia. The United States missile defense systems would be employed to defend the United States against limited missile launches, and to defend its deployed forces, allies and partners against regional threats. The United States intends to continue improving and deploying its missile defense systems in order to defend itself against limited attack and as part of our collaborative approach to strengthening stability in key regions.[87]

Some policy-makers expressed concern that the statements did not impose any obligations on either the United States or Russia. For Senator Lugar, the rhetoric was merely "in essence, editorial opinions," while Undersecretary of State, Ellen Tauscher argued that "Russia's unilateral statement on missile defenses is not an integral part of the New START Treaty. It's not legally-binding. It won't constrain US missile defense programs."[88] Although the statement did not provide Russia with "veto power" over US missile defense systems, it indicated that it could withdraw from the treaty should US missile defenses threaten "the potential of the strategic nuclear forces of the Russian Federation."[89] Conversely, the United States had no obligation to consult with Russia in assuring its planned defenses did not cross this threshold. It was permitted to construct and deploy whatever defenses it chose and Russia could then determine for itself whether such defenses impacted its strategic nuclear forces, and thereby, justified a withdrawal from the Treaty.[90]

While there were apparent positives relating to conversion and elimination, monitoring and verification, and ballistic missile defense, there were several analysts who argued that within the "fine print" of the terms of New START were "limits versus reduction."[91] As indicated earlier, the new limit of 1,550 deployed strategic warheads was 74 percent lower than the 6,000 warhead limit of the 1991 START Treaty, and 30 percent lower than the 2,200 deployed strategic warhead limit of the 2002 Moscow Treaty. However, while this is correct, the *limit* allowed by the treaty was not the actual *number* of warheads that could be deployed. The reason for this inconsistency can be attributed to a new counting rule that aligns one weapon to each bomber rather than the actual number of weapons assigned to them.[92] This "decoy" counting rule enables a rather large bank of warhead spaces under the treaty limit in which both states can deploy many more warheads than would otherwise be the case. Additionally, because there were no sub-limits for how warheads could be distributed on each of the three legs in the Triad, the "saved warheads" from the "fake" bomber count could be used to deploy more warheads on fast ballistic missiles.[93] The Moscow Treaty attributed real weapons numbers to bombers. The United States defined that weapons were counted as "operationally deployed" if they were "loaded on heavy bombers or stored in weapons storage areas of heavy bomber bases."[94] As a result, "large numbers of bombs and cruise missiles have been removed from US bomber bases to central storage sites over the past five years, leaving only those bomber weapons that should be counted against the 2,200-warhead Moscow Treaty limit."[95]

Since the new Treaty aligns only one warhead to each bomber, it no longer matters if the weapons are on the bomber bases or not; it's the bomber that counts not the weapons. Thereby, a base with 22 nuclear tasked B-52 bombers would only count as 22 weapons even though there may be hundreds of weapons on the base. As reaffirmed by Oelrich and Kristenen:

> while the treaty reduces the legal limit for deployed strategic warheads, it doesn't actually reduce the number of warheads. A peculiar counting rule increases the importance of bombers: each bomber counts only as one nuclear bomb although the B-52 can carry 20 nuclear armed cruise missiles and the Russian bombers, for example the Backfire and Blackjack, have similar payloads.[96]

If the New START Treaty counting rule was used in today's context, then the United States' deployment figure would be at 1,650 strategic warheads, not the actual 2,100 warheads, and Russia's deployment figure would be at 1,740 warheads instead of 2,600 warheads. In simple terms, the counting rule would "hide" approximately 450 and 860 warheads, respectively, or 1,310 warheads. As further emphasized by Oelrich and Kristensen:

> the paradox is that with the 'fake' bomber counting rule the United States and Russia could, if they chose to do so, deploy more strategic warheads under the New START Treaty by 2017 than would have been allowed by the Moscow Treaty by 2012.[97]

Indeed, the treaty does not require destruction of a single nuclear warhead and actually permits the United States and Russia to deploy almost the same number of strategic warheads that were permitted by the 2002 Moscow Treaty.[98]

US Ratification Process

Despite the apparent shortcomings, the Obama Administration submitted the New START Treaty to the Senate on May 13, 2010. The Treaty body encompassed the

Treaty text, the Protocol, the Annexes, the Article-by-Article analysis prepared by the Administration, and the 1251 report on future plans and budgets for US nuclear weapons required by Congress. It also included the text of the unilateral statements made by the United States and Russia when they signed the Treaty. The Treaty's approval required a vote of two-thirds of the Senate, or 67 Senators. The Senate Foreign Relations Committee held 12 hearings on the Treaty which began in April 2009, including testimony from former Secretaries of Defense William Perry and James Schlesinger. Overall, the committee received testimony from more than 20 witnesses from within and outside of the Obama Administration.[99] Additionally, it received statements from senior officials from the State Department, the Defense Department, the Department of Energy, and several former officials from past Administrations. The committee concluded its hearing process in mid-July, after receiving a National Intelligence Estimate on the future of Russian forces and a report on the verifiability of the treaty. The Senate Armed Services Committee held a total of eight hearings and briefings on the Treaty. On June 17, 2010, the Armed Services Committee heard testimony from Secretary of State Clinton, Secretary of Defense Gates, Secretary of Energy Chu, and Admiral Mullen, Administration officials and experts from outside the government. In addition, the Intelligence Committee held a closed hearing to discuss US monitoring capabilities and the verifiability of the Treaty.[100]

The Senate Foreign Relations Committee conducted talks to mark up the Resolution of Ratification for New START on September 16, 2010.[101] It began its discussion with a draft put forward by Senator Lugar and addressed a number of amendments proposed by members of the committee. The proposed amendments and the Lugar draft placated the members' concerns with US missile defense programs, US conventional prompt global strike capabilities, monitoring and verification, and Russian non-strategic nuclear weapons. While most of these amendments were defeated, the committee did modify and incorporate some into the resolution.[102] The Senate Foreign Relations Committee approved the Resolution of Ratification by a vote of 14–4 and sent the resolution to the full Senate. The Senate did not have time to address the Treaty before the November elections, however, the Administration pressed the Senate to debate the Treaty during the lame-duck session of Congress in December 2010. On December 22, 2010, the Senate gave final approval to the New START arms control Treaty with Russia. Senator John Kerry, the Massachusetts Democrat who led the floor debate over the Treaty, argued that the vote will shift the world away from the risk of nuclear disaster. "The winners are not defined by party or ideology," he said. "The winners are the American people, who are safer with fewer Russian missiles aimed at them."[103] Arms control advocates also welcomed the Senate vote. Richard Burt, head of an anti-nuclear advocacy group called Global Zero, described the vote as being "imperative for national security" and "will strengthen US Russian relations,"[104] while Daryl G. Kimball, executive director of the Arms Control Association, called the vote "remarkable in this time of hyper-partisanship," but still called on the Obama administration to move to bring down nuclear stockpiles further.[105]

Arms Control after New START

Despite the optimistic words of Kerry, Kimball, and Burt, many analysts hoped the New START Treaty would cut more deeply into US and Russian forces, reducing them to perhaps 1,000 warheads on each side. Others objected to the format because the Presidents agreed the new Treaty would not contain limits on non-strategic nuclear weapons or non-deployed nuclear warheads. Nonetheless, the New START Treaty was considered by many commentators as an important development in restarting relations with Russia, particularly given the nuclear assertion posited by the previous Administration. In terms of extending and updating the important verification regime, the document created a platform for transparency and confidence building. Additionally, the Treaty will also assist in strengthening the international non-proliferation regime and efforts to prevent other countries from developing nuclear weapons. Still, it has to be noted that the United States and Russia must be careful not to overemphasize the Treaty as creating defining reductions in nuclear arsenals and strategic delivery systems.[106] Although the Treaty reduced the limit, the achievement was undermined by a new counting rule that enables both states to deploy as many strategic warheads as under the Moscow Treaty. In essence, the New START Treaty was not so much a nuclear *reductions* treaty as it was a *verification* and *confidence building* treaty; a ballistic missile focused treaty that in essence removed strategic bombers from arms control.

As the document protected current force structures—rather than reducing them—it will inevitably engender increased attention to the large inventories of non-deployed weapons that both states retain. Whereas the US force structure is large enough to enable uploading of substantial numbers of reserve warheads, the Russian force is too small to provide a substantial upload capacity. Even with a significant production of new missiles, it is likely that Russia's entire Triad will drop to around 400 delivery vehicles by 2017—fewer than the United States has today in its ICBM arm alone. While there were those US critics who bemoaned that the United States' nuclear deterrent was dilapidating under New START, there were those who argued that the nuclear option had all but remained intact.[107] In the words of one senior White House official, the United States came away as a "clean winner" in retaining its option, echoing the sentiments espoused by candidate Obama during his election campaign of 2008. Indeed, while he supported the goal of working to eliminate all nuclear weapons, he also emphasized that "America will not disarm unilaterally" and that "as long as nuclear weapons exist, I will retain a strong, safe, secure, and reliable nuclear deterrent."[108]

2010 NPT Review Conference

Since the Prague speech, the Obama Administration has been consistent in linking its nuclear weapon position to the disarmament and non-proliferation commitments under the NPT Treaty; and that progress on arms control is "a means of strengthening our ability to mobilize broad international support for the measures needed to reinforce the non-proliferation regime and secure materials worldwide."[109] Entering into force in 1970 and extended indefinitely in 1995, the nuclear Non-Proliferation Treaty[110] can be deemed as the cornerstone of the nuclear non-proliferation regime.[111] The NPT is supported by International Atomic Energy Agency (IAEA) safeguards, national export control laws, coordinated export control policies under the Nuclear Suppliers Group (NSG), UN Security Council resolutions, and various other initiatives. The NPT recognizes five nations (the United States, Russia, France, Britain, and China) as nuclear-weapon states,[112] and 189 countries are parties to the NPT.[113] India, Israel, and Pakistan have never signed the Treaty and possess nuclear weapons. North Korea ratified the NPT but announced its withdrawal in 2003.[114]

Several states, including Argentina, Brazil, and South Africa, suspended their nuclear weapons programs and joined the NPT in the 1990s, while others—Ukraine, Belarus, and Kazakhstan—gave up former Soviet nuclear weapons on their territories and joined the NPT as non-nuclear-weapon states in the 1990s. Iraq and Libya are now in full compliance with the NPT after their respective nuclear weapons programs were dismantled. Iran was found in non-compliance with its IAEA safeguards obligations in 2005 and the matter was referred to the UN Security Council. The IAEA has reported as recently as February 2010 that Syria has not fully cooperated with an investigation into its nuclear activities. There are three key components, or "arteries," of the NPT: nuclear non-proliferation, nuclear disarmament, and the peaceful use of nuclear energy. In exchange for non-nuclear-weapon states (NNWS) pledging not to attain nuclear weapons, they are assured access to the peaceful use of nuclear energy. For their part, the NPT nuclear-weapon states agree to pursue nuclear disarmament and not assist another state in developing nuclear weapons. The IAEA attempts to implement the Treaty in that it is responsible for monitoring the peaceful use of nuclear energy and providing technical assistance to states.[115]

The 2010 Review Conference for the Treaty on the Non-Proliferation of Nuclear Weapons (NPT), held at United Nations Headquarters in New York from May 3 to 28, 2010 was expected to consider a number of issues. These included: universality of the Treaty; nuclear disarmament, including specific practical measures; nuclear non-proliferation, including the promoting and strengthening of safeguards; measures to advance the peaceful use of nuclear energy, safety, and security; regional disarmament and non-proliferation; implementation of the 1995 resolution on the Middle East; measures to address withdrawal from the Treaty; measures to further strengthen the review process; and ways to promote engagement with civil society in strengthening NPT norms and in promoting disarmament education.[116] Many analysts viewed the Conference as a significant test of the feasibility of the Treaty and how it would evolve to meet current and new challenges. In its declaratory policy and strategy documents, the Obama Administration has emphasized the NPT as the "centerpiece" of the non-proliferation regime and has pledged to strengthen the Treaty. As such, US officials emphasized that the primary objective for the Review

Conference was to "strengthen all three pillars" of the NPT.[117] For Susan Burk, the US ambassador to the NPT Review Conference, US priorities for the gathering included addressing cases of non-compliance, preventing abuse of the NPT's withdrawal provisions, garnering additional resources for the IAEA and broader adherence to the Additional Protocol, and improving IAEA safeguards. Regarding the importance of a final conference document, she said that "it would be very positive if we could agree on a statement, a forward-looking statement … [b]ut success can be defined in other ways as well."[118]

Additionally, Obama Administration officials emphasized the strengthening of the non-proliferation regime as a responsibility for non-nuclear-weapon states as well as nuclear weapon states,[119] and would include treating cases of non-compliance "honestly and seriously."[120] As Burk further stated, a significant US objective was that Review Conference discussions give "valuable momentum" to efforts of the IAEA, the United Nations, and the Conference on Disarmament to strengthen the non-proliferation regime.[121] US Secretary of State Hillary Clinton described the conference as a call "to strengthen a global non-proliferation regime … and focus on promoting practical solutions, not pursuing unrealistic agendas," adding that "[n]ow is the time to build consensus, not to block it."[122] She announced that the Obama Administration would seek Senate approval of the Protocols to the nuclear-weapon-free zones in Africa and the South Pacific, and announced a US pledge of $50 million to launch an IAEA Peaceful Uses Initiative. Aside from highlighting the US record on nuclear disarmament—including the size of the US nuclear arsenal[123] and the number of weapons it had dismantled since 1991—Clinton's opening speech included reference to the Nuclear Posture Review, the New START Treaty, and reductions in the US nuclear weapon stockpile:

> Our new START Treaty with Russia will limit the number of strategic nuclear weapons deployed by our countries to levels not seen since the 1950s. This agreement is consistent with the Secretary General's call to pursue nuclear disarmament through agreement on a framework of separate, mutually reinforcing instruments.… Our Nuclear Posture Review ruled out the development of new US nuclear weapons and new missions and capabilities for our existing weapons. It also stated we will not use nuclear weapons against non-nuclear-weapons states that are parties to the NPT and in compliance with their nuclear non-proliferation obligations. We have made a commitment to ratify the Comprehensive Test Ban Treaty, and we are ready—past ready—to start multilateral negotiations on a verifiable Fissile Material Cutoff Treaty.[124]

The Conference concluded with the adoption by consensus of a Final Document that included both a review of commitments and a forward looking action plan for nuclear disarmament, non-proliferation, and the promotion of the peaceful uses of nuclear energy. While the consensus document represented an achievement in comparison to the outcome of the 2005 Review Conference, much of the language in the action plan was watered down from previous versions, leaving it up to the next review in 2015 to see how far these initial steps will take the global community toward fulfilling the Nuclear Non-Proliferation Treaty's goals.[125]

Nonetheless, Obama lauded the agreement as being the "center of our global efforts to stop the spread of nuclear weapons around the world, while pursuing the ultimate goal of a world without them."[126] As he further emphasized, it reaffirms many "aspects of the agenda that I laid out in Prague, and which we have pursued together with other nations over the last year, and underscores that those nations that refuse to abide by their international obligations must be held accountable."[127] Additionally, in her closing statement at the conference on May 28, Under Secretary of State for Arms Control and International Security Ellen Tauscher described the agreement's action plan as "forward-looking and balanced." Along with recognizing steps that the United States and other countries have taken to advance nuclear disarmament, the document encourages "the early entry into force of the Comprehensive Nuclear Test Ban Treaty and the urgent need to get on with long-delayed talks on a fissile material cutoff treaty."[128] Lastly, National Security Advisor, General James L. Jones, "welcomed" agreements reached at the 2010 Non-Proliferation Treaty Review Conference in strengthening the global non-proliferation regime. As stated:

> The final document broadly supports our strategy to strengthen the NPT, which is essential to stopping the spread of nuclear weapons around the world and pursuing the ultimate goal of a world without them. The document includes balanced and practical steps to advance nuclear disarmament, non-proliferation, and peaceful uses of nuclear energy, which are critical pillars of the global non-proliferation regime. In particular, the document calls for measures to strengthen inspections and compliance with the Treaty, which will support our efforts to deal with countries like Iran who are seeking a nuclear weapons capability in violation of their international obligations.[129]

Several states pushed for the inclusion of deadlines in the framework for nuclear disarmament—such as a Nuclear Weapons Convention (NWC)—to be included in the final document.

While reference to this was evident in the review section,[130] the language only "notes" new proposals and initiatives for a nuclear weapon-free world, which was a lesser endorsement than if such proposals and initiatives had been "welcomed."[131] The Final Document also "notes" the UN Secretary-General's Five Point Plan for Nuclear Disarmament that included consideration of negotiating a NWC or "agreement on a framework of separate mutually reinforcing instruments, backed by a strong system of verification," and "affirms that the final phase of the nuclear disarmament process and other related measures should be pursued within an agreed legal framework, which a majority of States parties believe should include specified timelines." Despite the final document stating that "all States parties commit to pursue policies that are fully compatible with the Treaty and the objective of achieving a world without nuclear weapon,"[132] in real terms, the central focus of the NPT—disarmament for non-proliferation and access to peaceful uses of nuclear energy—remains unfulfilled.

Further, the conflict in the Middle East presents an increasingly significant impediment to the Treaty's future effectiveness. Indeed, the indefinite extension of the NPT in 1995 became possible only with the adoption of a resolution on the Middle East. Simply put, without further progress on the Middle East peace process, the non-proliferation regime will continue to be hindered in the future due to unresolved concerns about the slow pace of nuclear disarmament and the problems over the implementation of Article 4 of the NPT and the policies of the Nuclear Suppliers Group (NSG). Moreover, according to Jayantha Dhanapala, the 2010 NPT Review Conference Final Document "deviated from agreed upon policy by continuing with the India nuclear cooperation deal and creating special conditions for the Republic of Korea (ROK)—this, while China supplies reactors to Pakistan."[133] For James Traub, while some inroads were made, the 28-page document contained "no new commitments by the nuclear-weapons states to move toward the abolition of such weapons. Nor did the non-weapons states bind themselves to accept more intrusive inspections of their nuclear facilities. The parties made few other substantive new commitments."[134] As in the cases of both the NPR and New START processes, the achievements at the NPT review Conference were modest at best. This is not to say that the Obama Administration should not be commended in pursuing such efforts, but when measured against the vision of Prague, it appears that when such sentiments meet reality, limitations and compromises are often the result.

The Nuclear Security Summit

Of course, such limitations have not thwarted Obama's apparent enthusiasm on nuclear issues. In a significant landmark editorial posited in the *Wall Street Journal* in early 2008, George Shultz, William Perry, Henry Kissinger, and Sam Nunn urged world leaders to construct a pathway towards a nuclear-free world. They argued that one of the most important steps to be taken along the way was the acceleration of "work to provide the highest possible standards of security for nuclear weapons, as well as for nuclear materials everywhere in the world, to prevent terrorists from acquiring a nuclear bomb."[135] In response to the blueprint, in July 2009, President Obama proposed a summit to challenge world leaders as a means to "discuss steps … to secure loose nuclear materials; combat smuggling; and deter, detect, and disrupt attempts at nuclear terrorism."[136] On April 12–13, 2010, the United States hosted the first Nuclear Security Summit in Washington, DC, bringing together 49 world leaders in an effort to foster cooperation and consensus on one further step toward nuclear zero. According to David Sanger, the Summit was the largest gathering of heads of states called by a United States President since the 1945 United Nations Conference on International Organization.[137] Aside from the US, delegations from 46 governments attended—38 of which were represented by heads of state or government.[138]

Additionally, representatives from the European Union, the International Atomic Energy Agency, and the United Nations also attended.

In again expanding upon the sentiments espoused during the Prague speech, Obama stated the following:

> One year ago in Prague, I called for a new international effort to secure all vulnerable nuclear materials around the world in four years. This is one part of a broader, comprehensive agenda that the United States is pursuing—including reducing our nuclear arsenal and stopping the spread of nuclear weapons—an agenda that will bring us closer to our ultimate goal of a world without nuclear weapons.[139]

The United States government has undertaken work domestically and in partnership with other states to address this issue through several programs at the Departments of Defense, Energy, Homeland Security, and State. The International Atomic Energy Agency has also played a significant role in these efforts, particularly since the 9/11 terrorist attacks. Congressional interest in this issue has been focused on preventing a nuclear terrorist attack against the United States and providing funding for related programs.[140] Specifically, the US has removed HEU (Highly Enriched Uranium) from approximately 50 facilities internationally, while implementing security and accounting upgrades in 210 of an estimated 250 buildings with weapons-usable nuclear materials in Russia and Eurasia. As Matthew Bunn articulated in *Securing the Bomb 2010*, approximately 38 states "either possess nuclear weapons or have HEU or plutonium separated from spent fuel on their soil." Within this group, 18 states have sufficient amounts of fissile material to "require the highest international standards of security," which many do not yet have.[141]

Moreover, the huge stocks of global nuclear materials are maintained using "extremely varied accounting systems and the conditions for storing and protecting them from hijacking or sale to criminal elements are far from reliable."[142] In his opening message of the conference, Obama emphasized the concern posed by such materials:

> Nuclear materials vulnerable to being sold or stolen and fashioned into a nuclear weapon exist in dozens of nations. Just the smallest amount of plutonium—about the size of an apple—could kill and injure hundreds of thousands of innocent people. Terrorist networks such as al Qaeda have tried to acquire the material for a nuclear weapon, and if they ever succeeded, they would surely use it. Were they to do so, it would be a catastrophe for the world—causing extraordinary loss of life, and striking a major blow to global peace and stability.[143]

The summit concluded with a joint statement and a commitment to improve nuclear security standards, share best practices, and emphasized that international action was necessary to prevent an act of nuclear terrorism. As Vice President Biden stated, "we cannot wait for an act of nuclear terrorism before coming together to share best practices and raise security standards, and we will seek firm commitments from our partners to do just that."[144] The summit concentrated on the goal of securing weapons-usable nuclear materials (highly enriched uranium and plutonium), but did not address nuclear weapons security issues specifically. It was argued by some analysts that concentrating on nuclear materials may have been a means in which to attain the participation of states most sensitive to discussing nuclear weapons issues. Radiological material security was also not emphasized, although many nuclear security practices relevant to weapons-usable nuclear materials are also relevant to other nuclear materials, including radiological sources in the civilian fuel cycle.[145]

Despite this, proponents argued that the Nuclear Security Summit provided the platform for ongoing and new efforts to mitigate nuclear material development/transferral, including a Communiqué and an accompanying Work Plan. States attending the Summit agreed in the Communiqué that they would "commit to strengthen nuclear security and reduce the threat of nuclear terrorism" by endorsing Obama's initiative to secure within four years "all vulnerable nuclear material."[146] They also agreed on the need to improve security and accounting for HEU and plutonium, while strengthening regulations pertaining to such materials.[147] Without committing states to adherence to particular conventions or treaties, the Communiqué called for "promoting universality of key international treaties on nuclear security and nuclear terrorism."[148] States also "[reaffirmed] the essential role" of the International Atomic Energy Agency, calling for its ongoing support in implementing nuclear security practices. They also noted that additional radioactive materials (such as cesium and strontium) required similar security measures due to their potential use in dirty bombs.[149]

While there were apparent inroads made at the Obama-driven summit, critics such as Republican Sen. Jon Kyl of Arizona described the summit as failing to achieve progress on what he referred to as the most pressing issue: taking concerted international steps against Iran's efforts to develop a nuclear weapons program. As Kyl stated, "the summit's purported accomplishment is a non-binding communiqué that largely restates current policy and makes no meaningful progress in dealing with nuclear terrorism threats or the ticking clock represented by Iran's nuclear weapons program."[150] Contrary to this, Paul B. Stares argued that "along with the recently signed follow-on START Treaty reducing US and Russian strategic weapons and the findings of the Nuclear Posture Review," the Summit has enabled the Obama Administration to "put itself in a much stronger position to argue for increased international pressure against North Korea and Iran—not to mention other potential proliferators—to relinquish their nuclear ambitions."[151] For Kenneth Luongo, an expert on nuclear security at the Partnership for Global Security, Obama had "put his personal prestige on the line like no other world leader has before on the nuclear issue" and that the commitments were positive. However, he cautioned, "when the lights go down tonight, leaders need to hit the ground running on implementation."[152]

The Comprehensive Nuclear-Test-Ban Treaty (CTBT)

Indeed, one of the biggest tests in Obama's quest to transform vision into implementation pertains to CTBT ratification—particularly in trying to unhinge the staunch approach of his predecessor. The Bush Administration's standpoint on nuclear testing and the CTBT was very clear throughout its tenure in office: it wanted to keep the testing option open. In an unclassified briefing on January 9, 2002, former Assistant Secretary of Defense for International Security Policy, J.D. Crouch, clearly articulated its position. He stated there would be "no change in the Administration's policy at this point on nuclear testing. We continue to oppose CTBT ratification. We also continue to adhere to a testing moratorium." Further, "DOE is planning on accelerating its test-readiness program" to reduce the time needed between a decision to test and the conduct of a test, which was then 24 to 36 months. He also discussed new weapons:[153]

> At this point, there are no recommendations in the report about developing new nuclear weapons … we are trying to look at a number of initiatives. One would be to modify an existing weapon, to give it greater capability against … hard targets and deeply-buried targets. And we're also looking at non-nuclear ways that we might be able to deal with those problems.[154]

Similarly, in a *Washington Post* article on January 10, 2002, White House Press Secretary Ari Fleischer was quoted as saying that the President had not ruled out testing "to make sure the stockpile, particularly as it is reduced, is reliable and safe. So he has not ruled out testing in the future, but there are no plans to do so."[155]

As recently as June 25, 2007, former Secretary of State Condoleezza Rice also emphasized the Administration's position:

> The Administration does not support the Comprehensive Test Ban Treaty and does not intend to seek Senate advice and consent to its ratification. There has been no change in the Administration's policy on this matter. By reducing the likelihood of the need to return to underground nuclear testing, RRW [the Reliable Replacement Warhead] makes it more likely that the United States would be able to continue its voluntary nuclear testing moratorium. We cannot, however, provide guarantees regarding the voluntary moratorium. We may find at some future time that we cannot diagnose or remedy a problem in a warhead critical to the US nuclear deterrent without conducting a nuclear test.[156]

Such sentiments of the Bush Administration concerned many within the international community who viewed US ratification of the CTBT as being the cornerstone of compliance with Article VI. In a report by the international WMD Commission in 2006, it was argued that US ratification of the Treaty "would have more positive ramifications for arms control and disarmament than any other single measure."[157] Likewise, the 2010 International Commission on

Nuclear Non-proliferation and Disarmament Report described US CTBT ratification as being a significant "circuit-breaker" in gaining ratification by other hold-out states.[158] As posited earlier, two of the three pillars of the NPT regime are that the non-nuclear weapon states will forgo nuclear weapons and the nuclear-weapon states will move toward nuclear disarmament. A ban on future nuclear testing is seen as fulfilling both disarmament and non-proliferation goals by thwarting the qualitative development of nuclear weapons in weapons states and preventing new states from testing a nuclear weapon.[159]

NPT states have said in agreement documents at past review conferences that the CTBT is regarded as part of implementing Article VI commitments under the Treaty. One element of the 1995 Review Conference documents was a call for completing negotiations on a CTBT no later than 1996.[160] The latter decision was significant in attaining indefinite extension. The 2000 NPT Review Conference agreed to 13 "practical steps for the systematic and progressive efforts to implement Article VI" of the NPT, the first of which was the "early entry into force" of the CTBT.[161] To date, three of the five NPT nuclear-weapon states (Britain, France, and Russia) have ratified the CTBT, while China and the United States have not. The Senate voted not to give its advice and consent to ratification of the CTBT in 1999, and US policy-makers and analysts continue to debate the merits of ratifying it.

In what was viewed as a distinct shift from his predecessor, President Obama's Prague speech called for a global ban on nuclear testing and that his administration would "aggressively" pursue US ratification of the Comprehensive Nuclear-Test-Ban Treaty.[162] As echoed by Vice President Joseph Biden, "the President has made ratification of the Comprehensive Test Ban Treaty an Administration priority. He has asked me to guide the Administration's effort to gain Senate support for the Treaty."[163] Similarly, Secretary of State Hillary Clinton has stated that the CTBT is "an integral part of our non-proliferation and arms control agenda," and that the United States "will work in the months ahead both to seek the advice and consent of the United States Senate to ratify the Treaty, and to secure ratification by others so that the Treaty can enter into force."[164] While she subsequently participated in the Conference on Facilitating the Entry into Force of the Comprehensive Nuclear-Test-Ban Treaty—after years of the Bush Administration boycotting such events—the lack of follow-through on the President's promise has been considered by some commentators as "striking." This is particularly concerning as CTBT entry into force was viewed as a priority of the NPT members at the 1995 and 2000 review conferences.[165]

Additionally, Vice President Joe Biden's 18 February speech promising a ten percent increase to $7 billion for the budget of the National Nuclear Security Administration's stockpile management programs has been described "as a harbinger of a more specific pursuit effort to attract opponents in the Senate,"[166] while other analysts, such as Jon Medalia have noted that "there have been no hearings on CTBT in the 111th Congress, and it appears unlikely to be brought up in the lame duck session."[167] As always, domestic issues have consumed much of the Administration's time and political capital. In light of those demands and the priority that has been afforded to the ratification of New START, it would appear that the "aggressive" pursuit of CTBT ratification that the President promised in Prague is not going to be easy to attain.[168] This was apparent in a recent report by the bipartisan Congressional Commission on the Strategic Posture of the United States. While the commission supported further, unspecified reductions in US and Russian nuclear arsenals, it was divided on the goal of ratifying the test ban treaty and disagreed on the desirability of seeking a world without nuclear weapons.[169] As stated by William Perry:

> On the Comprehensive Test Ban Treaty, I believe the United States will not be able to assume leadership in the world on non-proliferation if we do not ratify the treaty, but I must say the commission is split by that issue.... About half our members disagree with the goal of ratifying CTBT; and indeed, if the Senate proceeds to hold hearings on that, I suspect some of our members may be testifying on one side of the issue and others will testify on the other side.[170]

Despite such concern, recent comments by Assistant Secretary of State Rose Gottemoeller indicate that Obama's optimism will remain intact, particularly given ratification of New START: "much has changed since the US Senate declined to provide its advice and consent to ratify the Treaty in 1999" and that "the Administration prepares for US Senate reconsideration of the Treaty."[171]

Yet there are huge challenges that must be addressed before the CTBT can be implemented. As in the case with New START, the challenge will be again be ratification. While former Republican secretaries of states George Shultz and Henry Kissinger are among those now favoring ratification, many Republican senators are firmly on record in their opposition. They have raised questions that will have to answered if a future CTBT ratification vote is to attain the support of ten to 15 or more Republican senators—the minimum that likely will be needed not only to ensure passage, which requires a two-thirds majority, but to establish strong bipartisan support for continuing the policy in the future. The main objection to the CTBT pertains to the extent to which it can be verified; the extent to which it enhances the non-proliferation agenda; the extent to which it allows the United States to ensure the long-term reliability of its existing arsenal in a manner that provides robust deterrence; and the extent to which the Treaty is consistent with future US nuclear weapons needs. It is it these objections and concerns that leave Obama's "aggressive" Prague aspirations—relating to CTBT ratification—precariously positioned in its slow, if not, tentative pace. Referring to the attitudes of the American people, Michael O'Hanlon affirms these limitations:

> Tired of incrementalism, the American public has long since lost its real interest in arms control. So has much of the rest of the world. As a result, when accords such as the Comprehensive Test Ban Treaty come up for

Senate ratification, there is little popular engagement and Treaty opponents can carry the day. Only a revolutionary proposal can break this logjam and lead to a true national debate in which obstructionist forces can be challenged and defeated—or so the argument might go.[172]

Closing words on Obama

From 2002 to 2008, the deeper nuclear dimension of the Bush Doctrine was reiterated, refined, accentuated, and guided through the 2002 National Strategy to Combat Weapons of Mass Destruction, the 2002 Nuclear Posture Review, the abandoned 2005 Doctrine for Joint Nuclear Operations, the 2006 Quadrennial Defense Review, the 2006 Strategic Operations Joint Operating Concept Version 2.0 and the Reliable Replacement Warhead program—foreshadowing a new nuclear era in which the once termed "weapon of last resort" became a usable and, according to the Bush Administration, necessary war-fighting device. In contrast, the Obama Administration has placed non-proliferation to the same level in US nuclear policy as the nuclear weapons posture. Moreover, it has emphasized that eventual nuclear disarmament is the central goal for US nuclear weapons policy and has attempted to establish the platform for possible future reductions in the role and numbers of nuclear weapons. However, the extent to which the Obama Administration actually does reduce the role and numbers of nuclear weapons remains to be seen. Some of the reduction options espoused in his NPR—including the amount of warheads that will be retired and the ICBMs, SSBNs, and bombers that will be cut—will only be fully conveyed in the months and years ahead. Indeed, it is here that Obama's nuclear policies—as reflected in the 2010 NPR—can be deemed as a pragmatic policy in its attempt to maintain a strong nuclear arsenal, modest reductions in nuclear weapons, non-proliferation efforts, and a vision of a world free of nuclear weapons.

Additionally, the second and other significant plank in Obama's nuclear policy—New START—while reducing the limit for how many weapons can be deployed on long-range ballistic missiles and heavy bombers, the agreement does not require destruction of a single nuclear warhead. Considering that the United States and Russia possess more than 90 percent of the world's nuclear weapons and will continue to do so when the treaty limit is reached seven years from now, the "changes" can also be viewed as moderate. Moreover, in an effort to ensure Congressional support for New START, 2010 saw the Obama Administration commit itself to significant increases in expenditure on modernizing nuclear weapons and the production complex over the next decade: well over $100 billion for modernization of missiles and bombers, and more than $85 billion for modernizing warheads and production facilities.[173] Such modernization will have to be balanced with the other significant goal of US nuclear policy pertaining to attaining international support for strengthening non-proliferation of nuclear weapons and materials. Demonstrating real intentions to reducing the number and role of nuclear weapons will be crucial to securing support for this agenda. Despite its modest limitations, the approval of the New START Treaty re-establishes a significant on-site inspection regime and potentially opens the way for negotiations on additional reductions in the future.

For many listeners in the Prague audience and beyond, the President's address was a reassuring assertion of US commitment to and leadership in the effort to rid the world of its most devastating weapons. In another part of the speech, however, Obama affirmed that "[w]ords must mean something." The Obama Administration's record thus far in transferring nuclear non-proliferation and disarmament rhetoric into reality has been limited. Despite the assertion that the NPR "will move beyond outdated Cold War thinking," the document is, to some extent, moribund in old postures. Nonetheless, 2010 can be viewed as a year in which Obama pressed forward with a wide array of initiatives, concluding with the ratification of the New START Treaty. Clearly, political factors have affected the president's follow-up on his Prague agenda. Gates' April 6 cover letter for the NPR noted that its implementation "will be the work of multiple administrations and Congresses, and will require sustained bipartisan consensus."[174]

Indeed, despite the New START ratification, a bipartisan consensus on nuclear non-proliferation and disarmament policy will continue to be an obstacle, and Obama will need all his intellect and powers of persuasion to obtain support for the program he outlined.[175] The real question is how successful Obama will be in sustaining his vision and his specific goals in the face of these constraints. While he struck bold rhetorical notes and promises in relation to limiting the role of nuclear weapons, he has stopped short of changing the status quo on critical issues that have lingered since the Cold War—such as tactical nuclear weapons and keeping missiles on alert. Having galvanized international hopes and expectations in which the United States would decisively move away from the Bush strategy to one of nuclear disarmament, the moderate NPR and New START, together with pragmatic developments at the Nuclear Summit, the May NPT Review Conference and Comprehensive Nuclear-Test-Ban Treaty, indicate that the significance of nuclear weapons in US security policy will remain intact. While Obama's nuclear strategy conveyed the marks of his avowed goal to reduce the nuclear danger, the shift away from the legacy of the Cold War arms race has been conservative. Obama's Prague speech "aimed for the mountaintop," but the aforementioned developments in 2010, left the vision of "US nuclear policy in the foothills."[176] Cautious rather than bold, the policies have won relatively strong backing from the leadership at the Pentagon and the military, but at a cost. Both the NPR and New START Treaty have ended up being transitional, rather than transformational. In order to realize fully the promise of a world without nuclear weapons, the Obama Administration has to do more to change outdated Cold War thinking and reduce the US reliance on nuclear weapons.[177] In essence, the Administration has pursued a policy of nuclear balance with steps towards disarmament, accompanied by measures to retain America's nuclear primacy.

Conclusion

The Bush Doctrine was developed incrementally over a span of approximately eight months. Beginning with the 2002 State of the Union address, President George W. Bush laid the foundation for a "newly" proactive strategy of counter-proliferation. In his address, states such as Iraq, Iran, and North Korea, and "their terrorist allies," were identified and defined as an "axis of evil" that was aiming to threaten and undermine the "peace of the world." In their pursuit of weapons of mass destruction, Bush argued that these regimes presented a "grave and growing danger," and that the United States would undertake what it deemed to be necessary as a means to preserve and ensure its security. Bush informed his audience that while time was "not on our side," his Administration would be deliberate and not "wait on events, while dangers gather." In one of his first hints of prevention, Bush stated that he would "not stand as peril draws closer and closer … and permit the world's most dangerous regimes to threaten us with the world's most destructive weapons."[1] Six months later, in a Commencement Speech to the US Military Academy at West Point, Bush elaborated upon the burgeoning national security doctrine, emphasizing the need for a more forward thinking strategy that (again) would not wait for "threats to fully materialize." Maintaining his assertive posture, Bush stated that the United States would "take the battle to the enemy, disrupt his plans, and confront the worst threats before they emerge … security will require … preventive action when necessary—to defend our liberty and to defend our lives."

For Bush and his Administration, the "new" post-9/11 world required a "path of action."[2] The West Point speech expressed such new world concerns in which the spread of chemical, biological, and nuclear weapons, along with ballistic missile technology—enabled "weak states and small groups" to attain a catastrophic power to strike "great nations." Furthermore, he argued, these "enemies" declared a very clear intention and were "seeking these terrible weapons" to "blackmail us, or to harm us, or to harm our friends…. [Thereby] we will oppose them with all our power."[3] Polarizing his description of the ensuing War on Terror conflict, Bush asserted that there could "be no neutrality between justice and cruelty" and that the United States and its allies were in a conflict between "good and evil." Again, emphasizing his Administration's dogmatic course, Bush informed his audience that he had no qualms in "confronting evil and lawless regimes" and was "prepared to lead the world" in this quest.[4]

Finally, in September 2002, the White House released the National Security Strategy of the United States of America—the most comprehensive articulation of the Bush Doctrine—thus officially adopting preventive self-defense as a key element of the US security strategy. Here, Bush further justified the use of preventive war and argued that the biggest threats the United States faced were entities at "the crossroads of radicalism and technology." Bush emphasized that the US must be prepared to stop rogue states and their terrorist clients before they were able to threaten or use WMD against the US and its allies. His depiction of rogue states and terrorists necessitated that the US could no longer solely rely on the "reactive posture" it had utilized in the past. Once again highlighting the "greater the risk of inaction," the Administration made it clear that a "compelling case" for "taking anticipatory action" to defend itself was required. Indeed, as some of the most defining words of his doctrine, Bush argued vehemently that in an era where "uncertainty remains as to the time and place of the enemy's attack—to forestall or prevent such hostile acts by our adversaries, the US, if necessary, will act pre-emptively."[5] In simple terms, the threat must be eliminated before it materialized.

The National Security Strategy was very conscious of its historical context and how this new phase would "harshly judge those who saw this coming danger but failed to act." In this new historical stage, the United States would undertake a strategy of action as a means of defending itself, "the American people, and our interests at home and abroad by identifying and destroying the threat before it reaches our borders."[6] Foreshadowing the creation of the Coalition of the Willing, the Bush Administration specified that it would strive to enlist the support of the international community, however, if there was a requirement to "exercise" its "right of self-defense by acting pre-emptively against such terrorists, to prevent them from doing harm against our people and our country … we will not hesitate to act alone."[7] Implicit in this strategy was a very important linkage: the declared enemy was not only terrorists but also anyone, including states, who aided them. Bush articulated this point on the night of 9/11: "We will make no distinction between the terrorists who committed these acts and those who harbor them."[8]

In contrast to the Cold War period of deterrence, the National Security Strategy of 2002 put forward what it deemed to be necessary in "today's" environment. During the Cold War, the document argued, deterrence was an effective form of defense. However, in the post-Cold War world the threat of retaliation was "far less likely to work against leaders of rogue states more willing to take risks, gambling with the lives of their people, and the wealth of their nations."[9] Indeed, during the Cold War, weapons of mass destruction were considered weapons of last resort whose use risked the destruction of those who used them. In the post-Cold War period, rogue actors viewed such weapons of mass destruction as weapons of choice: tools of intimidation and military aggression against their neighbors. Moreover, such actors saw these weapons as the best way of overcoming the conventional superiority of the United States.[10] For Bush's National Security Strategy of 2002, the threat confronting the US in the twenty-first century was the evolving nexus of transnational terrorism and WMD proliferation. It was this combination that engendered "new deadly challenges" from rogue states and terrorists whose nature and motivations, determination to obtain destructive powers hitherto available only to the world's strongest states, and the "greater likelihood that they will use weapons of mass destruction against us," that made the post-9/11 security environment "more complex and dangerous."[11] It was with this in mind that the Administration believed that notions of employing traditional concepts of deterrence would no longer be effective against a terrorist enemy whose avowed tactics were "wanton destruction and the targeting of innocents; whose so-called soldiers seek martyrdom in death and whose most potent protection is statelessness."[12]

The Bush Doctrine argued that states that sponsored terror and those that pursued WMD would compel the United States into preventive action. Interchanging the term preventive with the more "acceptable" term of pre-emption, Bush made it clear that "the United States had long maintained the option of pre-emptive actions to counter a sufficient threat to our national security."[13] Or in other words, the US had long reserved the right to take pre-emptive action in the face of an imminent security threat. However, it was "necessary" to adapt the concept of imminent threat to a new era of security circumstances—where the determination of rogue states and terrorists to use weapons of mass destruction in attacks aimed at the US had become very much apparent. While Bush was adamant that an adjustment to imminence was necessary, the concept itself can be considered a temporal, not a consequential condition. That is, the consequences of a rogue state or terrorist nuclear attack may be of critical—indeed, decisive—importance in the overall assessment of emerging threats, and may in the future provide the basis for permitting some form of anticipatory self-defense. But it is irrelevant to the temporal appreciation of that threat and should not be folded into the concept of imminence.[14] Whether a single rifle shot or a massive nuclear attack, an imminent threat is just that—one that is "instant, overwhelming, leaving no choice of means, and no moment for deliberation."[15] Bush's extended understanding of imminent threat connected logically to a consideration of "pre-emption" (or preventive war) as a strategic option in confronting that threat. The Bush Doctrine hastened to add that "pre-emption" would not necessarily be the first or the only option considered when confronting these threats. Nor, it warned, should other states use this option as a pretext for aggression. But henceforth, it insisted, the US retained the option of acting pre-emptively when the cause was just—in other words, pre-emption if necessary, but not necessarily pre-emption. As articulated, to forestall or impede such hostile acts by "our adversaries," the United States would be prepared to "act pre-emptively (preventively).... To support pre-emptive actions (preventive war), it will ... continue to transform its military forces (assert the nuclear option)."[16]

It was the above philosophy, rhetoric, ideology and security strategy of the Bush Administration's National Security Strategy of 2002 that provoked vigorous debate in the United States and abroad. Indeed, many argued that the Bush Doctrine symbolized a total break with American tradition in which the United States had undertaken a more cautious and defensive policy; a policy that was defined by the core arteries of containment and deterrence; a policy that advocated respect for legal norms and for the sovereign rights of other states.[17] It was argued that the United States had a history of refraining from the use of force until it or one of its allies had been attacked, and that the Bush Administration had dispelled this tradition and was now undertaking a far more assertive policy. As the Bush Administration articulated its National Security Strategy to both domestic and international audiences, the cessation of debate over United Nations action and Congressional approval for intervention in Iraq presented legitimating issues for these national and international institutions struggling to address security issues in an era of globalization. In the United States, an anti-terrorist narrative dominated post-9/11 security discourse and shifted the presumption against the acceptance of the Cold War analytical structures that had dominated foreign policy. Citizens and states opposed to US military action against Iraq invariably articulated their opposition through a narrative warning of the perils of US global hegemony. Conversely, advocates of Bush's policy in the US alluded to the inevitability of future security threats if the United States and a "willing coalition" failed to take preventive action against the state of Iraq. The Bush Administration, as well as international counterparts, all faced the common predicament of how to construct and reposition their arguments amid a frenzied global media environment, while fulfilling the challenging demands of creating a foreign policy rhetoric that addressed the dispositions of their national audiences.

The Bush Administration's arguments for redefining the United States' global security strategy depended on the shared premise that 9/11 engendered a new security environment. The National Security Strategy of 2002 explicitly presented rhetoric that worked to reinforce the threats presented by terrorism. The document defined the War on Terror, the nature of the enemy, and in detail, how "the United States of America" was "fighting a war against terrorists of a global reach.… The enemy (was) terrorism—premeditated, politically motivated violence perpetrated against innocents."[18] Consistent with Bush's post-September 11 public rhetoric was the emphasis of the "new war," presented and dramatized in the National Security Strategy of 2002 as a global security struggle that would be different from previous national struggles. Indeed, the document clearly identified how in the post-9/11 order the United States would champion aspirations for human dignity and "oppose those who resist it."[19] When looking at the rhetoric, philosophy, and security strategy espoused in the National Security Strategy it is not surprising that it came to dominate American political discourse from 2002 to 2004 as political leaders, academic scholars, and the general public debated the implications of this broad and contentious initiative. Whereas its proponents contended that an urgent and unprecedented threat revolution was well under way which required new and proactive approaches to using force, critics of the Bush Doctrine viewed its espousal of preventive war as a means to combat the expansion of WMD as further testimony to American unilateralism, and perhaps most importantly, a fundamental and unnecessary departure from the strategies of deterrence and containment.[20] Their political inclinations notwithstanding, both sides agreed that the Bush Doctrine was something entirely "new," "candid," "bold," and "revolutionary," a radical doctrine the likes of which the world had never seen and perhaps the most defining readjustment of US strategic thinking since the end of World War II.

However, as this book has conveyed, despite the recurrent depiction of being drastically "new" or "revolutionary," the Bush Doctrine in terms of counter-proliferation and preventive war advocacy was not the era-defining arrival that many at the time portended. In fact, as has been presented, such deliberations were very much implicit in previous US Administrations, in the context of both their National Security Strategy releases and preventive war considerations extending back to the end of World War II. However, if notions of assertive counter-proliferation and preventive war considerations were neither new nor groundbreaking, then what *was* defining about the Bush Doctrine? In simple terms, and as the second assertion of this book now documented, the "doctrine" attempted to position the nuclear option back to the fore; a defining policy that punctuated, updated, refined, and reaffirmed its core nuclear endorsement through the unclassified and classified documents it spawned.

Chapter One investigated the most controversial aspect of the National Security Strategy: its official adoption of "anticipatory self-defense" as a key element of the US security strategy, in which the United States was prepared to "act against such emerging threats before they are fully formed."[21] Simply put, the Administration's advocacy of "pre-emption" or, in reality, preventive war. The chapter established and perhaps even resolved some of the debates associated with the meanings and definitions pertaining to pre-emption and prevention. By confirming the core meanings and disparities associated between these two "strategic concepts," a clearly defined analysis was able to be undertaken in latter chapters in which the researcher was able to assess the extent to which preventive war had long been a deep and implicit consideration in US security strategy. It was evident that what Bush himself was advocating during the period after 9/11 (2001), the release of the National Security Strategy (September 2002), through to the Iraq War (March 2003), was the serious consideration, endorsement, and, ultimately, use of preventive war against those actors deemed to be a major threat to the United States' security and well-being. The chapter also investigated the extent to which such definitions and interpretations of pre-emption and prevention during this period challenged and transcended every facet of international relations and US security policy—within the context of history, doctrine, international law, and use within a Presidential rhetorical framework.

Having established the meanings and definitions associated with pre-emption and prevention; and the extent to which preventive war was considered a viable option, *Chapter Two* investigated the Bush Administration's task of "choosing" a state in which it would undertake the preventive war strategy. It was clear that from 2001 to 2003, Iraq, Iran, and North Korea were all perceived by the US to be "grave and gathering threats"—and were all considered rogue proliferators. It was also clear that the US was determined to act preventively against at least one of them. Although many arguments have been proposed to account for the US decision to attack Iraq rather than Iran or North Korea, given the varying similarities between them—it appeared that one of the major palatable differences between the three threatening states at the time was their relative military strength and relative military capabilities. However, even though Iraq may have been deemed as the weaker of the three states in the eyes of the Bush Administration, it was still perceived as being a dangerous "rogue proliferator." Regardless of some of the varying considerations posited in the chapter, it was clear that Bush and his Administration chose Iraq because it argued that it allegedly had WMDs, had supposed links to al Qaeda, and posed an extensive threat to the United States' security, but, more importantly, it had assessed the probability of a successful preventive war against Iraq as being fairly high based primarily upon practical considerations.

As posited, indications that the Bush Administration was considering a counter-proliferation strategy of preventive war were foreshadowed in statements made well before the publication of the National Security Strategy of 2002. Beginning with a speech given at the Citadel on September 23, 1999, through to the more defining words spoken at the State of the Union and West Point graduation ceremony of 2002—and formalized with the release of the document itself in September of the same year—the justification and emphasis of prevention and "action" was made abundantly clear. But also coinciding with such developments was a drive to link such notions of preventive war to the state of Iraq—deemed as the "rogue proliferator" of choice. Once the preventive doctrine had been made public in the National Security Strategy of 2002, Bush was both forthright and consistent in his quest to sway the American public of the "threat" that Saddam Hussein posed and of the possible ramifications should he acquire nuclear weapons—an attack similar to, but potentially more devastating than the events of 9/11. In terms of the "choice" of Iraq, the cultivation of the preventive war doctrine (rhetorically and formally in the context of the National Security Strategy of 2002), the alignment of the preventive war option to Iraq, as well as the orchestration and lead up to the preventive war itself—it appears that the Bush Doctrine could be deemed overzealous, extreme, and unprecedented. However, despite such appearances of a radically new approach, at its core, the Bush Doctrine's push for preventive war in Iraq in 2003 had long pervaded the strategic thought of policy-makers, officials, and military planners at the highest levels of the US government.

Indeed, as *Chapter Three* argued, since the dawning of the nuclear era in 1945, at least three other US Presidents (Dwight D. Eisenhower, Lyndon B. Johnson, and William J. Clinton) have faced the potential threat of nuclear technology in the hands of states hostile to their respective Administrations and each dealt with the same decision problem faced by President Bush in 2003: whether to use preventive military force as a means to counter the proliferation of such nuclear weapons technology. Each was forced to make their decision regarding the preventive use of force in the face of uncertainty. Each had to weigh the costs—many of them unknown—of preventively striking an adversarial state perceived to be developing nuclear weapons against the costs of refraining from preventive intervention and employing more conservative diplomatic methods, even while the threat of future military conflict hovered. The historical record of the last half century is replete with examples of high-level US decision-makers who seriously considered the undertaking of major unilateral preventive military actions as a means to thwart the proliferation of nuclear weapons by rogue states. Prior to the invasion of Iraq in 2003, the US had considered waging preventive war against no less than three additional rogue proliferators—the Union of Soviet Socialist Republics (Soviet Union) from 1945 to 1954; the People's Republic of China (China) from 1960 to 1964; and the Democratic People's Republic of North Korea (North Korea) from 1993 to 1994. By appraising these examples, it became clearly evident that several US Administrations had considered executing preventive war against their respective adversaries at the time, only to be inhibited in most instances by practical factors—and that what Bush himself advocated in 2003, was not new, radical, and certainly not revolutionary. It was clear that the Bush policy certainly qualified as a preventive war policy, however, the adoption of that strategy of prevention did not mark a total break with American tradition or earlier Administrations. As affirmed by Trachtenberg, when looking at various Administrations in the post-World War II era, it turns out that the "sort of [preventive] thinking" that one finds in the Bush policy documents, should "not to be viewed as anomalous. Under Roosevelt and Truman, under Eisenhower and Kennedy, and even under Clinton in the 1990s, this kind of thinking came into play in a major way."[22]

If the earlier chapters of this book dispelled arguments pertaining to the supposed "revolutionary," "new," or "radical" nature of the Bush Doctrine—based on comparisons with previous Administrations' penchant for prevention—it was apparent that what was "new" or "bold" about the Bush Administration's National Security Strategy of 2002 was its willingness to embrace "innovation within the armed forces ... experimentation with new approaches to warfare ... exploiting US intelligence advantages, and taking full advantage of science and technology"[23]—to the extent of reinvigorating a nuclear option which could ultimately be used in the context of prevention. While the motivation and consideration of preventive war has been an integral part of US policy-makers strategic thought since 1945, and while it can be argued that the preventive actions of the Bush Doctrine stalled in Iraq, the nuclear dimension encompassed in the Doctrine can be viewed as the truly "bold" assertion. Simply put, the prevention motivation embodied in the Bush Doctrine was not new, but the reinvigoration of the new nuclear option was. In its punctuating and reaffirming policy instruments (released through the period 2002–2008), Bush furthered the process towards increasing the role of nuclear weapons in US policy and security strategy. Indeed, the Bush documents and policy instruments signified a renewed role for nuclear weapons and the quest of his Administration to upgrade US offensive forces, deploy missile defenses, reconfigure communications and satellite systems, and overall, revitalize the nuclear complex.

However, to look at this development as purely a Bush Administration initiative would be both historically inaccurate and selective. As signified in *Chapter*

Four, it was evident that the Clinton Administration retained much of the existing US nuclear weapons policy and force posture in the decade after the demise of the Soviet Union and affirmed the role of nuclear weapons in US security strategy. Furthermore, the Clinton Administration flirted with targeting options for the use of nuclear weapons in response to chemical or biological attacks from states other than Russia, and in its declaratory policy, did not rule out the possible first use of nuclear weapons in extreme circumstances. It was here that military planners and policy-makers—through the Defense Counter-Proliferation Initiative (CPI) 1993, Nuclear Posture Review (NPR) 1994, Doctrine for joint Operations (Joint Pub 3-12) 1993/1995, Doctrine for Joint Theater Nuclear Operations 1996, Quadrennial Defense Review (QDR) 1997 and Presidential Decision Directive (PDD) 60 1997—maintained the significance of nuclear weapons despite the Soviet Union's demise. But as is revealed in *Chapter Five*, it was the Bush Doctrine and its accompanying guidance documents that amplified the Clinton "base," foreshadowing a new nuclear era in which the once-termed "weapon of last resort" became a usable and, according to the Bush Administration, necessary preventive war-fighting option. It is with this in mind that the National Security Strategy cannot be moribund to 2002 perceptions, but a document that must be viewed as a dangerous catalyst; a document that punctuated, updated, refined, and reaffirmed its core sentiments through the unclassified and classified documents it spawned. It cultivated and defined the resurgent role of nuclear weapons and the Bush Administration's push to modernize US offensive forces and the broader nuclear military complex.

In 1990, as the Cold War was coming to a close and the Soviet Union was entering its final year, the United States had more than 12,000 nuclear warheads deployed on 1,875 strategic nuclear delivery vehicles.[24] After completing the 2002 Nuclear Posture Review, the Bush Administration indicated that the United States would reduce its forces to 2,200 operationally deployed warheads, the number and concept codified in the Moscow Treaty, but it did not identify the specific combination of delivery vehicles or warhead loadings that the United States would maintain to reach the specified number. Subsequent Pentagon studies, including the Strategic Capabilities Assessment in 2005 and the 2006 Quadrennial Defense Review, offered further guidance on strategic nuclear force structure. As of January 1, 2009, according to the counting rules in the Strategic Arms Reduction Treaty (START), the United States had reduced this to 5,576 nuclear warheads on 1,198 strategic nuclear delivery vehicles.[25] In addition, according to the State Department, the United States reduced its number of operationally deployed warheads, a number that excluded many warheads that count under START, to 2,871 as of the end of December 2007.[26] While these figures do not count the same categories of nuclear weapons, they signify that the number of deployed warheads on US strategic nuclear forces has declined significantly in the two decades following the end of the Cold War. Yet, despite such figures, it is evident that nuclear weapons will remain important in the US national security strategy posture.[27] While the United States continued to reduce its deployed forces to meet the mandates of the Moscow Treaty, it is also likely to continue to pursue programs as a means to modernize and adjust its strategic forces. During the 2008 election campaign, then candidate Obama stated that he supported the goal of working to eliminate all nuclear weapons, but he also stated that "America will not disarm unilaterally," and that "as long as nuclear weapons exist, I will retain a strong, safe, secure, and reliable nuclear deterrent."[28] Indeed, despite Obama's nuclear reduction intentions, it is apparent that the significance of nuclear weapons in US security policy will continue as other replacement warheads and nuclear options emerge in the future under other names.

As discussed in *Chapter Six,* while Obama has posited bold words and promises in relation to limiting the role of nuclear weapons, he has stopped short of changing the status quo on critical issues that have lingered since the Cold War—such as tactical nuclear weapons and keeping missiles on alert. Having galvanized international hopes and expectations in which the United States would decisively move away from the Bush strategy to one of nuclear disarmament, the moderate NPR and New START, together with pragmatic developments at the Nuclear Summit, the May NPT Review Conference and Comprehensive Test Ban Treaty, indicate that the significance of nuclear weapons in US security policy will remain intact. In essence, the Obama Administration has pursued a policy of nuclear balance with steps towards disarmament, accompanied by measures to retain America's nuclear primacy—a primacy that the Bush Doctrine amplified, asserted, and revitalized through its guidance documents—the 2002 Nuclear Posture Review (NPR), the 2002 National Strategy to Combat Weapons of Mass Destruction (NSCWMD), CONPLAN (Concept Plan) 8022 (Global Strike), the 2005 Doctrine for Joint Nuclear Operations, the 2006 Quadrennial Defense Review, the 2006 Strategic Operations Joint Operating Concept Version 2.0, and Reliable Replacement Warhead (RRW).

It was the National Security Strategy of 2002/Bush Doctrine and aforementioned "editing documents" that revealed the significant contradiction between the Bush Administration's public rhetoric about reducing the role of nuclear weapons and the guidance issued to nuclear planners. Although the overall number of warheads was reduced, the doctrine guiding planning for the remaining arsenal reaffirmed an assertive posture with nuclear forces on high alert, ready to be used in an increasing number of strike scenarios against adversaries anywhere—even preventively. It was the National Security Strategy that provided the platform for the "quiet revolution" in US nuclear strategy undertaken by the Bush Administration during the period 2002–2008. Indeed, it was this deeper policy within the Bush Doctrine that foreshadowed a new nuclear era in which the Administration pursued a path of retaining and upgrading its enormous strategic arsenal as a means to defeat any adversary. It was a "radical" option that placed nuclear weapons back to the fore; "a strategy" that endorsed "repeated regime change … a steadily modernizing nuclear arsenal" and "a determination to retain deployed nuclear weapons forever."[29]

Notes

Introduction

1 Dan Balz and Robert U. Woodward, "America's Chaotic Road to War: Bush's Global Strategy Began to Take Shape in First Frantic Hours After Attack," *The Washington Post*, January 27, 2002.
2 George W. Bush, speech given at Washington National Cathedral for victims of terrorism, recorded by the Federal News, published in "After the Attacks," *New York Times*, September 15, 2001.
3 George W. Bush, Address to a Joint Session of Congress and the American People, September 20, 2001, available at www.whitehouse.gov.
4 Mark G. Mantho, "The Bush Doctrine: Origins, Evolution, Alternatives," Cambridge, MA: Guest Publication, The Project on Defense Alternatives, Commonwealth Institute, April 2004, p. 3.
5 *The National Security Strategy* is a document issued at various intervals by the Executive branch of the government of the United States for Congress. It illustrates and defines the major national security priorities of the United States of America and how the Administration of the day will undertake and execute such priorities in accordance to what it deems to be its national interest objectives. The legal structure for the National Security Strategy is defined in the Goldwater-Nichols Act. The document is intentionally broad in content and depends on elaborating the guidance provided in supporting documents. In specific relation to this book: *The National Security Strategy of the United States of America* of 2002 was a 36-page policy document (including cover and introduction) released by the White House. The nine-chapter document began with a different quote taken from a series of post-September 11 speeches given at West Point; the National Cathedral in Washington, DC; Berlin, Germany; Monterrey, Mexico; the Inter-American Development Bank, Washington, DC; and a Joint Session of Congress, Washington. *The National Security Strategy* began with an "Overview of America's International Security Strategy" (Chapter 1) and from there moved into the following: Chapter 2: "Champion Aspirations for Human Dignity;" Chapter 3: "Strengthen Alliances to Defeat Global Terrorism and Work to Prevent Attacks Against Us and Our Friends;" Chapter 4: "Work with Others to Defuse Regional Conflicts;" Chapter 5: "Prevent our Enemies from Threatening us, our allies, and our friends, with Weapons of Mass Destruction;" Chapter 6: "Ignite a New Era of Global Economic Growth through Free Markets and Free Trade;" Chapter 7: "Expand the Circle of Development by Opening Societies and Building the Infrastructure of Democracy;" Chapter 8: "Develop Agendas for Cooperative Action with Other Main Centers of Global Power;" and Chapter 9: "Transform America's National Security Institutions to Meet the Challenges and Opportunities of the Twenty-First Century."
6 George W. Bush, *The National Security Strategy of the United States of America*, Washington, DC: The White House, September 2002, p. 2.

7 Brian M. Jenkins, "A Nuclear 9/11?" This commentary appeared on CNN.com on September 11, 2008 and was republished on the RAND Corporation website: www.rand.org/commentary/2008/09/11/CNN.html.
8 Bush, *The National Security Strategy of the United States of America*, 2002, Opening Letter.
9 Ibid.; George W. Bush, *National Strategy to Combat Weapons of Mass Destruction (NSCWMD)*, Washington, DC: The White House, December 2002, p. l.
10 Jeffrey Record, "The Bush Doctrine and the War with Iraq," *Parameters*, 2003, 33, p. 9.
11 John L. Gaddis, "A Grand Strategy of Transformation," *Foreign Policy*, 2002, 133, pp. 50–57.
12 National Resources Defense Council, "Faking Nuclear Restraint, The Bush Administration's Secret Plan For Strengthening US Nuclear Forces," February 13, 2002, available at www.nrdc.org/nuclear/restraint.asp.
13 James Russell and James Wirtz, "A Quiet Revolution: The New Nuclear Triad," *Strategic Insight*, May, 2002, I(3), pp. 1–10.
14 Ibid., p. 29.

1 The Bush Doctrine: Definitions and interpretations of prevention and pre-emption

1 Bush, *The National Security Strategy of the United States of America*, 2002, Opening Letter; Bush, *National Strategy to Combat Weapons of Mass Destruction (NSCWMD)*, p. l.
2 Record, "The Bush Doctrine and the War with Iraq," p. 9.
3 Bush, *The National Security Strategy of the United States of America*, 2002, pp. 13–15.
4 Ibid., p. 15.
5 Ibid.
6 Ibid.
7 Ibid.
8 Ibid., p. 16.
9 Ibid.
10 Ibid., p. 3.
11 James Wirtz and James Russell, "US Policy on Preventive War and Pre-emption," *The Non-proliferation Review*, 2003, Spring, p. 116.
12 Anthony C. Arend, "International Law and the Pre-emptive Use of Force," *The Washington Quarterly*, 2003, 26, p. 91.
13 Jack S. Levy, "Declining Power and the Preventive Motivation for War," *World Politics*, 1987, 40, pp. 90–91.
14 Richard N. Lebow, "Windows of Opportunity: Do States Jump Through Them?" *International Security*, 1984, 9, p. 147.
15 Levy, "Declining Power and the Preventive Motivation for War," p. 91.
16 Thucydides, *The History of the Peloponnesian War*, New York: Penguin, 1972, p. 49.
17 François Heisbourg, "A Work in Progress: The Bush Doctrine and Its Consequences," *The Washington Quarterly*, 2003, 76, p. 78.
18 Robert Jervis, "Understanding the Bush Doctrine," *Political Science Quarterly*, 2003, 118, p. 370.
19 Victor D. Cha, "Hawk Engagement and Preventive Defense on the Korean Peninsula," *International Security*, 2002, 27, p. 48.
20 Colin S. Gray, *The Implications of Pre-emptive and Preventive War Doctrines: A Reconsideration*, Pennsylvania: Strategic Studies Institute Publications, 2007, pp. vii, xi.
21 Ibid.
22 Ibid., p. 13.

23 Recall George Friedman and Meredith Lebard, *The Coming War with Japan*, New York: St. Martin's Press, 1991; Richard Bernstein and Ross H. Munro, *The Coming Conflict with China*, New York: Alfred A. Knopf, 1997; Colin S. Gray, "The Quadrennial Defense Review (QDR), 2006, and the Perils of the 21st Century," *Comparative Strategy*, April-June 2006, 25(2), pp. 141–148.
24 Joseph Cirincione, Jessica T. Mathews, George Perkovich, and Alexis Orton, *WMD in Iraq: Evidence and Implications*, Washington: Carnegie Endowment for International Peace, 2004, p. 60.
25 Bush, *The National Security Strategy of the United States of America,* 2002, p. 15.
26 Glenn Frankel, "New US Doctrine Worries Europeans," *The Washington Post*, 30 September 2002, I(A) and 15(A).
27 John Steinbruner, "Confusing Ends and Means: The Doctrine of Coercive Preemption," *Arms Control Today*, January/February, 2003.
28 Michael O'Hanlon, Susan E. Rice, and James B. Sterling, "The New National Security Strategy and Pre-emption," Policy Brief #113, The Brookings Institution, December 2002.
29 Ibid., p. 7.
30 Jason D. Ellis and Geoffrey D. Kiefer, *Combating Proliferation: Strategic Intelligence and National Policy*, Baltimore, MD: Johns Hopkins University Press, 2004, p. 203.
31 Ibid.
32 This definition follows the work of Jack Levy who has written extensively about the preventive motivation in Levy, "Declining Power and the Preventive Motivation for War," pp. 90–92.
33 Levy, "Declining Power and the Preventive Motivation for War," p. 82.
34 Ibid., p. 84.
35 Ibid., p. 93.
36 Ibid., p. 94.
37 Randall L. Schweller, "Domestic Structure and Preventive War: Are Democracies More Pacific?" *World Politics*, January 1992, 44(2), pp. 235–269.
38 Lebow, "Windows of Opportunity," p. 155.
39 Chaim Kaufman, "Threat Inflation and the Failure of the Marketplace of Ideas: The Selling of the Iraq War," *International Security*, 2004, 29, p. 8.
40 Galia Press-Barnathan, "The War Against Iraq and International Order: From Bull to Bush," *International Studies Review*, 2004, 6(2), p. 204.
41 Levy, "Declining Power and the Preventive Motivation for War," p. 101.
42 Marc Trachtenberg, "Preventive War and US Foreign Policy," *Security Studies* January-March, 2007, 16(1), p. 1.
43 George W. Bush, Graduation Speech at West Point, June 1, 2002, available at www.whitehouse.gov/news/releases/2002/06/orint/20020601-3.html; Vice President Richard B. Cheney, "Vice President Speaks at VFW 103rd National Convention." The White House Archives, August 26, 2002, available at http://georgewbush-whitehouse.archives.gov/news/releases/2002/08/20020826.html; Bush, *The National Security Strategy of the United States of America,* 2002, Introduction.
44 Robert W. Tucker, *The Just War: A Study in Contemporary Doctrine*, Baltimore: John Hopkins University, 1960, p. 11.
45 Ibid., p. 12. Also, Tucker describes this history stretching from the 1932 Sino-Japanese crises to the United States action in 1956 to condemning the force exerted by Great Britain, France, and Israel against Egypt.
46 Richard Harries, "This War would not be a Just War," *The Observer*, August, 2002, p. 25, reprinted in *The Guardian*, available at www.guardian.co.uk/world/2002/aug/04/iraq.
47 Bush, *The National Security Strategy of the United States of America*, 2002, p. 15.
48 Neta C. Crawford, "Wrong War, Any Time," *Newsday*, March 16, 2003, p. A26.

49 Alberico Gentili, *De Jure Belli Libri Tres*, trans. by John C. Rolfe, Buffalo: William S. Hein, 1995 (1612), p. 66.
50 Ibid., p. 62.
51 Ibid., p. 66.
52 Hugo Grotius, *De Jure Belli Ac Pacis Libri Tres*, trans. by Francis W. Kelsey, Buffalo: William S. Hein, 1995 (1625), p. 173.
53 Ibid., pp. 174–175.
54 Emerich de Vattel, *Le Droit des gens, ou principes de la loi naturelle, appliqés à la conduite et aux affaires des nations et des souverains*, trans. by Charles G. Fenwick, Buffalo: William S. Hein, 1995 (1758), p. 249.
55 Ibid.
56 David M. Ackerman, *International Law and the Pre-emptive Use of Force Against Iraq*, CRS Report for Congress RS21314 (2003), available at www.usis.iVpdflother/RS21314.edf; and Michael N. Schmitt, "Pre-emptive Strategies in International Law," *Michigan Journal of International Law*, 2002, 24, pp. 513, 526.
57 UN Charter article 39, United Nations Charter, 26 June 1945. Available at www.un.org.aboutun/charter/.
58 UN Charter article 50, United Nations Charter, 26 June 1945. Available at www.un.org.aboutun/charter/.
59 Josef L. Kunz, "Individual and Collective Self-Defense in Article 5I of the Charter of the United Nations," *American Journal on International Law*, 1947, 41, pp. 872, 878; Ian Brownlie, *International Law and the Use of Force by States*, Oxford: Oxford University Press, 1963; Hans Kelsen, *The Law of the United Nations: A Critical Analysis of Its Fundamental Problems,* New York: Frederick A. Praeger, 1964, pp. 797–798; and Michael B. Akehurst, *A Modern Introduction to International Law*, 6th Edition, London: Routledge, 1987, p. 261.
60 Akehurst, *A Modern Introduction to International Law*, p. 261.
61 Derek W. Bowett, *Self Defence in International Law*, Manchester: Manchester University Press, 1958, pp. 193–195; and James L. Brierly, *The Law of Nations: An Introduction to the International Law of Peace.* 6th Edition, edited by Sir Humphrey Waldock, New York: Oxford University Press, 1963, p. 419. According to Akehurst it was expected in 1945 that all States would eventually join the UN. Therefore, the failure to mention protection of non-members from armed attack was "probably due to an oversight." See, Michael Akehurst, *A Modern Introduction to International Law*, 1987, p. 261.
62 Steve Fetter, "Ballistic Missiles and Weapons of Mass Destruction: What is the Threat? What Should be Done?" *International Security*, 1991, 16, p. 28.
63 Ibid.
64 Maria Ryan, "Inventing the 'Axis of Evil': The Myth and Reality of US Intelligence and Policy Making After 9/11," *Intelligence and National Security*, 2002, 17(4), p. 61.
65 Bush, *The National Security Strategy of the United States of America*, 2002, pp. 1–30.
66 Jervis, "Understanding the Bush Doctrine," p. 370.
67 Jeffrey Record, "Nuclear Deterrence, Preventive War and Counter-proliferation," *CATO Institute Policy Analysis*, 28 July 2004, p. 20.
68 O'Hanlon, Rice and Steinberg, "The New National Security Strategy and Preemption," pp. 5–6.
69 Lawrence J. Korb, *A New National Security Strategy in an Age of Terrorists, Tyrants, and Weapons of Mass Destruction*, New York: Council on Foreign Relations, 2003, p. 7.
70 John Mearsheimer and Stephen M. Walt, "An Unnecessary War," *Foreign Policy*, 2003, 134, p. 54.
71 Jeffrey Record, "Threat Confusions and its Penalties," *Survival*, 2002, 46, p. 60.
72 Ibid.
73 Neta C. Crawford, "The Best Defense: The Problem with Bush's Pre-emptive War Doctrine." *The Boston Review*, February/March, 2003.

74 Ibid.
75 Charles W. Kegley and Gregory A. Raymond, "Preventive War and Permissive Normative Order," *International Studies Perspectives*, 2003, 4, p. 389.
76 Schweller, "Domestic Structure and Preventive War," p. 236.
77 Scott A. Silverstone, "Can Democracies Initiate Preventive War? America's Confrontation with the Soviet Union and Iraq," paper prepared for presentation at the International Studies Association Annual Convention, Carnegie Council, Portland, Oregon, February 27, 2003, pp. 4, 7; and Crawford, "The Best Defense," p. 12.
78 Silverstone, "Can Democracies Initiate Preventive War?" p. 7.
79 Press-Barnathan, "The War Against Iraq and International order: From Bull to Bush," p. 202.
80 Ibid.
81 Walter R. Mead, *Power, Terror, Peace and War: America's Grand Strategy in a World at Risk*, New York: Alfred A. Knopf, 2004, p. 117.
82 Robert J. Pauly and Tom Lansford, *Strategic Pre-emption: US Foreign Policy and the Second Iraq War*, Burlington: Ashgate Publishing Company, 2005, pp. 154–155.
83 Ron Suskind, *Price of Loyalty: George W. Bush, the White House and the Education of Paul O'Neill*, New York: Simon & Schuster, 2004, p. 87.
84 Richard A. Clarke, *Against All Enemies: Inside America's War on Terror*, New York: Freedom Press, 2004, p. 266.
85 John L. Gaddis, *Surprise, Security and the American Experience: The Joanna Jackson Goldman Memorial Lectures on American Civilization and Government*, Massachusetts: Harvard University Press, 2003, p. 99.
86 Chris J. Dolan and Betty Glad, *Striking First: The Preventive War Doctrine and the Reshaping of US Foreign Policy*, New York: Palgrave Macmillan, 2004, p. 15.
87 Paul H. Nitze, "Atoms, Strategy and Policy," *Foreign Affairs*, 1955, 34, pp. 188–198.

2 The Bush Doctrine: preventive war in Iraq

1 Clarke, *Against All Enemies*, p. 264.
2 Robert U. Woodward, *Plan of Attack*, New York: Simon & Schuster, 2004, p. 1.
3 Robert S. Litwak, "The New Calculus of Pre-emption," *Survival*, 2002/2003, 44(4), p. 66.
4 Richard J. Durbin, "Assessing Iraq's Military Capabilities," US Congressional Record (Senate), September 10, 2002, pp. S8427–S8429.
5 Philip H. Gordon, Martin S. Indyk and Michael E. O'Hanlon, "Getting Serious About Iraq," *Survival*, 2002, Autumn, pp. 9–10.
6 US Department of State, *2002 Overview of State sponsored Terrorism*, Washington, DC: Office of the Coordinator for Counterterrorism, April 30, 2003.
7 Ibid.
8 National Commission on Terrorist Attacks, *The 9/11 Commission Report: Final Report of the National Commission on Terrorist Attacks Upon the United States*, New York: W.W. Norton, 2004, p. 61.
9 Clarke, *Against All Enemies*, p. 265.
10 National Threat Initiative, Iraq Profile, May 2004, available at www.nti.org/e_ressarch/profiles/Iraq/index.html.
11 US Congress, *Report of the Commission to Assess the Ballistic Missile Threat to the US*, Executive Summary, Pursuant to Public Law 201, 104th Congress, July 15, 1998, available at www.fas.org/irp/threat/missile/rumsfeld/index.html.
12 CIA Unclassified Report to Congress on the Acquisition of Technology Relating to Weapons of Mass Destruction and Advanced Conventional Munitions, January 1 through June 30, 2002, available at https://www.cia.gov/library/reports/archived-reports-1/jan_jun2002.html.

13 Joseph Cirincione, with Jon B. Wolfsthal and Miriam Rajkumar, *Deadly Arsenals: Tracking Weapon of Mass Destruction*, Washington, DC: Carnegie Endowment for International Peace, 2002, p. 271.
14 Thomas M. Franck, "What Happens Now? The United Nations after Iraq," *The American Journal of International Law*, 2003, 97, pp. 611–612.
15 Press-Barnathan, "The War Against Iraq and International Order," p. 202.
16 James L. Brierly, "International Law: Its Actual Part in World Affairs," *Royal Institute of International Affairs*, 20(3) July, 1944, p. 381.
17 Lawrence J. Korb, "A New National Security Strategy in the Age of Terrorisms, Tyrants, and Weapons of Mass Destruction," p. 50.
18 Lee Feinstein and Anne-Marie Slaughter, "A Duty to Prevent," *Foreign Affairs*, 2004, 83, p. 137.
19 Jane E. Stromseth, "Law and Force after Iraq: A Transitional Moment," *The America Journal of International Law*, 2003, 97, p. 639.
20 Richard N. Gardner, "Neither Bush nor the 'Jurisprudes,'" *The American Journal of International Law*, 2003, 97, p. 589.
21 Wirtz and Russell, "US Policy on Preventive War and Pre-emption," p. 120.
22 Thomas M. Franck, "What Happens Now? The United Nations after Iraq," p. 616.
23 Quoted in Woodward, *Plan of Attack*, p. 159.
24 Chaim Kaufman, "Threat Inflation and the Failure of the Marketplace of Ideas: The Selling of the Iraq War," p. 19.
25 Clarke, *Against All Enemies*, p. 284.
26 US Department of State, *2002 Country Report on Human Rights Practices*, the Bureau of Democracy, Human Rights and Labor, March 31, 2003.
27 Ibid.
28 Ibid.
29 Ibid.
30 Ibid.
31 Record, "Nuclear Deterrence, Preventive War and Counter-proliferation," p. 56.
32 Kaufman, "Threat Inflation and the Failure of the Marketplace of Ideas," p. 8; Press-Barnathan, "The War Against Iraq and International Order," p. 204.
33 US Department of Defense, *Nuclear Posture Review Report*, December 31, 2001.
34 US Congress, *Report of the Commission to Assess the Ballistic Missile Threat to the US*.
35 James Mann, *Rise of the Vulcans: The History of Bush's War Cabinet*, New York: Penguin, 2004, p. 242.
36 Clarke, *Against All Enemies*, p. 265.
37 British Petroleum, Statistical Review of World Energy, 2004, available at www.bp.com/liveassets/bp_internet/globalbp/globalbp_uk_english/publications/energy_reviews/STAGING/local_assets/downloads/pdf/oil_section_2004.pdf.
38 George W. Bush, Speech on the Future of Iraq, Office of the Press Secretary, February 26, 2002, available at www.guardian.co.uk/world/2003/feb/27/usa.iraq2.
39 Mann, *Rise of the Vulcans*, p. 346.
40 Quoted in Pejman Yousefzadeh, "Iraq: The 'Domino Effect,' We Can Get Behind," *Front Page Magazine*, April 8, 2004, pp. 1–2.
41 Lebow, "Windows of Opportunity," p. 182.
42 Gaddis, "A Grand Strategy of Transformation," p. 54.
43 George W. Bush, "A Period of Consequences," Address at The Citadel, South Carolina, September 23, 1999, available at www.citadel.edu/pao/addresses/pres bush.html.
44 M. Elaine Bunn, "Pre-emptive Action: When, How, and to What Effect?" *Strategic Forum*, 2003, 200, pp. 1–8.
45 US Department of Defense, *Quadrennial Defense Review* Report, September 30, 2001, available at www.defense.gov/pubs/pdfs/qdr2001.pdf.

46 Donald H. Rumsfeld, "Secretary Rumsfeld Speaks on '21st Century Transformation' of the US Armed Forces," January 31, 2002, available at www.defenselink.mi/speeches/2002/s20020131-secdef.html.
47 George W. Bush, "Remarks by the President to the Warsaw Conference on Combating Terrorism," November 6, 2001, available at http://usinfo.state.gov/topical/pol/terror/01 1 10604.htm.
48 Bush, State of the Union Address.
49 Ibid.
50 Ibid.
51 Bush, Graduation Speech at West Point.
52 Ibid.
53 See Thomas E. Ricks and Vernon Loeb, "Bush Developing Military Policy of Striking First," *The Washington Post*, 10 June 2002, A01.
54 Bush, *The National Security Strategy of the United States of America*, 2002, p. 6.
55 Ibid., p. 14.
56 Ibid.
57 Ibid., p. 15.
58 Ibid.
59 Ibid.
60 Ibid.
61 Ibid., p. 13.
62 Ibid., p. 15.
63 Ibid.
64 Ibid.
65 Ibid. Also, "transform its military forces" is a reference to what is extensively discussed in Chapters 6 and 7 of this thesis—that being, the reassertion of the "nuclear option."
66 Condoleezza Rice, "A Balance of Power That Favors Freedom," The Walter Wriston Lecture of the Manhattan Institute, Office of the Press Secretary, New York, Washington, DC: White House, October 1, 2002.
67 Colin L. Powell, "A Strategy of Partnerships," *Foreign Affairs*, January/February 2004, 83(1), pp. 22, 24. Powell's contention that pre-emption applied only to non-state actors such as terrorist groups was disingenuous, to say the least. The most prominent example of the Administration's use of preventive military force was the invasion of Iraq in March 2003 to overthrow the regime of Saddam Hussein. This was clearly not an instance of pre-emptive action against a non-state actor.
68 Rice, "A Balance of Power That Favors Freedom."
69 William H. Taft IV, "The Legal Basis for Pre-emption," *Council on Foreign Relations Journal*, 2002, available at www.cfr.org/publication print.php?id=5250&content=.
70 As Secretary of State Powell commented in his *Foreign Affairs* article: "Some at home have distorted the NSS for partisan reasons, attempting to make the Bush Administration look bad by turning fear of pre-emption into an early twenty-first-century equivalent of the Cold War era's 'rocket rattle.' Some abroad, meanwhile, have distorted US intentions through an apparent exercise in mirror imaging. Using their own mottled political histories as a reference point, they have asked what they would do with the power that the United States possesses and have mistakenly projected their own Hobbesian intentions onto our rather more Lockean sensibilities. But however it has happened, the distortion of US foreign policy strategy requires repair. This distortion does a disservice to honest observers trying to understand US Policy, and it contributes to irrational partisanship."
71 Richard B. Cheney, "Vice President Speaks at VFW 103rd National Convention."

72 George W. Bush, "President Discusses Growing Danger Posed by Saddam Hussein's Regime," Radio Address by the President to the Nation, The White House Archives, September 14, 2002, available at http://georgewbush-whitehouse.archives.gov/news/releases/2002/09/20020914.html.
73 Ibid.
74 Walter H. Pincus, "CIA learned in '02 That Bin Laden Had No Iraq Ties, Report Says," *The Washington Post*, September 15, 2006, A14.
75 "Top Bush Officials Push Case Against Saddam," Inside Politics, *CNN.com*, September 8, 2002, available at http://archives.cnn.com/2002/ALLPOLITICS/09/08/iraq.debate/.
76 Ibid.
77 Ibid.
78 George W. Bush, "Address to the Nation on Iraq," October 7, 2002, available at www.whitehouse.gov/news/releases/20021007-8.html.
79 Woodward, *Plan of Attack*, p. 69.
80 National Intelligence Council, "Iraq's Continuing Program for Weapons of Mass Destruction: Key Judgments," October 2002, p. 8, available at www.dni.gov/nic/special_keyjudgements.html.
81 Ibid.
82 George J. Tenet, "CIA Letter to Senate on Baghdad's Intentions," *Globalsecurity.org*, October 7, 2002, available at www.globalsecurity.org/WMD/library/news/iraq/2002/iraq-021007-cia01.htm.
83 Ibid.
84 Text of congressional joint resolution, published in *The Washington Post*, October 11, 2002, A12.
85 Mann, *Rise of the Vulcans*, pp. 332–334.
86 Ibid.
87 Interview with Bob Woodward, "The Choice of 2004," *Frontline*, available at www.pbs.org/wgbh/pages/frontline/shows/choice2004/interviews/woodward.html.
88 Woodward, *Plan of Attack*, p. 36.
89 For a detailed account of Rumsfeld's integral role in war planning, see Woodward's *Plan of Attack* or Tommy R. Franks' *American Soldier*. New York: Regan Books/Harper Collins, 2004.
90 Woodward, *Plan of Attack*, p. 38.
91 Ibid., pp. 98–99.
92 Ibid., p. 61.
93 Ibid., p. 135.
94 Ibid., p. 146.
95 Prepared Testimony of US Secretary of Defense Donald H. Rumsfeld before the House and Senate Armed Services Committees Regarding Iraq, September 18, 2002.
96 Thomas E. Ricks, *Fiasco*, New York: The Penguin Press, 2006, pp. 78–80.
97 Woodward, *Plan of Attack*, p. 206.
98 Ibid., p. 24.
99 Ibid., pp. 12 and 24.
100 George W. Bush, "President Bush's Address on Iraq," October 7, 2002, available at www.whitehouse.gov/news/releases/20021007-8.html.
101 Bush, State of the Union Address.
102 Woodward, *Plan of Attack*, pp. 253–254. Patrick Suskind corroborates the timeframe on Bush's decision in *One Percent Doctrine*, New York: Simon & Schuster, 2006.
103 Cirincione, Mathews, Perkovich, and Orton, *WMD in Iraq: Evidence and Implications*, p. 59
104 Ibid.
105 Before President Bush's decision on Iraq, Powell's language around the issue consistently referred to disarmament as opposed to regime change. However, once

Bush selected the preventive option, Powell fell in behind his commander-in-chief and supported the Administration's efforts to pull together a coalition at the UN. Powell himself has made very few public comments about his shift in stance but Greg Thielmann, former director of the Strategic Proliferation and Military Affairs Office at the State Department said Powell eventually supported the preventive military option because he was a "loyal secretary of state, a 'good soldier,' as it were, building the Administration' case before the international community." (Interview with Greg Thielmann, *Truth, War and Consequences,* PBS Frontline, August 13, 2003). Lawrence Wilkerson, Powell's chief of staff during the decision-making process on how to handle the perceived threat from Iraqi WMD, echoed Thielmann, calling Powell the "world's most loyal soldier," implying that Powell did not continue to push the LN option once it became clear that Bush had selected a different alternative. ("Weighing the Uniqueness of the Bush Administration's National Security Decision-Making Process: Boon or Danger to American Democracy?" *New America Foundation, American Strategy Program Policy Forum,* October 19, 2005). Whatever the case, though he remained committed to a philosophy of overwhelming force, popular support and well-defined mission, like his colleagues at the top of the Bush's foreign policy apparatus, Powell, in the end publicly supported a preventive attack on Iraq.

106 Colin L. Powell, "Remarks to the United Nations Security Council," February 5, 2003, available at www.globalsecurity.org/WMD/library/news/iraq/2003/iraq-030205-powell-un-17300pf.htm.

107 Woodward, *Plan of Attack*, p. 315.

108 Bush, State of the Union Address.

109 Interview with Dick Cheney, *Meet the Press*, NBC, March 16, 2003, available at www.mtholyoke.edu/acad/intrel/bush/cheneymeetthepress.htm.

110 Lebow, "Windows of Opportunity," p. 155.

111 George W. Bush, "President Outlines Priorities," Presidential Hall, Dwight D. Eisenhower Executive Office Building, November 7, 2002, available at http://georgewbush-whitehouse.archives.gov/news/releases/2002/11/20021107-2.html.

112 *Commission on the Intelligence Capabilities of the United States Regarding Weapons of Mass Destruction*, Report to the President, March 31, 2005, available at http://govinfo.library.unt.edu/wmd/report/wmd_report.pdf.

113 Greg Thielmann, "Preventive Military Intervention: The Role of Intelligence," Ridgway Center Policy Brief 04–1, October 2004.

114 George W. Bush, *The National Security Strategy of 2006*, Washington, DC: The White House, 2006, p. 23.

115 Condoleezza Rice, "Promoting the National Interest," *Foreign Affairs*, January-February, 2000, 79(1), pp. 45–62.

116 Condoleezza Rice, "Remarks by National Security Adviser Condoleezza Rice on Terrorism and Foreign Policy," speech to Paul H. Nitze School of Advanced International Studies, Johns Hopkins University, White House transcript, April 29, 2002.

117 Condoleezza Rice, "Dr. Condoleezza Rice Discusses President's National Security Strategy," Office of the Press Secretary, October 1, 2002, available at www.whitehouse.gov/news/releases/2002/10/print/20021001-6.

118 Ibid.

119 Ibid.

120 Ibid.

121 Woodward, *Plan of Attack*, p. 308.

122 Ibid., p. 251.

123 Bush, "President Outlines Priorities."

124 Cirincione, Mathews, Perkovich and Orton, *WMD in Iraq: Evidence and Implications*, p. 59.

125 Bush, *The National Security Strategy of 2006.*

3 The Bush Doctrine and prevention: evident in twentieth-century US foreign policy—case studies

1 Peter Lavoy, "What's New in the New US Strategy to Combat WMD?" *Strategic Insights*, I(10), December 2002, pp. 14–27.
2 US Department of State, *Foreign Relations of the United States*, Washington, DC, 1946, 1, p. 1201.
3 Barry R. Schneider, "Nuclear Proliferation and Counter-proliferation: Policy Issues and Debates," *Mershon International Studies Review*, 1994, 38, p. 225.
4 Gray, *The Implications of Pre-emptive and Preventive War Doctrines*, p. vii.
5 Ibid.
6 Ibid.
7 Ibid.
8 Ibid.
9 James B. Steinberg, "The Use of Preventive Force as an Element of US National Strategy," *The Princeton Project on National Security*, New Jersey, 2007, p. 1.
10 Trachtenberg, "Preventive War and US Foreign Policy," p. 1.
11 Russell D. Buhite and William C. Hamel, "War for Peace: The Question of an American Preventive War Against the Soviet Union, 1945–1955," *Diplomatic History*, 1990, 14(3), p. 370.
12 Michael L. Nacht, The Future Unlike the Past: Nuclear Proliferation and American Security Policy," *International Organisation*, 1981, 35, p. 194.
13 Marc Trachtenberg, "A Wasting Asset: American Strategy and the Shifting Nuclear Balance," *International Security*, 1988/89, 13, p. 5.
14 Quoted in Buhite and Hamel, "War for Peace," p. 374.
15 Trachtenberg, "A Wasting Asset," p. 14.
16 Craig Campbell, *Destroying the Village: Eisenhower and Thermonuclear War*, New York: Columbia University Press, 1998, p. 32.
17 Trachtenberg, "A Wasting Asset," p. 6.
18 Quoted in Buhite and Hamel, "War for Peace," p. 372.
19 Buhite and Hamel, "War for Peace."
20 US Department of State, Foreign Relations of the United States, p. 1163.
21 Quoted in Buhite and Hamel, "War for Peace," p. 373.
22 Quoted in Steven R. Prebeck, "Preventive Attack in the 1990s," Air University Press, posted on the Commonwealth Institute Website, May 28, 1993, p. 8, available at www.comw.org/qdr/fulltext/9305prebeck.pdf.
23 Buhite and Hamel, "War for Peace," p. 373.
24 Quoted in Buhite and Hamel, "War for Peace," p. 374.
25 Trachtenberg, "A Wasting Asset," pp. 7–8.
26 Quoted in Trachtenberg, "A Wasting Asset," pp. 7–8.
27 Quoted in Buhite and Hamel, "War for Peace," p. 378.
28 Eisenhower Memorandum to Dulles, September 1953, DDE Diary, August-September 1953, Folder 2, DDE Diary, Box 3, Ann C. Whitman File—Eisenhower Presidential Papers, Dwight D. Eisenhower Library.
29 US Department of State, *Foreign Relations of the United States*.
30 Basic National Security Policy, attached to National Security Council Report by James S. Lay Jr., NSC 5501, January 7, 1955, FRUS, 1955–1957, Vol. XIX, NARA, College Park, Maryland, 33.
31 Basic National Security Policy. All quotations in this paragraph are from the 1955 BNSP, NSC 5501, January 7, 1955, FRUS, 1955–1957, Vol. XIX.
32 Quoted in Ricks and Loeb, "Bush Developing Military Policy of Striking First," A01.
33 Richard Smoke, *National Security and the Nuclear Dilemma*, Reading: Addison-Wesley Publishing Company, 1984, p. 54.

34 Silverstone, "Can Democracies Initiate Preventive War?" p. 8.
35 Walter B. Slocombe, "Force, Pre-emption and Legitimacy," *Survival*, 2003, 45, p. 124.
36 Quoted in David A. Rosenberg, "The Origins of Overkill: Nuclear Weapons and American Strategy, 1945–1960," *International Security*, 1983, 7, p. 34.
37 NSC-68, *United States Objectives and Programs for National Security*, A Report to the President Pursuant to the President's Directive of January 31, 1950, released April 14, 1950 available at www.fas.org/irp/offdocs/nsc-hst/nsc-68.htm.
38 Quoted in Buhite and Hamel, "War for Peace," p. 382.
39 Quoted in Arthur M. Schlesinger, *War and the American Presidency*, New York: W.W. Norton, 2004, p. 22.
40 Quoted in Buhite and Hamel, "War for Peace," p. 382; Trachtenberg "A Wasting Asset," 1988/89, p. 26; Mike Moore, "Truman Got it Right," *Bulletin of the Nuclear Scientists*, January/February 2003, 59(1), p. 22.
41 George H. Quester, *Nuclear Monopoly*, New Brunswick: Transaction Publishers, pp. 57–58.
42 Rosenberg, "The Origins of Overkill," pp. 14–15.
43 Buhite and Hamel, "War for Peace," p. 383; Rosenberg, "The Origins of Overkill," pp. 14–15.
44 Ibid.
45 Quester, *Nuclear Monopoly*, p. 77.
46 Buhite and Hamel, "War for Peace," p. 383.
47 George H. Quester, *Nuclear Diplomacy: The First Twenty Five Years*, New York: The Dunellen Company, 1970, p. 39.
48 Quoted in Rosenberg, "The Origins of Overkill," p. 13.
49 Quoted in Trachtenberg, "A Wasting Asset," p. 40.
50 US Department of State, "Memorandum for the President: Implications of a Chinese Communist Nuclear Capability," College Park: US National Archives and Records Administration, April 30, 1964, p. 10.
51 Quoted in Gordon H. Chang, "JFK, China and the Bomb," *The Journal of American History*, 1988, 74, p. 1309.
52 Chang, "JFK, China and the Bomb," p. 1309.
53 Nacht, "The Future Unlike the Past," p. 198.
54 William Burr and Jeffrey T. Richelson, "Whether to 'Strangle the Baby in the Cradle,'" *Journal of American History*, 2000/2001, p. 67.
55 US Department of State Policy Planning Council, "China as a Nuclear Power: Some Thoughts Prior to the Chinese Test," College Park, US National Archives and Records Administration, October 7, 1964, p. 34.
56 Robert Garson, *The United States and China Since 1949: A Troubled Affair*. Madison: Fairleigh-Dickinson University Press, 1994, p. 81.
57 Burr and Richelson, "Whether to 'Strangle the Baby in the Cradle,'" p. 61.
58 Chang, "JFK, China and the Bomb," p. 1293; Burr and Richelson, "Whether to 'Strangle the Baby in the Cradle,'" p. 67.
59 Litwak, "The New Calculus of Pre-emption," pp. 53–80.
60 Alice L. Hsieh, "The Sino-Soviet Dialogue: 1963," *The Journal of Conflict Resolution*, 1964, 8, p. 110.
61 Ibid.
62 Quoted in Chang, "JFK, China and the Bomb," p. 1287.
63 Burr and Richelson, "Whether to 'Strangle the Baby in the Cradle,'" p. 95.
64 US Department of State, "Memorandum for the President," p. 2.
65 Ibid.
66 Burr and Richelson, "Whether to 'Strangle the Baby in the Cradle,'" p. 61.
67 Ibid., p. 77.
68 US Department of State, "Memorandum for the President," p. 3.

69 Ibid., p. 11.
70 US Department of State Policy Planning Council, "The Chinese Communist Nuclear Capacity and Some 'Unorthodox' Approaches to the Problem of Nuclear Proliferation," College Park, US National Archives and Records Administration, June 1, 1964, p. 1.
71 Burr and Richelson, "Whether to 'Strangle the Baby in the Cradle,'" pp. 62–93.
72 Ibid., p. 62.
73 Quoted in Chang, "JFK, China and the Bomb," p. 1301.
74 Chang, "JFK, China and the Bomb," p. 1306.
75 Quoted in Burr and Richelson, "Whether to 'Strangle the Baby in the Cradle,'" p. 73.
76 McGeorge Bundy, *Danger and Survival: Choices About the Bomb in the First Fifty Years*, New York: Random House, 1988, p. 532.
77 Quoted in Burr and Richelson, "Whether to 'Strangle the Baby in the Cradle,'" p. 55.
78 Bundy, *Danger and Survival*, p. 530.
79 "Memorandum From Robert W. Komer of the National Security Council Staff to the President's Special Assistant for National Security Affairs (Bundy)," November 5, 1963, FRUS, 196l-1963, Vol. 22, Lyndon B. Johnson Library, pp. 404–405.
80 Ibid.
81 "Memorandum From Robert W. Komer of the National Security Council Staff to the President's Special Assistant for National Security Affairs (Bundy)," February 26, 1964, FRUS, 1964–1968, Vol. 30, Lyndon B. Johnson Library, pp. 23–24; a marginal note in Bundy's handwriting connected to Komer's question read, "I'm for it."
82 Burr and Richelson, "Whether to 'Strangle the Baby in the Cradle,'" p. 54.
83 Quoted in Burr and Richelson, "Whether to 'Strangle the Baby in the Cradle,'" p. 67.
84 Editorial Note, Foreign Relations of the United States, 1961–1963, Vol. 21, Lyndon B. Johnson Library, p. 339.
85 "Remarks of President Kennedy to the National Security Council Meeting of 22 January 1963," January 22, 1963, Foreign Relations of the United States, 1961–1963, Vol. 8, p. 462.
86 Gordon Chang, *Friends and Enemies: The United States, China and the Soviet Union, 1948–72*, Stanford, CA: Stanford University Press, 1990, p. 232.
87 Burr and Richelson, "Whether to 'Strangle the Baby in the Cradle,'" p. 68.
88 Curtis E. LeMay, "Study of Chinese Communist Vulnerability," memorandum from the Acting Chairman, Joint Chiefs of Staff, to Secretary of Defense, April 29, 1963, Department of State Records, Office of the Country Director for the Republic of China, 1954–65, Box 4, Nuclear Capability.
89 Chang, *Friends and Enemies*, p. 1300.
90 Burr and Richelson, "Whether to 'Strangle the Baby in the Cradle,'" p. 67.
91 Chang, *Friends and Enemies,* p. 1297.
92 US Department of State Policy Planning Council, "The Chinese Communist Nuclear Capacity," p. 1.
93 Burr and Richelson, "Whether to 'Strangle the Baby in the Cradle,'" pp. 96–97.
94 Lyndon B. Johnson, *The Vantage Point: Perspectives of the Presidency, 1963–1969*, New York: Holt, Rinehart and Winston, 1971, pp. 469–470.
95 Burr and Richelson, "Whether to 'Strangle the Baby in the Cradle,'" p. 56.
96 Robert F. Kennedy, *Thirteen Days: A Memoir of the Cuban Missile Crisis*, New York: W.W. Norton, 1969, p. 49; quoted in Dan Reiter, "Exploding the Powder Keg Myth: Pre-emptive Wars Almost Never Happen," *International Security*, 1995, 20(2), p. 26.
97 Burr and Richelson, "Whether to 'Strangle the Baby in the Cradle,'" p. 82.
98 US Department of State Policy Planning Council, "The Chinese Communist Nuclear Capacity," p. 3.
99 Burr and Richelson, "Whether to 'Strangle the Baby in the Cradle,'" p. 69.

100 US Department of State Policy Planning Council, Memorandum: "Destruction of Chinese Nuclear Weapons Capabilities," College Park, US National Archives and Records Administration, April 14, 1964.
101 Burr and Richelson, "Whether to 'Strangle the Baby in the Cradle,'" p. 59.
102 US Department of State Policy Planning Council, "The Chinese Communist Nuclear Capacity," p. 1.
103 Ibid.
104 US Department of State Policy Planning Council, "The Chinese Communist Nuclear Capacity," pp. 1–2.
105 Statements of Lyndon B. Johnson, October 14–October 21, 1964, Lyndon B. Johnson Library, Box 127, file 16 October 1964.
106 National Security Files, Country Files, Lyndon B. Johnson Library, Box 238, file China Memos, Vol. II, 9/64–2/65, DOS telegram.
107 Burr and Richelson, "Whether to 'Strangle the Baby in the Cradle,'" p. 91.
108 Michael E. O'Hanlon and Mike Mochizuki, *Crisis in the Korean Peninsula: How to Deal with North Korea*. New York: McGraw-Hill, 2003, p. 23.
109 Ibid., p. 25.
110 Ibid., pp. 25–26.
111 Ashton B. Carter and William J. Perry, "Nuclear over North Korea: Back to the Brink," *The Washington Post*, October 20, 2002.
112 Joel S. Wit, Daniel B. Poneman, and Robert L. Gallucci, *Going Critical: The First North Korean Crisis*, Washington, DC: Brookings Institution Press, 2004, p. 390.
113 Carter and Perry, "Nuclear over North Korea."
114 Burr and Richelson, "Whether to 'Strangle the Baby in the Cradle,'" p. 62.
115 Carter and Perry, "Nuclear over North Korea."
116 Don Oberdorfer, *Two Koreas: A Contemporary History*, New York: Basic Books, 1997, p. 311.
117 Amy K. Furches, Interview with Dan Poneman, *Presidential Decision Making: When Do US Presidents Use Preventive Force to Counter Nuclear Proliferation?* George Washington University, 2007, p. 175.
118 Furches, Interview with Dan Poneman, p. 176.
119 Carter and Perry, "Nuclear over North Korea."
120 Wit *et al.*, *Going Critical*, p. 103.
121 Jack Anderson and Michael Binstein, "North Korea: Loose Nuclear Cannon," *The Washington Post*, March 29, 1992, p. C1; *North Korea News*, no. 702, September 27, 1993, p. 5; Wit *et al.*, *Going Critical*, p. 103.
122 William J. Perry, Testimony as Secretary of Defense at the Joint Hearing before the Senate Committee on Foreign Relations, 104 Congress, 1st session, Government Printing Office, January 1995, p. 15.
123 Wit *et al.*, *Going Critical*, p. 28.
124 Ibid., p. 241.
125 Quoted in Leon V. Sigal, *Disarming Strangers: Nuclear Diplomacy with North Korea*, Princeton: Princeton University Press, 1998, p. 71.
126 Sigal, *Disarming Strangers*, p. 81.
127 Ibid., p. 163.
128 Ibid., p. 82.
129 Ibid., p. 81.
130 Wit *et al.*, *Going Critical*, p. 200.
131 Quoted in Sigal, *Disarming Strangers*, p. 153.
132 Wit *et al.*, *Going Critical*, p. 210.
133 See Hon. Lee H. Hamilton, Extension Remarks, Congressional Record, "Anthony Lake on North Korea," 1994.
134 William Perry quoting Anthony Lake in "Remarks by Secretary of Defense William Perry to the Asia Society," Federal News Service, May 3, 1994.

135 Ibid.
136 Ibid.
137 Ibid.
138 Amy K. Furches, Interview with Samuel Berger, *Presidential Decision Making: When Do US Presidents Use Preventive Force to Counter Nuclear Proliferation?* George Washington University, 2007, p. 196.
139 Perry, "Remarks by Secretary of Defense William Perry to the Asia Society."
140 Wit *et al., Going Critical*, p. 204.
141 Amy K. Furches, Interview with William Perry, *Presidential Decision Making: When Do US Presidents Use Preventive Force to Counter Nuclear Proliferation?* George Washington University, 2007, p. 197.
142 Ibid., p. 197.
143 Amy K. Furches, Interview with James Woolsey, *Presidential Decision Making: When Do US Presidents Use Preventive Force to Counter Nuclear Proliferation?* George Washington University, 2007, p. 200.
144 Amy K. Furches, Interview with Robert Galluci, *Presidential Decision Making: When Do US Presidents Use Preventive Force to Counter Nuclear Proliferation?* George Washington University, 2007, p. 200.
145 Furches, Interview with James Woolsey, p. 200.
146 Ibid.
147 Ibid.
148 William J. Clinton, *My Life*, New York: Alfred A. Knopf, 2004, p. 591.
149 Ibid., pp. 602–603; and Oberdorfer, *Two Koreas*, p. 313.
150 Oberdorfer, *Two Koreas*, p. 313.
151 Ibid.
152 Ibid., p. 315.
153 Ibid.
154 Ibid.
155 CRS Report for Congress, CRS94–470F, *North Korea's Nuclear Weapons Program.*
156 Oberdorfer, *Two Koreas*, p. 315.
157 Clinton, *My Life*, p. 603.
158 CRS Report for Congress, CRS94–470F, *North Korea's Nuclear Weapons Program.*
159 Wit *et al., Going Critical*, p. 104.
160 Barton D. Gellman, "Trepidation at Root of US Korea Policy," *The Washington Post,* December 12, 1993, p. A1.
161 Wit *et al., Going Critical,* p. 104; Osirak refers to the Israeli strike against Iraq's nuclear facility at a location called Osirak.
162 Amy K. Furches, Interview with a Former US Military Official, *Presidential Decision Making: When Do US Presidents use Preventive Force to Counter Nuclear Proliferation?* George Washington University, 2007, p. 179.
163 Ibid.
164 Ibid.
165 It is important to note that the actual implementation of the options just described would lack the linearity implied by characterizing them as part of a sequence. Using continued talks with the US as a carrot also involved threatening North Korea with stick-sanctions—which the US would not be able to move to quickly unless it reinforced its military posture on the peninsula. But boosting the US force posture in South Korea could easily inflame an already tense situation and cause North Korea to accelerate instead of halt its nuclear program, which in turn would put pressure on the US to use force to destroy the nuclear facilities before it was too late. In short, the overlap between the options, specifically the force build-up needed to implement the second and third options, increased the riskiness of these options and arguably played a material role in how Clinton and his advisers viewed them.

166 Litwak, "The New Calculus of Pre-emption," p. 70.
167 Phillip C. Saunders, "Military Options for Dealing with North Korea's Nuclear Program," James Martin Center for Non-proliferation Studies, January 27, 2003.
168 Wit *et al.*, *Going Critical*, pp. 180–181.
169 Lebow, "Windows of Opportunity," p. 182.
170 Trachtenberg, "A Wasting Asset," pp. 40–43.
171 Quoted in Silverstone, "Can Democracies Initiate Preventive War?" p. 13.
172 Peter D. Feaver and Emerson M. S. Niou, "Managing Nuclear Proliferation: Condemn, Strike, or Assist?" *International Studies Quarterly*, 1996, 40, p. 215.
173 Sdney D. Drell and James E. Goodby, *The Gravest Danger: Nuclear Weapons*, Stanford: The Hover Institution Press, p. 41
174 Ibid.
175 Thucydides, *The History of the Peloponnesian War*, p. 110.
176 Trachtenberg, "Preventive War and US Foreign Policy," p. 29.
177 Ibid.

4 The Bush Doctrine and the nuclear option: the transition from Clinton to Bush

1 Amy F. Woolf, *US Nuclear Weapons: Changes in Policy and Force Structure*, CRS Report for Congress, Updated January 23, 2008, p. 1.
2 Joseph M. Siracusa and David G. Coleman, "Scaling the Nuclear Ladder: Deterrence from Truman to Clinton," *Australian Journal of International Affairs,* 54(3), 2000, p. 291.
3 Woolf, *US Nuclear Weapons: Changes in Policy and Force Structure*, p. 1.
4 William J. Perry, *Annual Report to the President and Congress*, Department of Defense, Washington, DC, February 1995, p. 84.
5 William J. Clinton, *A National Security Strategy for a New Century*, Washington, DC: The White House, 1998, p. 12.
6 Craig Cerniello, "Clinton Issues New Guidelines on US Nuclear Weapons Doctrine," *Arms Control Today*, November/December 1997.
7 R. Jeffrey Smith, "Clinton Directive Changes Strategy on Nuclear Arms; Centering on Deterrence, Officials Drop Terms for Long Atomic War," *The Washington Post*, December 7, 1997, p. A1.
8 Jason D. Ellis, "The Best Defense: Counter-proliferation and US National Security," *The Washington Quarterly,* 26(2) 2003, p. 17.
9 Harald Müller, David Fisher, and Wolfgang Kotter, *Nuclear Non-Proliferation and Global Order*, London: Oxford University Press, 1994, p. 131.
10 Thomas A. Keaney and Eliot A. Cohen (eds) *Gulf War Air Power Survey: Summary Report*, Washington, DC: USGPO, 1993, pp. 78–79.
11 Ibid., p. 82.
12 William M. Arkin, *Agnosticism When Real Values Are Needed: Nuclear Policy in the Clinton Administration*, Federation of American Scientist Public Interest Report, September/October 1994, p. 7.
13 Les Aspin, Address as Secretary of Defense to National Academy of Sciences on the Defense Counter-proliferation Initiative, Washington, DC, December 7, 1993.
14 Ellis, "The Best Defense," p. 17.
15 US Department of Defense, *Counter-proliferation and Treaty Activities*, DOD Office of the Executive Secretary, Chapter 6, available at www.DOD.gov/execsec/adr97/chap6.html.
16 Counter-proliferation Initiative, PDD/NSC 18, December 1993, Presidential Decision Directives, Clinton Administration 1993–2000, available at http://fas.org/irp/offdocs/pdd18.htm.

17 Barry R. Schneider, "Radical Responses to Radical Regimes: Evaluating Preemptive Counter-Proliferation," *McNair Paper 41*, Institute for Strategic National Studies, National Defense University, Washington, DC, May 1995, pp. 1–3.
18 Ibid.
19 Ibid.
20 Known as the Theater High Altitude Area Defense (THAAD) System. See "Aspin Emphasizes Missile Defense in Proliferation Approach," *Defense Daily*, December 8, 1993, p. 347.
21 "Aspin Emphasizes Missile Defense in Proliferation Approach." Also, Bill Gertz, "Aspin Outlines Threat of Arms Proliferation: Pentagon Unveils Counterstrategy," *Washington Times*, December 8, 1993, p. 4. During the Gulf War, the United States forces failed to stockpile enough vaccine to inoculate all personnel to prevent infection from germ warfare agents, had they been used by Iraq.
22 Schneider, "Radical Responses to Radical Regimes," pp. 1–3.
23 Ibid.
24 Ibid.
25 Aspin, Address to National Academy of Sciences.
26 Angus McColl, "Is Counter-proliferation Compatible with Non-proliferation? Rethinking the Defense Counter-proliferation Initiative," *Airpower Journal*, Spring, 1997, 11, p. 100.
27 Chris Williams, "DOD's Counter-proliferation Initiative: A Critical Assessment," *Fighting Proliferation: New Concerns for the Nineties*, edited by Henry Sokolski, Washington, DC: Air University Press, 1996, pp. 1–3.
28 Ibid.
29 "Jane's Interview: Ashton Carter," *Jane's Defence Weekly*, July 30, 1994, p. 40.
30 Joseph Pilat, "A Counter-proliferation Primer," Los Alamos, N. Mex.: Los Alamos National Laboratory, 1994, p. 3, cited in McColl, "Is Counter-proliferation Compatible with Non-proliferation?"
31 Anthony J. Tolin, Briefing, J-5, "Nuclear Posture Review: Key Issues For Review By The Strategic Advisory Group," March 15, 1994, slide 9. Partially declassified and released under the Freedom of Information Act.
32 Ibid.
33 STRATCOM's responsibility is directed in the Unified Command Plan. Apart from overall responsibility for maintaining the strategic nuclear war plans and reconnaissance forces, STRATCOM provides theater nuclear and counter-proliferation support to combatant commanders to assist them in developing tailored annexes designed to counter weapons of mass destruction. STRATCOM also provides specialized planning and consequence analysis, when requested by other combatant commanders. Additionally, CINCSTRAT works closely with other combatant commanders to initiate crisis action procedures contained in the Nuclear Supplement to the Joint Strategic Capabilities Plan. In crisis situations, when assigned as a supporting CINC, CINCSTRAT supports planning and execution of military operations for the combatant commander. See: Vice Admiral Richard W. Mies, US Navy, Director, Strategic Target Plans, US Strategic Command, Commander, Allied Submarines, Mediterranean, Commander, Submarine Allied Command, Atlantic, written response to Strom Thurmond, Chairman, Committee on Armed Services, US Senate, June 15, 1998, reprinted in US Senate, Committee on Armed Services, Nominations Before the Senate Armed Services Committee, Second Session, 195th Congress, Washington, DC: US Government Printing Office, 1999, S. HRG. 105–868, pp. 362–363.
34 US Strategic Command, J51 Memorandum, NPR Report #8, Working Group #5, November 4, 1993, p. 2.; USSTRATCOM Memorandum, NPR Report #5, Working Group #2, November 16, 1993, p. 2. Both documents partially declassified and released under the Freedom of Information Act.

35 US Department of Defense, "Listing, Group 5—Relationship Between US Nuclear Postures and Counter-proliferation Policy, Formal STRATCOM Answers as of November 22, 1993," pp. 12, 13. Partially declassified and released under the Freedom of Information Act.
36 Ibid.
37 US Strategic Command, J51 Memorandum, NPR Report #90, Working Group #5, March 7, 1994, p. 1. Partially declassified and released under the Freedom of Information Act.
38 US Strategic Command, J51 Memorandum, NPR Report #86, Working Group #5, March 2, 1994, p. 1; US Strategic Command Nuclear Posture Review Slides, Update Briefing, March 25, 1994, slide 3; US Strategic Command, J51 Memorandum, NPR Report #92, Working Group #5, March 9, 1994, p. 1; US Strategic Command, Nuclear Posture Review Slides, Update Briefing, March 11, 1994. All documents partially declassified and released under the Freedom of Information Act.
39 US Strategic Command, Nuclear Posture Review Slides, Update Briefing, December 3, 1993, slide 7. Partially declassified and released under the Freedom of Information Act.
40 US Strategic Command, J51 Memorandum, NPR Report #80, Working Group #5, February 23, 1994, p. 2. Partially declassified and released under the Freedom of Information Act.
41 This document is available online at the Joint Chief of Staff electronic library, available at www.dtic.mil/doctrine/jel/new_pubs/jp3_12_1.pdf.
42 Hans M. Kristensen, *US Nuclear Strategy Reform in the 1990s*, The Nautilus Institute, March 2000, p.16.
43 William J. Clinton, *A National Security Strategy of Engagement and Enlargement*, Washington, DC: The White House, February 1995, p. 15.
44 Ibid.
45 Nuclear Posture Review Implementation, PDD/NSC-30, September 1994, Presidential Decision Directives, Clinton Administration 1993–2000, available at www.fas.org/irp/offdocs/pdd30.htm.
46 Ibid.
47 Ibid.
48 Nuclear Posture Review Implementation, PDD/NSC-30.
49 Ibid.
50 William J. Perry, *Nuclear Posture Review*, Annual Report to the President and the Congress, Department of Defense, February 1995, available at www.fas.org/nuke/guide/usa/doctrine/DOD/95_npr.htm.
51 Ibid.
52 Ibid.
53 US Congress, Senate Committee on Armed Services, Briefing on Results of the Nuclear Posture Review, 103rd Congress, 2nd session, September 22, 1994, pp. 9, 10, 16, 17.
54 John M. Deutch, US Deputy Secretary of Defense, written answer in response to question submitted by Senator Strom Thurmond, in US Congress, Senate, Committee, on Armed Services, Briefing on Results of the Nuclear Posture Review, 103rd Congress, 2nd session, September 22, 1994, p. 56.
55 Hans M. Kristensen and Joshua Handler, "The USA and Counter-proliferation: A New and Dubious Role for US Nuclear Weapons," *Security Dialogue*, 27(4), December, 1996, p. 391.
56 Joint Chiefs of Staff, Doctrine for Joint Nuclear Operations, Joint Pub 3-12, April 29, 1993, p. 1, available at www.nukestrat.com/us/jcs/JCS_JP3-12_93.PDF.
57 Ibid.
58 Ibid.
59 Ibid.

60 Hans M. Kristensen, "Doctrine for Joint Nuclear Operations, December 1995," The Nuclear Information Project—Documenting Nuclear Policy and Operations, Federation of Atomic Scientist, available at www.nukestrat.com/us/jcs/jp3-12_95.htm.
61 Ibid.
62 Joint Chiefs of Staff, Doctrine for Joint Nuclear Operations, Joint Pub 3–12, December 1995, Chapter 1, p. 2, available at www.nukestrat.com/us/jcs/JCS_JP3-12_95.pdf.
63 Kristensen, "Doctrine for Joint Nuclear Operations."
64 Joint Chiefs of Staff, Doctrine for Joint Theater Nuclear Operations, Joint Pub 3–12.1, February 9, 1996, Chapter 1, p. 2, available at www.dtic.mil/jcs.
65 Joint Chiefs of Staff, Doctrine for Joint Theater Nuclear Operations, February 9, 1996, Chapter 3, p. 6.
66 Hans M. Kristensen, "Nuclear Futures: Proliferation of Weapons of Mass Destruction and US Nuclear Strategy," British American Security Information Council, March, 1998, p. 17.
67 See "Nuclear Posture Review Working Group 5—The Relationship Between Alternative Nuclear Postures and Counter-proliferation Policy," The Nuclear Information Project, Federation of Atomic Scientists, Nuclear Brief, July 11, 2005, available at www.nukestrat.com/us/reviews/wg5.htm.
68 The QDR is required by the Military Force Structure Review Act, which was included as part of the *National Defense Authorization Act for Fiscal Year 1997*. The Department of Defense designed the QDR to be a fundamental and comprehensive examination of America's defense needs from 1997 to 2015: potential threats; strategy; force structure; readiness posture; military modernization programs; defense infrastructure; and other elements of the defense program. The QDR is intended to provide a blueprint for a strategy-based, balanced and affordable defense program.
69 PDD/NSC 60, November 1997, Presidential Decision Directive, Clinton Administration 1993–2000, available at www.fas.org/irp/offdocs/pdd60.htm.
70 Office of the Secretary of Defense, "Design, Approach, and Implementation of the Quadrennial Defense Review," *Quadrennial Defense Review*, May 1997, available at www.fas.org/man/docs/qdr/.
71 Ibid.
72 Ibid.
73 Ibid.
74 Ibid.
75 Ibid.
76 James S. Thomason, Paul H. Richanbach, Sharon M. Fiore, and Deborah P. Christie, "The Quadrennial Defense Review Process: Lessons Learned from the 1997 Review and Options for the Future," the Commonwealth Institute website, Alexandria, VA: Institute for Defense Analyses, August 1998, p. 1, available at www.comw.org/qdr/thomason.pdf.
77 Ibid.
78 Ibid.
79 William S. Cohen, quoted in Carl Conetta, "Backwards Into the Future: How the Quadrennial Defense Review Prepares America for the Wrong Century," Project on Defense Alternatives, Cambridge, MA, June 1997.
80 Conetta, "Backwards Into the Future."
81 PDD/NSC 60.
82 R. Jeffrey Smith, "Clinton Directive Changes Strategy on Nuclear Arms."
83 PDD/NSC 60.
84 Ibid.
85 Ibid.
86 Smith, "Clinton Directive Changes Strategy on Nuclear Arms"; also, "Rogue Attackers May Face Nuclear Response," *Chicago Tribune*, December 8, 1997.

87 Kristensen, "Nuclear Futures," p. 23.
88 Ibid.
89 Associated Press, US-Nuclear, December 7, 1997, in Kristensen, "Nuclear Futures," Introduction.
90 Smith, "Clinton Directive Changes Strategy on Nuclear Arms."
91 Kristensen, "Nuclear Futures," p. 23.
92 Ibid.
93 Ibid.
94 William J. Clinton, *A National Security Strategy for a New Century*, Washington, DC: The White House, 1999.
95 Ibid.
96 The term "soft power" was coined by Joseph Nye, who served as Assistant Secretary of State during the Clinton Administration.
97 Clinton, *A National Security Strategy for a New Century*, 1999, p. 8.
98 Ibid.
99 Ibid.
100 Counter-proliferation Initiative, PDD/NSC 18.
101 Bush, *The National Security Strategy of the United States of America*, pp. 13–15.
102 Litwak, "The New Calculus of Pre-emption," pp. 54–60; Jason D. Ellis, "The Gravest Danger: Proliferation, Terrorism, and the Bush Doctrine," *Monitor*, Winter 2003, 9(1).
103 Ellis, "The Best Defense," pp. 115–133.
104 Bush, *The National Security Strategy of the United States of America*; reprinted in Bush, *National Strategy to Combat Weapons of Mass Destruction (NSCWMD)*, p. 1.
105 US Department of Defense, *Nuclear Posture Review*, p. 16.
106 "Nuclear Posture Review: What It Says … and What It Means. Nuclear Reduction/Disarmament Initiative," The Churches' Center for Theology and Public Policy, 4500 Massachusetts Avenue, NW, Washington, DC, p. 1.
107 Ibid.
108 Ibid.
109 Bush, *National Strategy to Combat Weapons of Mass Destruction (NSCWMD)*, p. 2.
110 Woolf, *US Nuclear Weapons: Changes in Policy and Force Structure*, p. 42.
111 Ibid.
112 Ibid.
113 Michael R. Gordon, "Nuclear Arms for Deterrence or Fighting?" *New York Times*, March 11, 2002, p. 1.
114 Doyle D. McManus, "Nuclear Use as 'Option' Clouds Issue," *The Los Angeles Times*, March 12, 2002, p. 1.
115 Richard D. Sokolsky and Eugene B. Rumer, "Nuclear Alarmists," *The Washington Post*, March 15, 2002, p. 23.
116 Woolf, *US Nuclear Weapons: Changes in Policy and Force Structure*, p. 43.
117 Comments attributed to Ivo H. Daalder, of the Brookings Institution. See James Dao, "Pentagon Study Urges Arms Shift, For Nuclear to High Tech," *The New York Times*, January 9, 2002.
118 Sam A. Nunn, William J. Perry, and Eugene E. Habiger, "Still Missing: A Nuclear Strategy," *The Washington Post*, May 21, 2002, p. 17.
119 J. Peter Scoblic, "Think Anew About US Nukes," *Christian Science Monitor*, March 19, 2002.
120 Woolf, *US Nuclear Weapons: Changes in Policy and Force Structure*, p. 44.
121 Douglas J. Feith, John A. Gordon, and James O. Ellis, Prepared statements before the Senate Armed Services Committee, Strategic Command, February 14, 2002, available at www.senate.gov/~armed_services.
122 Jack D. Crouch, United States Department of Defense Special Briefing on the Nuclear Posture Review, US Department of Defense, International Security Policy,

January 9, 2002, available at www.defenselink.mil/news/Jan2002/t01092002_t0109npr.html (transcript) and www.defenselink.mil/news/Jan2002/g020109-D-6570C.html (slides).

123 Feith *et al.*, Prepared statements before the Senate Armed Services Committee.

124 See, for example, William M. Arkin, "Not Just a Last Resort? A Global Strike Plan, with a Nuclear Option," *The Washington Post*, May 15, 2005.

125 Bush, *The National Security Strategy of the United States of America*, p. 14.

126 Comments of Stan Norris in Michael R. Gordon, "Nuclear Arms for Deterrence or Fighting?" p. 1.

127 Greg Miller, "Democrats Divide Over Nuclear Plan," *The Los Angeles Times*, March 13, 2002.

128 Comments of Joseph Cirincione in McManus, "Nuclear Use as 'Option' Clouds Issue," p. 1.

129 Sokolsky and Rumer, "Nuclear Alarmists," p. 23.

130 Ivo H. Daalder and James M. Lindsay, "A New Agenda for Nuclear Weapons," Policy Brief #94, Washington, DC: The Brookings Institution, February 2002, p. 6.

131 Woolf, *US Nuclear Weapons: Changes in Policy and Force Structure*, pp. 48–49.

132 Siracusa and Coleman, "Scaling the Nuclear Ladder: Deterrence from Truman to Clinton," p. 293.

133 Jack Mendelsohn, "The Muddle of US Nuclear Weapons Strategy," Arms Control Association, October 2005, available at www.armscontrol.org/act/2005_10/OCT-BookReviews.

5 The nuclear option: Bush and the "real" doctrine

1 Bush, *The National Security Strategy of the United States of America*, p. 5.

2 National Resources Defense Council, "Faking Nuclear Restraint, The Bush Administration's Secret Plan For Strengthening US Nuclear Forces."

3 Russell and Wirtz, "A Quiet Revolution," p. 1.

4 Robert M. Gates, letter to Senator Pete Domenici, May 4, 2007, available at www.nukestrat.com/us/guidance.htm.

5 The Reliable Replacement Warhead (RRW) was a new American nuclear warhead design and bomb family that was intended to be simple, reliable and to provide a long-lasting, low-maintenance future nuclear force for the United States. It was also the project name for the ongoing US Department of Energy National Nuclear Security Administration (NNSA) design project, started in 2004, to develop those designs.

6 Wright, "Iraq Occupation Erodes Bush Doctrine," p. A01.

7 Russell and Wirtz, "A Quiet Revolution," p. 1.

8 Jack D. Crouch, United States Department of Defense Special Briefing on the Nuclear Posture Review.

9 US Department of Defense, Office of the Secretary of Defense, *The Nuclear Posture Review*, January 8, 2002, submitted to Congress on December 31, 2001, available at www.globalsecurity.org.

10 Mark Bromley, David Grahame, and Christine Kucia, *Bunker Busters: Washington's Drive for New Nuclear Weapons*, Research Report, Washington, DC: British American Security Information Council, July 2002.

11 Russell and Wirtz, "A Quiet Revolution," p. 1.

12 Ibid.

13 Ibid.

14 Theresa Hitchens, "Slipping Down the Nuclear Slope: Bush Administration Nuclear Policy Lowers Bar Against Usage," paper presented at a conference on US Nuclear Policy and Counter-proliferation, February 26, 2003, available at www.cdi.org/nuclear/counter-proliferation-conference.cfm.

15 Ibid.
16 Bush, *The National Security Strategy of the United States of America,* 2002, Foreword/Introduction.
17 Ibid., p. 15.
18 Hitchens, "Slipping Down the Nuclear Slope."
19 US Department of Defense, *The Nuclear Posture Review*.
20 Crouch, Special Briefing on the Nuclear Posture Review; Donald H. Rumsfeld, unclassified cover letter for *Nuclear Posture Review* report to Congress, January 9 2002, available at www.defenselink.mil/news/Jan2002/d20020109npr.pdf; Office of Public Affairs, Office of the Secretary of Defense, "Pentagon Briefing: 2002 Nuclear Posture Review," fact sheet, January 10, 2002; Douglas J. Feith, Under Secretary of Defense for Policy, John A. Gordon, Administrator of the National Nuclear Security Administration, and Admiral James O. Ellis, USN, Commander in Chief, Strategic Command, prepared statements before the Senate Armed Services Committee, February 14, 2002, available at www.senate.gov/~armed_services. All information regarding the content of the NPR report is drawn from these and other published government sources.
21 US Department of Defense, *The Nuclear Posture Review*.
22 Ibid.
23 Ibid. See also US Department of Defense, *Annual Report to the President and the Congress*, Washington, DC: Office of the Secretary, 2002, pp. 83–92, available at www.DOD.mil/execsec/adr2001/Chapter06.pdf.
24 Robert S. Norris, Hans M. Kristensen, and Christopher E. Paine, *Nuclear Insecurity: A Critique of the Bush Administration's Nuclear Weapons Policies*, Natural Resources Defense Council, September 2004, p. 1.
25 Ibid., pp. 2–3.
26 US Department of Defense, *Quadrennial Defense Review, 2001*.
27 US Department of Defense, *The Nuclear Posture Review*.
28 Norris *et al*., pp. 3–4.
29 Ibid., p. 5.
30 Ibid., pp. 5–6.
31 Ferguson, Charles D. "Mini-Nuclear Weapons and the US Posture Review," James Martin Center for Non-proliferation Studies, April 8, 2002, available at http://cns.miis.edu/pubs/week/020408.htm.
32 Keith B. Payne, "The Nuclear Posture Review: Setting the Record Straight," *Washington Quarterly,* 28(3), Summer 2005, p. 147.
33 US Department of Defense, *The Nuclear Posture Review*, Foreword.
34 Hans M. Kristensen, "Nuclear Notebook—US Nuclear Forces 2006," *Bulletin of the Atomic Scientists*, January/February, 2006, 62(1), p. 71.
35 Ibid.
36 US Department of Defense, *The Nuclear Posture Review*.
37 Ibid.
38 CRS Report for Congress, *Nuclear Weapons and US National Security: A Need for New Weapons Programs*? Foreign Affairs, Defense, and Trade Division, Order Code RS21619, September 15, 2003, p. 1.
39 Bush, *The National Security Strategy of the United States of America*, pp. 14–15.
40 Ibid., p. 14.
41 Ibid., pp. 15–16.
42 Ibid., p. 29.
43 Bush, *National Strategy to Combat Weapons of Mass Destruction (NSCWMD)*, pp. vi, vii, viii, ix.
44 Ibid.
45 Ibid., p. 1.
46 Ibid.

47 Ibid.
48 Ibid., p. 2.
49 Ibid.
50 Ibid.
51 Bush, *National Strategy to Combat Weapons of Mass Destruction (NSCWMD)*, pp. vi, vii, viii, ix.
52 Ibid., p. 2.
53 Ibid., pp. 2–3.
54 Ibid.
55 Ibid., p. 3.
56 Ibid.
57 Hans M. Kristensen, "US Nuclear Weapons Guidance," The Nuclear Information Project: Documenting Nuclear Policy and Operations, Federation of Atomic Scientists, available at www.nukestrat.com/us/guidance.htm.
58 Ibid.
59 US Department of Defense, News Briefing, Richard B. Myers, Chairman of the Joint Chiefs of Staff, March 10, 2002; Interview with Wolf Blitzer, CNN Late Edition, distributed by the Office of International Information Programs, US Department of State, available at http://usinfo.state.gov.
60 "Defense Department Won't Comment on Leaked Nuclear Weapons Review (US Continues to Plan for Contingencies as Deterrence Strategy)," (360), March 10, 2002, distributed by the Office of International Information Programs, US Department of State, available at http://usinfo.state.gov.
61 Hans M. Kristensen, *Global Strike: A Chronology of the Pentagon's New Offensive Strike Plan*, Federation of American Scientists, March 2006, p. 75.
62 Hans M. Kristensen, "US National Security Strategy and Pre-emption," in *Defense Nationale and Securite Collective*, July 2006.
63 Ibid.
64 Richard B. Myers, General, USAF, Chairman, Joint Chiefs of Staff, statement before the Senate Armed Services Committee, 109th Congress, February 17, 2005, p. 32, available at http://armed-services.senate.gov/statemnt/2005/February/Myers%20 02-17-05.pdf.
65 The nuclear option in CONPLAN 8022 was first described in Arkin, "Not Just a Last Resort?" p. B01.
66 Kristensen, "US National Security Strategy and Pre-emption."
67 Nuclear Weapons Employment Policy (NUWEP), April 2004, quoted in Kristensen, *Global Strike*, p. 4.
68 Kristensen, *Global Strike*, p. 5.
69 Kristensen, "US National Security Strategy and Pre-emption."
70 Richard B. Myers, Change of Command/Retirement Ceremony, Offutt AFB, Omaha, Nebraska, July 9, 2004, p. 1.
71 Richard B. Myers, Posture Statement before House Armed Services Committee, February 16, 2005, p. 32, available at www.house.gov/hasc/testimony/109thcongress/ CJCSPostureStatement2-16-05.pdf.
72 Bush, *The National Security Strategy of the United States of America*, pp. 14–15.
73 Kristensen, *Global Strike*, p. 3.
74 Ibid.
75 Ibid.
76 Ibid.
77 Arkin, "Not Just A Last Resort?"
78 Ibid.
79 Kristensen, "Doctrine for Joint Nuclear Operations."
80 Ibid.
81 Ibid.

82 Joint Chiefs of Staff, Doctrine for Joint Nuclear Operations Final Coordination (2), Joint Pub 3–12, March 15, 2005, p. vii.
83 Ibid., p. ix.
84 Kristensen, *Global Strike*, pp. 37–38.
85 Joint Chiefs of Staff, Doctrine for Joint Nuclear Operations Final Coordination (2), Chapter 1, p. 6.
86 Ibid., p. 7.
87 Quoted in Walter H. Pincus, "Pentagon Revises Nuclear Strike Plan," *Washington Post*, September 11, 2005, p. A1.
88 Kristensen, *Global Strike*, pp. 37–38.
89 See Joint Pub 3–12, 1993; Joint Pub 3–12, 1995; Joint Pub 3–12.1, 1996.
90 Joint Chiefs of Staff, Doctrine for Joint Nuclear Operations Final Coordination (2), Joint Pub 3–12, p. 2.
91 Ibid., p. xi.
92 Hans M. Kristensen, "The Role of US Nuclear Weapons: New Doctrine Falls Short of Bush Pledge," *Arms Control Today*, September, 2005, available at www.armscontrol.org/act/2005_09/Kristensen.
93 Joint Chiefs of Staff, Doctrine for Joint Nuclear Operations Final Coordination (2), Joint Pub 3–12, p. xi.
94 Kristensen, "Doctrine for Joint Nuclear Operations."
95 Ibid.
96 Andrew Lichterman, "US Nuclear Weapons Doctrine: Disappearing from Public View, Nuclear Weapons," in *Disarmament Activist.org*, February 3, 2006, available at http://disarmamentactivist.org/2006/02/03/us-nuclear-weapons-doctrine-disappearing-from-public-view/.
97 US Department of Defense. Quadrennial Defense Review, Washington, DC, February 6, 2006, p. 49, available at www.globalsecurity.org/military/library/policy/DOD/qdr-2006-report.pdf.
98 Ibid., p. 29.
99 Ibid., p. 49.
100 Ibid.
101 Ibid.
102 Ibid.
103 Peter C.W. Flory, "Statement Before the Senate Armed Services Committee Strategic Forces Subcommittee Hearing Regarding Global Strike Issues, March 16, 2006," (hearing was delayed until March 29, 2006), United States Senate Committee on Armed Services, March 29, 2006, available at http://armed-services.senate.gov/e_witnesslist.cfm?id=1842.
104 US Department of Defense, *Quadrennial Defense Review*, 2006, p. ix.
105 Josh White and Ann S. Tyson, "Rumsfeld Offers Strategies for Current War Pentagon to Release 20-Year Plan Today," *The Washington Post*, February 3, 2006.
106 Bush, *The National Security Strategy of the United States of America,* 2002, p. 15.
107 Bush, *The National Security Strategy of 2006*, p. 18.
108 Ibid., p. 18.
109 Ibid., p. 23.
110 Ibid., pp. 22–23.
111 Hans M. Kristensen, quoted in "FAS Urges White House to Exclude Nuclear Weapons From National Security Strategy in War on Terrorism," Federation of Atomic Scientists, March 16, 2006, available at www.fas.org/press/news/2006/2006mar_natlsecstrategy.html.
112 US Department of Defense, *Strategic Operations Joint Operating Concept Version 2.0*, Secretary of Defense, Washington, DC, December 2006, p. 3.
113 US Department of Defense, *Strategic Operations Joint Operating Concept Version 2.0*, p. 3.

114 Ibid., p. 3.
115 Robert Nelson, "Complex 2030: DOE's Misguided Plan to Rebuild the US Nuclear Weapons Complex," *Nuclear Weapons and Global Security*, December 2006.
116 Ibid.
117 Ibid.
118 US Department of Energy, *Complex 2030: An Infrastructure Planning Scenario for a Nuclear Weapons Complex Able to Meet Threats of the 21st Century*, Office of Defense Programs, National Nuclear Security Administration (NNSA), October 23, 2006, p. 1.
119 Ibid.
120 Ibid.
121 Ibid.
122 Jacqueline Cabasso, "Complex 2030: US Plans for 'Nukes Forever,'" Western States Legal Foundation, available at www.wslfweb.org/docs/2030cabasso.pdf.
123 Ibid.
124 Ibid.
125 Ibid.
126 US Congress, Committee of Conference, "Making Appropriations for Foreign Operations, Export Financing, and Related Programs for the Fiscal Year Ending 30 September 2005, and For Other Purposes," report to accompany H.R. 4818, 108th Congress, 2nd session, 2004, H. Rept. 108–792, reprinted in US Congress, Congressional Record, November 19, 2004, Book II, p. H10556.
127 Jonathan Medalia, *The Reliable Replacement Warhead Program: Background and Current Develoments*, Foreign Affairs, Defense and Trade Division, Congressional Research Service, 2009, p. 1.
128 Daryl G. Kimball, "New Reasons to Reject New Warheads," *Arms Control Today*, January/February 2007.
129 "Busywork for Nuclear Scientists." *New York Times*, Editorial, January 15, 2007, p. 18.
130 NNSA Fact sheet, "NNSA's Reliable Replacement Warhead (RRW) Program: Modernizing the Nuclear Weapons Complex Today to Make it More Responsive to the Challenges of Tomorrow," available at www.nnsa.DOE.gov/docs/factsheets/2006/NA-06_FS03.pdf, in Jacqueline Cabasso, "Complex 2030: US Plans for 'Nukes Forever,'" Western States Legal Foundation, available at www.wslfweb.org/docs/2030cabasso.pdf, p. 2.
131 Linton F. Brooks, National Nuclear Security Administration Speech to the East Tennessee Economic Council, March 3, 2006, p. 4, available at www.nnsa.energy.gov.
132 Medalia, *The Reliable Replacement Warhead Program*, p. 3.
133 K. Henry O'Brien, Bryan L. Fearey, Michael R. Sjulin, and Greg A. Thomas, *Sustaining the Nuclear Enterprise: A New Approach*, Lawrence Livermore, Los Alamos, and Sandia National Laboratories, UCRL-AR- 212442, May 20, 2005, pp. 2–3.
134 Ibid., p. 3.
135 Ibid., p. 4.
136 Roger Speed and Michael M. May, "Assessing the United States' Nuclear Posture," in George Bunn and Christopher Chyba (eds) *US Nuclear Weapons Policy: Confronting Today's Threats*, Stanford University, CA: Center for International Security and Cooperation, and Washington, DC: Brookings Institution Press, 2006, pp. 256–264.
137 Medalia, *The Reliable Replacement Warhead Program*, p. 12.
138 Ibid., p. 16.
139 Ibid., p. 12
140 Ibid.
141 *Congressional Record*, 25 June 2004, p. H5085.

142 David L. Hobson, Congressman, "US Nuclear Security in the 21st Century," Address to the Arms Control Association, Washington, DC, February 3, 2005.
143 Thomas P. D'Agostino, "Statement before the House Armed Services Committee, Subcommittee on Strategic Forces, National Nuclear Security Administration," House Armed Services Committee Subcommittee, April 5, 2006, pp. 3, 6, available at www.globalsecurity.org/wmd/library/congress/2006_h/060405-dagostino.pdf.
144 The House Appropriations Committee reported the FY2006 Energy and Water Development Appropriations Bill, H.R. 2419, on May 18, 2005 (H.Rept. 109–86). Please note: The bill passed the House, 416–13, on May 24 with no amendments to the Weapons Activities section. In its report, the committee offered a "qualified endorsement" of RRW "contingent on the intent of the program being solely to meet the current military characteristics and requirements of the existing stockpile."
145 US Congress, Hearing on Department of Energy's FY2008 Budget for NNSA Programs, House Committee on Appropriations, Subcommittee on Energy and Water Development, March 29, 2007.
146 Jonathan Medalia, *The Reliable Replacement Warhead Program*, p. 50.
147 Ibid.
148 Ibid.
149 US Congress, Hearing on Nuclear Weapon Activities, House Committee on Appropriations, Subcommittee on Energy and Water Development, 109th Congress, 1st Session, March 29, 2007.
150 Ibid.
151 Robert S. Norris and Hans M. Kristensen, "Nuclear Forces, 2008," *Bulletin of the Atomic Scientist*, March/April 2008, 64(1), p. 53.
152 Ibid.
153 For a discussion of the Reliable Replacement Warhead, see Hugh Gusterson, "Understanding the Reliable Replacement Warhead," *Bulletin of Atomic Scientists*, July/August 2007, pp. 30–49; Nuclear Weapons Complex Assessment Committee. "The United States Nuclear Weapons Program: The Role of the Reliable Replacement Warhead." Washington, DC: AAAS, 2007, available at http://cstsp.aaas.org/content.html?contentid=899.
154 Senate Armed Services Committee, "National Defense Authorization Act for Fiscal Year 2008," Report 110–77, 110th Congress, 1st session, June 5, 2007, p. 395 (Section 1061).
155 US Department of Energy, FY2009 Congressional Budget Request, National Nuclear Security Administration, pp. 91–99.
156 US Department of Energy, FY2009 Congressional Budget Request, p. 25. The JASON study referenced is JSR-07-336E, "Reliable Replacement Warhead Executive Summary," September 7, 2007, p. 8, available at www.fas.org/irp/agency/DOD/jason/rrw.pdf.
157 US Congress, Hearing on FY2009 Budget for Strategic Defense Programs, House Committee on Armed Services, Subcommittee on Strategic Forces, 110th Congress, 2nd Session, February 27, 2008, transcript by CQ Transcriptions.
158 US Congress, Hearing on Nuclear Weapon Activities.
159 Elaine M. Grossman, "US General Calls for Faster Action on Reliable Replacement Warhead," *Global Security Newswire*, March 6, 2008.
160 Ibid.
161 Greg Webb, "Leading US Scientist Criticizes Warhead Effort," Global Security Newswire, February 27, 2008.
162 US Congress, House Committee on Armed Services, Duncan Hunter National Defense Authorization Act for Fiscal Year 2009, Joint Explanatory Statement to Accompany S. 3001, committee print, 110th Congress, 2nd session, September 2008, Committee Print HASC No. 10, Washington, DC, GPO, 2008, "Note from the Director of Legislative Operations," p. iii.

163 US Congress, House Committee on Armed Services, pp. 527, 816.

164 US Congress, House Committee on Appropriations, Energy and Water Development Appropriations Bill, 2009, Unnumbered committee print, 110th Congress, 2nd Session, 2008.

165 US Congress, House Committee on Appropriations, Energy and Water Development Appropriations Bill, pp. 123–124.

166 Ibid., p. 124.

167 US Congress, Senate Committee on Appropriations, Energy and Water Development Appropriations Bill, 2009, Report to Accompany S. 3258, 110th Congress, 2nd session, July 14, 2008, S.Rept. 110–416, Washington, DC, GPO, 2008, p. 120.

168 David R. Obey, "Explanatory Statement Submitted by Mr. Obey, Chairman of the House Committee on Appropriations, Regarding H.R. 1105, Omnibus Appropriations Act, 2009," Remarks in the House, Congressional Record, daily edition, February 23, 2009, p. H1962.

169 Quoted in Medalia, *The Reliable Replacement Warhead Program*, p. 40.

170 Medalia, *The Reliable Replacement Warhead Program*, 2009, p. 40.

171 US Congress, House Committee on Appropriations, Consolidated Security, Disaster Assistance, and Continuing Appropriations Act, 2009, Division C, Department of Defense Appropriations Act, 2009, unnumbered committee print, 110th Congress, 2nd session, October 2008, Washington, DC, GPO, 2008, p. 367.

172 US Executive Office of the President, Office of Management and Budget, Terminations, Reductions, and Savings: Budget of the US Government, Fiscal Year 2010, Washington, DC, 2009, p. 55, available at www.whitehouse.gov/omb/budget/fy2010/assets/trs.pdf.

173 US Congress, House Committee on Armed Services, National Defense Authorization Act for Fiscal Year 2010, Report on H.R. 2647 Together with Additional and Supplemental Views, 111th Congress, 1st session, June 18, 2009, H. Rept. 111–166, Washington, DC, GPO, 2009, p. 588.

174 US Congress, Senate Committee on Armed Services, National Defense Authorization Act for Fiscal Year 2010, Report to Accompany S. 1390, 111th Congress, 1st session, July 2, 2009, S. Rept. 111–35, Washington, DC, GPO, 2009, p. 254.

175 Hans M. Kristensen, "The Nuclear Posture of the United States," in Magnus Eriksson and Kari M. Osland (eds) *Nuclear Weapons in the 21st Century: Old Players, New Game—New Players, Old Game*, Oslo: Norwegian Defence Command and Staff College/Norwegian Institute of International Affairs, October 2008, pp. 53–66.

176 US Department of State, United States Relations with Russia: The Cold War, Office of the Historian, available at www.state.gov/r/palhoipubslfs/85895.htm#nsc68.

177 Hans M. Kristensen, "Dismantling Fewer, Not More, Nukes," *Los Angeles Times*, June 11, 2007.

178 Mark Thompson, "Obama's Showdown Over Nukes," *Time Magazine*, Washington, DC, January 26, 2009.

179 Ibid.

180 Ibid.

181 Ibid.

182 Hans Kristensen, "Nuclear Plan Shows Cuts and Massive Investments," FAS Strategic Blog, available at www.fas.org/blog/ssp/.

183 Kristensen, "The Nuclear Posture of the United States," pp. 53–66.

6 The nuclear option: from Bush to Obama

1 James Kitfield, "Road To Zero Nukes Remains Fraught," *National Journal*, June 1, 2009, available at http://gsn.nti.org/gsn/ts_20090601_8825.php.

2 George P. Schultz, William J. Perry, Henry A. Kissinger, and Sam Nunn, "A World Free of Nuclear Weapons," *Wall Street Journal*, January 4, 2007; George P. Schultz,

William J. Perry, Henry A. Kissinger, and Sam Nunn, "Toward a Nuclear- Free World," *Wall Street Journal*, January 15, 2008.

3 Barack Obama, "Remarks By President Barack Obama," Hradcany Square, Prague, Czech Republic, Washington, DC: The White House, Office of the Press Secretary, April 5, 2009, available at www.whitehouse.gov/the_press_office/Remarks-By-President-Barack-Obama-In-Prague-As-Delivered/.

4 Paul Meyer, "Prague One Year Later: From Words to Deed," *Arms Control Today*, May 2010, available at www.armscontrol.org/act/2010_05/LookingBack.

5 Ibid.

6 Obama, "Remarks By President Barack Obama," Hradcany Square, Prague.

7 Meyer, "Prague One Year Later: From Words to Deed."

8 Obama, "Remarks By President Barack Obama," Hradcany Square, Prague.

9 Ibid.

10 Meyer, "Prague One Year Later: From Words to Deed."

11 Obama, "Remarks By President Barack Obama," Hradcany Square, Prague.

12 Ibid.

13 Meyer, "Prague One Year Later: From Words to Deed."

14 Barack Obama, *The National Security Strategy of the United States of America*, Washington, DC: The White House, September 2010, p. 23.

15 Ibid.

16 Ibid.

17 Ibid.

18 Ibid., p. 24.

19 Ibid., p. 24.

20 David E. Hoffman, "Reviewing the Review: Obama's New Nuke Strategy is a Good Start. But the Cold War's Legacy Lives On," *Foreign Policy*, April 6, 2010, available at www.foreignpolicy.com/articles/2010/04/06/reviewing_the_review.

21 US Department of Defense, *The Nuclear Posture Review 2010*, Washington, DC, April 2010, available at www.defense.gov/npr/docs/2010%20Nuclear%20Posture%20Review%20Report.pdf, p. viii.

22 US Department of Defense, *The Nuclear Posture Review*, 2002.

23 Obama, "Remarks By President Barack Obama," Hradcany Square, Prague.

24 US Department of Defense, *The Nuclear Posture Review 2010*, p. 16.

25 Ibid., p. 17.

26 Daryl G. Kimball and Greg Thielmann, "Obama's NPR: Transitional, Not Transformational," *Arms Control Today*, May 2010, available at www.armscontrol.org/act/2010_05/Kimball-Thielmann.

27 US Department of Defense, *The Nuclear Posture Review 2010*.

28 Ibid., p. v.

29 Ralph A. Cossa, "Moving Toward 'No First Use,'" *International Security Network*, April 9, 2010, available at www.isn.ethz.ch/isn/Current-Affairs/Security-Watch/Detail/?lng=en&id=114713.

30 Kimball and Thielmann, "Obama's NPR: Transitional, Not Transformational."

31 US Department of Defense, *The Nuclear Posture Review 2010*, p. 30.

32 David J. Trachtenberg, "Assessing the NPR: A Closer Look," *Center for Defense Studies*, April 20, 2010, available at www.defensestudies.org/?p=2274.

33 Obama, "Remarks By President Barack Obama," Hradcany Square, Prague.

34 Hans M. Kristensen, "The Nuclear Posture Review," *FAS Strategic Security*, April 8, 2010, available at www.fas.org/blog/ssp/2010/04/npr2010.php#more-2908.

35 Ibid.

36 US Department of Defense, *The Nuclear Posture Review 2010*, p. 20.

37 Ibid., p. 25.

38 Hans M. Kristensen, "The Nuclear Posture Review."

39 US Department of Defense, *The Nuclear Posture Review 2010*, p. 16.

40 Ibid., p. 32.
41 Ibid., p. 28.
42 Ibid., p. 28.
43 Ibid., p. 39.
44 Hans Kristensen, "Nuclear Plan Shows Cuts and Massive Investments."
45 Ibid.
46 Ibid.
47 Ibid.
48 Ibid.
49 Office of the Press Secretary. *Joint Understanding by Obama, Medvedev on Weapon Negotiations*, Washington, DC: The White House, July 8, 2009, available at www.america.gov/st/texttransenglish/2009/July/20090708154724xjsnommis0.7355005.html.
50 Amy F. Woolf, *The New START Treaty: Central Limits and Key Provisions*, CRS Report for Congress, November 24, 2010, p. 1.
51 Office of the Press Secretary. *Joint Understanding by Obama, Medvedev on Weapon Negotiations*.
52 Ibid.
53 The text of the Treaty, its Protocol, annexes, and article-by-article analysis can be found at www.state.gov/t/vci/trty/126118.htm.
54 For a brief summary of the original START Treaty, as well as a review of the US-Russian negotiations on the new START Treaty, see CRS Report R40084, *Strategic Arms Control After START: Issues and Options*, by Amy F. Woolf.
55 For details on this agreement see CRS Report RL31448, *Nuclear Arms Control: The Strategic Offensive Reductions Treaty*.
56 Office of the Press Secretary. "Key Facts about the New START Treaty," Washington, DC: The White House, March 26, 2010, available at www.whitehouse.gov/the-press-office/key-facts-about-new-start-treaty.
57 Woolf, *New START Treaty: Central Limits and Key Provisions*, p. 1.
58 Office of the Press Secretary. "Key Facts about the New START Treaty."
59 US Department of State, *Comparison of START Treaty, Moscow Treaty, and New START Treaty*, Bureau of Verification, Compliance and Implementation, Washington, DC, April 8, 2010, available at www.state.gov/t/vci/rls/.139901.htm.
60 Woolf, *New START Treaty: Central Limits and Key Provisions*, p. 2.
61 Ibid.
62 Office of the Press Secretary. "Key Facts about the New START Treaty."
63 Woolf, *New START Treaty: Central Limits and Key Provisions*, p. 2.
64 Office of the Press Secretary. "Key Facts about the New START Treaty."
65 According to New START's Protocol 7 a deployed ICBM launcher is "an ICBM launcher that contains an ICBM and is not an ICBM test launcher, an ICBM training launcher, or an ICBM launcher located at a space launch facility." A deployed SLBM launcher is a launcher installed on an operational submarine that contains an SLBM and is not intended for testing or training. A deployed mobile launcher of ICBMs is one that contains an ICBM and is not a mobile test launcher or a mobile launcher of ICBMs located at a space launch facility. These deployed launchers can be based only at ICBM bases. A deployed ICBM or SLBM is one that is contained in a deployed launcher. Nondeployed launchers are, therefore, those that are used for testing or training, those that are located at space launch facilities, or those that are located at deployment areas or on submarines but do not contain a deployed ICBM or SLBM. The New START Treaty does not limit the number of nondeployed ICBMs or nondeployed SLBMs. It does, however, state that these missiles must be located at facilities that are known to be within the infrastructure that supports and maintains ICBMs and SLBMs. These include "submarine bases, ICBM or SLBM loading facilities, maintenance facilities, repair facilities for ICBMs or SLBMs, storage facilities for ICBMs or SLBMs,

conversion or elimination facilities for ICBMs or SLBMs, test ranges, space launch facilities, and production facilities." Nondeployed ICBMs and SLBMs may also be in transit between these facilities, although Article IV of the treaty indicates that this time in transit should be "no more than 30 days."

66 Each individual missile will be identified in the database by a "unique identifier," which will, in most cases, be the serial number affixed to the missile during production.

67 *Treaty between the United States of America and the Russian Federation on Measures for the Further Reduction and Limitation of Strategic Offensive Arms*, p. 3, available at www.nti.org/e_research/official_docs/inventory/pdfs/aptnewstart.pdf.

68 Woolf, *New START Treaty: Central Limits and Key Provisions*, p. 2.

69 *Protocol to the Treaty between the United States of America and the Russian Federation on Measures for the Further Reduction and Limitation of Strategic Offensive Arms*, p. 93, available at www.state.gov/documents/organization/140047.pdf.

70 Ibid.

71 Ibid., pp. 93–94.

72 Ibid.

73 Woolf, *New START Treaty: Central Limits and Key Provisions*, p. 9.

74 *Protocol to the Treaty between the United States of America and the Russian Federation.*

75 Woolf, *New START Treaty: Central Limits and Key Provisions*, p. 9.

76 Ibid., p. 11.

77 Ibid.

78 *Protocol to the Treaty between the United States of America and the Russian Federation.*

79 Woolf, *New START Treaty: Central Limits and Key Provisions*, p. 11.

80 Ibid.

81 Ibid., p. 14.

82 Ivan Oelrich and Hans M. Kristensen, *Verification Extended Public Interest Report*, The Federation of American Scientists, 63(2), Summer 2010, p. 7.

83 Office of the Press Secretary, *Joint Statement by President Dmitriy Medvedev of the Russian Federation and President Barack Obama of the United States of America.*

84 Office of the Press Secretary, *Joint Understanding by Obama, Medvedev on Weapon Negotiations.*

85 *Treaty Between The United States of America and the Russian Federation on Measures for the Further Reduction and Limitation of Strategic Offensive Arms*, p. 2.

86 Article 14, following the form of most previous arms control treaties, indicates that each party shall have the right to withdraw from the Treaty if it decides that extraordinary events related to the subject of the Treaty have jeopardized its supreme national interests. For the Russian statement, see http://eng.kremlin.ru/text/docs/2010/04/225214.shtml.

87 US Department of State. "Statement by the United States of America Concerning Missile Defense," Bureau of Verification, Compliance and Implementation, Washington, DC, April 7, 2010, available at www.state.gov/documents/organization/140406.pdf.

88 Ellen Tauscher, "Remarks at the Atlantic Council Panel Discussion," *The Case for New START Ratification*, Atlantic Council Panel Discussion, United States Mission to the United Nations and Other International Organizations in Geneva, Washington, DC, April 21, 2010, available at http://geneva.usmission.gov/2010/04/22/new-start-ratification/.

89 "Russian Statement on NEW Start Treaty," available at http://eng.kremlin.ru/text/docs/2010/04/225214.shtml.

90 Woolf, *New START Treaty: Central Limits and Key Provisions, p.* 16.

91 Oelrich and Kristensen, *Verification Extended Public Interest Report*, p. 8.

92 Ibid.
93 Ibid.
94 Ibid.
95 Ibid.
96 Ibid., p. 7.
97 Ibid., p. 8.
98 Ibid.
99 Woolf, *New START Treaty: Central Limits and Key Provisions*, p. 22.
100 Ibid., p. 22.
101 US Congress, Senate Committee on Foreign Relations, *Treaty with Russia on Measures for Further Reduction and Limitation of Strategic Offensive Arms (The New START Treaty)*, Executive Report, 111th Congress, 2nd session, October 1, 2010, Executive Report 111–6, Washington, DC, 2010.
102 Josh Rogin, "Kerry and DeMint Spar over Missile Defense," *Foreign Policy: The Cable*, September 16, 2010, available at http://thecable.foreignpolicy.com/posts/2010/09/16/kerry_and_demint_spar_over_missile_defense. See, also, John Isaacs, Analysis of the Senate Foreign Relations Committee Passage of the new START Treaty, *The Chain Reaction,* 16 September 2010, available at http://blog.livableworld.org/story/2010/9/16/16585/7341.
103 John Kerry, quoted in Peter Baker, "Senate Passes Arms Control Treaty With Russia, 71–26," *The New York Times*, December 22, 2010.
104 Richard Burt, quoted in Peter Baker, "Senate Passes Arms Control Treaty With Russia, 71–26," *The New York Times*, December 22, 2010.
105 Daryl G. Kimball, quoted in Peter Baker, "Senate Passes Arms Control Treaty With Russia, 71–26," *The New York Times*, December 22, 2010
106 Oelrich and Kristensen, *Verification Extended Public Interest Report*, p. 9.
107 Ibid.
108 Barack Obama, "Arms Control Today 2008 Presidential Q&A: Democratic Candidate Barack Obama," *Arms Control Today*, September 24, 2008, available at www.armscontrol.org/system/files/Obama_Q-A_FINAL_Dec10_2008.pdf.
109 Nuclear Posture Review, p. vii.
110 Full text of the treaty can be found at www.iaea.org/Publications/Documents/Infcircs/Others/infcirc140.pdf.
111 The "nuclear nonproliferation regime" refers to international efforts to prevent the spread of nuclear weapons through treaties, export control coordination and enforcement, UN Security Council resolutions and other initiatives.
112 The treaty defines nuclear-weapon states as those which have manufactured and exploded a nuclear weapon or other nuclear explosive device prior to 1 January 1967.
113 This number does not include North Korea.
114 Whether North Korea is still an official member has not been determined by the treaty depositaries. There was some early debate over the legitimacy of North Korea's withdrawal from the NPT for procedural reasons. However, UN Security Council resolutions call on North Korea to return to the NPT. White House Coordinator for Arms Control and WMD Proliferation Gary Samore said on April 22, 2010, that "as a technical legal matter we don't recognize that they have withdrawn from the treaty," available at www.carnegieendowment.org/files/0421_transcript_samore.pdf.
115 Paul K. Kerr, Mary Beth Nikitin, Amy F. Woolf, and Jonathan Medalia, *2010 Non-Proliferation Treaty (NPT) Review Conference: Key Issues and Implications*, CRS Report for Congress, May 3, 2010, Summary.
116 Ibid., p. 6.
117 For example, see Susan E. Rice, "Statement on the Fortieth Anniversary of the Nuclear

Non-Proliferation Treaty," U.S. Mission to the United Nations, New York, NY, March 5, 2010, available at http://usun.state.gov/briefing/statements/2010/137889.htm.

118 Susan Burk, "Taking Stock of the NPT: An Interview With US Special Representative Susan Burk," *Arms Control Today*, March 2010, available at www.armscontrol.org/act/2010_03/Burk.

119 Robert Einhorn, "Obama reaffirms his stance on nukes; South Africa has a crucial role to play in making the world a safer place," *The Star*, August 27, 2009, available at www.thestar.co.za/index.php?fArticleId=5138971.

120 US House of Representatives Committee on Foreign Affairs, Hearing on "Stopping the Spread of Nuclear Weapons, Countering Nuclear Terrorism: The NPT Review Conference and the Nuclear Security Summit," Washington, DC, April 21, 2010, available at www.cfr.org/terrorism/house-foreign-affairs-committee-testimony-stopping-spread-nuclear weapons-countering-nuclear-terrorism-npt-review-conference-nuclear-security-summit/p21940.

121 Ibid.

122 Hillary Clinton, "Remarks before the 2010 NPT Review Conference," New York, NY, 3 May 2010, available at www.cfr.org/publication/22042/hillary_clintons_remarks_before_the_2010_npt_review_conference.html.

123 To promote nuclear transparency and strengthen global arms control, the United States revealed that it has 5,113 operational warheads in its nuclear arsenal on May 3, coinciding with the opening of the NPT Review Conference.

124 Clinton, "Remarks before the 2010 NPT Review Conference."

125 Alicia Godsberg, *Nuclear Non-Proliferation Treaty Review Conference Concludes in Final Document*, The Federation of American Scientists, 63(2), Summer 2010, p. 10.

126 Office of the Press Secretary, "President Obama's Statement on NPT Review Conference Treaty must be at center of efforts to stop spread of nuclear weapons," Washington, DC: The White House, May 28, 2010, available at www.america.gov/st/texttransenglish/2010/May/20100528230427ptellivremos0.3599163.html#ixzz1COBJcOsE.

127 Ibid.

128 US Department of State. "Remarks by Under Secretary Tauscher on NPT Review Conference U.S. reaffirms NPT commitment to make progress toward nuclear disarmament," Office of the Spokesman, Washington, DC, May 28, 2010 available at www.america.gov/st/texttransenglish/2010/May/20100528170206ptellivremos0.5303766.html##ixzz1COCNBzMt.

129 Office of the Press Secretary. "Statement by the National Security Advisor, General James L. Jones, on the Non-Proliferation Treaty Review Conference," Washington, DC: The White House, May 28, 2010, available at www.america.gov/st/texttransenglish/2010/May/20100528225343ptellivremos6.870234e 02.html##ixzz1CNaFES98.

130 *2010 Review Conference of the Parties to the Treaty on the Non-Proliferation of Nuclear Weapons—Final Document*, Action 82: The Conference "notes the new proposals and initiatives from Governments and civil society related to achieving a world free of nuclear weapons … [and] notes the proposals for nuclear disarmament of the Secretary-General of the United Nations to inter alia consider negotiations on a nuclear weapons convention or agreement on a framework of separate mutually reinforcing instruments, backed by a strong system of verification," available at www.un.org/en/conf/npt/2010/.

131 Alicia Godsberg, *Nuclear Non-Proliferation Treaty Review Conference Concludes in Final Document*, p. 12.

132 *2010 Review Conference of the Parties to the Treaty on the Non-Proliferation of Nuclear Weapons—Final Document*, Action 1.

133 Jayantha Dhanapala, "Evaluating the 2010 NPT Conference," Special Report 258, United States Institute of Peace, October 2010, available at www.usip.org/publications/evaluating-the-2010-npt-review-conference.
134 James Traub, "Two Cheers for Multilateralism: Why the Nuclear Review Conference was a Minor Triumph for Obama," *Foreign Policy*, June 8, 2010, available at www.foreignpolicy.com/articles/2010/06/08/two_cheers_for_multilateralism.
135 George P. Schultz *et al.*, "Toward a Nuclear free World."
136 Office of the Press Secretary, "Press conference by President Obama in L'Aquila, Italy," Washington, DC: The White House, July 10, 2009, available at www.whitehouse.gov/the_press_office/Press-Conference-by-the-President-in-LAquila-Italy-7-10-09.
137 David Sanger and William J. Broad, "Leaders Gather for Nuclear Talks as New Threat Is Seen," *The New York Times*, April 11, 2010, available at www.nytimes.com/2010/04/12/world/12nuke.html.
138 Josh Rogin, "White House Announces Nuclear Summit Attendees," *Foreign Policy*, April 10, 2010, available at http://thecable.foreignpolicy.com/posts/2010/04/10/white_house_announces_nuclear_summit_attendees.
139 Barack Obama, "Obama's Speech at the Nuclear Security Summit."
140 Mary Beth Nikitin, *Securing Nuclear Materials: The 2010 Summit and Issues for Congress*, CRS Report for Congress, April 16, 2010, p. 2, available at www.fas.org/sgp/crs/nuke/R41169.pdf.
141 Matthew Bunn, *Securing the Bomb 2010: Securing All Nuclear Materials in Four Years, Project on Managing the Atom*, April 2010, p. 25, available at www.nti.org/e_research/Securing_The_Bomb_2010.pdf.
142 Gareth Evans and Yoriko Kawaguchi, *Eliminating Nuclear Threats: A Practical Agenda for Global Policymakers, International Commission on Nuclear Non-proliferation and Disarmament*, Canberra/Tokyo, 2009, p. 44.
143 Obama, "Obama's Speech at the Nuclear Security Summit."
144 Joseph R. Biden, "The Path to Nuclear Security: Implementing the President's Prague Agenda," National Defense University, February 18, 2010, Office of the Vice President, Washington, DC, available at www.whitehouse.gov/the-press office/remarksvice-president-biden-national-defense-university.
145 Mary Beth Nikitin, *Securing Nuclear Materials: The 2010 Summit and Issues for Congress.*
146 *Communiqué from Washington Nuclear Security Summit: Nations Pledge to Strengthen Nuclear Security, Reduce Nuclear Terrorism*, April 13, 2010, available at, www.america.gov/st/texttransenglish/2010/April/20100413171855eaifas0.6155773.html#.
147 Sarah J. Diehl and Paula Humphrey, "The April 2010 Nuclear Security Summit: One More Step Toward the Mountaintop," *Monterey Institute for International Studies James Martin Center for Nonproliferation Studies* April 20, 2010, available at www.nti.org/e_research/e3_nuclear_security_summit.html.
148 Ibid.
149 Ibid.
150 Jon Kyl, "Kyl Statement on Nuclear Security Summit," *Jon Kyl Senator of Arizona website*, April 13, 2010, available at http://kyl.senate.gov/record.cfm?id=323782.
151 Paul B. Stares, "Important Steps for Nuclear Security," *Council on Foreign Relations*, April 13, 2010, available at www.cfr.org/proliferation/important-steps-nuclear-security/p21894.
152 Kenneth Luongo, quoted in Mary Beth Sheridan, "Obama secures 47-nation pact at nuclear summit," *The Washington Post*, April 14, 2010, available at www.washingtonpost.com/wpdyn/content/article/2010/04/13/AR2010041300427.html.
153 Jonathan Medalia, *Comprehensive Nuclear-Test-Ban Treaty: Background and*

Current Developments, CRS Report for Congress, December 7, 2010, p. 3, available at www.fas.org/sgp/crs/nuke/RL33548.pdf.

154 Jack D. Crouch, Special Briefing on the Nuclear Posture Review.

155 Ari Fleischer quoted in Walter Pincus, "U.S. Aims for 3,800 Nuclear Warheads," *Washington Post*, January 10, 2002.

156 Condoleezza Rice, "Letter to Honorable Pete Domenici, United States Senate," June 25, 2007.

157 Weapons of Mass Destruction Commission, *Weapons of Terror: Freeing the World of Nuclear, Biological and Chemical Arms*, Stockholm, Sweden, 2006, p. 107, available at www.wmdcommission.org/files/Weapons_of_Terror.pdf.

158 Gareth Evans and Yoriko Kawaguchi, *Eliminating Nuclear Threats*, Report of the International Commission on Nuclear Non-proliferation and Disarmament, 2009, available at www.icnnd.org/reference/reports/ent/index.html.

159 Paul K. Kerr, Mary Beth Nikitin, Amy F. Woolf, and Jonathan Medalia, *2010 Non-Proliferation Treaty (NPT) Review Conference: Key Issues and Implications*, CRS Report for Congress, May 3, 2010, p. 8, available at www.fas.org/sgp/crs/nuke/R41216.pdf.

160 The CTBT was opened for signature on September 24, 1996. The CTBT decision is in Decision 2 of the 1995 package, "Principles and Objectives for Nuclear Non-Proliferation and Disarmament," available at www.un.org/disarmament/WMD/Nuclear/1995-NPT/1995NPT.shtml.

161 *2000 Review Conference of the Parties to the Treaty on the Non-Proliferation of Nuclear Weapons*, "Final Document," Volume 1, NPT/CONF/2000/28 (Parts I and II), available at www.armscontrol.org/act/2000_06/docjun.

162 Obama, "Remarks By President Barack Obama," Hradcany Square, Prague.

163 Joseph R. Biden, "Letter from Vice President to the Honorable Edward Pastor, Chairman, Subcommittee on Energy and Water Development, Committee on Appropriations," US House of Representatives, September 16, 2009.

164 Hillary R. Clinton, "Remarks at CTBT Article XIV Conference," New York, NY, September 24, 2009," p. 2, available at www.ctbto.org/fileadmin/user_upload/Art_14_2009/240909_Morning_Session/240909_US.pdf.

165 Meyer, "Prague One Year Later."

166 Biden, Joseph R., "The Path to Nuclear Security: Implementing the President's Prague Agenda."

167 Jonathan Medalia, *Comprehensive Nuclear-Test-Ban Treaty*, Summary.

168 Meyer, "Prague One Year Later."

169 Kitfield, "Road To Zero Nukes Remains Fraught."

170 William Perry, quoted in Kitfield, "Road To Zero Nukes Remains Fraught."

171 Rose Gottemoeller, quoted in Jonathan Medalia, *Comprehensive Nuclear-Test-Ban Treaty*, Summary.

172 Michael O'Hanlon, *A Skeptic's Case for Nuclear Disarmament*, The Brookings Institution, Washington, DC, 2010, p. 13.

173 Hans M. Kristensen, "Senate Approval of New START Moves Nuclear Arms Control Forward," FAS Security Strategy, December 22, 2010, available at www.fas.org/blog/ssp/2010/12/newstart-3.php.

174 US Department of Defense, *The Nuclear Posture Review 2010, Cover Letter*.

175 Meyer, "Prague One Year Later."

176 Kimball and Thielmann, "Obama's NPR: Transitional, Not Transformational."

177 Ibid.

Conclusion

1 Bush, State of the Union Address.

2 Bush, Graduation Speech at West Point.

3 Ibid.
4 Ibid.
5 Bush, *The National Security Strategy of the United States of America*, pp. 13–15.
6 Ibid., p. 1.
7 Ibid., p. 5.
8 George W. Bush, Statement by the President in His Address to the Nation, Washington, DC, September 11, 2001, available at www.whitehouse.gov/news/releases/2001/09/20010911 16.html, p. 1.
9 Bush, *National Security Strategy of the United States of America*, pp. 13–15.
10 Ibid., pp. 13–15.
11 Ibid., p. 13.
12 Ibid., p. 15.
13 Ibid.
14 For the contrary view on this point see, Christopher Greenwood, "International Law and the Pre-emptive Use of Force: Afghanistan, al-Qaida, and Iraq," *International Law Journal*, 2003, 7(16); and Terence Taylor, "The End of Imminence?" *The Washington Quarterly*, 2004, 57: pp. 66–67.
15 *Webster's Revised Unabridged Dictionary.*
16 Bush, *National Security Strategy of the United States of America*, p. 16.
17 Trachtenberg, "Preventive War and US Foreign Policy," p. 2.
18 Bush, *The National Security Strategy of the United States of America*, p. 5.
19 Ibid., p. 4.
20 Record, "The Bush Doctrine and the War with Iraq," p. 9.
21 Bush, *National Security Strategy of the United States of America*, 2002, pp. 13–15.
22 Trachtenberg, "Preventive War and US Foreign Policy," p. 29.
23 Bush, *National Security Strategy of the United States of America*, 2002, pp. 1–3.
24 Natural Resources Defense Council, Table of US Strategic Offensive Force Loadings, Archive of Nuclear Data, available at www.nrdc.org/nuclear/nudb/datab1.asp. The same source indicates that the Soviet Union, in 1990, had just over 11,000 warheads on 2,332 strategic nuclear delivery vehicles.
25 Russia, by the same accounting, had 3,909 warheads on 814 delivery vehicles. See US Department of State, START Aggregate Numbers of Strategic Offensive Weapons, Fact Sheet, Bureau of Verification, Compliance and Inspection, Washington, DC, April 1, 2009.
26 The State Department did not provide an unclassified estimate for Russia's current force of operationally deployed warheads. See US Department of State, *Annual Report on Implementation of the Moscow Treaty*, Bureau of Verification, Compliance, and Inspection, May 13, 2008, p. 2.
27 The Bush Administration emphasized this point in early 2002, when presenting the results of the 2001 Nuclear Posture Review (NPR). Douglas Feith, the Undersecretary of Defense for Policy, stated that nuclear weapons "continue to be essential to our security, and that of our friends and allies." See Feith, Prepared statements before the Senate Armed Services Committee.
28 "Arms Control Today 2008 Presidential Q&A: Democratic Candidate Barack Obama," *Arms Control Today*, September 24, 2008, available at www.armscontrol.org/2008election.
29 George Perkovich, "Bush's Nuclear Revolution: A Regime Change in Nonproliferation," *Foreign Affairs*, March/April 2003, 82(2), p. 4.

Bibliography

Primary sources

2000 Review Conference of the Parties to the Treaty on the Non-Proliferation of Nuclear Weapons, "Final Document," Volume 1, NPT/CONF/2000/28 (Parts I and II), available at www.armscontrol.org/act/2000_06/docjun.

2010 Review Conference of the Parties to the Treaty on the Non-Proliferation of Nuclear Weapons – Final Document, available at www.un.org/en/conf/npt/2010.

Aspin, Les. Address as the Secretary of Defense to National Academy of Sciences on the Defense Counter-proliferation Initiative, Washington, DC, December 7, 1993.

Basic National Security Policy, attached to National Security Council Report by James S. Lay Jr., NSC 5501, January 7, 1955. Foreign Relations of the United States, 1955–1957, Vol. XIX, NARA, College Park, Maryland, 33.

Biden, Joseph R. "Letter from Vice President to the Honorable Edward Pastor, Chairman, Subcommittee on Energy and Water Development, Committee on Appropriations," US House of Representatives, September 16, 2009.

Biden, Joseph R. "The Path to Nuclear Security: Implementing the President's Prague Agenda," National Defense University, February 18, 2010, Office of the Vice President, Washington, DC, available at www.whitehouse.gov/the-press office/remarksvice-president-biden-national-defense-university.

Brooks, Linton F. National Nuclear Security Administration Speech to the East Tennessee Economic Council, March 3, 2006, available at www.nnsa.energy.gov/.

Bush, George W. "A Period of Consequences." Address at The Citadel, South Carolina, September 23, 1999, available at www.citadel.edu/pao/addresses/presbush.html.

Bush, George W. Address to the Joint Session of Congress, February 27, 2001, from http://whitehouse.gov/news/releases/2001/02/20010228.html.

Bush, George W. Address to a Joint Session of Congress and the American People, September 20, 2001, available at www.whitehouse.gov.

Bush, George W. Address to the Nation on Iraq: Denial and Deception, October 7, 2002, available at www.whitehouse.gov/news/releases/20021007-8.html.

Bush, George W. Graduation Speech at West Point, June 1, 2002, available at www.whitehouse.gov/news/releases/2002/06/orint/20020601-3.html.

Bush, George W. *The National Security Strategy of 2006.* Washington, DC: The White House, 2006.

Bush, George W. *The National Security Strategy of the United States of America.* Washington, DC: The White House, September 2002.

Bush, George W. *National Strategy to Combat Weapons of Mass Destruction (NSCWMD).* Washington, DC: The White House, December 2002.

Bush, George W. "President Bush's Address on Iraq." October 7, 2002, available at www.whitehouse.gov/news/releases/20021007-8.html.

Bush, George W. "President Bush Holds Roundtable with Arab – and Muslim – American Leaders." Embassy at Afghanistan, Washington, DC, available at www.dhs.gov/xnews/speeches/speech_0026.shtm.

Bush, George W. "President Discusses Growing Danger Posed by Saddam Hussein's Regime." Radio Address by the President to the Nation, The White House Archives, September 14, 2002, available at http://georgewbush-whitehouse.archives.gov/news/releases/2002/09/20020914.html.

Bush, George W. "President Outlines Priorities." Presidential Hall, Dwight D. Eisenhower Executive Office Building, November 7, 2002, available at http://georgewbush-whitehouse.archives.gov/news/releases/2002/11/20021107-2.html.

Bush, George W. "Remarks by the President in Address to the United Nations General Assembly." New York, September 12, 2002, from www.globalsecurity.org/wmd/library/news/iraq/2002/iraq-020912-wh01.htm.

Bush, George W. "Remarks by the President to the Warsaw Conference on Combating Terrorism." November 6, 2001, available at http://usinfo.state.gov/topical/pol/terror/01 1 10604.htm.

Bush, George W. Speech on the Future of Iraq, Office of the Press Secretary, February 26, 2002, available at www.guardian.co.uk/world/2003/feb/27/usa.iraq2.

Bush, George W. Speech at Washington National Cathedral for Victims of Terrorism, recorded by the Federal News, published in "After the Attacks," *The New York Times*, September 15, 2001.

Bush, George W. State of the Union Address, January 29, 2002, available at www.whitehouse.gov/new/releases/2002/01/print/2002l0l/print/20020129.html.Burk

Bush, George W. Speech to the National Press Club, Washington, DC, May 23, 2000, available at www.foreignpolicy2000.org/library/index.html.

Cheney, Richard B. "Vice President Speaks at VFW 103rd National Convention." The White House Archives, August 26, 2002, available at http://georgewbush-whitehouse.archives.gov/news/releases/2002/08/20020826.html.

CIA. Unclassified Report to Congress on the Acquisition of Technology Relating to Weapons of Mass Destruction and Advanced Conventional Munitions, January 1 through June 30, 2002, available at https://www.cia.gov/library/reports/archived-reports-1/jan_jun2002.html.

Clinton, Hillary R. "Remarks at CTBT Article XIV Conference," New York, NY, September 24, 2009," available at www.ctbto.org/fileadmin/user_upload/Art_14_2009/240909_Morning_Session/240909_US.pdf.

Clinton, Hillary R. "Remarks before the 2010 NPT Review Conference," New York, NY, May 3, 2010, available at www.cfr.org/publication/22042/hillary_clintons_remarks_before_the_2010_npt_review_conference.html.

Clinton, William J. *A National Security Strategy for a Global Age*. Washington, DC: The White House, December 2000.

Clinton, William J. *A National Security Strategy of Engagement and Enlargement*. Washington, DC: The White House, July 1994.

Clinton, William J. *A National Security Strategy of Engagement and Enlargement*. Washington, DC: The White House, February 1995.

Clinton, William J. *A National Security Strategy for a New Century*. Washington, DC: The White House, 1998.

Clinton, William J. *A National Security Strategy for a New Century.* Washington, DC: The White House, 1999.

Commission on the Intelligence Capabilities of the United States Regarding Weapons of Mass Destruction. Report to the President, March 31, 2005, available at http://govinfo.library.unt.edu/wmd/report/wmd_report.pdf.

Communiqué from Washington Nuclear Security Summit: Nations Pledge to Strengthen Nuclear Security, Reduce Nuclear Terrorism, April 13, 2010, available at www.america.gov/st/texttransenglish/2010/April/20100413171855eaifas0.6155773.html#.

Counterproliferation Initiative. PDD/NSC 18, December 1993, Presidential Decision Directives, Clinton Administration 1993–2000, available at http://fas.org/irp/offdocs/pdd18.htm.

Crouch, Jack D. Special Briefing on the Nuclear Posture Review, US Department of Defense, International Security Policy, January 9, 2002, available at www.defenselink.mil/news/Jan2002/t01092002_t0109npr.html (transcript) and www.defenselink.mil/news/Jan2002/g020109-D-6570C.html (slides).

D'Agostino, Thomas P. Statement before the House Armed Services Committee, Subcommittee on Strategic Forces, National Nuclear Security Administration, House Armed Services Committee Subcommittee, April 5, 2006 available at www.globalsecurity.org/wmd/library/congress/2006_h/060405-dagostino.pdf.

Deutch, John M. Written answer in response to question submitted by Senator Strom Thurmond, in US Congress, Senate, Committee, on Armed Services, Briefing on Results of the Nuclear Posture Review, 103rd Congress, 2nd session, September 22, 1994.

Durbin, Richard J. “Assessing Iraq's Military Capabilities.” US Congressional Record (Senate), September 10, 2002.

Editorial Note, Foreign Relations of the United States, 1961–1963, Vol. 21, Lyndon B. Johnson, Library.

Eisenhower Memorandum to Dulles, September 1953. DDE Diary, August-September 1953, Folder 2, DDE Diary, Box 3, Ann C. Whitman File – Eisenhower Presidential Papers, Dwight D. Eisenhower Library.

Feith, Douglas J., John A. Gordon, and James O. Ellis. Prepared statements before the Senate Armed Services Committee, Strategic Command, February 14, 2002, available at www.senate.gov/~armed_services.

Flory, Peter C.W. “Statement Before the Senate Armed Services Committee Strategic Forces Subcommittee Hearing Regarding Global Strike Issues, March 16 2006,” (hearing was delayed until March 29, 2006), United States Senate Committee on Armed Services, March 29, 2006, available at http://armed-services.senate.gov/e_witnesslist.cfm?id=1842.

Foreign Relations of the United States. 1946–1954. Washington, DC: US Department of State.

Gates, Robert M. Letter to Senator Pete Domenici, available at www.nukestrat.com/us/guidance.htm, May 4, 2007.

Hamilton, Lee H. Extension Remarks, Congressional Record, “Anthony Lake on North Korea,” US House of Representatives, March 8, 1994.

Hobson, David L. “US Nuclear Security in the 21st Century.” Address to the Arms Control Association, Washington, DC, February 3, 2005.

Joint Chiefs of Staff. Doctrine for Joint Nuclear Operations Final Coordination (2). Joint Pub 3-12, March 15, 2005.

Joint Chiefs of Staff. Doctrine for Joint Nuclear Operations. Joint Pub 3-12, April 29, 1993, available at www.nukestrat.com/us/jcs/JCS_JP3-12_93.PDF.

Joint Chiefs of Staff. Doctrine for Joint Nuclear Operations. Joint Pub 3-12, December 1995, available at www.nukestrat.com/us/jcs/JCS_JP3-12_95.pdf.

Joint Chiefs of Staff. Doctrine for Joint Theater Nuclear Operations. Joint Pub 3-12.1, February 9, 1996, available at www.dtic.mil/jcs.

LeMay, Curtis. "Study of Chinese Communist Vulnerability." Memorandum from the Acting Chairman, Joint Chiefs of Staff, to Secretary of Defense, April 29, 1963, Department of State Records, Office of the Country Director for the Republic of China, 1954–65, Box 4, Nuclear Capability.

"Memorandum from Robert W. Komer of the National Security Council Staff to the President's Special Assistant for National Security Affairs (Bundy)." November 5, 1963, Foreign Relations of the United States, 1961–1963, Vol. 22, Lyndon B. Johnson Library.

"Memorandum from Robert W. Komer of the National Security Council Staff to the President's Special Assistant for National Security Affairs (Bundy)." February 26, 1964, Foreign Relations of the United States, 1964–1968, Vol. 30, Lyndon B. Johnson Library.

Mies, Richard W. Strategic Target Plans, US Strategic Command, Commander, Allied Submarines, Mediterranean, Commander, Submarine Allied Command, Atlantic, written response to Strom Thurmond, Chairman, Committee on Armed Services, US Senate, June 15, 1998, reprinted in US Senate, Committee on Armed Services, Nominations before the Senate Armed Services Committee, Second Session, 195th Congress, Washington, DC: GPO, 1999, S. HRG. 105–868.

Myers, Richard B. Change of Command/Retirement Ceremony, Offutt AFB, Omaha, Nebraska, July 9, 2004.

Myers, Richard B. Posture Statement Before House Armed Services Committee, February 16, 2005, available at www.house.gov/hasc/testimony/109thcongress/CJCSPostureStatement2-16-05.pdf.

Myers, Richard B. Statement before the Senate Armed Services Committee, 109th Congress, February 17, 2005, available at http://armed-services.senate.gov/statemnt/2005/February/Myers%2002-17-05.pdf.

National Defense Authorization Act for Fiscal Year 2001 (Public Law 106–398), October 30, 2000.

National Defense Authorization Act for Fiscal Year 2001, Rpt. 106–292, Senate Armed Services Committee, 106th Congress, 2nd session, Washington, DC: GPO, 2000.

National Security Files. Country Files, Lyndon B. Johnson Library, Box 238, file China Memos, Vol. II, 9/64–2/65, DOS telegram.

National Threat Initiative. Iraq Profile, May 2004, available at www.nti.org/e_ressarch/profiles/Iraq/index.html.

NSC-68. *United States Objectives and Programs for National Security*. Report to the President Pursuant to the President's Directive of January 31, 1950, released April 14, 1950, available at www.fas.org/irp/offdocs/nsc-hst/nsc-68.htm.

Nuclear Posture Review Implementation. PDD/NSC-30, September 1994, Presidential Decision Directives, Clinton Administration 1993–2000, available at www.fas.org/irp/offdocs/pdd30.htm.

"Nuclear Posture Review Working Group 5 – The Relationship Between Alternative Nuclear Postures and Counterproliferation Policy." The Nuclear Information Project, Federation of Atomic Scientists, Nuclear Brief, July 11, 2005, available at www.nukestrat.com/us/reviews/wg5.htm.

NUWEP (Nuclear Weapons Employment Policy) April 2004, taken from *The Nuclear Information Project*, available at www.nukestrat.com/us/guidance.htm.

Obama, Barack. "Arms Control Today 2008 Presidential Q&A: Democratic Candidate Barack Obama," *Arms Control Today*, September 24, 2008, available at www.armscontrol.org/system/files/Obama_Q-A_FINAL_Dec10_2008.pdf.

Obama, Barack. *The National Security Strategy of the United States of America*. Washington, DC: The White House, September 2010.

Obama, Barack. "Obama's Speech at the Nuclear Security Summit," April 13, 2010, available at www.cfr.org/publication/21889/obamas_speech_at_the_nuclear_security_summit_april_2010.html.

Obama, Barack. "Remarks by President Barack Obama," Hradcany Square, Prague, Czech Republic, Washington, DC: The White House, Office of the Press Secretary, April 5, 2009, available at www.whitehouse.gov/the_press_office/Remarks-By-President-Barack-Obama-In-Prague-As-Delivered/.

Obey, David R. "Explanatory Statement Submitted by Mr. Obey, Chairman of the House Committee on Appropriations, Regarding H.R. 1105, Omnibus Appropriations Act, 2009." Remarks in the House, Congressional Record, daily edition, February 23, 2009.

Office of Homeland Security. *National Strategy for Homeland Security*. Washington, DC: White House, July 2002.

Office of the Press Secretary. *Joint Understanding by Obama, Medvedev on Weapon Negotiations*. Washington, DC: The White House, July 8, 2009, available at www.america.gov/st/texttransenglish/2009/July/20090708154724xjsnommis0.7355005.html.

Office of the Press Secretary. "Key Facts about the New START Treaty," Washington, DC: The White House, March 26, 2010, available at www.whitehouse.gov/the-press-office/key-facts-about-new-start-treaty.

Office of the Press Secretary. "President Obama's Statement on NPT Review Conference Treaty must be at center of efforts to stop spread of nuclear weapons," Washington, DC: The White House, May 28, 2010, available at www.america.gov/st/texttransenglish/2010/May/20100528230427ptellivremos0.3599163.html#ixzz1COBJcOsE.

Office of the Press Secretary. "Press conference by President Obama in L'Aquila, Italy," Washington, DC: The White House, July 10, 2009, available at www.whitehouse.gov/the_press_office/Press-Conference-by-the-President-in-LAquila-Italy-7-10-09.

Office of the Press Secretary. "Statement by the National Security Advisor, General James L. Jones, on the Non-Proliferation Treaty Review Conference," Washington, DC: The White House, May 28, 2010, available at www.america.gov/st/texttransenglish/2010/May/20100528225343ptellivremos6.870234e 02.html##ixzz1CNaFES98.

Office of Public Affairs Office of the Secretary of Defense. "Pentagon Briefing: 2002 Nuclear Posture Review." Fact sheet, January 10, 2002.

Office of the Secretary of Defense. "Design, Approach, and Implementation of the Quadrennial Defense Review." Quadrennial Defense Review, May 1997, available at www.fas.org/man/docs/qdr/.

Office of the Secretary of Defense. *Proliferation: Threat and Response*. Washington, DC: Department of Defense, January 2001.

PDD/NSC 60, November 1997, Presidential Decision Directive, Clinton Administration 1993–2000, available at www.fas.org/irp/offdocs/pdd60.htm.

Perry, William J. *Annual Report to the President and Congress*. Department of Defense, Washington, DC, February 1995.

Perry, William J. *Nuclear Posture Review*. Annual Report to the President and the Congress, US Department of Defense, February 1995, available at www.fas.org/nuke/guide/usa/doctrine/dod/95_npr.htm.

Perry, William J. Testimony as Secretary of Defense at the Joint Hearing before the Senate Committee on Foreign Relations, 104 Congress, 1st session, Government Printing Office, January 1995.

Powell, Colin L. "Remarks to the United Nations Security Council." February 5, 2003, available at www.globalsecurity.org/WMD/library/news/iraq/2003/iraq-030205-powell-un-17300pf.htm.

Protocol to the Treaty between the United States of America and the Russian Federation on Measures for the Further Reduction and Limitation of Strategic Offensive Arms, available at www.state.gov/documents/organization/140047.pdf.

"Remarks of President Kennedy to the National Security Council Meeting of January 22, 1963." January 22, 1963, Foreign Relations of the United States, 1961–1963, Vol. 8.

Rice, Condoleezza. "A Balance of Power that Favors Freedom." The Walter Wriston Lecture of the Manhattan Institute, Office of the Press Secretary, New York, Washington, DC: White House, October 1, 2002.

Rice, Condoleezza. "Dr. Condoleezza Rice Discusses President's National Security Strategy." Office of the Press Secretary, October 1, 2002, available at www.whitehouse.gov/news/releases/2002/10/print/20021001-6.

Rice, Condoleezza. "Letter to Honorable Pete Domenici, United States Senate," June 25, 2007.

Rice, Condoleezza. "Remarks by National Security Adviser Condoleezza Rice on Terrorism and Foreign Policy." Speech to Paul H. Nitze School of Advanced International Studies, Johns Hopkins University, White House transcript, April 29, 2002.

Rice, Susan E. "Statement on the Fortieth Anniversary of the Nuclear Non-Proliferation Treaty," U.S. Mission to the United Nations, New York, NY, March 5, 2010, available at http://usun.state.gov/briefing/statements/2010/137889.htm.

Rumsfeld, Donald H. Prepared testimony before the House and Senate Armed Services Committees Regarding Iraq, September 18, 2002.

Rumsfeld, Donald H. "Secretary Rumsfeld Speaks on '21st Century Transformation' of the US Armed Forces." January 31, 2002, available at www.defenselink.mi/speeches/2002/s20020131-secdef.html.

Rumsfeld, Donald H. Unclassified cover letter for *Nuclear Posture Review* report to Congress, January 9, 2002, available at www.defenselink.mil/news/Jan2002/d20020109npr.pdf.

"Russian Statement on NEW Start Treaty," available at http://eng.kremlin.ru/text/docs/2010/04/225214.shtml.

Senate Armed Services Committee. "National Defense Authorization Act for Fiscal Year 2008." Report 110–77, 110th Congress, 1st session, June 5, 2007.

Statements of Lyndon B. Johnson, October 14–October 21, 1964, Lyndon B. Johnson Library, Box 127, file October 16, 1964.

Tauscher, Ellen. "Remarks at the Atlantic Council Panel Discussion," *The Case for New START Ratification*, Atlantic Council Panel Discussion, United States Mission to the United Nations and Other International Organizations in Geneva, Washington, DC, April 21, 2010, available at http://geneva.usmission.gov/2010/04/22/new-start-ratification/.

Thielmann, Greg. "Preventive Military Intervention: The Role of Intelligence." Ridgway Center Policy Brief 04–1, October 2004.

Tolin, Anthony J. "Nuclear Posture Review: Key Issues For Review By The Strategic Advisory Group." Briefing, J-5, March 15, 1994.

Treaty between the United States of America and the Russian Federation on Measures for the Further Reduction and Limitation of Strategic Offensive Arms, available at www.nti.org/e_research/official_docs/inventory/pdfs/aptnewstart.pdf.

UN Office for Disarmament Affairs, *1995 Review and Extension Conference of the Parties to the Treaty on the Non-Proliferation of Nuclear Weapons*, New York, NY, available at www.un.org/disarmament/WMD/Nuclear/1995-NPT/1995NPT.shtml.

US Congress. Committee of Conference. "Making Appropriations for Foreign Operations, Export Financing, and Related Programs for the Fiscal Year Ending September 30, 2005, and for Other Purposes." Report to accompany H.R. 4818, 108th Congress, 2nd session, 2004, H. Rept. 108–792, reprinted in US Congress, Congressional Record, November 19, 2004, Book II.

US Congress. Hearing on Department of Energy's FY2008 Budget for NNSA Programs. House Committee on Appropriations, Subcommittee on Energy and Water Development, March 29, 2007.

US Congress. Hearing on FY2009 Budget for Strategic Defense Programs. House Committee on Armed Services, Subcommittee on Strategic Forces, 110th Congress, 2nd Session, February 27, 2008, transcript by CQ Transcriptions.

US Congress. Hearing on Nuclear Weapon Activities. House Committee on Appropriations, Subcommittee on Energy and Water Development, 109th Congress, 1st Session, March 29, 2007.

US Congress. House Committee on Armed Services. Duncan Hunter National Defense Authorization Act for Fiscal Year 2009, Joint Explanatory Statement to Accompany S. 3001, committee print, 110th Congress, 2nd session, September 2008, Committee Print HASC No. 10, Washington: GPO, 2008.

US Congress. House Committee on Armed Services. National Defense Authorization Act for Fiscal Year 2010, Report on H. R. 2647 Together with Additional and Supplemental Views, 111th Congress, 1st session, June 18, 2009, H. Rept. 111–166, Washington: GPO, 2009.

US Congress. House Committee on Appropriations, Energy and Water Development Appropriations Bill, 2009. Unnumbered committee print, 110th Congress, 2nd Session, 2008.

US Congress. House Committee on Appropriations. Consolidated Security, Disaster Assistance, and Continuing Appropriations Act, 2009. Division C, Department of Defense Appropriations Act, 2009, unnumbered committee print, 110th Congress, 2nd session, October 2008, Washington: GPO, 2008.

US Congress. *Report of the Commission to Assess the Ballistic Missile Threat to the US*, Pursuant to Public Law 201, 104th Congress, July 15, 1998.

US Congress. Senate Committee on Armed Services, Briefing on Results of the Nuclear Posture Review, 103rd Congress, 2nd session, September 22, 1994.

US Congress. Senate Committee on Armed Services, National Defense Authorization Act for Fiscal Year 2010, Report to Accompany S. 1390, 111th Congress, 1st session, July 2, 2009, S. Rept. 111–35, Washington: GPO, 2009.

US Congress. Senate Committee on Foreign Relations, *Treaty with Russia on Measures for Further Reduction and Limitation of Strategic Offensive Arms (The New START Treaty)*, Executive Report, 111th Congress, 2nd session, October 1, 2010, Executive Report 111–6, Washington, DC, 2010.

US Department of Defense. *Annual Report to the President and the Congress*. Washington, DC: Office of the Secretary, 2002, pp. 83–92, available at www.dod.mil/execsec/adr2001/Chapter06.pdf.

US Department of Defense. *Counterproliferation (CP) Implementation.* ASD(ISP), July 9, 1996.

US Department of Defense. *Counterproliferation and Treaty Activities.* Office of the Executive Secretary, available at www.dod.gov/execsec/adr97/chap6.html.

US Department of Defense. "Listing, Group 5 – Relationship Between US Nuclear Postures and Counterproliferation Policy, Formal STRATCOM Answers as of 22 November 1993."

US Department of Defense. News Briefing, Richard B. Myers, Chairman of the Joint Chiefs of Staff, March 10, 2002.

US Department of Defense. *Nuclear Posture Review Report.* January 8, 2002, submitted to Congress on December 31, 2001. Excerpt available at www.globalsecurity.org.

US Department of Defense. *The Nuclear Posture Review 2010*, Washington, DC, April 2010, available at www.defense.gov/npr/docs/2010%20nuclear%20posture%20review%20report.pdf.

US Department of Defense. *Quadrennial Defense Review Report.* September 30, 2001, available at www.defense.gov/pubs/pdfs/qdr2001.pdf.

US Department of Defense. *Quadrennial Defense Review*, Washington, DC, February 6, 2006, available at www.globalsecurity.org/military/library/policy/dod/qdr-2006-report.pdf.

US Department of Defense. Special Briefing on the Nuclear Posture Review. News Transcript, January 9, 2002.

US Department of Defense. *Strategic Operations Joint Operating Concept Version 2.0.* Secretary of Defense, Washington, DC, December 2006.

US Department of Defense and NNSA. "FY08 Refurbishment Planning Schedule." As of January 25, 2008, obtained from National Nuclear Security Administration.

US Department of Energy. *Complex 2030: An Infrastructure Planning Scenario for a Nuclear Weapons Complex Able to Meet Threats of the 21st Century.* Office of Defense Programs, National Nuclear Security Administration, October 23, 2006.

US Department of Energy. *FY2006 Congressional Budget Request* Vol. I. National Nuclear Security Administration.

US House of Representatives Committee on Foreign Affairs. Hearing on "Stopping the Spread of Nuclear Weapons, Countering Nuclear Terrorism: The NPT Review Conference and the Nuclear Security Summit," Washington, DC, April 21, 2010, available at www.cfr.org/terrorism/house-foreign-affairs-committee-testimony-stopping-spread-nuclear-weapons-countering-nuclear-terrorism-npt-review-conference-nuclear-security-summit/p21940.

US Department of State. *2002 Country Report on Human Rights Practices.* The Bureau of Democracy, Human Rights and Labor, March 31, 2003.

US Department of State. *2002 Overview of State Sponsored Terrorism.* Washington, DC: Office of the Coordinator for Counterterrorism, April 30, 2003.

US Department of State. *Annual Report on Implementation of the Moscow Treaty.* Bureau of Verification, Compliance, and Inspection, May 13, 2008.

US Department of State. *Comparison of START Treaty, Moscow Treaty, and New START Treaty*, Bureau of Verification, Compliance and Implementation, Washington, DC, April 8, 2010, available at www.state.gov/t/vci/rls/.139901.htm.

US Department of State. *Foreign Relations of the United States.* Washington, DC, 1946.

US Department of State. "Memorandum for the President: Implications of a Chinese Communist Nuclear Capability." College Park: US National Archives and Records Administration, April 30, 1964.

US Department of State. "Remarks by Under Secretary Tauscher on NPT Review Conference U.S. reaffirms NPT commitment to make progress toward nuclear disarmament," Office of the Spokesman, Washington, DC, May 28, 2010 available at www.america.gov/st/texttransenglish/2010/May/20100528170206ptellivremos0.5303766.html##ixzz1COCNBzMt.

US Department of State. START Aggregate Numbers of Strategic Offensive Weapons, Fact Sheet. Bureau of Verification, Compliance and Inspection, Washington, DC, April 1, 2009.

US Department of State. "Statement by the United States of America Concerning Missile Defense," Bureau of Verification, Compliance and Implementation, Washington, DC, April 7, 2010, available at www.state.gov/documents/organization/140406.pdf.

US Department of State, "United States Relations with Russia: The Cold War," Office of the Historian, available at www.state.gov/r/palhoipubslfs/85895.htm#nsc68.

US Department of State Policy Planning Council. "China as a Nuclear Power: Some Thoughts Prior to the Chinese Test." College Park, US National Archives and Records Administration, October 7, 1964.

US Department of State Policy Planning Council. "The Chinese Communist Nuclear Capacity and Some 'Unorthodox' Approaches to the Problem of Nuclear Proliferation." College Park, US National Archives and Records Administration, June 1, 1964.

US Department of State Policy Planning Council. "Destruction of Chinese Nuclear Weapons Capabilities." College Park, US National Archives and Records Administration, April 14, 1964.

US Executive Office of the President. Budget of the US Government, Fiscal Year 2010, Office of Management and Budget, Terminations, Reductions, and Savings; Washington, DC, 2009, available at www.whitehouse.gov/omb/budget/fy2010/assets/trs.pdf.

US Strategic Command. J51 Memorandum. NPR Report #5, Working Group #2, November 16, 1993.

US Strategic Command. J51 Memorandum. NPR Report #8, Working Group #5, November 4, 1993.

US Strategic Command. J51 Memorandum. NPR Report #80, Working Group #5, February 23, 1994.

US Strategic Command. J51 Memorandum. NPR Report #86, Working Group #5, March 2, 1994.

US Strategic Command. J51 Memorandum. NPR Report #90, Working Group #5, March 7, 1994.

US Strategic Command. J51 Memorandum. NPR Report #92, Working Group #5, March 9, 1994.

US Strategic Command. Nuclear Posture Review Slides, Update Briefing, December 3, 1993.

US Strategic Command. Nuclear Posture Review Slides, Update Briefing, March 11, 1994.

US Strategic Command Nuclear Posture Review Slides, Update Briefing, March 25, 1994.

Weapons of Mass Destruction Commission, *Weapons of Terror: Freeing the World of Nuclear, Biological and Chemical Arms,* Stockholm, Sweden, 2006, available at www.wmdcommission.org/files/Weapons_of_Terror.pdf.

Secondary sources

Books

Akehurst, Michael B. *A Modern Introduction to International Law*. 6th Edition. London: Routledge, 1987.

Bailyn, Bernard. *The Ideological Origins of the American Revolution.* Cambridge, MA: Harvard University Press, 1967.

Bernstein, Richard and Ross H. Munro. *The Coming Conflict with China*. New York: Alfred A. Knopf, 1997.

Blix, Hans. *Disarming Iraq*. New York: Pantheon Books, 2004.

Bostdorff, Denise M. *The Presidency and the Rhetoric of Foreign Crisis*. Columbia: University of South Carolina Press, 1994.

Bowett, Derek W. *Self Defence in International Law*. Manchester: Manchester University Press, 1958.

Brierly, James L. *The Law of Nations: An Introduction to the International Law of Peace*. 6th Edition, edited by Sir Humphrey Waldock. New York: Oxford University Press, 1963.

Brownlie, Ian. *International Law and the Use of Force by States*. Oxford: Oxford University Press, 1963.

Bundy, McGeorge. *Danger and Survival: Choices About the Bomb in the First Fifty Years*. New York: Random House, 1988.

Bush, George H. W. and Brent Scowcroft. *A World Transformed.* New York: Knopf, 1998.

Campbell, Craig. *Destroying the Village: Eisenhower and Thermonuclear War*. New York: Columbia University Press, 1998.

Chang, Gordon. *Friends and Enemies: The United States, China and the Soviet Union, 1948–72*. Stanford, CA: Stanford University Press, 1990.

Cirincione, Joseph with Jon B. Wolfsthal and Miriam Rajkumar. *Deadly Arsenals: Tracking Weapon of Mass Destruction*. Washington, DC: Carnegie Endowment for International Peace, 2002.

Cirincione, Joseph, Jessica T. Mathews, George Perkovich, and Alexis Orton. *WMD in Iraq: Evidence and Implications*. Washington: Carnegie Endowment for International Peace, 2004.

Clarke, Richard A. *Against All Enemies: Inside America's War on Terror*. New York: Freedom Press, 2004.

Clinton, William J. *My Life*. New York: Alfred A. Knopf, 2004.

Cooper, Phillip J. *By Order of the President: The Use and Abuse of Executive Direct Action*. Lawrence: University Press of Kansas, 2002.

Dolan, Chris J. and Betty Glad. *Striking First: The Preventive War Doctrine and the Reshaping of US Foreign Policy*. New York: Palgrave Macmillan, 2004.

Drell, Sidney D. and James E. Goodby. *The Gravest Danger: Nuclear Weapons*. Stanford: The Hoover Institution Press, 2003.

Ellis, Jason D. and Geoffrey D. Kiefer. *Combating Proliferation: Strategic Intelligence and National Policy*. Baltimore, MD: Johns Hopkins University Press, 2004.

Elwood, William N. *Rhetoric in the War on Drugs: The Triumphs and Tragedies of Public Relations*. Westport, CT: Praeger, 1994.

Evans, Gareth and Yoriko Kawaguchi. *Eliminating Nuclear Threats: A Practical Agenda for Global Policymakers, International Commision on Nuclear Non-proliferation and Disarmament.* Canberra/Tokyo, 2009.

Franks, Tommy R. *American Soldier*. New York: Regan Books/Harper Collins, 2004.

Friedman, George and Meredith Lebard. *The Coming War with Japan*. New York: St. Martin's Press, 1991.

Gaddis, John L. *Surprise, Security and the American Experience: The Joanna Jackson Goldman Memorial Lectures on American Civilization and Government.* MA: Harvard University Press, 2003.

Garson, Robert. *The United States and China Since 1949: A Troubled Affair*. Madison: Fairleigh-Dickinson University Press, 1994.

Gentili, Alberico. *De Jure Belli Libri Tres.* Translated by John C. Rolfe. Buffalo: William S. Hein, 1995 (1612).

Gray, Colin S. *The Implications of Pre-emptive and Preventive War Doctrines: A Reconsideration.* Pennsylvania: Strategic Studies Institute Publications, 2007.

Grotius, Hugo. *De Jure Belli Ac Pacis Libri Tres.* Translated by Francis W. Kelsey. Buffalo: William S. Hein, 1995 (1625).

Hersman, Rebecca K.C. *Friends and Foes.* Washington, DC: Brookings Institution Press, 2000.

Johnson, Lyndon B. *The Vantage Point: Perspectives of the Presidency, 1963–1969.* New York: Holt, Rinehart and Winston, 1971.

Kennedy, Robert F. *Thirteen Days: A Memoir of the Cuban Missile Crisis.* New York: W.W. Norton, 1969.

Korb, Lawrence J. *A New National Security Strategy in an Age of Terrorists, Tyrants, and Weapons of Mass Destruction.* New York: Council on Foreign Relations, 2003.

Kelsen, Hans. *The Law of the United Nations: A Critical Analysis of Its Fundamental Problems.* New York: Frederick A. Praeger, 1964.

Lanham, Richard A. *A Handlist of Rhetorical Terms.* 2nd Edition. Berkeley: University of California Press, 1991.

Mann, James. *Rise of the Vulcans: The History of Bush's War Cabinet.* New York: Penguin, 2004.

Mead, Walter R. *Power, Terror, Peace and War: America's Grand Strategy in a World at Risk.* New York: Alfred A. Knopf, 2004.

Müller, Harald, David Fisher and Wolfgang Kotter. *Nuclear Non-Proliferation and Global Order.* London: Oxford University Press, 1994.

National Commission on Terrorist Attacks, *The 9/11 Commission Report. Final Report of the National Commission on Terrorist Attacks Upon the United States.* New York: W.W. Norton & Company, 2004.

Oberdorfer, Don. *Two Koreas: A Contemporary History.* New York: Basic Books, 1997.

O'Hanlon, Michael E. and Mike Mochizuki. *Crisis in the Korean Peninsula: How to Deal with North Korea.* New York: McGraw-Hill, 2003.

Pauly, Robert J. and Tom Lansford. *Strategic Pre-emption: US Foreign Policy and the Second Iraq War.* Burlington: Ashgate Publishing Company, 2005.

Quester, George H. *Nuclear Diplomacy: The First Twenty Five Years.* New York: The Dunellen Company, 1970.

Quester, George H. *Nuclear Monopoly.* New Brunswick: Transaction Publishers, 2000.

Ricks, Thomas E. *Fiasco.* New York: The Penguin Press, 2006.

Schlesinger, Arthur M. *War and the American Presidency.* New York: W.W. Norton, 2004.

Sigal, Leon V. *Disarming Strangers: Nuclear Diplomacy with North Korea.* Princeton: Princeton University Press, 1998.

Siracusa, Joseph M. *Into the Dark House: American Diplomacy and the Ideological Origins of the Cold War.* Claremont, CA: Regina Books, 1998.

Siracusa, Joseph M. *Nuclear Weapons: A Very Short Introduction.* New York: Oxford University Press, 2008.

Smoke, Richard. *National Security and the Nuclear Dilemma.* Reading: Addison-Wesley Publishing Company, 1984.

Suskind, Patrick. *One Percent Doctrine.* New York: Simon & Schuster, 2006.

Suskind, Ron. *Price of Loyalty: George W. Bush, the White House and the Education of Paul O'Neill.* New York: Simon & Schuster, 2004.

Thucydides. *The History of the Peloponnesian War.* New York: Penguin, 1972.

Tucker, Robert W. *The Just War: A Study in Contemporary Doctrine.* Baltimore: John Hopkins University, 1960.

de Vattel, Emerich. *Le Droit des gens, ou principes de la loi naturelle, appliqés à la conduite et aux affaires des nations et des souverains.* Translated by Charles G. Fenwick. Buffalo: William S. Hein, 1995 (1758).

Vagts, Alfred. *Defense and Diplomacy: The Soldier and the Conduct of Foreign Relations.* New York: Columbia University Press, 1956.

Webster's Revised Unabridged Dictionary. 1913, available at http://dict.die. net/imminent.

Wit, Joel S., Daniel B. Poneman, and Robert L. Gallucci. *Going Critical: The First North Korean Crisis.* Washington, DC: Brookings Institution Press, 2004.

Woodward, Robert U. *Plan of Attack.* New York: Simon & Schuster, 2004.

Book chapters

Andre, David J. "Competitive Strategies: An Approach against Proliferation." In Henry Sokolski (ed.), *Fighting Proliferation.* Alabama: Air University Press, 1996, 257–276.

Condit, Celeste M. and April M. Greer. "The Particular Aesthetics of Winston Churchill's 'War Situation I.'" In J. Michael Hogan (ed.) *Rhetoric and Community: Studies in Unity and Fragmentation.* Columbia, SC: University of South Carolina Press, 1998, 167–203.

Furches, Amy K. Interview with Dan Poneman. *Presidential Decision Making: When Do US Presidents Use Preventive Force to Counter Nuclear Proliferation?* Washington, DC: George Washington University, 2007, 162–205.

Furches, Amy K. Interview with a former US Military Official. *Presidential Decision Making: When Do US Presidents Use Preventive Force to Counter Nuclear Proliferation?* Washington, DC: George Washington University, 2007, 162–205.

Furches, Amy K. Interview with James Woolsey. *Presidential Decision Making: When Do US Presidents Use Preventive Force to Counter Nuclear Proliferation?* Washington, DC: George Washington University, 2007, 162–205.

Furches, Amy K. Interview with Robert Galluci. *Presidential Decision Making: When Do US Presidents Use Preventive Force to Counter Nuclear Proliferation?* Washington, DC: George Washington University, 2007, 162–205.

Furches, Amy K. Interview with Samuel Berger. *Presidential Decision Making: When Do US Presidents Use Preventive Force to Counter Nuclear Proliferation?* Washington, DC: George Washington University, 2007, 162–205.

Furches, Amy K. Interview with William Perry. *Presidential Decision Making: When Do US Presidents Use Preventive Force to Counter Nuclear Proliferation?* Washington, DC: George Washington University, 2007, 162–205.

Kristensen, Hans M. "The Nuclear Posture of the United States." In Magnus Eriksson and Kari M. Osland (eds) *Nuclear Weapons in the 21st Century: Old Players, New Game – New Players, Old Game.* Oslo: Norwegian Defence Command and Staff College/Norwegian Institute of International Affairs, October 2008, 53–66.

Snider, Don M. and John A. Nagl. "The National Security Strategy: Documenting Strategic Vision." In Joseph R. Cerami and James F. Holcomb Jr (eds) *US Army War College Guide to Strategy*. Carlisle: Strategic Studies Institute, 2001, 127–143.

Speed, Roger and Michael M. May. "Assessing the United States' Nuclear Posture." In George Bunn and Christopher Chyba (eds) *US Nuclear Weapons Policy: Confronting Today's Threats*. Stanford University, CA: Center for International Security and Cooperation, and Washington, DC: Brookings Institution Press, 2006, 256–264.

Steinberg, James B. "The Use of Preventive Force as an Element of US National Strategy." *The Princeton Project on National Security*. New Jersey, 2007, 1–16.

Williams, Chris. "DOD's Counterproliferation Initiative: A Critical Assessment." In Henry Sokolski (ed.) *Fighting Proliferation: New Concerns for the Nineties*. The Nonproliferation Policy Education Center, Washington, DC: Air University Press, 1996, 228–252.

Journal articles

Alvarez, Jose E. "Hegemonic International Law Revisited." *American Journal of International Law*, 2003, 97: 873–888.

Andréani, Gilles. "The Disarray of US Non-Proliferation Policy." *Survival*, Winter 1999–2000, 41(4): 42–61.

Arend, Anthony C. "International Law and the Pre-emptive Use of Force." *The Washington Quarterly*, 2003, 26: 89–103.

Bitzer, Lloyd F. "The Rhetorical Situation." *Philosophy and Rhetoric*, 1968, 1: 1–14.

Bostdorff, Denise M. and Daniel J. O'Rourke. "The Presidency and the Promotion of Domestic Crisis: John Kennedy's Management of the 1962 Steel Crisis." *Presidential Studies Quarterly*, 1997, 27(2): 343–361.

Brierly, James L. "International Law: Its Actual Part in World Affairs." *Royal Institute of International Affairs*, July, 1944, 20(3): 381–389.

Buhite, Russell D. and William C. Hamel. "War for Peace: The Question of an American Preventive War Against the Soviet Union, 1945–1955." *Diplomatic History*, 1990, 14(3): 367–384.

Bunn, M. Elaine. "Pre-emptive Action: When, How, and to What Effect?" *Strategic Forum*, 2003, 200: 1–8.

Burr, William and Richelson, Jeffrey T. "Whether to 'Strangle the Baby in the Cradle.'" *Journal of American History*, 2000/2001: 54–89.

Cha, Victor D. "Hawk Engagement and Preventive Defense on the Korean Peninsula." *International Security*, 2002, 27: 40–78.

Chang, Gordon H. "JFK, China and the Bomb." *The Journal of American History*, 1988, 74: 1287–1310.

Dow, Bonnie J. "The Function of Epideictic and Deliberative Strategies in Presidential Crisis Rhetoric." *Western Journal of Speech Communication*, 1989, 53: 294–310.

Ellis, Jason D. "The Best Defense: Counter-proliferation and US National Security." *The Washington Quarterly*, 2003, 26(2): 115–133.

Ellis, Jason D. "The Gravest Danger: Proliferation, Terrorism, and the Bush Doctrine." *Monitor*, Winter 2003, 9(1): 5–9.

Feaver, Peter D. and Emerson M.S. Niou. "Managing Nuclear Proliferation: Condemn, Strike, or Assist?" *International Studies Quarterly*, 1996, 40: 209–233.

Feinstein, Lee and Anne-Marie Slaughter. "A Duty to Prevent." *Foreign Affairs*, 2004, 83: 136–150.

Fetter, Steve. "Ballistic Missiles and Weapons of Mass Destruction: What is the Threat? What Should be Done?" *International Security*, 1991, 16: 5–42.

Franck, Thomas M. "What Happens Now? The United Nations after Iraq." *The American Journal of International Law*, 2003, 97: 610–619.

Gaddis, John L. "A Grand Strategy of Transformation." *Foreign Policy*, 2002, 133: 50–57.

Gardner, Richard N. "Neither Bush nor the 'Jurisprudes.'" *The American Journal of International Law*, 2003, 97: 585–590.

Gordon, Philip H., Martin S. Indyk and Michael E. O'Hanlon. "Getting Serious About Iraq." *Survival*, 2002, Autumn: 9–22.

Gray, Colin S. "The Quadrennial Defense Review (QDR), 2006, and the Perils of the 21st Century." *Comparative Strategy*, April–June 2006, 25(2): 141–148.

Greenwood, Christopher. "International Law and the Pre-emptive Use of Force: Afghanistan, al-Qaida, and Iraq." *International Law Journal*, 2003, 7(16).

Gusterson, Hugh. "Understanding the Reliable Replacement Warhead." *Bulletin of Atomic Scientists*, July/August 2007: 30–49.

Heisbourg, François. "A Work in Progress: The Bush Doctrine and Its Consequences." *The Washington Quarterly*, 2003, 76: 75–88.

Hsieh, Alice L. "The Sino-Soviet Dialogue: 1963." *The Journal of Conflict Resolution*, 1964, 8: 99–115.

Jentleson, Bruce W. "The Pretty Prudent Public: Post-Vietnam American Opinion on the Use of Military Force." *International Studies Quarterly*, 1992, 36: 49–73.

Jervis, Robert. "Understanding the Bush Doctrine." *Political Science Quarterly*, 2003, 118: 365–388.

Kamp, Karl-Heinz. "Pre-emption: Far from Forsaken." *Bulletin of the Atomic Scientists*, March–April 2005, 61(2): 21–35.

Kaufman, Chaim. "Threat Inflation and the Failure of the Marketplace of Ideas: The Selling of the Iraq War." *International Security*, 2004, 29: 5–48.

Kegley, Charles W. and Gregory A. Raymond. "Preventive War and Permissive Normative Order." *International Studies Perspectives*, 2003, 4: 385–394.

Kristensen, Hans M. "Nuclear Notebook – US Nuclear Forces 2006." *Bulletin of the Atomic Scientists*, January/February, 2006, 62(1): p. 71.

Kristensen, Hans M. and Joshua Handler. "The USA and Counterproliferation: A New and Dubious Role for US Nuclear Weapons." *Security Dialogue*, December 1996, 27(4): 387–399

Kunz, Josef L. "Individual and Collective Self-Defense in Article 5I of the Charter of the United Nations." *American Journal on International Law*, 1947, 41: 872, 878.

Lake, Anthony K. "Confronting Backlash States." *Foreign Affairs,* 1994, 73: 45–55.

Lavoy, Peter. "What's New in the New US Strategy to Combat WMD?" *Strategic Insights*, December 2002, 1(10): 14–27.

Lebow, Richard N. "Windows of Opportunity: Do States Jump Through Them?" *International Security*, 1984, 9: 147–186.

Levy, Jack S. "Declining Power and the Preventive Motivation for War." *World Politics*, 1987, 40: 82–107.

Lieber, Keir A. and Robert J. Lieber. "The Bush National Security Strategy." *US Foreign Policy Agenda*, December 2002: 12–28.

Litwak, Robert S. "The New Calculus of Pre-emption." *Survival*, Winter 2002/2003, 44(4): 53–80.

McColl, Angus. "Is Counterproliferation Compatible with Non-proliferation? Rethinking the Defense Counterproliferation Initiative." *Airpower Journal*, Spring 1997, 11: 99–109.

Mahnken, Thomas G. "A Critical Appraisal of the Defense Counterproliferation Initiative." *National Security Studies Quarterly,* Summer 1999, 5(3): 91–102.

Mearsheimer, John J. and Stephen M. Walt. "An Unnecessary War." *Foreign Policy,* 2003, 134: 50–59.

Moore, Mike. "Truman Got it Right." *Bulletin of the Nuclear Scientists,* January/February 2003, 59(1): 20–30.

Müller, Harald and Mitchell Reiss. "Counterproliferation: Putting New Wine in Old Bottles." *The Washington Quarterly,* Spring 1996, 18(2): 145–149.

Nacht, Michael."The Future Unlike the Past: Nuclear Proliferation and American Security Policy." *International Organisation,* 1981, 35: 193–212.

Nitze, Paul H. "Atoms, Strategy and Policy." *Foreign Affairs,* 1955, 34: 188–198.

Norris, Robert S. and Kristensen, Hans M. "Nuclear Forces, 2008." *Bulletin of the Atomic Scientist,* March/April 2008, 64(1): 50–53.

Olson, Kathryn M. "Constraining Open Deliberation in Times of War: Presidential War Justifications for Grenada and the Persian Gulf." *Argumentation and Advocacy,* 1991, 78(2): 129–15.

Payne, Keith B. "The Nuclear Posture Review: Setting the Record Straight." *Washington Quarterly,* Summer 2005, 28(3): 135–151.

Perkovich, George. "Bush's Nuclear Revolution: A Regime Change in Non-proliferation." *Foreign Affairs,* March/April 2003, 82(2): 2–8.

Powell, Colin L. "A Strategy of Partnerships." *Foreign Affairs,* January/February 2004, 83(1): 22–34.

Press-Barnathan, Galia. "The War Against Iraq and International Order: From Bull to Bush." *International Studies Review,* 2004, 6(2): 195–212.

Record, Jeffrey. "The Bush Doctrine and the War with Iraq." *Parameters,* 2003, 33: 4–21.

Record, Jeffrey. "Threat Confusions and its Penalties." *Survival,* 2002, 46: 51–72.

Reiter, Dan. "Exploding the Powder Keg Myth: Pre-emptive Wars Almost Never Happen." *International Security,* 1995, 20(2): 5–34.

Rice, Condoleezza. "Promoting the National Interest." *Foreign Affairs,* January–February, 2000, 79(1): 45–62.

Roberts, Brad. "Proliferation and Non-proliferation in the 1990s: Looking for the Right Lessons." *Non-proliferation Review,* Fall 1999, 6(4): 70–82.

Rosenberg, David A. "The Origins of Overkill: Nuclear Weapons and American Strategy, 1945–1960." *International Security,* 1983, 7: 3–71.

Russell, James and James Wirtz, "A Quiet Revolution: The New Nuclear Triad." *Strategic Insight,* May, 2002, I(3): 1–10.

Rubin, Barry. "US Foreign Policy and Rogue States." *The Middle East Review of International Affairs,* 1999, 3: 1–7.

Ryan, Maria. "Inventing the 'Axis of Evil': The Myth and Reality of US Intelligence and Policy Making After 9/11." *Intelligence and National Security,* 2002, 17(4): 55–76.

Schmitt, Michael N. "Pre-emptive Strategies in International Law." *Michigan Journal of International Law,* 2002, 24: 513–548.

Schneider, Barry R. "Nuclear Proliferation and Counter-proliferation: Policy Issues and Debates." *Mershon International Studies Review,* 1994, 38: 209–34.

Schweller, Randall L. "Domestic Structure and Preventive War: Are Democracies More Pacific?" *World Politics,* January 1992, 44(2): 235–269.

Siracusa, Joseph M. and David G. Coleman. "Scaling the Nuclear Ladder: Deterrence from Truman to Clinton." *Australian Journal of International Affairs,* 2000, 54(3): 277–296.

Slocombe, Walter B. "Force, Pre-emption and Legitimacy." *Survival*, 2003, 45: 117–130.

Snauwaert, Dale T. "The Bush Doctrine and Just War Theory." *The Online Journal of Peace and Conflict Resolution*, Fall 2004, 6(1): 121–135.

Stromseth, Jane E. "Law and Force after Iraq: A Transitional Moment." *The America Journal of International Law*, 2003, 97: 628–642.

Taft IV, William H. "The Legal Basis for Pre-emption." *Council on Foreign Relations Journal*, 2002, available at www.cfr.org/publication print.php?id=5250&content=.

Taylor, Terence. "The End of Imminence?" *The Washington Quarterly*, 2004, 57: 66–67.

Trachtenberg, Marc. "A Wasting Asset: American Strategy and the Shifting Nuclear Balance." *International Security*, 1988/89, 13: 5–49.

Trachtenberg, Marc. "Preventive War and US Foreign Policy." *Security Studies* January–March, 2007, 16(1): 1–31.

Wirtz, James and James Russell. "US Policy on Preventive War and Pre-emption." *The Non-proliferation Review*, 2003, Spring: 113–122.

Wirtz, James and James Russell. "A Quiet Revolution: The New Nuclear Triad." *Strategic Insight*, May, 2002, I(3), pp. 1–10.

Wolfers, Arnold. "National Security as an Ambiguous Symbol." *Political Science Quarterly*, 1952, 67(4): 481–502.

Reports

Ackerman, David M. *International Law and the Pre-emptive Use of Force Against Iraq*. CRS Report for Congress. RS21314, 2003, available at www.usis.iVpdflother/RS21314.edf.

Arkin, William M. *Agnosticism When Real Values Are Needed: Nuclear Policy in the Clinton Administration.* Federation of American Scientists Public Interest Report, September/October 1994.

Bromley, Mark, David Grahame, and Christine Kucia. *Bunker Busters: Washington's Drive for New Nuclear Weapons.* Research Report, Washington, DC: British American Security Information Council, July 2002.

Bunn, Matthew. *Securing the Bomb 2010: Securing All Nuclear Materials in Four Years*. Project on Managing the Atom, April 2010, available at www.nti.org/e_research/Securing_The_Bomb_2010.pdf.

CRS Report for Congress. *Nuclear Weapons and US National Security: A Need for New Weapons Programs?* Foreign Affairs, Defense, and Trade Division, Order Code RS21619, September 15, 2003.

CRS Report for Congress. *North Korea's Nuclear Weapons Program: US Policy Options.* CRS94–470F.

Daalder, Ivo H. and James M. Lindsay, "A New Agenda for Nuclear Weapons," Policy Brief #94, Washington, DC: The Brookings Institution, February 2002, p. 6.

Dale, Catherine. *National Security Strategy: Legislative Mandates, Execution to Date, and Consideration for Congress*. Congressional Research Service, 7–5700, RL34505, December 2008, available at www.crs.gov.

Evans, Gareth and Yoriko Kawaguchi. *Eliminating Nuclear Threats*. Report of the International Commission on Nuclear Non-proliferation and Disarmament, 2009, available at www.icnnd.org/reference/reports/ent/index.html.

Godsberg, Alicia. *Nuclear Non-Proliferation Treaty Review Conference Concludes in Final Document.* The Federation of American Scientists, 63(2), Summer 2010.

Hoffman, David E. "Reviewing the Review: Obama's New Nuke Strategy is a Good Start. But the Cold War's Legacy Lives On," *Foreign Policy*, April 6, 2010, available at www.foreignpolicy.com/articles/2010/04/06/reviewing_the_review.

Keaney, Thomas A. and Eliot A. Cohen (eds) *Gulf War Air Power Survey: Summary Report.* Washington, DC: USGPO, 1993.

Kerr Paul K., Mary Beth Nikitin, Amy F. Woolf, and Jonathan Medalia. *2010 Non-Proliferation Treaty (NPT) Review Conference: Key Issues and Implications.* CRS Report for Congress, May 3, 2010, available at www.fas.org/sgp/crs/nuke/R41216.pdf.

Kimball, Daryl G. and Greg Thielmann, "Obama's NPR: Transitional, Not Transformational," *Arms Control Today*, May 2010, available at www.armscontrol.org/act/2010_05/Kimball-Thielmann.

Kitfield, James. "Road To Zero Nukes Remains Fraught," *National Journal*, June 1, 2009, available at http://gsn.nti.org/gsn/ts_20090601_8825.php.

Kristensen, Hans M. "US National Security Strategy and Pre-emption." *Defense Nationale and Securite Collective.* July 2006, available at www.defnat.com/en/acc_frames/resultat.asp?cid_article=20060718&ccodoper=3&cid=200607&ctypeencours=0.

Kristensen, Hans M. *Global Strike: A Chronology of the Pentagon's New Offensive Strike Plan.* Federation of American Scientists, March 2006, available at www.fas.org/ssp/docs/GlobalStrikeReport.pdf.

Medalia, Jonathan. *Comprehensive Nuclear-Test-Ban Treaty: Background and Current Developments*, CRS Report for Congress, December 7, 2010, available at www.fas.org/sgp/crs/nuke/RL33548.pdf.

Medalia, Jonathan. *The Reliable Replacement Warhead Program: Background and Current Developments.* Foreign Affairs, Defense and Trade Division, Congressional Research Service, 2009.

Meyer, Paul. "Prague One Year Later: From Words to Deed," *Arms Control Today*, May 2010, available at www.armscontrol.org/act/2010_05/LookingBack.

Nelson, Robert. "Complex 2030: DOE's Misguided Plan to Rebuild the US Nuclear Weapons Complex." *Nuclear Weapons and Global Security.* December 2006, available at www.ucsusa.org/nuclear_weapons_and_global_security/nuclear_weapons/policy_issues/complex-2030-does-misguided.html.

Nikitin Mary Beth. *Securing Nuclear Materials: The 2010 Summit and Issues for Congress.* CRS Report for Congress, April 16, 2010, available at www.fas.org/sgp/crs/nuke/R41169.pdf.

Norris, Robert S., Hans M. Kristensen and Christopher E. Paine. *Nuclear Insecurity: A Critique of the Bush Administration's Nuclear Weapons Policies.* Natural Resources Defense Council, September 2004.

O'Brien, K. Henry, Bryan L. Fearey, Michael R. Sjulin, and Greg A. Thomas. *Sustaining the Nuclear Enterprise: A New Approach.* Lawrence Livermore, Los Alamos, and Sandia National Laboratories, UCRL-AR- 212442, May 20, 2005.

O'Hanlon, Michael. *A Skeptic's Case for Nuclear Disarmament.* The Brookings Institution, Washington, DC, 2010.

Oelrich, Ivan and Hans Kristensen. *Verification Extended Public Interest Report,* The Federation of American Scientists, 63(2), Summer 2010.

Record, Jeffrey. "Nuclear Deterrence, Preventive War and Counter-proliferation." *CATO Institute Policy Analysis.* July 28, 2004, 1–32.

Sachs, Richard C. *Hearings in the US Senate: A Guide for Preparation and Procedure.* Government and Finance Division, CRS Report for Congress, August 19, 2003.

Samore, Gary. "International Perspectives on the Nuclear posture Review." Carnegie Endowment for International Peace, Washington, DC, April 22, 2010, available at www.carnegieendowment.org/files/0421_transcript_samore.pdf.

Schneider, Barry R. "Radical Responses to Radical Regimes: Evaluating Pre-emptive Counter-Proliferation." *McNair Paper 41.* Institute for Strategic National Studies, National Defense University, Washington, DC, May 1995.

Snider, Don M. *Strategy, Forces, and Budgets: Dominant Influences in Executive Decision-making: Post-Cold War, 1989–1991.* Strategic Studies Institute, USAWC, 1993.

Stares, Paul B. "Important Steps for Nuclear Security." *Council on Foreign Relations*, April 13, 2010, available at www.cfr.org/proliferation/important-steps-nuclear-security/p21894.

Woolf, Amy F. *The New START Treaty: Central Limits and Key Provisions.* CRS Report for Congress, November 24, 2010, available at www.fas.org/sgp/crs/nuke/R41219.pdf.

Woolf, Amy F. *US Nuclear Weapons: Changes in Policy and Force Structure.* CRS Report for Congress, Updated January 23, 2008.

Papers and other documents

Burk, Susan. "Taking Stock of the NPT: An Interview with US Special Representative Susan Burk," *Arms Control Today*, March 2010, available at www.armscontrol.org/act/2010_03/Burk.

Cabasso, Jacqueline. "Complex 2030: US Plans for 'Nukes Forever.'" Western States Legal Foundation, available at www.wslfweb.org/docs/2030cabasso.pdf.

Conetta, Carl. "Backwards Into the Future: How the Quadrennial Defense Review Prepares America for the Wrong Century." Project on Defense Alternatives. Cambridge, MA: Briefing Memo 13, June 1997.

Cossa, Ralph A. "Moving Toward 'No First Use,'" *International Security Network*, April 9, 2010, available at www.isn.ethz.ch/isn/Current-Affairs/Security-Watch/Detail/?lng=en&id=114713.

Dean, Jonathan. "Report of the Task Force on Peace and Security: The US Doctrine of Preventive Attack – Real Problem, Wrong Answer." United Nations Association, June 17, 2003.

"Defense Department Won't Comment on Leaked Nuclear Weapons Review – US Continues to Plan for Contingencies as Deterrence Strategy." (360) distributed by the Office of International Information Programs, US Department of State, March 10, 2002, available at http://usinfo.state.gov.

Dhanapala, Jayantha. "Evaluating the 2010 NPT Conference," Special Report 258, United States Institute of Peace, October 2010, available at www.usip.org/publications/evaluating-the-2010-npt-review-conference.

Diehl, Sarah J. and Paula Humphrey. "The April 2010 Nuclear Security Summit: One More Step Toward the Mountaintop," *Monterey Institute for International Studies – James Martin Center for Nonproliferation Studies*, April 20, 2010, available at www.nti.org/e_research/e3_nuclear_security_summit.html.

"FAS Urges White House to Exclude Nuclear Weapons from National Security Strategy in War on Terrorism." Federation of Atomic Scientists, March 16, 2006, available at www.fas.org/press/news/2006/2006mar_natlsecstrategy.html.

Ferguson, Charles D. "Mini-Nuclear Weapons and the US Posture Review." James Martin Center for Non-proliferation Studies, April 8, 2002, available at http://cns.miis.edu/pubs/week/020408.htm.

Hitchens, Theresa. "Slipping Down the Nuclear Slope: Bush Administration Nuclear Policy Lowers Bar Against Usage." Paper presented at a conference on US Nuclear Policy and Counter-proliferation, February 26, 2003, available at www.cdi.org/nuclear/counterproliferation-conference.cfm.

Isaacs, John. "Analysis of the Senate Foreign Relations Committee Passage of the new START Treaty." *The Chain Reaction,* September, 16, 2010, available at http://blog.livableworld.org/story/2010/9/16/16585/7341.

Kristensen, Hans M. "Doctrine for Joint Nuclear Operations." The Nuclear Information Project – Documenting Nuclear Policy and Operations, Federation of Atomic Scientists, December 1995, available at www.nukestrat.com/us/jcs/jp3-12_95.htm.

Kristensen, Hans M. "Nuclear Futures: Proliferation of Weapons of Mass Destruction and US Nuclear Strategy." British American Security Information Council, March, 1998.

Kristensen, Hans M. "Nuclear Plan Shows Cuts and Massive Investments." FAS Strategic Blog, June, 2010, available at www.fas.org/blog/ssp/.

Kristensen, Hans M. "The Nuclear Posture Review." *FAS Strategic Security*, April 8, 2010, available at www.fas.org/blog/ssp/2010/04/npr2010.php#more-2908.

Kristensen, Hans M. "Senate Approval of New START Moves Nuclear Arms Control Forward." *FAS Security Strategy*, December 22, 2010, available at www.fas.org/blog/ssp/2010/12/newstart-3.php.

Kristensen, Hans M. "US Nuclear Strategy Reform in the 1990s." The Nautilus Institute, March 2000.

Kristensen, Hans M. "US Nuclear Weapons Guidance." The Nuclear Information Project: Documenting Nuclear Policy and Operations, Federation of Atomic Scientists, available at www.nukestrat.com/us/guidance.htm.

Kyl, Jon. "Kyl Statement on Nuclear Security Summit." Jon Kyl Senator of Arizona website, April 13, 2010, available at http://kyl.senate.gov/record.cfm?id=323782.

Lichterman, Andrew. "US Nuclear Weapons Doctrine: Disappearing from Public View, Nuclear Weapons." Disarmament Activist.org, February 3, 2006, available at http://disarmamentactivist.org/2006/02/03/us-nuclear-weapons-doctrine-disappearing-from-public-view/.

Mantho, Mark G. "The Bush Doctrine: Origins, Evolution, Alternatives." Cambridge, MA: Guest Publication, The Project on Defense Alternatives, Commonwealth Institute, April 2004.

Mendelsohn, Jack. "The Muddle of US Nuclear Weapons Strategy." Arms Control Association, October 2005, available at www.armscontrol.org/act/2005_10/OCT-BookReviews.

National Intelligence Council, "Iraq's Continuing Program for Weapons of Mass Destruction: Key Judgments." October 2002, p. 8, available at www.dni.gov/nic/special_keyjudgements.html.

National Resources Defense Council, "Faking Nuclear Restraint, The Bush Administration's Secret Plan For Strengthening US Nuclear Forces." February 13, 2002, available at www.nrdc.org/nuclear/restraint.asp.

Natural Resources Defense Council. Table of US Strategic Offensive Force Loadings. Archive of Nuclear Data, available at www.nrdc.org/nuclear/nudb/datab1.asp.

NNSA Fact Sheet. "NNSA's Reliable Replacement Warhead (RRW) Program; Modernizing the Nuclear Weapons Complex Today To Make It More Responsive to the Challenges of Tomorrow." Available at www.nnsa.doe.gov/docs/factsheets/2006/NA-06_FS03.pdf.

"Nuclear Posture Review: What It Says … and What It Means?" Nuclear Reduction/Disarmament Initiative, The Churches' Center for Theology and Public Policy, Washington, DC, available at www.nrdi.org/nuclear/FinalNPR.htm.

"The United States Nuclear Weapons Program: The Role of the Reliable Replacement Warhead." Nuclear Weapons Complex Assessment Committee. Washington, DC: AAAS, 2007, available at www.aaas.org.

O'Hanlon, Michael E. "Should the War on Terrorism Target Iraq?" Policy Brief #93, Washington, DC: The Brookings Institution Press, January 2002.

O'Hanlon, Michael, Susan E. Rice, and James B. Sterling. "The New National Security Strategy and Pre-emption." Policy Brief #113, The Brookings Institution, December 2002.

"Pentagon Cancels Controversial Nuclear Doctrine." Nuclear Brief, February 2, 2006, taken from The Nuclear Information Project, available at www.nukestrat.com/us/guidance.htm.

Pilat, Joseph. "A Counter-proliferation Primer." Los Alamos, N. Mex.: Los Alamos National Laboratory, 1994.

Prebeck, Steven R. "Preventive Attack in the 1990s." Air University Press, posted on the Commonwealth Institute website, May 1993, available at www.comw.org/qdr/fulltext/9305prebeck.pdf.

Rogin, Josh. "Kerry and DeMint Spar over Missile Defense." *Foreign Policy: The Cable*, September 16, 2010, available at http://thecable.foreignpolicy.com/posts/2010/09/16/kerry_and_demint_spar_over_missile_defense.

Rogin, Josh. "White House Announces Nuclear Summit Attendees." *Foreign Policy*, April 10, 2010, available at http://thecable.foreignpolicy.com/posts/2010/04/10/white_house_announces_nuclear_summit_attendees.

Saunders, Phillip C. "Military Options for Dealing with North Korea's Nuclear Program." James Martin Center for Non-proliferation Studies, January 27, 2003.

Silverstone, Scott A. "Can Democracies Initiate Preventive War? America's Confrontation with the Soviet Union and Iraq." Paper prepared for presentation at the International Studies Association Annual Convention, Carnegie Council, Portland, Oregon, February 27, 2003.

Snider, Don M. "The National Security Strategy: Documenting Strategic Vision." Strategic Studies Institute, USAWC, March 15, 1995.

Thomason, James S. Paul H. Richanbach, Sharon M. Fiore, and Deborah P. Christie. "The Quadrennial Defense Review Process: Lessons Learned from the 1997 Review and Options for the Future." Commonwealth Institute Website, Alexandria, VA: Institute for Defense Analyses, August 1998, available at available at www.comw.org/qdr/thomason.pdf.

Trachtenberg, David J. "Assessing the NPR: A Closer Look," *Center for Defense Studies*, April 20, 20101, available at www.defensestudies.org/?p=2274.

Traub, James. "Two Cheers for Multilateralism: Why the nuclear review conference was a minor triumph for Obama." *Foreign Policy*, June 8, 2010, available at www.foreignpolicy.com/articles/2010/06/08/two_cheers_for_multilateralism.

"Weighing the Uniqueness of the Bush Administration's National Security Decision – Making Process: Boon or Danger to American Democracy?" New America Foundation, American Strategy Program Policy Forum, October 19, 2005.

News media

Anderson, Jack and Michael Binstein. "North Korea: Loose Nuclear Cannon." *The Washington Post*, March 29, 1992.

Arkin, William M. "Not Just a Last Resort? A Global Strike Plan, with a Nuclear Option." *The Washington Post*, May 15, 2005.

"Arms Control Today 2008 Presidential Q&A: Democratic Candidate Barack Obama." *Arms Control Today*, September 24, 2008.

"Aspin Emphasizes Missile Defense in Proliferation Approach." *Defense Daily*, December 8, 1993.

Baker, Peter. "Senate Passes Arms Control Treaty With Russia, 71–26," *The New York Times*, December 22, 2010.

Balz, Dan and Bob Woodward. "America's Chaotic Road to War: Bush's Global Strategy Began to Take Shape in First Frantic Hours After Attack." *The Washington Post*, January 27, 2002.

Bromley, Marc, David Grahame and Christine Kucia. "Bunker Busters: Washington's Drive for New Nuclear Weapons." Research Report, *Guardian Unlimited*, July 2002.

"Busywork for Nuclear Scientists." *The New York Times*, Editorial, January 15, 2007.

Carter, Ashton B. and William J. Perry. "Nuclear over North Korea: Back to the Brink." *The Washington Post*, October 20, 2002.

Cerniello, Craig. "Clinton Issues New Guidelines on US Nuclear Weapons Doctrine." *Arms Control Today*, November/December 1997.

Crawford, Neta C. "The Best Defense: The Problem with Bush's Pre-emptive War Doctrine." *The Boston Review*, February/March, 2003.

Crawford, Neta C. "Wrong War, Any Time." *Newsday*, March 16, 2003.

Dao, James. "Pentagon Study Urges Arms Shift, For Nuclear to High Tech." *The New York Times*, January 9, 2002.

Einhorn, Robert. "Obama Reaffirms his Stance on Nukes; South Africa has a Crucial Role to Play in Making the World a Safer Place," *The Star*, August 27, 2009, available at www.thestar.co.za/index.php?fArticleId=5138971.

"End Game." Television documentary, *Frontline*, PBS, 2007.

Frankel, Glenn. "New US Doctrine Worries Europeans." *The Washington Post*, September 30, 2002.

Garamone, Jim. "Cooperative Defense Initiative Seeks to Save Lives." *American Forces Information Service News Articles.* Washington, DC: Defense Link News, April 10, 2000, available at www.defenselink.mil/cgibin/dlprint.cgi?www.defenselink.mil/news/Apr2000/n04102000_20004104.html.

Gellman, Barton D. "Trepidation at Root of US Korea Policy." *The Washington Post*, December 12, 1993.

"Germany 'Very Concerned' after Bush's Iraq Speech." *Deutche Presse-Agenteur*, September 13, 2002.

Gertz, Bill. "Aspin Outlines Threat of Arms Proliferation: Pentagon Unveils Counterstrategy." *Washington Times*, December 8, 1993.

Gordon, Michael R. "Nuclear Arms for Deterrence or Fighting?" *The New York Times*, March 11, 2002.

Grossman, Elaine M. "US General Calls for Faster Action on Reliable Replacement Warhead." *Global Security Newswire,* March 6, 2008.

Hanson, Victor. "Wars New and Old." *National Review*, April 19, 2004.

Harries, Richard. "This War would not be a Just War," *The Observer*, August, 2002, reprinted in *The Guardian*, available from www.guardian.co.uk/world/2002/aug/04/iraq.

Interview with Bob Woodward. "The Choice of 2004." *Frontline*, available at www.pbs.org/wgbh/pages/frontline/shows/choice2004/interviews/woodward.html.

Interview with Dick Cheney. *Meet the Press*, NBC, March 16, 2003, available at www.mtholyoke.edu/acad/intrel/bush/cheneymeetthepress.htm.

Interview with Greg Thielmann. "Truth, War and Consequences." *Frontline*, PBS, August 13, 2003.

Interview with Wolf Blitzer. *CNN Late Edition*, CNN, distributed by the Office of International Information Programs, US Department of State, available at http://usinfo.state.gov.

"Jane's Interview: Ashton Carter." *Jane's Defence Weekly*, 30 July 1994.

Jenkins, Brian M. "A Nuclear 9/11?" CNN.com, September 11, 2008, republished on the RAND Corporation website, available at www.rand.org/commentary/2008/09/11/CNN.html.

Kristensen, Hans M. "Dismantling Fewer, Not More, Nukes." *Los Angeles Times*, June 11, 2007.

Kristensen, Hans M. "The Role of US Nuclear Weapons: New Doctrine Falls Short of Bush Pledge." *Arms Control Today*, September, 2005.

Kimball, Daryl G. "New Reasons to Reject New Warheads." *Arms Control Today*, January/February, 2007.

McManus, Doyle M. "Nuclear Use as 'Option' Clouds Issue." *Los Angeles Times*, March 12, 2002.

Miller, Greg. "Democrats Divide Over Nuclear Plan." *Los Angeles Times*, March 13, 2002.

North Korea News, no. 702, September 27, 1993.

Nunn, Sam A., William J. Perry, and Eugene E. Habiger. "Still Missing: A Nuclear Strategy." *The Washington Post*, May 21, 2002.

Perry, William. "Remarks by Secretary of Defense William Perry to the Asia Society." *Federal News Service*, May 3, 1994.

Pincus, Walter H. "CIA Learned in '02 that Bin Laden Had No Iraq Ties, Report Says." *The Washington Post*, September 15, 2006.

Pincus, Walter H. "Pentagon Revises Nuclear Strike Plan." *The Washington Post*, September 11, 2005.

Pincus, Walter. "US Aims for 3,800 Nuclear Warheads," *The Washington Post*, January 10, 2002.

Pollack, Kenneth M. "Why Iraq Can't Be Deterred." *The New York Times*, September 26, 2002.

Ricks, Thomas E. and Vernon Loeb. "Bush Developing Military Policy of Striking First." *The Washington Post*, June 10, 2002.

"Rogue Attackers May Face Nuclear Response." *Chicago Tribune*, 8 December, 1997.

Sanger, David and William J. Broad, "Leaders Gather for Nuclear Talks as New Threat Is Seen," *The New York Times*, April 11, 2010, available at www.nytimes.com/2010/04/12/world/12nuke.html.

Schultz, George P., William J. Perry, Henry A. Kissinger, and Sam Nunn, "A World Free of Nuclear Weapons," *The Wall Street Journal*, January 4, 2007.

Schultz, George P., William J. Perry, Henry A. Kissinger, and Sam Nunn, "Toward a Nuclear- Free World," *The Wall Street Journal*, January 15, 2008.

Scoblic, J. Peter. "Think Anew About US Nukes." *Christian Science Monitor*, March 19, 2002.

Sheridan, Mary Beth, "Obama secures 47-nation pact at nuclear summit," *The Washington Post*, April 14, 2010, available at www.washingtonpost.com/wpdyn/content/article/2010/04/13/AR2010041300427.html.

Smith, R. Jeffrey. "Clinton Directive Changes Strategy on Nuclear Arms; Centering on Deterrence, Officials Drop Terms for Long Atomic War." *The Washington Post*, December 7, 1997.

Sokolsky, Richard D. and Eugene B. Rumer. "Nuclear Alarmists." *The Washington Post*, March 15, 2002.

Steinbruner, John. "Confusing Ends and Means: The Doctrine of Coercive Pre-emption." *Arms Control Today*, January/February, 2003.

Tenet, George J. "CIA Letter to Senate on Baghdad's Intentions." Globalsecurity.org, October 7, 2002, available at www.globalsecurity.org/WMD/library/news/iraq/2002/iraq-021007-cia01.htm.

Thompson, Mark. "Obama's Showdown Over Nukes." *Time Magazine*, Washington, DC, January 26, 2009.

"Top Bush Officials Push Case Against Saddam." Inside Politics, CNN.com, September 8, 2002, available at http://archives.cnn.com/2002/ALLPOLITICS/09/08/iraq.debate/.

Webb, Greg. "Leading US Scientist Criticizes Warhead Effort." *Global Security Newswire*, February 27, 2008.

White, Josh and Ann S. Tyson. "Rumsfeld Offers Strategies for Current War Pentagon to Release 20-Year Plan Today." *The Washington Post*, February 3, 2006.

Wright, Robin. "Iraq Occupation Erodes Bush Doctrine." *The Washington Post*, June 28, 2004.

Yousefzadeh, Pejman. "Iraq: The 'Domino Effect,' We Can Get Behind." *Front Page Magazine*, April 8, 2004.

Index

90–45–90 plan 43

active defenses 131
adversaries, expansion of 122–3, 125
al Qaeda 27, 29–30, 40, 41–2; *see also* Bin Laden, Osama
American doctrine, legal and ethical standards 14
Anderson, E.E. 59
anti-terrorist narrative 187
anticipatory self-defense 7, 8, 17–18, 188
Arkin, William N. 135
Arnold, Henry H. 58
Article 51, interpretations of 17–18
Asia, threat of proliferation 69
Aspin, Les 96, 97–8
assertive counter-proliferation 121–2
axis of evil 32, 35

Basic National Security Policy (NSC-5501) 60
Bell, Robert 109
Biden, Joseph 177–8, 180
Bin Laden, Osama 26; *see also* al Qaeda
Biological Weapons Convention (BWC) 111
Bismarck, Otto von 22
Blair, Tony 46
Blix, Hans 46
Brookings Institution 11
Brooks, Linton 146, 147
Buchwald, Todd 27–8
Buhite, Russell 55, 58
Bullit, William 57, 59
Bundy, McGeorge 69–70, 71
Bunn, Matthew 177
Bureau of Intelligence and Research (INR) 41
Burk, Susan 174
Burnham, James 89
Burr, William 66, 67, 69, 70–1, 74
Burt, Richard 171
Bush Administration: argument for pre-emption 122; preventive war in historical context 88–92; response to 9/11 1, 6; transition from Clinton Administration *see* Clinton-Bush transition ; transition to Obama Administration *see* Bush-Obama transition
Bush Doctrine 5; vs. Clinton Doctrine 111; as continuation of US policy 119; criticism of 6, 10–11, 115–16, 117, 120; debate 186–7; development 184; in historical context 188; nuclear amplification 112–16, 117–18; nuclear dimension 190–1; overview 2–3; proponents' arguments 22; summary and conclusions 184–92; theoretical basis 53; *see also* National Security Strategy
Bush, George W.: announcement of attack 47; argument for pre-emptive war 7; decision-making 48–9; Iraq as threat 39–40; post 9/11 statements 34–5; return to UN 46; view of deterrence 36–7; West Point speech, 2002 35, 184
Bush-Obama transition: Comprehensive Nuclear Test Ban Treaty (CTBT) 179–82; National Security Strategy, 2010 158–9; New Strategic Arms Reduction Treaty (New START) 164–72; NPT Review Conference, 2010 172–6; Nuclear Security Summit 176–8; overview 156; Prague speech 156–8, 160, 161, 180

Cabasso, Jacqueline 145, 146
Campbell, Craig 57
Carter, Ashton 76–7, 78, 99
Carter, Jimmy 84–5
Cha, Victor 9
Chang, Gordon 69
Cheney, Dick 23, 39, 40, 47, 48, 96
Chilton, Kevin 151
China 65–76, 190; Bundy's attitude 69–70; Johnson's attitude 72–3; Kennedy's attitude 70–2; military and nuclear development 67–8; preventive considerations 65–9; reasons for not acting against 73–6; response to NSS 123; risk of retaliation against US bases 75; statement on nuclear weapons 75–6
"China as a Nuclear Power" 66–7
Clarke, R.A. 30
Clinton Administration 4–5; transition to Bush Administration *see* Clinton-Bush transition
Clinton, Bill: attitude to North Korea 83–4; change of approach to North Korea 84–5; Counter-Proliferation Initiative. 97
Clinton-Bush transition: Clinton to Bush 111–18; Counter-Proliferation Initiative.

96–9; Doctrine for Joint Nuclear Operations, 1993 (Joint Pub 3–12) 103–4; Doctrine for Joint Nuclear Operations,1995 (Joint Pub 3–12) 104–5; National Security Strategy, 1999 110–11; Nuclear Posture Review (NPR) 99–104; overview 93–6; Presidential Decision Directive 60, 1997 108–10; Quadrennial Defense Review, 1997 (QDR) 106–8
Clinton Doctrine, vs. Bush Doctrine 111
Clinton, Hillary 174, 180
Cohen, Eliot A. 96
Cohen, William 108
Cold War: deterrence 36; US nuclear forces 94
Coleman, David G. 94, 118
Complex 2030 144–5
Comprehensive Nuclear Test Ban Treaty (CTBT) 110, 157, 158, 179–82
Congress, need to convince 41
CONPLAN (Concept Plan) 8022 (Global Strike) 132–5
containment 61
costs, of war 47
Counter-Proliferation Initiative, 1993 96–9, 111
counter-proliferation strategy 34
Crawford, Neta 15, 21
credibility 22–3
Crouch, J.D. 179

D'Agostino, Thomas 148, 151
Daalder, Ivo 114, 117
De Vattel, E. 16–17
declaratory doctrine 24
democratization 33
Department of Defense reviews 94
deterrence 36–7; under Bush 116; changed concept of 129, 130–1, 144–5, 185–6; under Clinton 95; Cold War 57; under Eisenhower 60–1; range of 123; regional 103, 105; seen as likely to fail 154; traditional concepts no longer effective 127
Dhanapala, Jayantha 176
DiRita, Larry 79
disarmament 157, 158, 177
dismantlement 163
doctrine, active and declaratory 24
Doctrine for Joint Nuclear Operations,1993 (Joint Pub 3–12) 103–4
Doctrine for Joint Nuclear Operations,1995 (Joint Pub 3–12) 104–5
Doctrine for Joint Nuclear Operations, 2005 (Joint Pub 3–12) 136–40
Doctrine for Joint Theater Nuclear Operations 1996 105–6
doing something big 22–3
domestic factors, in preventive war 12–13
Drell, Sydney E. 91–2
Durbin, Richard 25

Eisenhower, Dwight D. 59–61
Elliot House, Karen 80
Ellis, J.D. 11
evidence, lack of 48–9

Feaver, P.D. 91
Feith, Douglas 44, 116
Fetter, Steven 100
first use 95
Fleischer, Ari 179
foreign policy, change of direction 49–51, 54–5
Fortress Bagdad 43
Foster, William 71
Franks, Tommy 43

Gaddis, John Lewis 23
Gaffney, Frank Jr 79
Gallucci, Bob 82, 84–5
Gardner, Richard N. 29
Garson, Robert 67
Gates, Robert 120, 154
Generated Start Plan 43
Gentili, A. 16
Glaspie, April 21
Global Strike 133, 135
Global Strike Alert Order (ALERTORD) 133
Global Strike Interim Capability Operations Order (OPORD) 133
Goodby, James E. 91–2
Gordon, Michael 114
Gordon, P.H. 26
Gore, Al 85
Gottemoeller, Rose 181
Gray, Colin 9–10, 54
Grotius, H. 16
Groves, Leslie 53
Gulf War 95
Gulf War Air Power Survey (GWAPS) 95–6

Haas, Richard 79
Habiger, Eugene 115
Hamel, William 55, 58
Harries, R. 14
Harriman, Averell 71
Hilsman, Roger 66
Hobson, David 148
Hoffman, David 159
horizontal proliferation 89–90
human rights 30–1
Hussein, Saddam 21, 23, 189
Hybrid Plan 43–4

ideology 51–2
imminence 18
imminent threat 127–8, 186
Indyk, M. 26
intelligence: capacity to gather and assess 19; disregard of 48; Gulf War Air Power Survey (GWAPS) 95–6; Iraq as threat 41
International Atomic Energy Agency (IAEA) 110
International Commission on Nuclear Non-proliferation and Disarmament Report, 2010 179–80
international law: historical viewpoints 16–17; horizontal proliferation 89–90; and Iraq invasion 28–9; preventive war 7, 11, 13–19

international security environment, US responses to changes 94
Iran 31, 32
Iraq: alleged role in 9/11 29–30; announcement of attack 47; choice as site of preventive action 26–34, 47–9, 52, 91, 188–9; human rights 30–1; military capability 33–4; military weakness 44; nuclear program 27; plan for regime change 42–3; as preferred target 3–4, 25; principles underlying invasion 120; as rogue proliferator 26; as strategic choice 33; as threat to US 36, 39–40; UN inspections 46
Iraqi Osirak nuclear reactor 9

Johnson, Lyndon B. 72–5
Johnson, Robert H. 65, 68–9, 74–5
Joint Stealth Task Force 35
Jones, James L. 175
jus ad bellum 17
just war 13–14
justice, vigilante 11

Kanter, Arnold 80
Kaufman, Chaim 30
Keaney, Thomas A. 96
Kegley, Charles W. 21
Kennedy administration, moral aversion to war 74
Kennedy, John F. 67, 70–2
Kennedy, Robert 73
Kerrey, Bob 79
Kerry, John 117, 171
key goals, for pre-emption 137–8
Khalizad, Zalmay 42
Kiefer, G.D. 11
Kimball, Daryl 151, 171
Kissinger, Henry 176
Komer, Robert 70
Korb, Lawrence 20, 28–9
Korean War 59
Kosovo 14
Krauthammer, Charles 79
Kristensen, Hans M. 105–6, 109–10, 137–8, 161, 168, 170
Kuwait 21
Kyl, John 178

Lake, Anthony 80
Langley Hsieh, Alice 67
Lansford, Tom 23
last resort 18
Laurence, William 59
Lavoy, Peter 53
Lebow, Richard Ned 12–13, 33, 47, 88
legal standards 14
legality, of Iraq invasion 28–9
legitimacy 11, 13, 17–18
LeMay, Curtis 71
Levy, Jack S. 8, 9, 12
Life Extension Program 155
Lindsay, James M. 117
Litwak, R.S. 87
lower yield weapons 138

Luck, Gary 84, 86
Lugar, Richard 84, 171
Luongo, Kenneth B 178

Mann, J. 33
Matthews, Francis 58
May, Michael M. 147
McCain, John 79–80
McColl, Angus 98–9
McCone, John 71
McManus, Doyle 114
McNamara, Robert 69
Mead, W.R. 23
Medalia, Jonathan 147–8, 180
Medvedev, Dmitri 164
Meyer, Paul 158
military capability 33–4, 48
Mochizuki, Mike 76
moral standards 14
morality 74, 89–91
Moscow Treaty 191
motivation, for preventive action 12
Myers, Richard B. 133, 134

Nacht, Michael 56, 66
National Intelligence Estimate, October, 2002 41
national interest 14, 19–20
National Security Presidential Directive (NSPD) 17 129
national security, redefinition of 14–15
National Security Strategy, 1999 110–11
National Security Strategy, 2002 36–7, 111–12, 126–8; as active doctrine 24; as change of direction 50–1, 54–5; depiction of US 20; historical perspective 185; on international law 15–16; nuclear proliferation as unacceptable 19–20; origin and overview 1–2; on preventive war 35; primacy of preventive option 54; rhetoric of 187; strategic options 38; summary and conclusions 185–92; undermining diplomacy 116–17; *see also* Bush Doctrine
National Security Strategy, 2006 141–3
National Security Strategy, 2010 158–9
National Security Strategy of Engagement and Enlargement paper 101
National Security Strategy of the United States of America see National Security Strategy
National Strategy to Combat Weapons of Mass Destruction (NSCWMD) 118, 128–32
necessity 18
negative security assurance 117
New Strategic Arms Reduction Treaty (New START) 164–72, 182–3; arms control 172; ballistic missile defense 168–70; conversion and elimination 166–7; core limits 165–6; monitoring and verification 167–8; US ratification process 170–1; *see also* Strategic Arms Reduction Treaty (START)
New Triad of capabilities 3, 120, 121, 126, 133, 153
Niou, E.M.S. 91
Nitze, Paul 24, 71

"no first use" declaration 160
non-proliferation 11
Non-Proliferation Treaty (NPT) 104, 110, 157, 180; *see also* NPT Review Conference, 2010
non-state actors 106
North Korea 76–88, 190; 1994 nuclear crisis 77; case for military action 29; human rights 31; as irritant 32; preventive considerations 76–80; reasons for not acting against 85–8; risk of regional arms race 77; turning point 83–4
NPT Review Conference, 2000 180
NPT Review Conference, 2010 172–6; *see also* Non-Proliferation Treaty (NPT)
NSC-68 62
nuclear capability, limited 63–4
nuclear enticement 159
nuclear expansion, bases of 124
nuclear monopoly 56
nuclear parity 57
Nuclear Posture Review Implementation Plan 133
Nuclear Posture Review (NPR) 99–104, 111, 116, 121–6
Nuclear Posture Review (NPR), 2010 159–64
nuclear proliferation: as threat in Asia 69; as unacceptable 19–20
Nuclear Security Summit 176–8
nuclear tests, suspension of 155
nuclear threat, historical perspective 4–5, 53–5
Nuclear Threat Initiative 27
nuclear war, planning 124
nuclear weapons: argument for reduction 114; Bush Administration focus 154; as deterrent 95; dismantling 154; lower yield 138; pledge to reduce 161–2; policy continuity 191; possibility of use 35; reduction 191–2; renewed role for 4, 5; scenarios for use 136; strategic significance 162; threshold of utilization 125, 139
Nuclear Weapons Employment Policy (NUWEP) 96
Nunn-Lugar Cooperative Threat Reduction (CTR) Program 110
Nunn, Sam 84, 115, 149–50, 151, 176

O'Brien, K. Henry 146–7
O'Hanlon, Michael 20, 26, 76, 154, 181–2
O'Neill, Paul 23
Obama Administration 5, 192; planned modernization of nuclear weapons 155; Reliable Replacement Warhead (RRW) program 153; summary and conclusions 182–3; *see also* Bush-Obama transition
Obama, Barack 176, 177; Prague speech 156–8, 160, 161, 180
Oelrich, Ivan 168, 170
Office of Reconstruction and Humanitarian Assistance 44
oil rationale 32–3
OPLAN 8044 Revision 05 133
options, review of 42

passive defenses 131
Patton, George S. 57
Pauly, Robert J. 23
Peloponnesian War 9
Perry, William 76–7, 78, 81, 84, 95, 102, 115, 150, 176, 181
Pilat, Joseph 99
planning, for preventive war 42–6
policy instruments 119–20
policy objective, change in 42
Poneman, Daniel 77–8, 86
post- Cold War restraint 120
post-Cold War, role of US nuclear forces 94
post-war planning 44
Powell, Colin 38, 40, 46–7, 48
power shift, as basis of preventive action 12, 20
Prague speech 156–8, 160, 161, 180
prediction, behavior of adversaries 21–2
pre-emption: articulated in NSS 126; defining 12; goals for 137; international law 16; vs. preventive war 8–11; supportive infrastructure 8
pre-emptive action, history of 14
pre-emptive counter-proliferation strategies, international law 17
Presidential Decision Directive 60, 1997 108
Press-Barnathan, Galia 22, 28
prevention, defining 12
preventive considerations 19–23
preventive counter-proliferation strike, necessary circumstances for 54
preventive restrictions, USSR 61–5
preventive strategy: clarification 37–9; linking to Iraq 39–42
preventive war: Bush's argument for 7; as counter-proliferation strategy 189; criticism of strategy 20–1; decision to undertake 11–13; disguised as pre-emption 18; early indications 34–5; Eisenhower's rejection of 60–2; historical perspective 53–5, 88–92, 189–90; international law 11, 13–19; as key element of security 185; lead up 46–7; legitimacy 11, 13; as part of war on terrorism 50; vs. pre-emption 8–11; reason for 19; reasons against 61–5; theoretical understanding 9–10; Truman's rejection of 62–3; two-pronged requirement of necessity 38–9; as war of aggression 62
proactive counter-proliferation 127
Project Solarium 59–60
proliferation, horizontal 89–90
proportionality 18, 19
protest, against Bush policy 139–40
public opinion 31–2, 41

Quadrennial Defense Review (QDR), 1997 106–8
Quadrennial Defense Review (QDR), 2001 124
Quadrennial Defense Review (QDR), 2006 140–1
Quester, G.H. 63, 64

radicalism, as security threat 2, 6
Raymond, Gregory A. 21

reasonable presumption 17
Record, J. 20
regime change 42–3
regional powers, nuclear threat 105
Reliable Replacement Warhead (RRW) program 120, 141, 144–55, 163; Bush Administration support 148; criticism of 149; debate 146; goals for 146; Obama Administration 153; opposition to 150–1; withdrawal of funding 151–3, 155
Responsibility to Protect (R2P) 29
retaliation, fear of 64
Reuther, Ray 62
Rice, Condoleezza 20, 38, 40, 49–51, 179
Rice, Susan E. 20
Richelson, Jeffrey T. 66, 67, 69, 70–1, 74
Ridgway, Matthew 62
risks, of preventive attack 44–5
rogue states: deterrence 21; intentions 21, 186; possibility of preventive war 20
Rosenberg, David Allen 63
Rumer, Eugene B. 114
Rumsfeld Commission 27, 32
Rumsfeld, Donald 34, 44, 48, 125, 133, 141
Running Start Plan 43
Rusk, Dean 69, 77
Russell, J. 30, 120, 121
Russia 123, 164–72

Sanger, David 176
Saunders, Philip 87
Schneider, B.R. 54, 97, 98
Schultz, George 176
Schweller, Randall 12, 22
Scoblic, Peter 115–16
Scott Tyson, Ann 141
Scowcroft, Brent 30, 80
self-deterrence 64–5
September 11, 2001: alleged Iraqi complicity 29–30; basis for questioning international law 15; emotive response 7; influence on Bush's thinking 45–6; as motive for prevention 34; response to 1, 6, 13
Shalikashvili, John 84
Silverstone, Scott 62
Siracusa, Joseph M. 94, 118
Six-Day War 8
Slocombe, Walter 62
Smith, Harold 99
Smoke, Richard 61–2
Sokolsky, Richard D. 114
Soviet Union *see* USSR
Speed, Roger 147
Stares, Paul B. 178
State War Navy Coordinating Committee 58
Steinberg, James B. 20, 55
Steinbruner, John 11
stockpile 162
Stockpile Stewardship Program (SSP) 145
Strategic Arms Reduction Treaty (START) 94, 157, 158, 161, 191; *see also* New Strategic Arms Reduction Treaty (New START)
Strategic Command (STRATCOM) 100–1, 103
Strategic Operations Joint Operating Concept Version 2.0, 2006 143–4
strategic options 38

Taft, William 27–8, 38–9
Tauscher, Ellen 175
Tenet, George 41–2
terrorism 26, 186
"The Future of Iraq" 44
The Just War 13–14
Thielmann, Greg 48
Trachtenberg, M. 55, 57, 88, 91–2, 190
Tratchenberg, David 161
Traub, James 176
Tucker, Robert 13–14

Unified Command Plan 133
unilateralism 2, 52, 120, 185, 187
United Nations Charter: acts of defense 15–16; interpretations of 17–18; US adherence to 14; use of pre-emptive or preventive force 17
United Nations Security Council Resolutions: 578 28; 678 28; 687 28; 1373 29; 1441 28
UN resolutions, Iraqi breaches 27–8
US Department of Defense 32
US Department of State 30–1
USSR 55–65, 190; call for preventive war against 57–9; Eisenhower administration 59–61; nuclear capability 56; preventive considerations 55–9; reasons for not acting against 61–5; as threat to US 56

Vanderberg, Hoyt 65
Velvet Revolution 157
Viclosky, Peter 149
vigilante justice 11
vital interests 78–9

war, costs of 47
War on Terror 50, 184, 187
Warsaw Conference on Combating Terrorism 34–5
weapons, flexibility and range of 122–3
weapons of mass destruction (WMD): attitudes to 36–7; as security threat 2, 6; UN inspections 46; as weapons of choice 127
White, Josh 141
Wirtz, J. 30, 120, 121
Wit, J.S. 77, 80, 87
WMD Commission Report 2006 179
Wolfowitz, Paul 48
Woolf, Amy F. 126
Woolsey, James 82–3
worst-case scenario planning 19

yield-to-weight ratio 147–8